International Marketing Strategy

Visit the *International Marketing Strategy*, 5e Companion Website at
www.pearsoned.co.uk/bradley to access **students** weblinks

International Marketing Strategy

FIFTH EDITION

FRANK BRADLEY

University College Dublin

FT Prentice Hall
FINANCIAL TIMES

An imprint of **Pearson Education**
Harlow, England • London • New York • Boston • San Francisco • Toronto • Sydney • Singapore • Hong Kong
Tokyo • Seoul • Taipei • New Delhi • Cape Town • Madrid • Mexico City • Amsterdam • Munich • Paris • Milan

Pearson Education Limited
Edinburgh Gate
Harlow
Essex CM20 2JE
England

and Associated Companies throughout the world

Visit us on the World Wide Web at:
www.pearsoned.co.uk

First published under the Prentice Hall imprint 1991
Second edition 1995
Third edition 1999
Fourth edition 2002
Fifth edition 2005

© Prentice Hall Europe 1991, 1995, 1999
© Pearson Education Limited 2002, 2005

ISBN 0 273 68688 7

British Library Cataloguing-in-Publication Data
A catalogue record for this book is available from the British Library

Library of Congress Cataloguing-in-Publication Data
A catalog record for this book is available from the Library of Congress

10 9 8 7 6 5 4 3 2 1
08 07 06 05 04

Typeset in 9/12pt Stone Serif by 35
Printed by Ashford Colour Press Ltd., Gosport

The publisher's policy is to use paper manufactured from sustainable forests.

This book is dedicated to my wife Breda,
my daughters Siobhán and Maedhbh
and my sons Jonathan and Simon with love

Contents

Part I   Understanding the international marketing environment

Part II   Product and brand strategies in international markets

8   The consumer products firm 143

9   The industrial products firm 159

Part III   Strategic challenge of international market entry

13   Market entry – exporting   225

14   Market entry – strategic alliances   240

15 Market entry – acquisition and direct investment 263

16 Market entry – a strategic approach 280

Part IV   International marketing operations

17 Channels of international distribution   301

18 Pricing in international markets   328

Companion Website and Instructor resources

Visit **www.pearsoned.co.uk/bradley** to find valuable online resources

For students
■ Links to relevant sites on the web

For instructors
■ Complete, downloadable Instructor's Manual
■ PowerPoint slides that can be downloaded and used as OHTs

For more information please contact your local Pearson Education sales representative or visit **www.pearsoned.co.uk/bradley**

Preface

The study of international marketing strategy is concerned with the strategic and operational marketing issues that arise in response to continuing growth in trade. It also involves the concomitant availability of a myriad of new products and services, the dramatic increase in mobile foreign investment, the widespread movement of people and the pervasiveness of international competition at the level of the firm.

Two major forces shape the global economy today – political and economic convergence and market consolidation shaped by information technology. First, the increasing political and economic convergence manifested in new and enlarging trade blocs and increased militarism and global terrorism is forcing international firms to reconsider their marketing strategies. To survive in this environment, companies must adopt flexible international marketing strategies. Firms that avoid international markets or do not have flexible or well-developed international strategies often discover that they face competition not just from agile internationally oriented domestic firms but also from aggressive foreign competitors seeking to expand abroad. The firm competes, therefore, in a global marketplace. Second, the impact of improvements in communications technologies, especially electronic communications, is forcing change on the international firm. These improvements are due to the rapid changes in all forms of technology that have resulted in access for many to low-cost communications that has opened markets to customers throughout the world.

The growth of brands in international markets represents the most powerful way the company responds to the two forces identified above. The provision of information through corporate, product and service branding has become a phenomenon of the global marketplace. The firm develops its international marketing strategies and implements them in the context of a complex and changing technological and competitive environment. In doing so it must also respond to the needs and demands of a myriad of customers located in many different countries and influenced by many different cultures. At the same time the firm must cope with competition in each of its markets.

There are few companies that are not affected, therefore, by trends in international markets. More open and integrated international markets create opportunities and competitive challenges for the firm seeking profitable growth. To succeed in such an environment managers must be flexible and be able to develop and implement dynamic international marketing strategies. It is necessary, therefore, for the international firm to be able to develop cost-effective and international marketing strategies that can be implemented. Managers of international firms face two challenges: to ensure that strategy does not reflect the biases rooted in the company's successes in the domestic market; and once a viable strategy is discovered, to ensure that resources are allocated in a way that accurately reflects the strategy.

Objectives

International Marketing Strategy, 5e engages readers and helps them understand the full range of tasks facing the firm in international marketing. The book explains how to integrate the various market entry and development strategies into a series of decisions that reflect an interplay of the international marketing environment, technological forces and the strengths and weaknesses of the firm. After reading this book the reader should be able to:

■ evaluate and integrate a wide range of management concepts with a focus on the international marketing tasks facing the firm

■ analyze management problems facing the firm in international markets

■ select and evaluate appropriate conceptual frameworks

■ identify courses of international marketing action

■ develop international marketing strategies for consumer products firms, industrial products firms and services firms, irrespective of size or ownership structure

■ decide the appropriate way of entering chosen foreign markets

■ know how to implement the international marketing strategy selected through suitable methods of pricing and distribution supported by appropriate international marketing negotiations strategies.

Target audience

The fifth edition has been written specifically for:

■ postgraduate students specializing in international business with marketing as a major topic

■ senior undergraduates who already have studied a marketing management course

■ research students in other areas of business who are interested in the internationalization of the firm and who require a managerial orientation in their study

■ senior executives pursuing management development courses in global strategy.

The book should also be of special interest to the manager who thinks strategically about the development and growth of the firm in international markets and to managers who wish to keep abreast of the most recent thinking in their specialized field.

Unique features

International Marketing Strategy, 5e is international both in terms of the sourcing of its material and in the treatment of the subject matter – it is not merely a book on marketing management to which an international emphasis has been added. The material has been written from the point of view of the firm competing in international markets irrespective of country of origin and is strongly research based. This book has three important content features:

- it is based on tested frameworks and concepts that have been consolidated and integrated with a focus on the strategic development of the firm in international markets
- the practice of international marketing by actual companies is illustrated throughout the text and a series of specially selected chapter exhibits, drawn from reports of international marketing in action, provides further detail and case illustrations of international marketing in practice, and
- learning objectives and convenient summaries in each chapter provide a clear, cogent understanding of the subject matter.

Changes in the fifth edition

The fifth edition has been extensively rewritten and contains many changes that improve the content. The same structure used in previous editions has been retained as it provides strong pedagogic support and reflects the international process followed by many firms. Much of the material has, however, been reorganized to provide greater clarity and a flow more in keeping with the process of evolution followed by firms. A number of chapters have been expanded, e.g. *Chapter 1 Scope of international marketing strategy*, *Chapter 2 International marketing in the global economy*, *Chapter 3 Company resources and capabilities* and *Chapter 5 Culture values and technology*. The chapter on pricing, Chapter 18, has been reduced in size. Two new chapters have been added or restructured substantially – a chapter on consumer products (Chapter 8) and a chapter on international market selection (Chapter 12).

Outline

The material in *International Marketing Strategy, 5e* is developed from the perspective of the firm competing in international markets. The book develops and evaluates international marketing strategies for firms at different stages of their development – firms new to internationalization, firms at the growth stage and the experienced firm attempting to extend into many additional markets using a multiplicity of entry strategies to suit the circumstances faced by the firm. The focus of *International Marketing Strategy* is on how the firm copes in the international arena, not on individual elements of the international marketing mix. The material is presented in four interrelated parts:

■ The first chapter, *Scope of international marketing strategy*, acts as an introduction to the rest of the book. The discussion here focuses on providing a conceptual framework to evaluate the firm in the international marketing system.

■ The material in Part I, **Understanding the international marketing environment**, consists of six chapters. First we look at international marketing in the global economy. An internal analysis of the company itself is provided next, followed by an evaluation of competitors. Then a series of three chapters examines the broader environment – culture values and technology in international marketing; the political economy and created advantage – how governments attempt to create competitive advantage for their firms; and public policy and regulation – how firms cope with political risk and uncertainty.

■ Part II, **Product and brand strategies in international markets**, comprises five chapters that identify approaches to developing international marketing strategies for different types of firm – the consumer products firm, the industrial products firm and the services firm. The first chapter in this section is new, Chapter 8 *The consumer products firm*. This chapter examines consumer product issues in international markets, especially product adaptation, new product development and the role of product platforms. The chapters on industrial products and services have been updated and given a greater international focus. Branding issues for all three types of firm, but especially consumer products, are discussed in Chapter 11 *Building the global brand*. Another new chapter, Chapter 12 *Selecting international markets*, has been prepared by drawing on material in Chapter 8 *Profiling international product markets* of the fourth edition and by adding new material.

■ The third part, **Strategic challenge of international market entry**, comprises the same four chapters as in the fourth edition, extensively rewritten. The emphasis has changed, however. In the new edition the focus is on first understanding the various modes of international market entry and then integrating these cohesively in a strategic approach to market entry.

■ The last part, **International marketing operations**, contains four chapters – channels of international distribution, pricing in international markets, selling and negotiating in international markets and assessing international marketing operations and performance. The pricing chapter has been rewritten and shortened and now emphasizes exchange rate volatility and flexible pricing. The chapter on negotiations has been focused much more on the linkage between culture, selling and negotiations and the need for effective cross-cultural communications. The last chapter now contains an outline of the planning process and a discussion of the application of strategy in the context of the firm's distinctive competencies, in addition to the established material on financial and non-financial methods of performance evaluation.

The following schematic outline of the book shows how each chapter and part fits together in a logical and structured way:

1. Scope of international marketing strategy

Part I: Understanding the international marketing environment
2. International marketing in the global economy
3. Company resources and capabilities
4. Analysis of international competitors
5. Culture, values and technology
6. Political economy and created advantage
7. Public policy risk and regulation

Part II: Product and brand strategies in international markets
8. The consumer products firm
9. The industrial products firm
10. The services firm
11. Building the global brand
12. Selecting international markets

Part III: Strategic challenge of international market entry
13. Market entry – exporting
14. Market entry – strategic alliances
15. Market entry – acquisition and direct investment
16. Market entry – a strategic approach

Part IV: International marketing operations
17. Channels of international distribution
18. Pricing in international markets
19. Selling and negotiating in international markets
20. International marketing operations and performance

Note to instructors

To further enhance teaching and learning, visit **www.pearsoned.co.uk/bradley** to access the Instructor's Manual which contains the following sections:

- Teaching methods applicable to international marketing
- Designing the international marketing course
- Evaluating and selecting case studies for an international marketing course
- Twenty files corresponding to chapters in the book containing learning objectives, chapter overview, detailed summary and relevant essay questions and outline answers. These files also contain 20 powerpoint files corresponding to book chapters containing slides for teaching purposes, and
- Links – a list of useful hyperlinks to pertinent international marketing websites.

Acknowledgements

As with previous editions, I am especially grateful for the stimulation and challenge provided by MBA and Masters of Marketing students at the Michael Smurfit Graduate School of Business at University College Dublin, and by students at universities and business schools in Europe, North America and the Far East where I have had the privilege of visiting and teaching seminars and short courses. I very much appreciate unsolicited comments I have received on the fourth edition. In particular, I am indebted to a number of colleagues at other institutions who use the book and who have provided very useful detailed contributions regarding content and structure. I am also very grateful to Simon Bradley who helped with background research and the accumulation of research materials and to Anita Wade who prepared diagrams for this edition. I also extend thanks to the following reviewers for their pre-revision review comments:

Alice Maltby, Bristol Business School, University of the West of England
Dr A. Pecotich, Information Management and Marketing Business School, The University of Western Australia
Dr Per Servais, Department of Marketing, University of Southern Denmark

The people I owe most gratitude to are the students and lecturers who have used the previous four editions and have in a most practicable way supported the preparation of this edition. I look forward to a partnership with them and others in the future and welcome their comments and suggestions for improvement. I would also like to thank the Marketing publishing team at Pearson Education headed by Senior Acquisitions Editor Thomas Sigel, for helping bring this edition to market. While these and others have helped in many ways, I remain responsible for any errors and other shortcomings in the book. Nevertheless, I hope that students, colleagues, and managers will find the book valuable as they prepare for the challenge of international markets.

Frank Bradley
R & A Bailey Professor of Marketing
Michael Smurfit Graduate School of Business
University College Dublin
May 2004

Publisher's acknowledgements

We are grateful to the following for permission to reproduce copyright material:

Figure 1.3 from 'Strategic interfacing of R & D and marketing' in *Research Management*, January, 28–33, Industrial Research Institute, Inc., Carroad, P. A. and Carroad, C. A. (1982); Figure 2.2 from Ghosal, S. 'Global Strategy: an organizing framework', in *Strategic Management Journal*, 8, September-October, p. 435. 1987 © John Wiley & Sons Limited. Reproduced with permission; Figure 3.3 *Journal of Marketing* **59**, (April), 9, American Marketing Association, Hunt, S. D. and Morgan, R. M., 1995; Figure 3.7 from 'The internationalisation process of the firm – a model of knowledge development and increasing foreign market commitments' in *Journal of International Business Studies*, **8** (1) 22–30, Palgrave Macmillan, Johnson, J. and Vahine, J., 1997; Figure 4.1 F. M. Scherer *Industry Market Structure and Economic Performance*, second edition, copyright © 1980 by Houghton Mifflin Company; Table 5.1 from *The Science of Man in the World Crises* by Murdock, G. P., © 1945 Columbia University Press. Reprinted with the permission of the publisher; Table 5.2 reprinted from *Industrial Marketing Management*, **25**, Bush, V. D. and Ingram, T., 'Adapting to diverse customers: a training matrix for international marketers', pp. 373–83, © (1996), with permission from Elsevier; Figure 6.2, p. 63, from *Human Development Report 2004: Identity, Diversity and Globalization* by United Nations Development Programme, copyright – 2004 by the United Nations Development Programme. Used by permission of Oxford University Press, Inc.; Figure 9.4 from 'Identifying and qualifying industrial market segments', from *European Journal of Marketing*, **20** (2), 8–21, Emerald Group Publishing Ltd, Hlavacek, J. D. and Reddy, N. M., 1986; Figure 9.5 from 'Developing communication strategies for foreign market entry' in *Research in International Marketing*, Routledge Ltd., Bradley, M. F., 1986; Figure 11.5 from Quelch, J. (1999), 'Global brands: taking stock', in *Business Strategy Review*, **10** (1), 8. Reprinted with permission of Blackwell Publishing; Table 13.1 from 'The export behaviour of Smaller Wisconsin manufacturing firms' in *Journal of International Business Studies*, **8** (2), 93–8, Palgrave Macmillan, Bilkey, W. J. and Tesar, G., 1977; Figure 13.4 from '*Developing markets for new products and services through joint exporting by innovative SMEs Seminar*' Commission of the European Communities, Luxembourg, 6–7 March, Bradley, M. F., 1985; Figure 14.5 reprinted from *Long Range Planning*, **17** (December), Lassere, P. 'Selecting a foreign partner for technology transfer' pp. 43–9, © (1984) with permission from Elsevier; Figure 16.2 from 'Towards a composite theory of foreign market entry mode choice: the role of marketing strategy variables' in the *Journal of Strategic Marketing*, **1**, 48, Taylor and Francis, http://www.tandf.co.uk/journals. Gannon, M., 1993; Figure 16.6 reprinted from 'Entering new business: selecting strategies for success' by Roberts, E. B. and Berry, C. A., *MIT Sloan Management Review*, Spring 1985, pp. 5–6, by permission of publisher. Copyright © 1985 by Massachusetts Institute of Technology. All rights reserved; Figure 17.8 reprinted by permission of *Harvard Business Review*. From '*Blown to Bits*' by Evans, Philip and Thomas S. Wurster, (2000). Copyright © 2000 by the Harvard Business School Publishing Corporation, all rights reserved; Figure 17.9 from *Reconfiguring European Logistics Systems*, Council of Logistics Management, O'Laughlin, K. A., Cooper, J. and

Cabocel, E. (1993). Reproduced with permission; Figure 19.6 from *Journal of Marketing*, **51**, (April), 15, American Marketing Association, Dwyer R. F., Schurr, Paul M. and Oh, Sejo, 1987; Figure 20.7 adapted from Mobley, L. and McKeown, K. (1987), 'ROI Revisited' in *Intrapreneurial Excellence*, and 'Balanced Growth Plans: An ROI Breakthrough', in *Growth Strategies*, Copyright © 1987, American Management Association. Used by permission of the publisher, American Management Association, New York. All rights reserved. www.amanet.org.

The Market Research Society for an extract adapted from the article 'Asian culture – the marketing consequences' by C. Robinson published in *Journal of the Market Research Society* (38)1; The Irish Times for extracts adapted from *The Irish Times* 2 April 2004; Editions Gallimard for an extract about the Gallimard Publishing Company; The Sunday Business Post for an extract published in *The Sunday Business Post* 25 February 2001; Elsevier for an extract from the article 'Starting out right: negotiation for lessons for domestic and cross cultural business alliances' by K. K. Reardon and R. E. Spekman published in *Business Horizons* (37)1 1994; Asia Inc. for an extract adapted from the article 'Pewter King' by Cindy Tham published in *Asia Inc.* April 2004; The Wall Street Journal Europe for extracts adapted from articles published in *The Wall Street Journal Europe*; and The Economist Newspaper Limited for extracts adapted from articles published in *The Economist* © The Economist Newspaper Limited, London. Exhibit 1.5 Big names seek the safety of camouflage, from *The Financial Times Limited*, 5 February 2004, © Sarah Murray; Exhibit 5.1 The American dream gets a Latino beat, from *The Financial Times Limited*, 25 March 2004, © Sarah Murray.

We are grateful to the Financial Times Limited for permission to reprint the following material:

Exhibit 4.1 Business proceeds at jogging pace, Financial Times Special Report – Watches & Jewelry, © *Financial Times*, 17 April 2004; Exhibit 4.2 Europe's big hope for future of airline travel takes shape, © *Financial Times*, 8 April 2004; Exhibit 5.3 Supplement: Mastering Management: Culture is of the essence in Asia, even global companies can make major mistakes when dealing with Asian cultures, © *Financial Times*, 27 November 2000; Page 117, quote, Aventis 'white knight' hopes hit, © *Financial Times*, 20 April 2004; Table 8.1 A History of Innovation, © *Financial Times*, 17 April 2004; Exhibit 8.1 Nokia's dominance in question after wrong call on handsets, © *Financial Times*, 8 April 2004; Exhibit 10.1 Far from resting on his laurels, chief executive Sir Terry Leahy has already announced a further £1.7bn of investment to take . . . , © *Financial Times*, 20 April 2004; Exhibit 11.3 Lessons on how to leverage the heritage, Financial Times Special Report – Watches & Jewelry, © *Financial Times*, 17 April 2004; Exhibit 13.1 Daewoo deal gives Tata SK foothold, © *Financial Times*, 8 April 2004; Exhibit 18.1 Europe's exporters get the greenback blues, © *Financial Times*, 11 March 2004.

In some instances we have been unable to trace the owners of copyright material, and we would appreciate any information that would enable us to do so.

1 Scope of international marketing strategy

The firm in international markets operates in an environment of opportunities and threats in which it is necessary to develop appropriate international marketing strategies configured to compete with other firms while providing value to customers. In such circumstances the firm responds by developing new products or by adapting existing products to the needs of customers in domestic and international markets. International marketing also means deciding which markets to enter and develop and the sequence and timing of entry. A most important issue is the firm's decision on how to enter international markets. The nature, scope and significance of international marketing for the firm are described in this chapter.

After studying this chapter you should be able to:

- understand the general environment of international marketing and the impact of globalization on the firm;
- specify the driving forces behind the internationalization of the firm;
- describe and explain the scope of international marketing strategy in the firm;
- outline the firm's generic strategic responses facing international marketing opportunities;
- discuss the process of international marketing strategy development and performance improvement for the international firm in the context of the process framework of internationalization which underlies and integrates the material covered in this book.

Strategic approaches to international markets

A major difficulty facing many firms in attempting to internationalize is that they respond to an unknown but complex environment and international competition by trial and error or as a process of incrementalism based on an opportunistic response to market development rather than as a strategic choice to grow profitably through internationalization. As a result, beneficial small changes are gradually adopted in a process of adapting to the existing situation, an evolutionary, expedient process. Because it is expedient and evolutionary it frequently produces meagre short-term results which are opportunistic and, therefore, not coupled with their long-run consequences. In contrast, the requirement for firms seeking to survive in international markets is to adopt a revolutionary or strategic perspective on international competition. Strategic competition is comprehensive in its commitment; it involves the dedication of the whole firm (Mitchell and Bradley, 1986).

In formulating a strategy, the company must distinguish between purpose, what it exists to do, and constraints, what it must do in order to survive. The purpose of most firms evolves over time and for some it eventually encompasses the idea of serving potential customers in diverse international markets. Having a clear focus on the benefits required by international customers limits the range of strategic choices that must be evaluated and, therefore, helps to simplify strategy development. The more focused and detailed the purpose is, the more likely it is that a company will be able to develop a winning strategy. The firm's purpose can define the product or technology, the markets to be targeted, the type of positioning to be achieved and the values that must guide the firm's behaviour. A well-defined company purpose gives long-term directional stability to the firm without forcing it into an unrealistic strategy.

For firms new to competing in international markets the reluctance to compete on strategic terms rather than on the basis of increments is understandable. Incumbents in foreign markets frequently possess a competitive advantage over new entrants especially if these are unprepared and lack commitment. Strategic success depends on an understanding of the culture and competitors in the foreign market and the possession of positive perceptions within the firm.

A strategic approach also implies that there are uncommitted resources in the firm which may be dedicated permanently to uses which have a long-term payoff. It also implies that management has the training and skill to predict risk and return with sufficient accuracy and confidence to justify the commitment of such resources. Finally, it means that firms must be willing to act deliberately to make the commitment to invest in international markets.

International marketing strategy

The distinctive attribute of the strategic development of the firm in international markets is that the firm transfers products, services, technologies and ideas as intellectual property, tangible and intangible assets, across national borders. In some circumstances the transfer is through exporting. In other situations ownership or management control over the transfer is retained by entering into alliances with like-minded companies, or the firm may invest directly in foreign markets to transfer the assets. There are many reasons why a firm decides to internationalize:

■ small or saturated domestic market or better opportunities abroad;
■ shortening product and technology life cycles;

- excess capacity and resources or unique competence in the firm;
- desire to follow competitors or customers abroad;
- growth aspirations and international orientation of the firm;
- an opportunistic response to unsolicited order or request from abroad;
- backward or forward integration to reduce costs and increase control.

The function of the firm in international markets combines international marketing decisions with newer forms of resource transfer, thus blurring the distinction between the equity and contractual forms of international transactions. In international marketing we examine the selling activities associated with exporting and the investment activities associated with the other modes of resource transfer such as licensing, joint ventures and other forms of strategic alliance and foreign direct investment.

Definitions of international marketing

Many writers have offered different suggestions as to what the discipline of international marketing should study. For Cateora and Ghauri (1999) it is the complexity and diversity found in international marketing operations which distinguishes the discipline. Terpstra (1983) also stresses the complexity of international marketing. Keegan (1989) distinguishes between domestic and global marketing and states that the differences between the two derive entirely from differences in national environments, company organization and strategies in different national markets. For Kahler and Kramer (1977) international marketing is broader and consists of exporting or producing and marketing in more than one country without the goods crossing national borders. This definition begins to recognize the key role of the firm in international marketing. The dominant actor in the international marketing process is the firm which has permanent operations in two or more countries with businesses that cross national borders (Fayerweather 1982). These processes include economic, cultural and political interactions.

International marketing is, therefore, the process by which individuals and companies:

- identify needs and wants of customers in different international markets;
- provide products, services, technologies and ideas competitively to satisfy needs and wants of different customer groups in different markets;
- communicate information about the assets being transferred across political and cultural boundaries;
- deliver the products and services internationally using one or a combination of foreign entry modes.

As a working definition of international marketing the following is offered:

International marketing means identifying needs and wants of customers in different markets and cultures, providing products, services, technologies and ideas to give the firm a competitive marketing advantage, communicating information about these products and services and distributing and exchanging them internationally through one or a combination of foreign market entry modes.

Figure 1.1
Generic
international
marketing
strategies

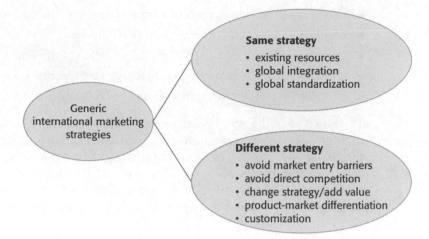

Generic international marketing strategies

Generic international marketing strategies include ways of entering foreign markets which are broadly similar to strategies used in the domestic market and other strategies adapted for various reasons to the requirements of foreign markets. Many firms that have been successful in large domestic markets such as the United States or Japan use the same strategy when they enter new international markets. Other firms modify the strategy or use a very different approach (Figure 1.1). Following the same strategy abroad as at home is facilitated when the firm operates with low unit costs having achieved scale economies in the domestic market. Alternatively the firm may have access to resources which give it an absolute cost advantage over incumbents in the foreign market or the firm may have relatively easy access to the capital required for unadapted foreign market entry.

Usually such firms possess a well-known brand name which gives them a powerful means of developing new markets abroad. In the absence of a well-known brand name small companies sometimes use a country of origin reference especially at the embryonic stage of the life cycle if such associations are positive in the minds of consumers. For smaller firms particularly it may be necessary to adapt the foreign market entry strategy to avoid direct competition from strong local suppliers or other large international companies active in the new market. It may be possible to select a different market segment that would allow the company to build share before attempting a broad-scale approach to the market. The Japanese photocopying company Canon followed this indirect approach by providing small machines for smaller businesses before providing products for the larger office market in competition with companies such as Rank Xerox. Some companies respond to environmental changes by providing customized products more suited to the needs of customers.

Many companies are successful in international markets because they avoid market entry barriers by changing the accepted business structure. They offer competitive products through different distribution channels, the Internet or direct marketing, thereby by-passing foreign wholesalers and agents. Perhaps a more powerful alternative strategy is to build more reliability into the firm's products which can overcome service network barriers. In the car business new manufacturers such as Korean companies have actively built reliability, advanced technology and high quality into small cars which provides the greatest benefits in terms of a retaliation barrier. This approach gives the new entrant credibility and it is also difficult for incumbents to copy.

Opportunistic approach to international markets

While most successful firms adopt a strategic approach in international markets, some firms enter them in an opportunistic way. In these circumstances it is necessary to avoid the following opportunistic cost traps:

■ providing customized capacity for opportunistic business arising in foreign markets;
■ high front-end design and engineering investment to obtain the first international order;
■ possible substantial costs of unsuccessful bidding in different cultures; and
■ the opportunity costs of resources devoted to such business.

Firms operating in opportunistic markets avoid these cost traps by setting conservative capacity levels for such business, separating core markets both organizationally and procedurally and implementing screening processes throughout.

The meaning of strategy for the international firm refers, therefore, to an integrated set of actions taking account of the firm's resources, aimed at increasing the long-term well-being of the firm through securing a sustainable advantage with respect to its competition in serving customer needs in domestic and international markets. The key words in this definition are integrated; actions; sustainable; competition. Part of overall strategy is a marketing mix strategy which refers to the development of specific marketing programmes focused on the unique characteristics of selected target markets and customers.

Standardization or customization

There is considerable debate in the marketing literature on the appropriateness of niche versus global strategies (Levitt, 1983; Quelch and Hoff, 1986). This is the old standardization debate in new clothes, which is not very different from the issue as debated in the late 1960s when the questions 'can you standardize multinational marketing?' and 'are domestic and international markets dissimilar?' were raised (Bartels, 1968; Buzzell, 1968). Conceptualization of the problem is the key to understanding the behaviour of international firms but so too is their actual behaviour, which is often much further advanced than the prescriptions of theoreticians.

Many writers have argued for a standardized, instead of a differentiated, approach to international markets. Accordingly a standardized approach is desirable because sales may be higher owing to a consistent product image across different geographic markets. Furthermore, costs can be reduced by amalgamating production activities, moving to low-cost locations without sacrificing quality and obtaining the economies associated with formulating and implementing a single standardized marketing plan (Walters, 1986; Yip, 1989). In a study of the US, UK, Canadian and European markets, mostly in the EU, Szymanski *et al.* (1993, p. 11) conclude that businesses may be better off standardizing their strategic resource mix to capture the benefits purported to be associated with a standardized approach to serving multiple national markets. According to proponents of the arguments for standardization, global companies drive down unit costs which allows them to price-penetrate markets and force non-global competitors out of the markets. 'The global corporation operates with resolute constancy, at low relative cost, as if the entire world, or major regions of it, were a single entity; it sells the same things in the same way everywhere' (Levitt, 1983, pp. 92–93).

The second school of thought, those who favour differentiation, argues that because few markets are exactly alike it is necessary to adapt the marketing mix to ensure that sufficient customization exists to satisfy buyer needs in each market (Quelch and Hoff, 1986; Wills *et al.*, 1991). The idea that the same product can be sold everywhere in the same way has, however, been discredited. Most large consumer products companies exploit national differences. Even in a product category such as beer, local tastes prevent rampant globalization of the dominant brands (Exhibit 1.1). Even well-known brands, such as Coca-Cola and McDonald's, make concessions to local tastes in order to succeed in international markets. Coca-Cola no longer views the world soft drinks market as being entirely fizzy. The company has introduced a range of non-carbonated drinks including teas to meet the beverage needs of customers in different parts of the world. McDonald's hamburgers are served with teriyaki sauce in Japan, with chili peppers in Mexico, with beer in Portugal and tea is a feature of the company's product portfolio in France and Hong Kong. Levitt assumes that customer needs and interests have become increasingly homogenous worldwide but there is no clear evidence that this is a universal trend. Furthermore, timing of market entry and market barriers may allow incumbents to develop strong local brands which sometimes form an antidote to the charms of strong aggressive international brands. Even within markets, there is great diversity of behaviour and tastes.

Exhibit 1.1   Difficult to see the big pitcher

Global is a buzzword in most industries, and beer is no exception. Holland's Heineken, the world's second biggest brewer, boasts that its brew, drunk in more than 170 countries is the most international beer brand in the world. Belgium's Interbrew calls itself 'the world's local brewer'. And everybody has heard of, if not gulped, the watery fizz known as Budweiser, made by the US company Anheuser Busch, the world's largest brewer. In this context, it is sobering to learn that beer is one of the least global consumer goods of all. Nine out of every ten cans of Budweiser are still drunk in the US; some 61 per cent of Heineken's and 68 per cent of Carlsberg's are drunk in the European Union. Nor is beer all that strongly branded. Only two beers figure in Interbrand's 75 top global brands, Budweiser and Heineken – and they are well behind such names as Coca-Cola, McDonald's and Marlboro.

Source: adapted from *The Economist*, 20 January 2001, p. 65 and Heineken website. The Economist © The Economist Newspaper Limited, London (20 January 2001)

Figure 1.2
Impact of culture
and scale on
standardization

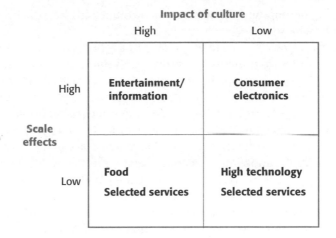

Clearly, therefore, there are differences in different markets; high-technology markets are highly standardized especially in product categories such as consumer electronics whereas for products affected by culture, circumstances dictate the extent of standardization: teenage clothing and music are highly standardized while food and beverages such as prepared meats and beer in general are highly culture bound and not standardized.

Levitt's (1983) assumption that people around the world are willing to sacrifice preferences in product features, functions and design for lower prices and higher quality is also challenged by the evidence available. A number of price-sensitive markets exist, but differentiation remains a powerful marketing strategy. A major source of differentiation and competition in international markets derives from brand loyalty. Branding, however, is unlikely to be a major consideration in a price-sensitive and commodity-like market.

Sometimes standardized brand strategies appear to succeed whereas in other cases they fail dismally. Standardization of strategy is a means to an end, not an end in itself it should be flexible to ensure continued commitment by local management. The impact of culture is a special consideration in international markets as it challenges the scale benefits which the firm may expect. This may force the firm to consider the relationship between scale and culture in their product-markets (Figure 1.2). In some businesses such as entertainment, scale and culture effects are high, while in certain medical and engineering services both effects are low. In consumer electronics and personal computers the impact of culture is low but the scale effects are significant. In contrast, in food and other medical services such as gynecological treatments cultural effects are high but scale effects are low. The appropriate marketing strategy for each of these sets of circumstances is likely to be very different as each requires a different understanding of customer needs in different countries and cultures.

Implications of standardizing strategy

In a literal sense choosing to use a standardized international marketing strategy involves offering identical product lines at identical prices through identical distribution systems, supported by identical promotional programmes, in several different countries, the opposite of localized marketing strategies which contain no common elements whatsoever.

Not all companies are able to adopt a standardized strategy as its appropriateness varies from industry to industry. At one end of the spectrum are multidomestic firms, in which competition in each country, or a small group of countries, is essentially independent of competition in other countries. In these industries a firm may enjoy a competitive advantage from a one-time transfer of know-how from its home base to foreign countries. The firm may adapt its intangible assets for each country, however, and, accordingly, the competitive advantage of the firm is largely specific to each country. Examples of industries operating in this mode would be some retailing, distribution, insurance and retail banking. At the other end of the spectrum are what are termed global industries. The term global, like the word strategy, has become somewhat overused and perhaps misunderstood; it should not be taken literally but, rather, should be applied to a collection or a region of markets. A global industry is one in which a firm's competitive position in one country is significantly influenced by its position in other countries. In these industries firms do not operate with a collection of individual markets but a series of linked markets in which rivals compete against each other across these markets (Exhibit 1.2).

A firm may choose to compete with a country-centred strategy, thus focusing on specific market segments or countries, when it can carve out a niche by responding to whatever local country differences are present. The firm that follows this approach does so at considerable risk to itself from competitors that follow a global strategy. It also misses opportunities for cost savings and scale economies. The purest global strategy would be to concentrate as many activities as possible in one country and to serve markets from this base with a tightly coordinated market offering. This is not only the domain of companies such as Toyota or Xerox, but smaller international firms could clearly also gain by coordinating their international marketing endeavours through joint ventures and other alliances. As a result of such a strategy, clear advantages may accrue in the rapid attainment of scale and learning thresholds, the sharing of development and commercialization costs and establishing significant if shared positions in international markets.

Exhibit 1.2 Nestlé invests in core categories

Strong brands and Nestlé's 'be everywhere' strategy of global market penetration are major reasons behind the company's policy of holding on to its more than 6,000 brands including Kit Kat chocolate, Buitoni pasta and sauces and Alpha dog food. The company recognizes that it needs to have a portfolio of brands to compete in different product categories and at different organizational levels worldwide. Hence, it has allocated its brands into four broad categories:

■ *Worldwide corporate brands*: Nestlé, Carnation, Buitoni, Maggi, Perrier, Nescafé, Friskies.
■ *Worldwide strategic brands*: Kit Kat, Polo, Mighty Dog, After Eight
■ *Regional strategic brands*: Vittel, Alpo, Stouffer's
■ *Local brands*: Texicana, Rocky

Market integration, standardization and differentiation

Production scale economies of themselves may be of little value but, if they can be combined in a marketing system that integrates knowledge from different countries, they are much more useful. Two types of integration, simple and complex, must be considered. In simple integration, some companies keep their most sophisticated operations at home but contract out other production to low-cost countries. Smaller multinationals seem to favour this strategy, whereby product development and marketing are performed in the home base while production takes place in numerous overseas subsidiaries. These subsidiaries are highly mobile and their location is often dependent on wage rates.

Larger companies locate their production activities according to the dictates of the market. Decision-making is dispersed throughout the company, irrespective of location, and the entire company is held together as a complex information system. Knowledge management within such companies is complex and integration of activities on the basis of information across different countries is a challenging task. Many companies, especially the large-scale well-known brand companies, attempt complex market integration by centralizing organizational decisions at headquarters and standardizing international marketing strategies.

Even once dyed-in-the-wool large-scale brand market standardizers have begun to recognize the value of differentiation. As may be seen below, standardization is based on management's perception of similarities between markets. In this context it is likely that US multinational companies with large and relatively uniform domestic markets perceive fewer differences when they internationalize. Coca-Cola is a good example of such a company; things changed, however, when Douglas Daft, the first non-US person to run the company, who also had spent most of his career outside the United States, began to recognize the myopia of a standardized strategy for the company (Exhibit 1.3).

Exhibit 1.3   Seeing the world through open eyes

When Douglas Daft became the boss of Coca-Cola one of his first moves was to decentralize management. He moved the group's regional managers out of headquarters in Atlanta to locate them closer to their local market. In making this decision Daft cited Coca-Cola's launch of a new carbonated tea in north-east China in 1999, several months behind its rivals: 'We had the formula, we had the flavour, we had done all the taste testing, but Atlanta kept saying "are you sure?" Now local managers are free to take the decision and the flack for any mistakes.' The head of Coke's Eurasia division, Ahmet Bozer, says it took him only 13 days to win approval to launch two new brands, Apple and Pear Fresca, in Kazakhstan. Three months used to be the norm.

With local responsibility go local brands. Daft recognizes that Coca-Cola is not always 'it'. 'People don't buy drinks globally,' he says. 'You can't pander to similarities between people: you have to find the differences.'

Source: adapted from *The Wall Street Journal Europe*, Thursday 18 May 2000, p. 1,
The Economist, 12 February 2000, p. 74 and various issues of *Business Week*

Entering foreign markets

Where the capacity and incentive to internationalize are strong enough, the firm is likely to concentrate on those products that seem in most demand in the home market. After initial success in the domestic market the firm attempts to exploit the competitive advantage internationally in a series of stages. Exporting the product is sometimes the first and only stage and is sufficient to accomplish the firm's objectives. Exporting to exploit a technological lead is likely at the early stage of the development of a product because managers are not acutely concerned with production cost. Later on, however, costs may become a concern and other entry modes become more attractive.

Firms with very narrow product lines are generally committed to maintaining their lead in a limited, well-defined market. Confined to that market they have a high stake in maintaining quality standards, in protecting and preventing disclosure of their technological skills and in maintaining tight control over market strategy to be applied to their products. Strategic decisions may be relatively few but each is highly important and each affects the firm as a whole. Such firms show a strong preference for wholly owned subsidiaries. They usually enter and stay in foreign markets through foreign direct investment.

Firms with very broad product lines which exploit technological leads see themselves as comparatively efficient at developing those technological advantages. Because they know that such advantages are perishable, their strategy is usually to make the widest, and presumably the quickest, application of any technological lead they may develop. Since such leads can be exploited over many products in many markets, these firms rely on others to provide the specific market information and specialized distribution needed to exploit them. Because of the necessity to penetrate markets quickly, they are more tolerant of joint ventures and other forms of strategic alliance as the means of entering and staying in international markets.

An alternative means of internationalizing the firm is to exploit a strong brand name. In the modern world of easy international movement and communication, brand names can sometimes gain strength without much conscious effort on the part of the firm that owns the name. Strength of a foreign brand name is associated with the fact or illusion of superior or predictable performance. The expectation of this performance is often strengthened and fortified by extensive promotional expenditures, as is commonly the case for branded pharmaceuticals and foods, beverages and confectionery products. With regard to predictable performance, the strong brand may depend on some technological capability, e.g. Nestlé's ability to deliver worldwide packaged confectionery products in a reasonably standardized condition on a reasonably reliable basis can be a technically exacting job that has been mastered by only a limited number of firms.

Increasingly, smaller firms have been able to establish a strong presence in international markets through innovative use of the Internet. Provided they have the capability to fulfil orders, small firms can build a corporate brand through the Internet particularly in multiple niche markets abroad. Many such firms cope successfully with the fulfilment aspect of their international business by working closely with the postal and other courier services to provide delivery, often difficult to accomplish for a small firm.

Product-market development

In order to avoid opportunistic responses there are a number of things that successful firms do and a number they eschew. In a period of rapid change and discontinuity in the environment, the successful firm is patient and plans carefully to avoid knee-jerk reactions to opportunistic business in developing international product-markets. Only products or product attributes with a very short life cycle can be introduced at short notice; instant new products that become successful are a rarity. Successful companies also avoid attempting to develop instant new markets. There are very few left and those that remain should be treated in a deliberate and strategic way.

It is usually a mistake to jump into markets; since they follow certain rhythms the company may miss the opportunity. A more powerful strategy is to get in ahead of the crowd and to enjoy the benefits of a developing marketing infrastructure. In this way the firm avoids the bandwagon effect when the costs of serving the market begin to increase and the market then declines or disappears.

One way some companies have of beating the crowd is to use their products and services as platforms. This is a recognition that competition has moved firms beyond the business of supplying a product alone. Products and services have become platforms for information, additional technology and service. Indeed many products and services have changed from being a goal in themselves to being a means of establishing close, long term, interactive customer relationships.

Technology, product and market decisions

The simplest internationalization strategy, as seen above, is to sell existing products abroad. Rarely, however, does such a simple strategy work. Usually the firm must adapt its products, and sometimes even its technology, when considering entry to new international markets, thus innovating on three dimensions: product, technology and market (Figure 1.3). The origin in this diagram, Point 1, represents present circumstances

Figure 1.3
Technology–
product–market
decisions

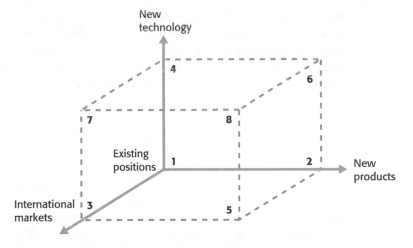

Source: adapted from Carroad, P. A. and Carroad, C. A. (1982) 'Strategic interfacing of R&D and marketing', *Research Management*, January, 28–33

and any distance in any of the three directions specified represents an innovation (Carroad and Carroad, 1982). The firm might innovate by developing a new product based on existing technology, Point 2. An example of this would be the introduction by a Scottish distillery of a private label brand of whisky on behalf of a Japanese supermarket chain to position against brand leaders.

Selling an existing product overseas without any change is represented by Point 3 which is itself an innovation since it involves a whole new marketing programme for a different market. Parts of the marketing mix may have to be adapted. Another possibility is for the firm to reduce its production costs by introducing a new technology, Point 4. For example, a change to computer process technology in the food industry could mean improved product and or lower product cost. Here the product is unchanged and so are the markets but the technology is modernized which may subsequently be the basis of a new foray into international markets.

Frequently, firms develop new products for new international markets but based on present technology, Point 5. The introduction to Greece of branded regato cheese by the Irish Dairy Board under its Kerrygold brand is an example. In this case product development was substantial but a large lucrative market in Greece was discovered and developed. The technology of regato cheese manufacture was known as the Irish Dairy Board had previously exported similar, but unbranded, cheeses to other European countries, especially Italy.

When Heineken developed its alcohol-free beer, Brükner, it required a new technology to remove alcohol from the beer, which resulted in the development of a new product for an existing market, Point 6. Alcohol-free beers have successfully entered the beer market. For some beer consumers alcohol-free beers have replaced ordinary beers, especially under certain circumstances, e.g. before driving, after a long drinking session or for health and dietary reasons. Interactive Internet based educational programmes are an example of a new technology with an existing product which has entered the new and growing worldwide educational and training market, Point 7. Lastly, Point 8, when Baileys Original Irish Cream was launched in 1974 it was a new product based on a new technology, aimed at a new market. The new product was made from whiskey and cream but with lower alcohol than products it was designed to replace. It was based on a new technology which allowed the successful mixing of spirits and cream, a technology that did not previously exist. The product was developed in Ireland but from the start it was developed for the large lucrative international markets throughout the world, especially the US. Clearly, any innovation which takes the firm along any two, e.g. product and market, or all three dimensions, e.g. product, market and technology, requires considerable planning and company resources. Innovating on any one dimension requires considerable care but innovation on more than one dimension requires considerable synergy among parts of the company and between the company and outside partners in the wider business system.

Clearly, the firm may pursue a number of the strategies encompassed in the mix of possible strategies outlined. In deciding the best way forward, however, the firm is constrained by the needs of customers in the market, by growth in the market and by its competitors. Four factors, each discussed elsewhere, form the basis on which the firm can grow in international markets:

- the business should be defined in terms of the firm's capabilities which provides a durable basis for strategy;

- ability to earn profits depends on competitive advantage and attractiveness of the industry;

- a recognition that the sources of competitive advantage are low costs and differentiation;

- attractiveness of industry depends on the firm's power in the business system which is derived from market entry barriers.

Strategic differentiation in the international firm

Successful companies invest in products and markets but they also invest in people to ensure that they are capable of managing in different cultures and under different political regimes. They must also invest heavily in adapting their existing products and services and in developing new products and services specifically for international markets; this means seeking to differentiate themselves strategically from competitors (Figure 1.4). Strategic differentiation means providing new customer benefits and focusing on customer value in selected international markets.

Important sources of differentiation include knowledge of the market, the product and customers and the relationships within the organization and with suppliers. This means obtaining a complete understanding of customer needs and behaviour in each foreign market to be considered. It also means determining the key elements of differentiation that the firm will be required to develop and it means focusing on key elements that enter into the customer's buying decision process.

The company may also differentiate itself based on its unique product and process technologies that give it a platform to compete internationally. Increasingly, the human values of senior managers in the firm are being treated as dominant in providing the basis of competitive advantage. The capacity of the firm to perform in international markets based on the traditional (Porter, 1985) view of competitive

Figure 1.4
Strategic differentiation and international marketing performance

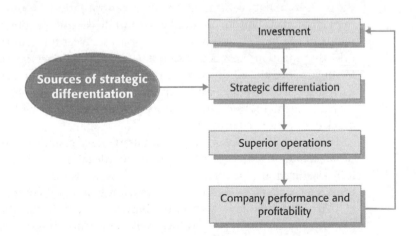

advantage may have been eroded as human values have recently been identified as the single most important antecedent in maintaining competitive advantage and in supporting firm performance (Pfeffer, 2002). Congruence of human values among the firm's decision-makers and the consequences for corporate cultures, therefore, is an important influencing factor in the performance of international firms (Craig and Douglas, 1996; Ralston *et al.*, 1997). The style of decision-makers also influences company performance (Kroeber, 1952; White, 1993), the innovation of technology and cross-border alliances (Dyer and Ouchi, 2002; Tidd *et al.*, 2002).

By differentiating the product or service through customization, low cost and speed to the market, the company creates superior operations and increases value for its customers. In this way performance in terms of returns, sales growth and cash flow is improved which in turn leads to greater investment in the company, thereby allowing further differentiation, thereby creating a virtuous circle as suggested in the figure.

International marketing strategy and organization

There are various dimensions to this issue. International companies may standardize and centralize their activities by business function; marketing is usually the last to be centralized. Alternatively the company may centralize selected marketing mix elements; product positioning is usually standardized and control over it centralized whereas some freedom over distribution and pricing is often given to subsidiaries. Some firms standardize and centralize decisions by product according to the impact of culture and scale economies. Standardization and centralization may also occur by country; smaller or poorer-performing countries and newer country markets may need more support from the centre and so may be more susceptible to a standard and centralized approach. There are distinct advantages and disadvantages of standardization and centralization. Such an approach may offer scale economies but the firm may be slow to react to changes in the environment and lose customers. On the other hand decentralization allows the company to be quick and connected to the customer but the cost effect of extra capacity and resources may be unwarranted.

In theory back-office shared services become a model whereby the company obtains the benefits of both centralization and decentralization. Front-office services, e.g. sales, marketing, distribution, should be decentralized and customized to suit the requirements of the market, and back-office services are centralized. In Europe, in particular, now that most business is transacted in euro, a single service centre may be sufficient for the finance and administrative functions, e.g. accounts receivable. A pan-European shared services system may be optimal for back-office activities in the future. With such arrangements the company obtains scale economies while retaining the close and quick connection to customers.

Using these principles and by simultaneously examining the company's international marketing strategy regarding standardization and centralization and the way it is organized, it is possible to classify firms into various categories (Figure 1.5). Large firms such as Nestlé would be considered a command company since it operates in globally integrated markets and the business system is controlled from headquarters in Switzerland. Nestlé is considered as standardized and centralized. At the other extreme very small companies new to international marketing recognize global market

Figure 1.5
International
marketing
strategies and
organization

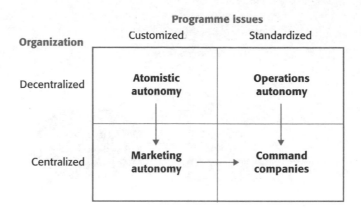

segments, develop focused market strategies and operate with local autonomy in the business system. These firms are decentralized and customized or differentiated. In between these two extremes there are firms which possess marketing autonomy or operations autonomy.

International marketing environment

The international marketing environment is a complex constellation of demands and constraints which the firm faces as it attempts to compete and grow. Identifying customer values in international markets requires a sophisticated understanding of differentiated expressions of customer needs, many of which are influenced by culture. Similarly, the task of communicating the values provided and their delivery in international markets is complex, requiring a great deal of understanding of the environment and its influences. International marketing is characterized by the convergence of the company's marketing process, usually in one country, and the customer's purchase decision process in another. In a competitive world, it is difficult to provide, communicate, and deliver added value. If, however, the company cannot provide added value in the international business system it has no reason to be part of that system. This international marketing environment consists of a number of elements most of which lie outside the control of the firm (Figure 1.6). Each of these elements is discussed and integrated in the firm's decision-making process.

In the international marketing environment the firm may have a number of goals. For example an international firm might attempt to position itself as a leader in its declared product-market; to be a leader in the use of defined product and communications technologies in providing value to customers in different countries; or to broaden the firm's international appeal by expanding its product portfolio and strengthening its international network links and introducing new ones.

In regard to objectives and targets the company might set itself three- or five-year objectives which it considers achievable. The type of general objectives which might be set include the following:

Figure 1.6
International
marketing
environment

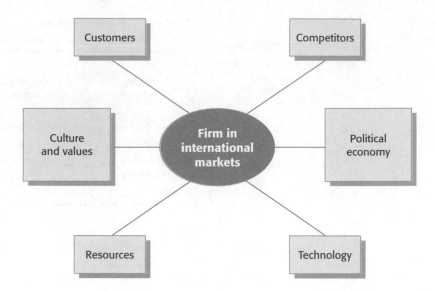

- to maximize company effectiveness by removing internal and external obstacles to international product-market development;
- to differentiate itself from existing and future competitors in selected international markets;
- to seek long-term financial equilibrium while protecting revenue flows into the company.

Market fragmentation and consolidation

Market fragmentation arises when market entry costs are low and exit costs are high, where there are few positive experience curve effects, where cost structures are atypical and governments interfere in the market. The strong determination of national governments to support the development of industries believed to be of strategic importance can also contribute to market fragmentation, which is especially true, but waning, in public transport, telecommunications, airports and airlines.

Persistent differences in consumer tastes, differences in culture and language and variation in technical standards also contribute to the process of fragmentation (Figure 1.7). In addition tariffs and non-tariff barriers force manufacturers to think locally. At the same time, with the exception of the EU, retailers are still very much national organizations focused on one country only, although this is changing. In the regime of international markets characterized by these barriers large firms are deprived of one of their favourite weapons, cost leadership stemming from manufacturing scale effects, while smaller firms proliferate and compete by serving speciality niches.

In traditional consumer mass markets, population age structures, the increase in the number of women working away from the home and the recognition of a multilingual and multicultural society have forced many companies to cope with fragmented markets by developing niche strategies. At the same time the mass media advocate standardized products while consumers increasingly seek variety.

Figure 1.7
Fragmentation
of international
markets

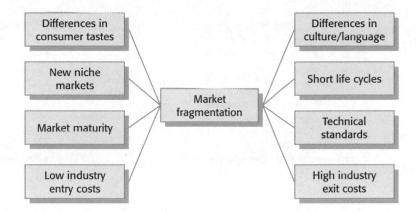

These are among the more important factors which have influenced trends toward increased fragmentation in markets. They are more influential in some markets than others and the ability of firms to cope with them varies correspondingly. High culture-bound items such as food, clothing and medicine are more likely to be sold in fragmented markets, whereas consumer electronics and music, especially music aimed at the youth market, will probably continue to serve a standardized consolidated market. In summary, the reasons for international market fragmentation are.

- differences in tastes, languages, culture and technical standards represent obstacles to market consolidation which force managers to 'think local';
- recognition of multilingual and multicultural societies forces many companies to develop niche strategies in coping with fragmentation;
- retailers are still nationally focused, especially outside the EU;
- large firms are deprived of a favourite competitive weapon – cost leadership arising from scale effects in manufacturing and marketing;
- regulated markets, low industry entry costs and high industry exit costs contribute to market fragmentation;
- new information technologies may be used effectively to serve fragmented markets.

Consolidation of markets is achieved when low-cost, standardized products are provided, marketing expenditures are systematically raised, a spate of acquisitions occurs and large capital investments raise the minimum scale to be efficient (Figure 1.8). Other factors which promote the consolidation of markets are attempts by companies to rationalize production capacity across a number of markets and increases in investment in knowledge to raise labour productivity. These are the kinds of strategies pursued by the large well-known multinational companies. In recent years throughout the EU, large retailers have become effective multinational companies. Observing the advanced convergence in consumer tastes and preferences in different countries they have internationalized through their efficient private-label operations and now challenge the large established brand manufacturers for supremacy. Large retailers such as Carrefour and Aldi are in effect consolidating and integrating the EU retail markets.

Figure 1.8
Consolidation of
international
markets

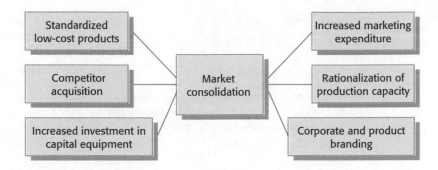

Similarly, the large multinational brewing companies, recognizing the product differences among brands, local and global, have been attempting to gain entry to new international markets. For example, 'thinking local', some international brewers believe, may be the solution to gain a solid foothold in the beer market in China (Exhibit 1.4). In summary, international markets may be consolidated when:

■ successful international firms introduce low-cost standardized products covering most market needs, replacing many specialized products;

■ large marketing expenditures force less well funded competitors to leave the market; this is a common strategy in packaged consumer goods markets, especially among large-scale international retailers using private-label brands;

■ acquiring competitors and rationalizing production capacity consolidates markets, a strategy often followed by alcoholic beverage and electrical products companies.

The continuous process of market fragmentation followed by consolidation presents firms with growth and development opportunities for international product-market development.

Exhibit 1.4   Global brewers tap into local brands in China

China's beer market has leapt from 50 million barrels a year in 1990 to 200 million barrels just thirteen years later, and most of the world's big brewers have been there since the start to witness the boom, but alas, few are reaping the rewards. Well-known international brands like Foster's, Budweiser and Beck's have foundered despite the potentially lucrative market, and they have done so for two reasons: brand value and a fragmented market. Mr Wai Kee Tan, recently appointed VP of corporate operations for Interbrew SA in Asia, is succinct when he asserts, 'China is a nation, but not a national market.' Breweries are often confined to city-size markets because of production and distribution strategies where value brands prevail in a price-conscious market. Most breweries like KK, market leaders in Ningbo, recycle bottles to minimize costs, and while the network of small local distributors is often effective in meeting demand fluctuations – 90 per cent of beer distribution in Ningbo, a city of five million, is effected through the city's 6,000 corner shops and stands – market coverage is limited to a 200km radius beyond which this strategy becomes prohibitively expensive.

When it all began in the 1990s, China was swimming in beer with over 800 breweries, many commercially inefficient, but their brands were readily available. Interbrew's Beck's brand, Anheuser Busch's Budweiser and Foster's Group Ltd's Foster's brand were among other international brewers who failed to understand the market and tap into the Chinese consumer's mindset. In Interbrew's case, this was something that almost destroyed their 1997 acquisition of Jinling brewery in Nanjing, another city of more than five million. Jinling was promoted by Interbrew as a premium brand, alienating its customer base. Saved by its old chief, Mr Tan's intervention, Jinling remained just part of Interbrew who ultimately lacked a national brand and a national strategy. Eventually the company directors came round to Mr Tan's advice: forget a national brand, forget a regional brand, even; think locally. And so an aggressive acquisitions drive for local holdings, among them KK, resulted in Interbrew holding 9 per cent of the market as number three brewer in the country by concentrating on just a few bubbles of the Chinese brewing market.

Source: adapted from *The Wall Street Journal Europe*, Wednesday 10 March 2004, pp. 1–3

Globalization of markets

Globalization, or the trend toward global markets, means many things to different people. Many elements affect globalization and its impact on countries, companies and people. The technological capacity of a country and its ability to adapt to changing needs is a major element in globalization of business. Another factor which underlies the concept is access to large integrated markets, such as the United States or the EU, especially the newly enlarged EU. The competitiveness of people and enterprise, increasingly dependent on their ability to create new assets, provides an attraction for mobile foreign investment and the surge in international migration as people seek a better life. These factors, when combined with a political capacity to adapt and change, are additional elements to be considered in the globalization debate. Related to these is the need to establish and promote international institutions which provide the necessary framework for globalization of business to take place. Lastly, there is the role of governments which is becoming increasingly important in influencing the location decisions of companies, particularly those engaged in mobile foreign investment.

These aspects of globalization have been responsible for increases in material wealth but at the same time there are many reservations concerning unbridled globalization of markets. 'We are delighted to buy our cars from Ford, our televisions from Sony and perhaps our soft drinks from Coca-Cola, but we still want our pensions to be underwritten by our own government. . . . Globalization is great if you are in the United States, not so comfortable if you see your language threatened by Internet English and your children influenced by Hollywood violence' (*The Economist*, 15 July 2000, Review Section, p. 4). Indeed in recent years anti-western sentiment has adversely affected the image of what were once thought to be the unassailable global brands. Many such brands struggle to manage the localization issue in the context of global aspirations but a number have adapted positions in an attempt to be more acceptable locally (Exhibit 1.5). Globalization also refers to the enormous growth in international trade on the one hand and profound concerns about the social consequences on the other hand.

Aspects of the globalization debate which directly affect international firms include:

- new information and communications technologies which enable the firm to have a global presence – a key role for the Internet;
- communication technology which integrates suppliers into their customers' buying processes and consumers' lifestyle;
- growth of non-profit businesses in international markets;
- call for more ethical and social responsibility among international firms;
- emergence of a global culture based on music, clothing and entertainment;
- influence of global branding incorporating services and products.

In regard to the last point many firms now outsource all their manufacturing to become research and development and marketing companies where the value added is carefully appropriated in the brand, e.g. Nike, Levis, 3M.

Exhibit 1.5   Big names seek the safety of camouflage

Whoever thought a McArabia could defend what a Big Mac once stood for? That is essentially the lesson McDonald's and many other global retailers have learnt as a means to coping with general anti-western sentiment. It is a struggle by brands to manage localization. Some do it more effectively than others perhaps because of their business structures, like that of franchising. It allows the licensee's input on local matters like consumer trends and preferences. Some licensees have gone to great lengths, such as Bambang Rachmadi who pre-empted US protests in his Indonesian McDonald's chain by placing green flags of Islam in his restaurants along with religious music and Islamic security guards. This ploy of adapting to the local market is an established marketing strategy for multinational companies, albeit from the top down, devising products to fit with local values and tastes. It explains why Coca-Cola offers more than 200 products worldwide and McDonald's offers Teriyaki Burgers in Japan and Chicken Maharaja Macs in India where beef is not typically eaten. However, this approach also seems to help insure highly visible brands from terrorism and other attacks by fostering a community orientation. Whatever they do, in most countries surveyed by a Harvard Business School study of 1,800 consumers in 12 countries including Turkey, Egypt and Indonesia, 80 per cent of respondents chose global brands over local alternatives. So whereas in some cases firms may opt to leave in place local company names as a security buffer, for others the option is to assimilate to the local culture.

Source: adapted from Murray, S., 'Big names seek the safety of camouflage',
Financial Times, Thursday 5 February 2004, p. 11

Until recently, globalization meant a slow global product roll-out by a large company. Nowadays, relatively small companies engage in global marketing even of sophisticated products. Globalization as a phenomenon is the product of the freeing of trade and technological developments that allow integrated global communications and the possibility of real-time financial transactions and worldwide manufacturing.

Three aspects of globalization are of interest here: the impact of industry structure, influences on the business system and country market interdependence (Ohmae, 1989, 1990; Solberg, 1997). In regard to industry structure, some industries are highly fragmented and serve niche markets which are very segmented, e.g. services, building materials and furniture. Other industries such as consumer electronics, soft drinks and tobacco are highly consolidated and firms in these industries serve mass markets. Competition in fragmented markets is diffuse with the result that small, poorly resourced firms can survive. Consolidated industries and markets tend to be dominated by high-technology multinational firms with low-cost facilities. The type of industry structure is determined by entry barriers and their resistance to attack. Scale economies, product differentiation and blocked distribution channels are barriers to market access and help to determine industry structure.

Technology and market liberalization

Cheap and efficient communications allow firms to locate various parts of their production and marketing processes in different countries while maintaining close contact. Modern information technology reduces the need for physical contact between providers and consumers which allows previously untradeable services to be sold internationally. New technologies and advances in existing ones enable companies to concentrate on producing standardized, reliable and low priced products that alleviate life's burdens and expand discretionary time and spending power without worrying about the details of what everyone thinks they might like (Levitt, 1983, p. 99). In this world manufacturers gain global scale economies and experience curve benefits in production, distribution, marketing and management through improvements in information and communications; transportation; and manufacturing technologies.

Firms in regional markets

In reality, global markets are a figment of cosy imaginative thinking; many international companies expand only to nearby markets of close business distance. European companies, typically, expand to other nearby European countries, US companies expand into Canada and Mexico, and increasingly to Europe, and Japanese companies concentrate their overseas ventures in the south-east Asian region and in the United States.

For many years, large well-known international companies were in fact a series of national entities held together in ownership, but not for any strategic reason. These companies coped with high tariffs, high transport costs and very restrictive local content rules by establishing subsidiaries in each country in which they operated. The lowering of trade barriers, transport and communications costs helped to reduce manufacturing and transaction costs. For example, by 2004, about 20 per cent of Unilever's ice-cream production in Europe was sold across borders compared with about 3 per cent in 1990. This consolidation and trade expansion resulted in the closure of many production plants. By producing regionally for local markets, Unilever achieves production scale economies. The circumstances in marketing were different. Unilever ice-cream brands are different in most markets, indicating that market convergence is yet to manifest itself in a major way. Unilever recognizes this diversity in international markets but attempts to balance local and global demands primarily through the astute management of its brands. While the company has a range of ice-cream brands in different markets, after much effort to standardize, only the logo has been standardized for global markets.

Understanding international marketing: a framework

The firm decides whether to internationalize by determining the scope of international marketing and the strategies available to it and by establishing a framework to understand the internationalization process in the firm. In order to make such a decision and develop an appropriate analytical framework, it is necessary to understand the scope of international marketing in the firm (Chapter 1). A framework consisting of four parts has been developed to assist in understanding the process (Figure 1.9).

In Part I: Understanding the international marketing environment we explore the value of the various theories and conceptualizations of the firm in international markets (Chapter 2). We then attempt to understand the impact of organizational issues on the internationalization process – the firm's resource base and managerial capacity (Chapter 3). A key aspect of this part is also to understand competitors (Chapter 4) and the broader environment of international marketing (Chapters 5–7). Topics examined include an analysis of culture in international marketing (Chapter 5); the political economy of international markets and how competitive advantage may be created (Chapter 6); how to cope with political risk, uncertainty and the regulations and directives of governments and international organizations (Chapter 7).

In Part II: Product and brand strategies in international markets, the dimensions of the international marketing strategy for three different types of firms are examined. Chapter 8 examines international marketing strategies pursued by consumer products companies, while the circumstances facing industrial products and services companies are examined in Chapters 9 and 10 respectively. These three sets of circumstances cover the broad range of experiences facing the international firm at any one time or at different stages in their evolution. Acknowledging the trend toward corporate and global branding, Chapter 11 explicitly examines the issues associated with international marketing communications and building the global brand. The matter of selecting international markets and international market segmentation is treated in Chapter 12.

In Part III: Strategic challenge of international market entry, the ways of entering international markets are examined. The concept of entering foreign markets through the principal modes of entry, exporting (Chapter 13), strategic alliances (Chapter 14) and foreign direct investment and acquisition (Chapter 15), are examined in detail. This section ends with an evaluation of the strategic choices open to the firm in entering foreign markets in particular circumstances and how best to choose among them (Chapter 16).

In Part IV: International marketing operations, ways of implementing the international marketing programme are examined. This means strategically aligning strategy and performance by ensuring that the company's products and services are delivered

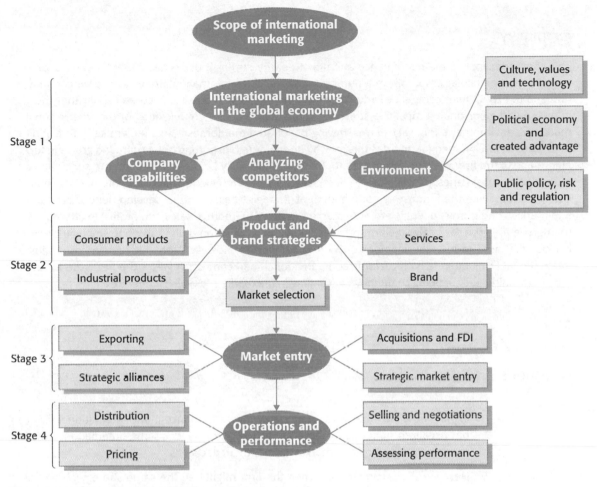

Figure 1.9 Understanding international marketing: a framework

efficiently and effectively to international customers (Chapter 17) and priced to meet the requirements of the company and its customers while remaining competitive (Chapter 18). It also means communicating, negotiating and selling in myriad international markets while taking account of the cultural and business factors already examined (Chapter 19). In Chapter 20, the overall operations of the firm are examined to ensure that performance objectives and strategic targets established for the firm in international markets are attained.

Summary

This chapter examines the performance and growth of the firm as it diversifies into new international markets with particular emphasis on a number of issues. Firms internationalize to overcome competition and to exploit their competitive advantages in new markets. In order to succeed usually they must adopt multidimensional competitive strategies more suited to the complexities of the international marketing environment. Innovative firms, having penetrated the domestic market, are keen to exploit their leads in foreign markets. Initially, this may be done through exporting but as demand grows in foreign markets the firm may increase its commitment progressively by moving through the spectrum of foreign sales subsidiaries, joint ventures or direct investments. In seeking to improve international marketing performance the firm uses a combination of strategies based on the development of products and markets and modes of entry into new markets in order to improve sales and profits. In attempting to improve the growth in sales the firm pursues one or a combination of the following strategies: market penetration; product development; market integration to increase profits or reduce costs. Most international firms operate with customized international marketing strategies – the key issue for the firm is obtaining and retaining competitive advantage in the markets in which it operates.

Questions

1. Explain how the improvement of marketing performance in the international firm can be visualized in terms of new product/technology decisions, international market investment decisions and market development decisions.

2. Describe the circumstances when the firm might use the same strategy abroad as it does in the domestic market.

3. One of the arguments for internationalizing are the associated scale benefits. Describe situations where scale benefits may not apply.

4. Many factors affect the environment facing the international firm. Identify and describe the more important of these. Explain how the international firm can cope with this environment.

5. Demonstrate that by differentiating itself strategically the firm can improve its international marketing performance.

6. Describe the forces leading to fragmented international markets and show how firms attempt to consolidate these markets.

7. What is the meaning of globalization for marketing and what are the principal arguments for and against it?

References

Bartels, R. (1968) 'Are domestic and international marketing dissimilar?', *Journal of Marketing*, **32**, 56–61.

Buzzell, R. D. (1968) 'Can you standardize multinational marketing?', *Harvard Business Review*, **46** (November–December), 102–13.

Carroad, P. A. and Carroad, C. A. (1982) 'Strategic interfacing of R&D and marketing', *Research Management* (January), 28–33.

Cateora, P. R. and Ghauri, P. N. (1999) *International Marketing – European Edition*, Maidenhead, Berkshire, England: McGraw Hill.

Craig, C. S. and Douglas, S. P. (1996) 'Developing strategies for global markets: an evolutionary perspective', *The Columbia Journal of World Business*, Spring, pp. 71–103.

Dyer, J. H. and Ouchi, W. G. (2002) 'Japanese style partnerships – giving companies a competitive edge', in *Managing Innovation and Change*, J. Henry and D. Mayle, Eds, London: Sage.

Fayerweather, J. (1982) *International Business Strategy and Administrative*, 2nd edn, Cambridge, MA: Ballinger.

Kahler, R. and Kramer, R. L. (1977) *International Marketing*, 4th edn, Cincinnatti, OH: Southwestern Publishing.

Keegan, W. J. (1989) *Global Marketing Management*, 4th edn, Hemel Hempstead: Prentice Hall International.

Kroeber, A. L. (1952) *The Nature of Culture*, University of Chicago Press.

Levitt, T. (1983) 'The globalization of markets', *Harvard Business Review*, **61** (May–June), 92–102.

Mitchell, O. and Bradley, F. (1986) 'Export commitment in the firm – strategic or opportunistic behaviour', *Journal of Irish Business and Administrative Research*, **8** (Part 2), 12–19.

Ohmae, K. (1989) 'Managing in a borderless world', *Harvard Business Review*, **67** (May–June), 152–61.

Ohmae, K. (1990) *The Borderless World*, New York, NY: Harper Business.

Pfeffer, J. (2002) 'Competitive advantage through people' in *Managing Innovation and Change*, J. Henry and D. Mayle, Eds, London: Sage.

Porter, M. E. (1985) *Competitive Advantage*, New York: Free Press.

Quelch, J. A. and Hoff, E. J. (1986) 'Customizing global marketing', *Harvard Business Review*, **64** (May–June), 59–68.

Ralston, D., Holt, D. H., Terpstra, R. H. and Yu, K.-C. (1997) 'The impact of national culture and economic ideology on management work values: a study of the United States, Russia, Japan and China', *Journal of International Business Studies*, **28**, First Quarter, (1), pp. 177–207.

Solberg, C. A. (1997) 'A framework for analysis of strategy development in globalizing markets', *Journal of International Marketing*, **5** (1), 9–30.

Szymanski, D. M., Bharadwrj, S. G. and Varadarajan, P. R. (1993) 'Standardization versus adaptation of international marketing strategy: an empirical investigation', *Journal of Marketing*, **57** (October), 1–17.

Terpstra, V. (1983) *International Marketing*, 3rd edn, Chicago, IL: The Dryden Press.

Tidd, J., Bassant, J. and Pavitt, K. (2002) 'Learning through alliances' in *Managing Innovation and Change*, J. Henry and D. Mayle, Eds, London: Sage.

Walters, P. G. (1986) 'International marketing policy: a discussion of the standardization construct and the relevance for corporate policy', *Journal of International Business Studies*, **17** (Summer), 55–69.

White, H. C. (1993) 'Values come in styles, which mate to change' in *The Origin of Values*, M. Hechter, L. Nadel and R. E. Michod, Eds, Aldine, New York: de Gruyter.

Wills, J., Samli, A. C. and Jacobs, L. (1991) 'Developing global products and marketing strategies: a construct and research agenda', *Journal of Academy of Marketing Science*, **19** (Winter), 1–10.

Yip, G. S. (1989) 'Global strategy: in a world of nations?', *Sloan Management Review*, **31** (Fall), 29–41.

Part I Understanding the international marketing environment

Part I consists of six chapters. Chapter 2 presents the various theories that help to understand the process of international marketing in the global economy. The emphasis in on developing a managerial framework to support decision-making in international markets. Chapter 3 is devoted to evaluating the capability of the firm to compete in international markets and to recommend possible development paths for the company. Chapter 4 turns attention to an evaluation of competing firms and attempts to determine the nature and extent of international competition likely to be faced by the firm. Three major aspects of the international marketing environment are then examined. Chapter 5 examines the impact of culture on managerial decision-making and buyer behaviour, how human values possessed by people affect their lives and how technology or material culture and aesthetics affects the nature of products and services demanded. Influences from the political economy and the effects of created advantage on the firm are examined in Chapter 6 and the last chapter in this section examines how public policies and regulations affect the international transfer of products, services and ideas (Chapter 7).

2 International marketing in the global economy

To understand the role of international marketing in the firm it is necessary to consider decisions being made as part of a continuum and not as discrete components corresponding to the various modes used to transfer assets internationally. It is limiting, therefore, to treat exporting behaviour as something very different from licensing, joint ventures or foreign direct investment in the establishment of an international firm. This artificial separation is a reflection of the 'production–selling' versus 'marketing' syndrome. Successful firms adopt a marketing approach which is more comprehensive as it integrates all managerial aspects of the international firm in the context of the international marketing system.

After studying this chapter you should be able to:

■ describe major trade and transaction theories of the firm in international markets;

■ apply the concept of comparative advantage to the international firm;

■ specify the importance of a market orientation for the international firm;

■ design a framework to analyze the international marketing behaviour of the firm in the context of strategically positioning the firm in the international marketing system.

Theory and practice of international marketing

Managers and firms have for a long time given explicit attention to the international marketing dimension of business and have recognized it as a separate field with regard to strategy formulation and organizational requirements. In contrast to purely domestic operations, marketing activities which take place across national boundaries require considerable familiarity with multiple marketing environments and their culture and business practices, international exchange rate determination and the various geopolitical pressures which affect the firm. The context for international marketing activities is additional market and exchange risk, conflict among firms of different cultures, environmental adjustments and the influences of economic, political and cultural differences.

Because of this contextual variability a differentiated approach to international marketing is required. A strategy for international marketing which assumes a non-differentiated approach is, however, prevalent in this literature (Bartels, 1968; Buzzell, 1968; Levitt, 1983). These authors have argued that markets are global and that marketing strategies should also be global and, therefore, standardized and non-differentiated. Because of this focus, many scholars and some managers ignore market heterogeneity and in the circumstances of a differentiated world market, a non-segmented strategy is inevitably suboptimal. The simple standardized international marketing models are weak in predicting outcomes in the complex and often turbulent environment which characterizes international marketing.

Managerial theory of international marketing

Marketing in the business system

A long-term marketing orientation draws together suppliers, customers, competitors and partners to create value in the entire business system. It is the business system as a whole that creates value (Lanning and Michaels, 1988) within a set of dynamic relationships (Brandenburger and Nalebuff, 1996) among customers, suppliers, competitors, partners and the company itself. The international marketing system consists of five major participant groups:

- customers;
- competitors;
- partners;
- suppliers; and
- the company itself.

In this system the company is the focus of attention as it establishes relationships with all the other participants who are located in the domestic market and abroad. In establishing relationships in this international marketing system the company considers the environment of international marketing which reflects the influence of culture, economics and politics on the system (Figure 2.1). Developing an appropriate international marketing strategy involves coping with the specified relationships within this international marketing system.

Orientation of the company in the business system

The business system succeeds if it produces value for its participants – otherwise it perishes. Each participant must add value, otherwise there is no reason to be there. An effective business system is a value system, where added value is the source of power in

Figure 2.1
International
marketing
system

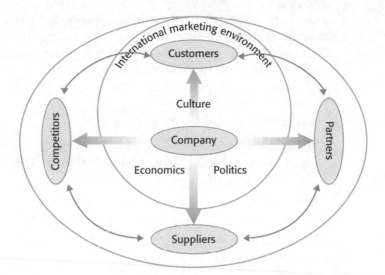

the business system. The question is one of determining the importance of the company to all other participants in the business system.

Firms which participate in the business system as partners complement the company and its suppliers, thereby increasing the value to customers. Partners are most important in international markets: agents, distributors, joint venture partners, and other service organizations. By including such firms in the framework a much richer and more accurate view of the business system in which international marketing activity takes place is obtained.

Many firms are both competitors and partners with respect to their suppliers. British Airways and Singapore Airlines compete for passengers, landing slots and gates, but they played a partnership role in the development of the Airbus superjumbo for which both are major customers.

As we move further into the knowledge based economy, such complementary partnerships on the supply side are likely to become standard practice. This is especially true where there is a large front-end investment and where the variable costs are relatively modest. Practically all the costs in designing computer software are front-end, so the larger the market, the greater the leverage and the more development costs can be spread.

Viewing the value in the business system as the result of a network of important relationships highlights two important facts. First, decisions made by one company affect and are affected by decisions made by other firms. Second, some companies often make decisions that are normally associated with those of other participants in the system. Thus, the firm makes important decisions which affect suppliers, just as suppliers make important decisions which are normally thought of as being in the purview of the firm. Because so many decisions are part of a network in which a decision in one company directly or indirectly influences decisions in other firms, major decisions must be consistent with the goals of participants in the network and their products. Decisions must also complement each other to maximize their overall impact (Barabba and Zaltman, 1991, pp. 212–16). These notions of consistency and complementarity apply to the network of firms in the business system and are important elements which focus on synergy among diverse firms. The company in the business system is a member of a network in which added value and synergy are created. In summary, the firm is a member of a business system:

- that produces value and synergy;
- that reflects a system of customer relationships;
- in which knowledge is an integral part of a value provision system;
- which manifests dynamic relationships among the company, customers, suppliers, competitors and partners;
- that competes as a system in international markets;
- that seeks consistency and complementarity of marketing action;
- in which decisions made by one firm affect and are affected by decisions of other firms in the business system.

A framework for international marketing

Firms with broad resource bases tend to pursue diversification (Penrose, 1959; Montgomery and Hariharen, 1991). Such firms tend to enter new markets where the resource requirements match their resource capabilities. International market diversification results from excess capability in resources which have multiple uses. In order to utilize more fully its R&D or its new product development skills, capabilities which are imperfectly mobile across international markets and face high transaction costs, a firm might seek opportunities outside its original market. The more generalizable the resources, the wider the opportunities available. In developing their product-markets, therefore, many firms, especially larger firms, are able to exploit the scope economies associated with shared physical assets, downstream activities, knowledge and learning (Figure 2.2).

International marketing is a discipline containing a number of paradigms which draw on a number of theories. Theories are operationalized through the decisions taken by managers in dealing with the international environment. Identifying suitable paradigms is important since a paradigm indicates what a discipline should study, what questions it should ask and what rules should be followed in interpreting the answers obtained (Cateora, 1993). International marketing is not a single theory but, rather, a discipline containing a number of theories which when applied become the operating technologies of practitioners engaged in the international marketing process (Carman, 1980). The objective of any theory of international marketing should be to explain marketing behaviour as it crosses international boundaries including:

- impact of different value systems and culture on needs, wants and demands for products and services;
- buyer behaviour in different markets;
- company reaction to changes in culture – global convergence or divergence;
- flows of imports and exports worldwide;

Figure 2.2
Sources of scope
economies in
the international
firm

Shared assets	Product diversification	Market diversification
Physical assets	Flexible manufacturing, e.g. Ford, Caterpillar, Komatsu	Global brand name, e.g. Philips
Channel activities	Same distribution channel, e.g. Matsushita, Gillette	Servicing customers worldwide, e.g. Citiqroup, HP
Knowledge/ learning	Research and development, e.g. NEC	Knowledge integration, e.g. Procter & Gamble, Cap Gemini

Source: adapted from Ghosal, Sumantra (1987) 'Global strategy: an organizing framework', *Strategic Management Journal*, 8, 5, September–October, p. 435

- joint venture and licensing activities;
- location and direction of overseas investment.

Trade and transaction costs

There are a number of theories which attempt to explain international business patterns that include the worldwide flow of imports and exports, the pattern of joint ventures and licensing arrangements and the location and direction of overseas investment.

Absolute advantage and the international firm

Trade between countries arises because of the possession of an absolute or comparative advantage in the basis for trade. This explains trade between two countries, the first with an absolute advantage in the production of one product and the second in the production of a different product. Absolute advantage, the trade theory developed by Adam Smith, the eighteenth-century British economist, may arise because of differences in factors such as:

- climate;
- quality of land;
- natural resource endowments including:
  - labour, capital;
  - technology; or
  - entrepreneurship.

According to this theory it is sensible for each country to specialize in the product in which it has an absolute advantage and to secure its needs of the products in which it has a disadvantage through foreign trade. It is mere common sense that if one country is very good at making hats and another is very good at making shoes, then total output can be increased by arranging for the first country to concentrate on making hats and the second on making shoes. Then, through trade in both goods, more of each can be consumed in both places. That refers to absolute advantage. Each country is better than the other at making a certain good, and so profits from specialization and trade.

The extent of benefit from specialization and trade will depend, of course, on the prices at which trading takes place. This brings in the concept of 'opportunity cost', meaning what a country will have to give up of one product in order to secure another. Like other trade theories this one assumes that a regime of 'free and fair' trade exists between countries, something much in dispute. The activities of the World Trade Organization and UNCTAD (UN Commission for Trade and Development) and GATT (General Agreement on Tariffs and Trade) are focused on these matters.

Comparative advantage and the international firm

If a country possesses an absolute advantage in the two products traded, however, there may not be any trade since the country with the absolute advantage in producing both products has nothing to gain. An alternative explanation may be sought in the possession of comparative advantage, the trade theory associated most closely with David Ricardo, the nineteenth-century British economist. With this theory, a country may have an absolute advantage in producing both products but, as long as the weaker country has a comparative advantage in the production of one of the products, trade will occur.

Comparative advantage exists in every country, even in situations where the country has a poor reputation in the activity concerned. Indeed, each country can have a comparative advantage in making a certain product even if it is worse at making that product than any other country. This is a matter of definition: a country has a comparative advantage where its margin of superiority is greater, or its margin of inferiority smaller.

Accordingly, when commentators on African countries, or Australia or wherever else, state that such countries have no comparative advantage in anything, they are simply confusing absolute advantage, for which their claim may or may not be true, with comparative advantage, for which it is certainly false. The distinction must be understood because the case for free trade is often thought to depend on the existence of absolute advantage – and is therefore thought to collapse whenever absolute advantage does not exist. But economic theory shows that gains from trade follow from comparative advantage. Since comparative advantage is never absent, this gives the theory far broader scope than most popular critics suppose.

In particular, it shows that even countries which are desperately bad at making everything can expect to gain from international competition. If countries specialize according to their comparative advantage, they can prosper through trade regardless of how inefficient, in absolute terms, they may be in their chosen speciality.

The comparative advantage concept, especially with exchange rates incorporated, is less restrictive and more general. It also serves the useful purpose of demonstrating the importance of exchange rate movements to the marketing strategies of the firm in international markets. An adverse movement in exchange rates could easily wipe out the benefits of an otherwise excellent international marketing programme. The comparative advantage concept, in particular, leads to a good first approximation in regard to exchange of goods and services between countries.

The theory of comparative advantage provides important guidelines in the formulation of a theory appropriate to understanding the firm in international markets. Trade between countries is beneficial for all countries involved if each specializes in those products for which its factors of production, confined to land, labour and capital, make it, compared with other countries, more efficient. The country need not have an absolute advantage in producing any product over all countries; it need only be relatively more efficient in producing some products than others. Trade theories provide a first approximation of what might exist in a theoretical world but with government interference and changing political agencies they are unlikely to be found in practice.

Transactions costs in international markets

Practically every firm, by virtue of its history, possesses some kind of unique asset that is the potential source of a stream of profits to the owner. These assets may consist of a technological, marketing or managerial capability or a natural resource position not fully possessed by other firms.

Suppose that for any reason a firm cannot export; then it must sell its special assets or services – licensing in the case of know-how – to a foreign firm or it must establish a foreign affiliate. Suppose the source of the firm's competitive advantage is its technological know-how. If the regime of appropriability in which the firm operates permits only weak legal enforcement of rights over intellectual property, transactional problems will abound, and alternative control modes are likely to be preferred (Teece, 1981). Know-how often cannot be codified since it has an important tacit component. Even when it can, it is not always readily understood by the receiver, and it is extremely difficult to transfer without intimate personal contact involving training, demonstration and participation. Even when transaction difficulties are apparent, establishing a foreign subsidiary is an extreme response to the needs of a one-off transfer.

The above arrangements, although expressed in the context of assets which are based on technological know-how, extend to many different kinds of asset which are difficult to trade, e.g. managerial and organizational know-how, goodwill or brand loyalty. These represent types of assets for which markets may falter as effective exchange mechanisms. Accordingly, the existence of high transaction costs is one of the major issues which lies behind foreign direct investment.

Limitations of trade theory and transaction cost explanations

There are a number of limitations in the traditional trade and transactions cost explanations of the firm in international markets, flowing in part from the simplifying assumptions of the model. Some key assumptions are that factors of production, land, labour and capital are immobile between countries, that perfect information exists as to international trade opportunities and that trading firms in different countries are independent entities. Also, the model assumes perfect competition and does not allow for oligopoly or monopoly. Trade theory does not explicitly recognize technology, know-how or management and marketing skills as significant factors of production which can be the basis for comparative advantage. Probably the most important limitation of trade theory is that it assumes that traditional importing and exporting is the only way of transferring products and services across borders. It does not recognize that the firm may supply foreign demand through, for example, licensing or foreign production.

It also misses the rationale behind the twentieth-century development of marketing by assuming that products sold in the international marketplace are standard, basic and transferable – wheat, cotton and wine, for example.

The principal deficiency of international trade theory and transaction cost economics explanations is that while they contribute to our understanding of the greater wealth-producing potential of countries on efficiency grounds they cannot explain differences in innovation or in the quality of products and services produced in different countries. Trade theory is based on an assumed homogeneity of firms as opposed to the diversity of firms observed. Transaction cost economics can contribute to explaining firm diversity only by diverging from such neo-classical assumptions as homogeneous demand. In addition there is considerable difficulty in operationalizing transactions costs which limits the contribution of this aspect of the theory. An alternative theory of competition which explains firm diversity by building on the concepts of comparative advantage and which can be applied to the international marketing arena is required.

Nature of the international firm

Until the mid-1960s, there was little interest in the phenomenon of the firm in international markets. Neither was there much interest in internationalization as a process culminating in foreign direct investment. Later, the international company was seen as one that exports capital, moves products and equity from countries where returns are low to markets where returns are higher, earning the profits of arbitrage while simultaneously contributing to the more efficient worldwide allocation of capital (Teece, 1981). The predictions of capital arbitrage theories, however, are quite different from the resource transfer activities of international firms, who invest, borrow, buy and sell in different markets. There are considerable cross-flows of investments and products between markets, which make the role of the international firm worth examining.

A more plausible theory of foreign direct investment appeals to oligopoly theory and suggests two major reasons why firms should operate beyond their borders (Hymer, 1970):

■ bypass competition by acquiring it or displacing it;
■ to employ the firm's special competitive advantages abroad, such as financial skills, access to capital, entrepreneurship and marketing skills. There are various ways to ensure that the benefits accrue to the firm.

The product in which the competitive advantage is embodied could be exported or the technology used to make the product could be licensed to, or produced under, a joint venture with a foreign firm. The firm prefers to invest abroad in many situations to avoid technological misappropriation and to prevent the costly bargaining between licensor and licensee, on the one hand, and the inherent instability and danger of technological misappropriation of joint ventures on the other (Hymer, 1970; Killing, 1982). It is the costs associated with these forms of transfer and the extent of control under each which decides the hierarchical mode of organization. These insights shift emphasis away from international trade and finance toward industrial organization and marketing.

Resource theory of international marketing

From the previous discussion there is considerable evidence that traditional comparative advantage and transaction cost theories should be modified to allow for significant resource heterogeneity and immobility among firms in an industry and between markets. In this context the firm gains a comparative advantage over other firms by making the best use of heterogeneous resources which are much more sophisticated than the land, labour and capital, homogenous resources, assumed in traditional theories. Intangible resources such as organizational culture, knowledge and capabilities should also be included. These higher-order, complex resources are most important for modern companies and their countries, as attested to by Hong Kong, Japan and Singapore which have virtually no natural resources. While these resources are not considered 'natural' endowments they form the most important resources that collectively constitute the capabilities of the firm and provide the firm with its competitive advantage.

Sources of competitive advantage

Until recently managers, customers and society generally were conditioned by a scarcity paradigm which emanated from the industrial age, where the focus was on managing and allocating scarce resources, managing risk and seeking efficiencies. In the knowledge age, capitalizing on new technologies, international competition and widespread product parity in industrial and consumer goods markets, the focus is on abundance, where considerations such as growth, adding value, creating wealth and exceeding customer expectations, not just meeting them, have become the centre of the firm's attention. Knowledge and its tangible manifestation, technology, is the principal source of value and power in the modern economy. Technology raises returns on investment and living standards, while by-passing the laws of diminishing returns, the centrepiece of traditional economic thinking. In these circumstances the greater the knowledge and technological intensity of the firm's output, the greater the likelihood that the firm can distinguish itself in international markets.

Knowledge may be defined as objective, knowing the facts, which can be taught, or experiential knowledge, knowing how something is done (Penrose, 1959). The critical distinction is between knowledge which is explicit and capable of articulation and, therefore, transferable at low cost, and knowledge which is tacit and manifested only in its application and not amenable to transfer. These two forms of knowledge underlie the firm's international competitive advantage. By distinguishing between these two forms of knowledge, it is easier to consider the issue of transferability across space and through time and between individuals, especially when located in different countries and conditioned by different cultures. Explicit knowledge is revealed by its communication whereas tacit knowledge is revealed through its application. This distinction is important for the manner and mode of transfer of products, services and technology in international markets.

Analyzing the firm's capability in terms of its knowledge base provides an understanding of the conditions under which competitive advantage is both built and sustained (Grant, 1991, p. 452). In many cases, competitive advantage depends on the firm's procedures for integrating knowledge. Branding illustrates the successful integration of product and customer knowledge into a brand name and logo that distinguishes the brand from myriad other competing products in the market. Most successful firms use complex sets of routines, attitudes and operations, supported by sophisticated communications technologies which are manifest in the firm's culture and management practices. For international marketing firms, the greater the span of knowledge being integrated, and the more sophisticated the procedures used, the more difficult it is for rivals to copy.

If, however, the firm's competitive advantage is insufficient or is short lived, so too will be the benefit for the firm. Durability is a key factor influencing the speed with which the resource depreciates. Most resources have a limited life span and earn only temporary profits; hence the benefits of speed to market and pioneering. Durability relates to issues of the life cycle. For this reason, firms attempt to reduce the possibility of substitution and imitation. Preventing imitation by establishing property rights to scarce resources, marketing information and other factors which impede imitative competition protects the benefits accruing to the firm (Lippman and Rumelt, 1992). Appropriability deals with the issue of who captures the value that the resource creates. The value of the resource may by subject to bargaining among customers, suppliers, distributors and employees. In many situations the firm that owns the resource does not capture the full value of the resource; the value dissipates to other firms in the business system. This is a matter of concern in the foreign market entry decision whereby some modes of entry favour the appropriation of value to the firm while others do not.

The dilemma for the international firm is to sustain competitive advantage by building barriers to imitation while effectively replicating that knowledge internally, but across markets. Imitability means that the resources must have a physical uniqueness which may be patented or are unique in some way and accumulated over time, e.g. brand loyalty. It also means that it should be impossible for outsiders to disentangle what the resource is or how to create it. Such causal ambiguity is often associated with organizational capabilities. To protect a resource, firms often engage in a strategy of economic deterrence whereby they make large investments in the asset relative to current market share. Causal ambiguity, uncertainty regarding the causes of differences among firms, prevents would-be imitators from knowing exactly what to imitate or how to do it (Peteraf, 1993, p. 183). Such uncertainty about differences among competitors arises from:

- special product formulations;
- brand management capabilities;
- internal company management routines; and
- processes which can be patented or copyrighted to limit imitation.

Building equity into brands, competitive alliances and foreign direct investments are alternative ways of addressing the dilemma in international markets. Superior market positions depend on the firm's customer base, relations with suppliers and partners, relations with customers (e.g. brand equity), facilities and systems, and the firm's own endowment of technology and complementary property rights. These are the company's assets or resource endowments which the company has accumulated over time. In addition, the company possesses certain capabilities, the glue that binds the firm's assets together and enables them to be used to advantage (Day, 1994, p. 38). Capabilities are so deeply embedded in the organization's routines and practices that they cannot easily be traded or imitated (Dierickx and Cool, 1989). The firm's competitive advantages are derived, therefore, from the nature of the firm's products, markets, technological orientation, resources and knowledge. Thus, firms which provide competitively priced, knowledge based and technically superior products in the domestic market have clear marketing advantages which can be exploited on international markets. In a study of the internationalization process among medium-sized companies, Yip, Gomez Biscarri and Monti (2000) discover that a sequence process exists – from competitive advantage in the domestic market to internationalization which is more common than from internationalization to advantage. These authors conclude that it is important to start with an initial competitive advantage that can be leveraged abroad.

International transfer of knowledge based assets

To control and manage their knowledge base, companies attempt to establish property rights on their technology and products. The appropriability of a knowledge base depends on whether it is tacit or explicit. Tacit knowledge is not directly appropriable because it cannot be directly transferred. It can be appropriated only through its application in production. Explicit knowledge, because it is in the public domain, may be re-sold by anyone who acquires it; it is a public good. Except for patents, brands and copyrights, knowledge is generally inappropriable by means of market transactions. Hence, the preponderance of brands, patents and copyrighted knowledge in international markets on the one hand, and intrafirm transfers such as joint ventures or foreign direct investment on the other. This assumes that the company is operating in countries where knowledge owners are protected by legally established property rights.

The transferability and appropriability of knowledge together provide a reason for the dominance of the firm in international marketing. Explicit knowledge is transferred internationally by means of finished products and services which are usually exported. Tacit knowledge, as found in high technology systems and products, is transferred internationally by means of strategic alliances or foreign direct investment, depending on the degree of application involved, because individuals are the principal repositories of such knowledge and the movement of people is required.

Summary

Analytical frameworks in international marketing have depended on theories and paradigms developed in other areas, especially international trade, industrial organization and strategic marketing. In this context the dominant position of the firm in the international marketing system is recognized and the key role of value added and its provision within a business system that is increasingly international in its activities and orientation must be considered.

Each of these areas has provided elements which allow us to build a framework in which to develop international marketing strategies. Valuable insights into the conditions under which international exchange of assets (products and services) occurs may be gleaned from international trade theory, especially the effect of fluctuating exchange rates on marketing programmes. From industrial organization theory the role of the firm in the internationalization process, and especially the reasons for foreign direct investment, may be understood. Because the firm in international markets must deal with relatively high transaction costs it is necessary to consider various modes of foreign market entry used in transferring assets abroad. There is, however, a need for a managerial theory of international marketing within the business system which integrates decisions on manufacturing and marketing. The managerial theory of international marketing developed here provides a framework to identify and evaluate generic product-market and business system strategies for international marketing.

Questions

1. Describe the international marketing task facing the firm and outline an approach to the study of international marketing.

2. What are the principal contributions of international trade theory and transaction cost theory, to the study of the firm in international markets?

3. The firm in international markets does not compete on its own but rather it competes within an international marketing system in which there are many independent organizations, some of whom complement the firm's endeavours while others compete directly. Discuss.

4. Explain how product and market diversification can be considered sources of scope economies for the international firm.

5. Describe how the resource based theory of international marketing can help in explaining how the firm engages in the internationalization process.

6. What special difficulties does the firm face in transferring knowledge based assets to customers abroad?

References

Barabba, V. P. and Zaltman, G. (1991) *Hearing the Voice of the Market*, Boston, MA: Harvard Business School Press.

Bartels, R. (1968) 'Are domestic and international marketing dissimilar?', *Journal of Marketing*, **32**, 56–61.

Brandenburger, A. M. and Nalebuff, B. J. (1996) *Co-opetition*, New York, NY: Currency-Doubleday.

Buzzell, R. D. (1968) 'Can you standardize multinational marketing?', *Harvard Business Review*, **46** (November–December), 102–13.

Carman, J. M. (1980) 'Paradigms for marketing theory', *Research in Marketing*, **3**, 1–36.

Cateora, P. R. (1993) *International Marketing*, 8th edn, Homewood, IL: Irwin.

Day, G. (1994) 'The capabilities of market-driven organizations', *Journal of Marketing*, **58** (October), 37–52.

Dierickx, I. and Cool, K. (1989) 'Asset stock accumulation and sustainability of competitive advantage', *Management Science*, **35** (December), 1504–11.

Ghosal, S. (1987) 'Global strategy: an organizing framework', *Strategic Management Journal*, **8** (5), September–October, 425–40.

Grant, R. M. (1991) 'The resource-based theory of competitive advantage: implications for strategy formulation', *California Management Review*, Spring 1991, p. 118.

Hymer, S. (1970) 'The efficiency (contradictions) of multinational corporations', *American Economic Review*, **60**, 441–8.

Killing, P. J. (1982) 'Technology acquisition: license agreement or joint venture', *Columbia Journal of World Business*, **15** (3), 38–46.

Lanning, M. J. and Michaels, E. G. (1988) 'A business is a value delivery system', *McKinsey Staff Paper*, **41**.

Levitt, T. (1983) 'The globalization of markets', *Harvard Business Review*, **61** (May–June), 92–102.

Lippman, S. A. and Rumelt, R. P. (1992) 'Uncertain imitability: an analysis of interfirm differences in efficiency under competition', *The Bell Journal of Economics*, **13**, 418–38.

Montgomery, C. A. and Hariharen, S. (1991) 'Diversified expansion by larger established firms', *Journal of Economic Behaviour and Organization*, **12**, 71–89.

Penrose, E. (1959) *The Theory of the Growth of the Firm*, Oxford. Basil Blackwell.

Peteraf, M. A. (1993) 'The cornerstones of competitive advantage: a resource based view', *Strategic Management Journal*, **14**, 179–91.

Teece, D. (1981) 'The market for know how and the efficient international transfer of technology', *Annals of the American Academy of Political and Social Science*, **458**, 81–96.

Yip, G., Biscarri, J. G. and Monti, J. A. (2000) 'The role of the internationalization process in the performance of newly internationalizing firms', *Journal of International Marketing*, **8** (3), 10–25.

3 Company resources and capabilities

This chapter provides guidance to a resource audit or internal assessment of the firm. The chapter is divided into two parts. The first part examines the firm as an organization and deals with the products it makes and the firm's advantages. The second part focuses on the people in the firm, especially the characteristics of those people who make strategic decisions in the firm – the management.

After studying this chapter students should be able to:

- describe and explain the characteristics of the international firm;
- determine the importance of size, scale of operations, location, technology and product range for the firm in international markets;
- develop management profiles of successful international firms;
- specify the various resources required for internationalization;
- determine the role of management aspirations, commitment and expectations in the internationalization of the firm;
- evaluate how the firm allocates resources in the context of the product-market business system.

Characteristics of the international firm

Sustainable success for the company derives from growth, market share, customer loyalty, image and positioning but primarily from profits and cash flow. Cash flow compared with sales is a fundamental prerequisite for flexible action, especially in the face of the strategic uncertainty, in international markets. There are a number of factors, including the criteria used to judge success, the firm's objectives and goals, its technology and innovation capability, its products, its location and its size, which are believed to influence the performance on international markets and the likelihood of success (Figure 3.1).

Figure 3.1
Factors
influencing
internationalization
of the firm

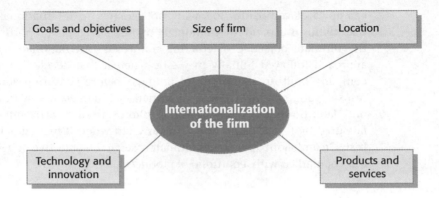

Goals and objectives of the international firm

Managers are concerned with the goals of the firm and the extent to which they are achieved. Avoiding undue instability in sales performance is related to a basic goal, i.e. security and survival. The more unpredictable the firm perceives variations in its sales, the more concerned it is to find diversified sources of sales and growth in order to insulate it from overconcentrating on the domestic market. Diversification into international markets may provide the firm with a degree of insulation ensuring that if it suffers a loss in one market it is less likely to experience losses in all markets. Thus, when the basic security of the firm is threatened by market fluctuations, a powerful motivation to enter international markets may exist.

The strategies that the firm adopts are constrained by its past behaviour and actions. The firm's history of previous investments and its operating routines constrain its future behaviour. A type of market expansion process within the domestic market may have to be experienced before the firm is prepared for international markets.

The strategic decisions facing the firm in international marketing collapse into two groups – those related to products and those related to markets. The firm examines its existing product portfolio and decides whether new products are necessary. Initially, the firm may provide additional products and services for the domestic market before expanding into international markets (Figure 3.2). Alternatively, the company may decide to internationalize on the basis of a single successful product. There are many

Figure 3.2
International
product market
portfolios

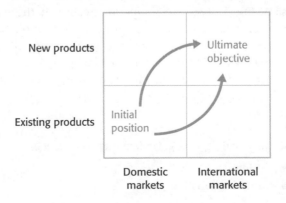

examples of companies following both routes to international markets. More frequently firms expand internationally by first developing a portfolio of products with the ultimate objective of entering numerous international markets. This was the approach followed initially by Nestlé when it first decided to internationalize. The company built up a portfolio of products before venturing abroad. Less frequently firms expand rapidly into many international markets first with a single product and only later do they develop a full portfolio of products. The single product route was favoured by R & A Bailey and Company Ltd when it first launched 'Baileys Original Irish Cream'. Both approaches ultimately serve the objective of being present in a portfolio of markets with a portfolio of products.

Access to resources

A major incentive for internationalization arises when the firm possesses excess or unused resources. These may be resources such as excess capacity in production or special knowledge, highly specialized labour and machinery, by-products from existing operations or financial resources. By excess capacity we mean any slack in any resource under the firm's control. Firms are endowed with different amounts and types of resources and capabilities, which allow them to compete in different ways. Firms which are better endowed have lower average costs than competitors and can provide products and services at lower cost or provide greater customer value.

These resources are difficult to transfer among firms because of transaction costs and because the assets may contain tacit knowledge (Teece *et al.*, 1996, p. 15). Such resources and core capabilities of the firm, particularly those which involve collective learning and are knowledge based, are enhanced as they are applied (Prahalad and Hamel, 1990). Resources and capabilities which are distinctive and superior, relative to those of rivals, may become the basis for competitive advantage if they are matched appropriately to market opportunities (Thompson and Strickland, 1996, pp. 94–5). These resources may, therefore, provide both the basis and direction for the growth of the firm itself, i.e. there may be a natural trajectory embedded in a firm's knowledge base (Peteraf, 1993, p. 182). Hence, the importance of studying the firm itself when attempting to predict its likely performance in international markets.

According to Hunt and Morgan (1995) competition consists of a constant struggle among firms for a comparative advantage in resources which will yield a competitive advantage to them in the market and, in turn, a superior financial performance. The same process produces superior quality in the goods and services in the country, greater efficiency in their production and innovation. Hence, comparative advantage in resources at the company level drives competitive advantage for the company in the market which in turn benefits the company itself and the economy at large.

Firms have access, in varying degrees, to a multitude of potential tangible resources which may be classified as:

■ financial;
■ physical, legal (e.g. trademarks and licences);
■ human;
■ organizational;

Figure 3.3
Comparative
advantage
theory of
competition

Source: adapted from Hunt, S. D. and Morgan, R. M. (1995) 'The competitive advantage theory of competition', *Journal of Marketing*, **59** (April), 9. (Reprinted with permission from the American Marketing Association)

- informational (e.g. consumer and competitor intelligence); and
- relational (e.g. supplier and customer relationships).

These tangible resources are heterogeneous in that every firm possesses an assortment of resources that is in some way unique. When a firm possesses a unique or rare resource it has the potential for producing a comparative advantage for itself (Barney, 1991). According to Hunt and Morgan (1995, p. 7) a comparative advantage in resources exists when a firm's resource assortment enables it to produce a product or service that, relative to existing competitors, is perceived by some market segments to be of superior value and/or can be produced at lower cost. Company resources provide the firm's comparative advantage that in turn allows the firm to develop a competitive advantage. Competitive advantage introduces the possibility of superior quality in the firm's products and services and superior financial performance (Figure 3.3).

Different countries have different competitive strengths often reflecting access for their firms to intangible resources. Germany excels in sophisticated engineering industries and chemicals, Japan in electronics and miniaturization, the United States in computers and the cinema and the British in books, theatre and television drama programmes (Porter, 1986). Local roots appear to be important; a German company does not necessarily become better at engineering if it globalizes. Three reasons are cited for the benefits of being local; the ability to:

- cultivate good suppliers;
- recruit good workers; and
- respond to challenging competitors, facing the same customers and markets.

Areas and regions which immediately fit this description are the Prato region of northern Italy for design and fashion, Silicon Valley in California for computers and the Valencia area in Spain for ceramics. The resources which form the basis of the economic strength of these regions are immobile and the skills and competitive advantages are intimately bound to the local culture and are not easily copied.

Size of the firm in international markets

When a firm's horizons are very limited, even if it has an excellent product, it will have little knowledge of the market. In general, small firms are:

■ less aware of the potential of exporting;
■ less confident of their ability to export;
■ less knowledgeable about how to export;
■ less certain where to find the relevant information about customers and markets abroad.

Many small businesses wrongly believe that only a large enterprise can handle the technical complexity of international markets. Company size may, however, dictate the size of a business opportunity that can be undertaken. Thus small companies frequently find the risks too great and the financial demands too high to undertake very large international projects. There are three main considerations with respect to size:

■ resources;
■ lack of market knowledge;
■ perceived inability to survive in international markets.

The availability of resources such as managerial and foreign marketing know-how, adequate financing and research and development tend to be limited in the small firm, which has less spare resources to devote to internationalization activity. The larger firm's needs for financial assistance may be met by corporate funds and venture capital. Small firms do not have ready access to these sources. Furthermore, small firms generally do not have sufficient people to devote to overseas markets; it also typically lacks expertise in market research and planning. Finally, the smaller firm is usually not as expert as a large firm in processing documentation, the complexity of which increases manifold in overseas dealings.

On the second and third points, company size is no longer much of an impediment to success in international marketing. The small firm usually has no less knowledge and information about markets than the larger firm with 'market scanning' ability and may be just as capable of successful international business. With deregulation, the decline or removal of trade barriers and the fall in transport and communications costs, small companies can serve global markets successfully. The new communications technologies enable most companies to participate in world markets. Large companies no longer have a monopoly on managerial abilities since modern management techniques are also accessible to smaller companies.

Companies active in international markets have access to a much larger pool of management resources than small local firms and they experience a wider range of environmental changes, consumer needs and competitive reactions. By integrating and using this information effectively, the international firm is better prepared for global markets. In many instances, the successful international firm's most valuable resource is a culture reflecting its ability to integrate and use diverse marketing information. Information about information has become a key resource. Communication technologies integrate suppliers into the business processes of customers, which ensures closer communication and efficiency.

Location of the firm

By expanding into additional regions in a large domestic market, the company extends its communication network and develops its skills in marketing a product at a distance. From the extended communications network, there is a greater likelihood of exposure to attention-evoking factors – those influences which cause a firm to consider an international strategy; an unsolicited overseas enquiry, for example. This process is probably more likely to operate in a large country such as the United States or Australia than in a small country such as Belgium, Ireland or New Zealand.

The location of the firm affects the transport costs of products and also, more importantly, information flows. One of the reasons given for higher efficiency in urban regions is that a large number of firms and places of work, concentrated in a small area, improves the conditions for production and creates a favourable 'enterprise environment', e.g. Hong Kong and Singapore. This is especially true in the case of 'information production' that contains a high proportion of face-to-face contacts, since direct personal contacts are often more efficient than other means of contact. These are preferable when the exchange of information involves uncertainty or when it is impossible to foresee what will happen when the information transmitted creates new situations demanding a new exchange of information.

Technology and innovation

There are increasing returns to scale in innovation which means that companies located in countries with advanced technologies like the United States are better placed to innovate further. New ideas often derive by recombining the impacts of existing ideas so that countries and firms with a reputation for ideas produce a continuous stream of innovations. The size of the market also matters; the incentive to innovate is related to the number of potential customers in the market. As innovation involves large fixed costs, e.g. R&D, a larger domestic market initially supports innovation with ease. For this reason US and Japanese firms are better positioned than are their European counterparts. By drawing on two different branches of science to recombine the impact of chemically based photosensitive paper and digitalization, Kodak attempts to drive digital imaging to new markets (Exhibit 3.1).

Exhibit 3.1 Has Kodak missed the moment?

Kodak boss George Fisher's strategy 'to drive digital imaging to new markets' may be eight years old, but its new chief, Daniel Carp, has been credited as the man who might just eventually secure the centenarian camera company's foothold in the digital future with a $3 billion investment and acquisitions drive. Kodak aims to rebalance revenues from 70:30 in favour of film products as of 2000 to 60:40 in favour of digital products by 2006, all the more challenging as revenues crept up by a mere 1.5 per cent while net profits shrank by 63 per cent and film sales continue to dwindle in western and Japanese markets. However, it is easier said than done for a firm whose past is steeped in processing chemicals and photosensitive paper.

For someone who promised no further big investments in traditional film, a $100m purchase of 20 per cent of Lucky Film in China may raise questions about Kodak's ability to kick the celluloid habit. When expected growth rates for film sales in emerging markets of 7–9 per cent per annum for India and 6–8 per cent for China are considered, this sort of purchase may seem an astute move. However, digital photography is becoming increasingly cheaper while performance improves such that new consumers in the emerging markets may more easily skip a generation of technology, which could present problems for Kodak. Indeed, shareholders already suffering a dividend cut, slashed to finance this merger and acquisition drive, may prefer a safer investment in market niches where specialization may lead to smaller revenues but longer sustainability. While the firm has achieved some of Mr Fisher's original dream – Kodak is rivalled only by Sony in the US digital camera market sales – digital technology has opened up the playing field to an array of competitors from HP to Seiko, Epson and Nokia, and it may be down to the shareholders to decide whither the lens points next.

Source: adapted from *The Economist*, 3 January 2004, pp. 46–7.
The Economist © The Economist Newspaper Limited, London (3 January 2004)

Product range in the firm

Another important factor is the type of product line produced by the firm. Products may be described according to the level of knowledge intensity involved. In some cases the knowledge is explicit while in other cases it is tacit. The more explicit the knowledge, the smaller the information flow needed between seller and buyer and, therefore, the greater the chance for a potential seller of being exposed to export stimuli. Complex high-technology products in which knowledge is tacit require a more extensive flow of information and closer contacts between seller and buyer in different countries and cultures, thus exacerbating the communications problem.

Some firms have successfully internationalized their activities by concentrating on knowledge based products for which demand is highly income elastic. With the revolution in technological applications in many industries, the knowledge intensity in many products has increased, e.g. consumer electronics, prescription drugs, animal feed-additives. At the same time rising real incomes in many parts of the world allow consumers to switch from buying income inelastic products such as food commodities, to income elastic products such as luxury goods and sophisticated electronic products. Over time it may be possible for the firm to change its product portfolio in the direction of knowledge intensity while at the same time seeking product markets which are

Figure 3.4
Product-market
income elasticity
and knowledge
intensity

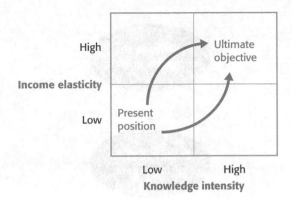

income elastic (Figure 3.4). During the 1960s Japanese firms followed this strategy quite successfully by shifting from producing cheap low-quality products to producing income elastic knowledge intensive products such as highly sophisticated optical equipment and components, fine chemicals, specialized motors and engines and miniaturized consumer electronics.

Management of the international firm

The management of the international firm depends on the possession of an appropriate level of six key success factors:

■ attitudes toward company growth;
■ cognitive style of managers;
■ managerial aspirations for internationalization;
■ commitment to international markets;
■ managerial expectations and internationalization;
■ motivation to internationalize.

Attitudes to company growth

In a general sense, expanding abroad usually involves company growth. Hence, management attitudes to growth in general must be considered. At the same time the disposition of managers to international activities or their intellectual or cognitive styles influence the manner and extent of internationalization in the firm.

Management attitudes towards company growth

Attitudes towards the growth of the firm are determined largely by perceptions of senior management regarding opportunities and barriers to expansion. Many factors influence the manager's attitude to growth through internationalization: managerial

Figure 3.5
Company growth,
cognitive style
and stage of
internationalization

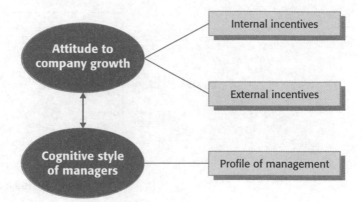

time and expense which must be devoted to sales, visiting foreign markets and collecting market information. As a result of these search and information gathering activities, the manager is more likely to develop a balanced positive attitude toward internationalization. Indeed, successful internationalization is unlikely to occur without the acquisition of relevant knowledge through a process of information internalization in the firm (Liesch and Knight, 1999). The experience thus gained allows the manager to perceive problems as a series of small manageable issues that are more easily resolved. Market changes, therefore, constitute a major force in forming attitudes toward growth of the firm.

At all times, the firm faces a variety of incentives to grow in one or more directions, but at the same time there are barriers to be overcome in implementing an expansion programme. The incentives to expand or grow may originate outside the firm or within it (Figure 3.5). Internal incentives to grow arise largely from the existence within the firm of a pool of unused productive services, resources and special knowledge. In many cases the firm will have a supply of these resources, but in others some resources may have to be acquired or somehow introduced. The presence of unused management services or their ready availability to the firm means that it can grow by increasing total investment. Clearly, then, 'Whenever a firm's management feels that the firm's capacity for growth is greater than that permitted by existing market and existing products, it will have an incentive to diversify' (Penrose, 1959, pp. 144–5). Consequently, the critical internal restriction on growth is that imposed by existing resources, including management.

External incentives to growth include increasing demand for a particular product or service, reflecting changes in the marketing environment and changes in the product technology environment which call for development. External incentives in the institutional environment to grow internationally might include new or improved government-assisted business development schemes or favourable changes in tariffs and other policies designed to encourage international marketing activities.

Cognitive style of managers

International outlook, foreign market orientation and dynamic firm management all refer to the same underlying management construct – a cognitive style which gives rise

Figure 3.6
Management
values dictate
strategic
direction

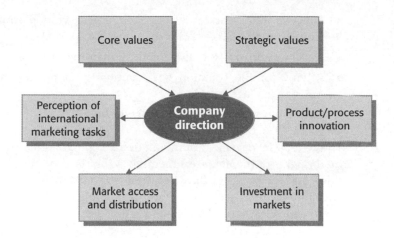

to an attitudinal propensity toward internationalization, reflecting the manager's innovativeness and open-mindedness toward new foreign markets. The more open-minded the cognitive style of the manager, the more favourably will negative export-ing outcomes be accepted (Welch and Wiedersheim-Paul, 1980). Closed-minded as opposed to open-minded managers display a closed cognitive style and are unlikely to adapt to a changing ill-structured international business environment (Bradley, 1984). Firms with a high proportion of such managers are, therefore, less likely to export than their less dogmatic or more open-minded counterparts.

Closed-minded managers favour business environments and management tasks which are structured and familiar (Faschingbauer *et al.*, 1978). Such managers are unlikely to exhibit a high propensity to internationalize. International markets are demonstrably unstructured, involve considerable risk, require considerable innovation and adoption of new ideas and management processes and are characterized by the need for information and the assistance of government support agencies. It is expected, therefore, that active international companies will be much less closed-minded than their passive counterparts. Managers' human values dictate the strategic direction of the firm. The core values of the manager influence the broad thrust of the company while strategic values are directed at more immediate concerns, each of which influ-ences perception, innovation, investment and strategy implementation within the firm (Figure 3.6).

In a general sense, therefore, the origins of the manager may influence decision-making depending on whether the location of the firm may be classified as high-context or low-context, a topic discussed in Chapter 5. As will be noted later, the US has been classified as a low-context society while many European countries, though not all, have been classified as high-context. The location of the firm may, therefore, affect the style of management and the approach to internationalization. As a general statement, two broad styles of management are identified – European and North American (Table 3.1).

In an attempt to be more specific, a survey of European managers (Kakabadse, 1993, p. 31) discovered four distinct styles of management:

- directive autocratic leadership, determinate and passionate – Spanish, British, Finnish, and 50 per cent of Irish managers surveyed;
- consensus-driven – Swedish and the remaining Irish managers;
- striving for the common goal; emphasis on professional skills – German and Austrian managers; and
- managing as élites – French managers.

The style of management of international companies has some of its roots in the cultural origins of the managers themselves, but is also influenced by the way managers think and the way they have been trained to think. It is generally believed that there are national differences among firms competing in international markets – firms in different countries respond to different sets of values:

- different time horizons for investments;
- strategic control combined with poor communications leads to unwieldy corporate bureaucracy in some countries;
- in many countries strategic strength is obtained from consensus at all levels in the firm;
- in some countries, especially in the east, family and group interests provide inner trust, which, with devotion, produces strong competitive firms.

Table 3.1 Styles of management in the international firm

European	North American
• Management of cultural diversity	• Emphasis on shareholders' profits
• People-oriented and internal negotiation important (unions)	• Emphasis on individual – personal achievement and professional mobility
• Long-term and short-term focus	• Functionalism and professionalism
• Emphasis on stakeholders not just shareholders	• Strong competition which is expected to lead to customer satisfaction
• Adaptation to customer needs	• Emphasis on product orientation rather than customer orientation – relationship with customers can border on the adversarial
• Integration of individual into the company	
• Little distinction between personal and professional life	

Aspirations, commitment and expectations of managers

Three characteristics of management are responsible for stimulating internationalization of the firm: managerial aspirations; commitment by the firm to international market development; and management expectations (Johanson and Vahlne, 1977). The interaction of the firm, its resources and characteristics, with the manager's aspirations, commitment and expectations, result in certain international marketing behaviour and outcomes (Figure 3.7).

Figure 3.7
Internal
influences on
international
marketing
behaviour

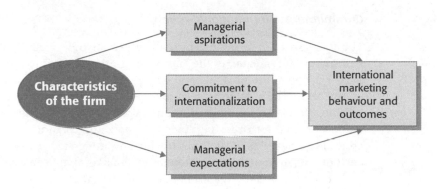

Source: adapted from Johanson, J. and Vahlne, J. E. (1977) 'The internationalization process of the firm – model of knowledge development and increasing foreign marketing commitments', *Journal of International Business Studies*, **8** (1), 22–30

Managerial aspirations for internationalization

Management aspirations reflect the importance the decision-maker places on the achievement of various business goals such as growth, profits and market development and are believed to be a direct determinant of decision-making behaviour. A positive relationship between export marketing behaviour and the decision-maker's aspirations (Simmonds and Smith, 1968) and the development and integration of new knowledge occurs incrementally within the firm (Penrose, 1959; Madhok, 1997). An incremental approach to knowledge acquisition enables managers to form more realistic perceptions on how best to internationalize (Eriksson *et al.*, 1997). Incremental resource commitments lead to increased experiential knowledge which is stored in the procedures and routines of the firm that are directed at the internationalization process (van Ittersum and Candel, 1998, p. 304).

Successful exporters recognize that growth and long-term profitability are achievable only through the adoption of an international marketing outlook. Differences between individuals in international orientation may explain differences in behaviour (Cunningham and Spigel, 1971; Reid, 1981). It is likely that an individual with a high degree of international orientation will have a higher probability both of being exposed to attention-evoking factors and of perceiving them. The value system and past history of the principal decision-maker are also important. The decision-maker's international outlook, i.e. the extent to which he or she perceives and considers as interesting events occurring outside his or her own country, is of central importance (Wiedersheim-Paul *et al.*, 1978, p. 48).

The firm new to international marketing has, however, no previous experience or measure of performance in international markets on which to base a level of aspiration regarding the outcomes of this new activity. For this reason the objective criterion of successful feedback will vary widely from company to company and is likely to be directly related to the perception and expectations of the key decision-makers in each instance (Welch and Wiedersheim-Paul, 1980, p. 338).

Commitment to internationalization

The more specialized resources are in respect of the specific international marketing endeavour, the greater is the firm's commitment to international marketing. The degree of commitment is higher the more the resources are integrated with other parts of the firm. Their value is derived from these integrated activities (Johanson and Vahlne, 1977). An example of resources which cannot easily be directed to another market or used for other purposes is a marketing organization which is specialized around the products of the firm in which an integrated system for maintaining good customer relations in various international markets has been established.

The other aspect of organizational commitment to international marketing refers to the amount of resources committed. This refers to the size of the investment in the market – investment in marketing, organization, personnel and other functional areas. Included are the gathering of foreign market information, assessment of foreign market potential and formulation of basic policies towards international marketing and planning.

Commitment to international markets requires that the firm devotes financial and human resources, as well as management attention, to carrying out new tasks and for building the infrastructure required for international marketing.

Commitment is also related to risk and uncertainty perceptions, where instability or a decline in the domestic market may increase the firm's search for diversification possibilities, thus decreasing the risk previously associated with international markets. Firms classified as committed exhibit a higher propensity to engage in certain planning activities than do non-committed firms. These activities are likely to lead to a more favourable attitude and probably increased commitment. The likelihood of withdrawal from international markets as a result of perceived negative early experience of such markets is thought to be strongly related to the degree of commitment to the internationalization process. In this regard psychological commitment as manifested through changes in attitude is more important than financial commitment. Lack of such commitment frequently shows itself as passive performance in international markets responding to unsolicited requests from foreign potential customers instead of actively seeking new foreign business. A passive disposition usually results in the firm eventually withdrawing from international markets.

Managerial expectations and internationalization

Expectations reflect the decision-maker's present knowledge as well as perceptions of future events. Managers tend to form expectations or opinions about the profitability and riskiness of international marketing on the basis of their own knowledge and/or the experience of other firms. Environmental variables, e.g. unsolicited orders from foreign buyers or fluctuations in the exchange rate, play an important role in management's subjective assessment of the desirability of internationalization.

The single most important determinant of a manager's expectations regarding the performance and behaviour of the firm given a certain level of effort committed to the internationalization process, is the actual business situation facing the firm. As managers gain more experience of a given situation, they are better able to develop more accurate expectations regarding the behaviour and performance of the firm in international markets. Herein lies the role of experiential knowledge, trade missions and trade fairs and other schemes to encourage companies to evaluate international markets.

Company resources in the business system

Resources and capabilities determine the firm's long-run strategy in the business system and their interaction is the primary source of profit. In an environment which is changing rapidly and where consumer tastes and preferences are volatile and myriad, as found in international markets, a definition of the business in terms of what the firm is capable of doing may offer a more durable basis for strategy than a traditional definition, based solely on needs and wants of consumers. Defining markets too broadly is of little help to the firm that cannot easily develop the capabilities to serve such a broad market. The firm's ability to earn profits depends on two factors:

■ the success of the firm in establishing competitive advantage over rivals; and

■ the attractiveness of the industry in which the firm competes.

The two sources of competitive advantage are:

■ the ability of the firm to reduce costs; and

■ its ability to differentiate itself in ways that are important to customers.

The ability to establish a cost advantage requires the possession of scale-efficient plants, access to low-cost raw materials or labour and superior process technology. Differentiation advantages derive from brand reputation, proprietary and patented technology and an extensive marketing network covering distribution, sales and services.

The attractiveness of an industry depends on the power the firm can exert over customers, rivals and others in the business system, which derives from the existence of market entry barriers. Market entry barriers are based on brands, patents, price and the power of competitive retaliation. These are resources which are accumulated slowly over time and a new entrant can only obtain at disproportionate expense (Grant, 1991, p. 115). Other sources of market power such as price-setting abilities depend on market share which is a consequence of cost efficiency, firm size and financial resources. Figure 3.8 integrates these ideas in a way which serves as a very convenient summary of this discussion. An important aspect of the framework for international marketing is that the resources which confer market power may be owned individually by firms or by independent firms located in different countries.

The resource based or core competency view of the firm urges the manager to focus on internal competencies or resources of the firm as the primary driver of performance. Other features that operate at the industry or national economy levels, however, also

Figure 3.8
Influence of
resources on the
profitability of
the firm

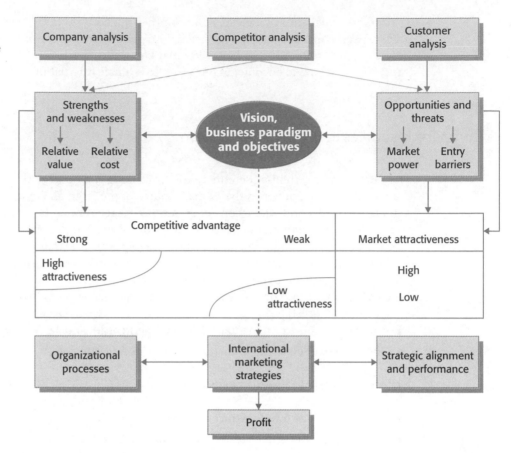

influence performance. A focus on businesses in addition to a focus on core competencies, therefore, may be necessary. By focusing on businesses in which profits are good or in which the firm can obtain an insulated position and by divesting activities in businesses that are unprofitable may bring success; for example, a focus on businesses where the firm has a monopoly or duopoly or where the installed customer base allows the firm to compete on relatively favourable terms.

Following this approach we would look at the firm as a portfolio of businesses rather than a portfolio of competencies. Adhering to a resource based or core competency view limits the ability of individual business units to fully exploit innovative product development opportunities which will usually cross business unit lines. An exclusive focus on resources or core competencies may lead to competing in industries that are fundamentally unattractive in terms of profit potential.

The firm must focus on circumstances both internal and external to itself to understand how to improve its performance. A tendency to look only outward can prevent the firm from developing its own potential while a tendency to look only inward can prevent the firm from understanding the threats and opportunities provided by the external environment. What goes on inside the firm, its positioning, activities, resources and knowledge bases influence performance. The nature of the industries or businesses in which the firm competes also has an important impact. Some industries are inherently more or less profitable than other industries. In this case the industry effect is more important than the firm effect.

The national environment in which the firms do most of their business also has an important impact through overall macroeconomic forces and government policies. The industries that surround industries in which firms compete, for example the supplier, the buyer and complementary industries, also have an impact. Any one or two of these levels might dominate the business system in which the firm operates so the impact of each needs to be assessed.

Managing costs and prices in international markets

In managing the cost side the successful firm is concerned with factor costs, scale and technology effects and exchange rate fluctuations. Factor costs refer to the location specific advantages that accrue to a manufacturer, e.g. labour cost differentials, availability of cheap raw materials and components, access to low-cost capital and government-sponsored industrial promotion incentives. Size, location and technological sophistication of manufacturing plants in different countries can present the firm with significant cost advantages. This is most apparent in comparing a single-plant firm which exports to serve international markets and a multiplant firm serving a selected portfolio of markets. The portfolio of markets allows the firm to leverage differences in competitive market structures to exploit the resulting price differentials.

Exchange rate fluctuations can eliminate cost advantages or make certain locations more attractive. Successful competitors learn how to manage three elements of cost:

■ labour costs;

■ manufacturing scale and technology; and

■ exchange rate fluctuations.

The successful firm does not attempt to reduce the impact of any one of these elements while ignoring the others. It is a question of seeking a balance among the three factors while maintaining flexibility. To do so the firm may have a portfolio of manufacturing locations that allows it to exploit both factor cost advantages and exchange rate differentials. With much of the world's trade denominated in US dollars, the euro or other stable currencies this factor is now less of an issue than it was but every now and again it must be considered. The depreciation of the $ in 2003–04 against the € resulted in more expensive imports into the United States from Europe, causing severe difficulty for many European firms, especially those that depended on exporting as a mode of market entry.

A portfolio of manufacturing locations, however, provides the firm with the opportunity of leveraging factor cost advantages with the objective of integrating them into a global network which would also consider exchange rate fluctuations. Changes in the firm's cost base encourages it to pay close attention to the need to seek improvements in technology and productivity.

On the price side the firm usually attempts to obtain the highest net price possible. A number of factors influence the ability of the firm to derive such prices:

- market structure;
- distribution and branding; and
- product line.

With regard to the first issue, the market in each country is unique in terms of its competitive structure; the intensity of competition determines the level of prices and is dependent on the number and type of competitors in the market. In order to exploit the resulting price differentials, especially when competitor costs are the same as those of the firm, it is advisable to be present in a portfolio of markets. Differential pricing in different international markets can give rise to problems, however, especially when parallel importing is possible.

Access and command of distribution channels is also a well-known competitive advantage. Well-known brands with a quality image and established reputation command a price premium. A broad product line also may give the firm control over the distribution channels and give rise to a premium suggesting that in addition to being present in a portfolio of markets the firm should also attempt to develop a brand and distribution presence in its key markets. Lastly, a wide product line can be as effective in allowing the firm to compete on price especially if it is present in many markets.

Product-market and business system resource allocation

Process positioning for competitive advantage is based on the company's ability to organize the business system to provide the final customer with the desired perceived value at the lowest delivered cost, which requires superior performance in at least one of the business system activities (Gilbert and Strebel, 1988).

High perceived value strategies are more appropriate in the emerging stages of the product life cycle when the manufacturing process is not a significant competitive factor. Technology is still evolving, the business system has not stabilized and competition tends to be confined to product innovation and development. High perceived value strategies tend to favour product markets with short life cycles. Low delivered cost strategies, however, are more appropriate at the standardization phase of the product life cycle which is characterized by rapid market development. Attention is focused on the production process and resources are directed to the entire business system with process technology, market positioning and distribution efficiency becoming critical.

Concentration on competitive products, attractive markets and on critical cost areas of the business system is the route to international market success for many companies, especially small firms in small open economies. Concentration on such products and markets is concerned with the company's marketing strategy, while concentrating on the critical cost areas of the business considers the importance of the business system. In this context the company considers how to allocate its resources and concentrates its endeavours among the various market segments identified (Figure 3.9). It may wish to concentrate on one or a few segments or serve all segments with the same strategy. Similarly, the firm has to consider where in the business system to allocate its resources. It may wish to devote most of its resources to manufacturing, some to assembly and less to distribution and customers, depending on circumstances. Large

Figure 3.9
Generic product-market and business system strategies

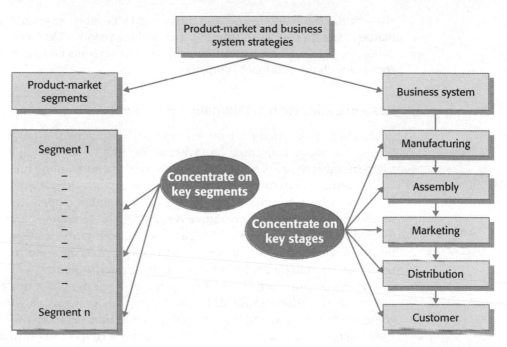

brand companies, especially in industrial product-markets, often follow the opposite strategy – concentrating on branding, distribution and customers; letting others manufacture under their control. 3M discovered many years ago that it made sense to let somebody else do its manufacturing. 3M's skills were in research and development, marketing and distribution. In 1995 the Timberland Company produced 80 per cent of its shoes in its own plants but by 2004 this figure had dropped to 15 per cent and it is likely to fall further. A generic market-business system resource allocation strategy attempts to identify the key product markets and the key stages in the business system to concentrate resources in order to be successful (Figure 3.9).

Underlying the second assumption is the view that the key success factor is to find a source of competitive advantage through reorganization of the business system. The objective of this reorganization is to achieve a superior cost–quality combination in a way which makes it difficult for competitors to emulate. The argument is that the key to success is to use the flexibility which the firm enjoys to unbundle the business system so as to focus on those elements of the value-added chain which yield the greatest return, while rearranging the provision of the other elements of the chain as cost-effectively as possible.

Concentrating on key stages in the business system often involves outsourcing and contract manufacturing. Contract manufacturing is less about reducing costs than about getting products to market quickly. Flexibility helps electronics firms cope with technological change. Because market leaders can suddenly fall from favour, contracting out manufacturing is less risky than building new factories. The extreme form of such behaviour is the virtual electronic firm Cisco Systems which makes Internet routing equipment. Although the firm is the market leader, it has only three plants, for its high-technology equipment and prototypes. Contract manufacturers make everything else – 'without the Internet none of this would be possible,' explains Carl Redfield who manages Cisco's manufacturing and logistical operations (*The Economist*, 12 February 2000, p. 66). In such a world entrepreneurial start-up firms no longer need a factory to compete with the dominant companies.

Resource allocation in international markets

In deciding its international market coverage, two generic strategies are available: diversification and concentration (Ayal and Zif, 1979). The first implies fast entry into a large number of product markets and diffusion of effort among them and the second is based on concentration of resources in a few product markets and slow expansion. Product-market concentration appears to be a rewarding approach especially for the smaller firm because it allows attractive markets to be targeted and resources to be focused on these markets only. Using a market concentration strategy, the first international market then acts as a bridgehead both for diversification into other international markets and for launching other products internationally.

Market concentration involves the purposeful selection of a small number of the most promising markets initially for more intensive development. For the smaller firm going international for the first time from a small home market, two or three markets would appear to constitute a reasonable span for a concentration strategy. A concentration strategy may be particularly attractive for the smaller firm as it requires a relatively low initial investment in marketing facilities, avoids the cost of dealing with small orders to less well-known markets, limits the span of managerial control and enables more visits to be made to each market. It also keeps the costs of international market research within the limits of the company's resources. Market concentration may also provide a springboard for subsequent diversification and consequent stabilization of the firm's exports. The outcomes regarding product concentration may be developed in an analogous way.

Market diversification involves the simultaneous entry into as many markets as possible. The objective of a market diversification strategy is to obtain a high rate of return through market development rather than market penetration, while maintaining a low level of resource commitment by selecting more accessible target markets. A market diversification strategy involves a greater risk for the firm since it requires a larger initial investment in markets. Greater risk attaches to market spreading but where it is successful it can be more profitable. In the longer term, this strategy is usually followed by a period of market consolidation in which the number of markets is reduced as less profitable ones are abandoned.

In practice, a firm is unlikely to select a position at the extremities of the spreading–concentration spectrum but more probably will pursue a mixed strategy, selling to a relatively large number of markets while concentrating resources on a selection of these. The advantage of such a mixed strategy is that it allows a firm to focus its strategy on the most promising markets, while leaving sufficient flexibility to accept opportunistic business in others. The outcome regarding product diversification may be developed in a similar manner.

Investment in product-markets usually occurs between the extremes of complete concentration and complete diversification. Product-market allocation strategies are

Figure 3.10
International market and product allocation strategies

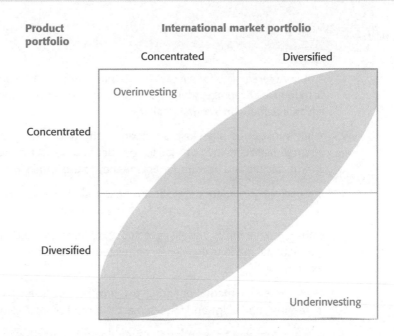

closely interlinked; market allocations impose constraints on the range of feasible product allocation strategies for the firm to sustain its competitive position.

For most companies that combine market and product diversification strategies it is unlikely that they would have sufficient resources to make the required marketing effort for all markets and products. This is the risk of underinvesting in markets, a problem which arises in rapid growth markets especially (Figure 3.10). The risk of overinvesting arises if the company serves only a few markets with a small range of products which may leave some important markets open to competitors. This difficulty is most likely to occur in companies with new innovative products for which it is important to be the first mover in international markets. To avoid the risk of under- or over-investing it may be necessary to balance product and market allocation strategies by selecting a position in the shaded area of the figure.

Summary

The resources and managerial capacity in the firm required for successful internationalization are linked to aspirations in the firm and also determine the extent of its competitive advantage in international markets. The characteristics of the firm in terms of objectives, technology and innovation, product location and size influence the aspirations of managers and hence the success of the firm. An important resource is open-minded management which seeks to develop the firm in international markets. In this context, by committing resources in a strategic way the firm can succeed in international markets. Firms tend to evolve through progressive stages of internationalization that require a differential resource commitment by management.

Questions

1. A major prerequisite for success in international markets is possession by the firm of a competitive advantage. Identify and discuss the most common sources of competitive advantage found in international firms.

2. While most firms pay close attention to the importance of external factors as they internationalize, many firms fail to consider internal factors adequately. What are these internal factors and how important are they to the firm in international markets?

3. Is it necessary to adopt a specific business outlook for success in international markets? Is such an outlook a prerequisite for the motivation in firms to internationalize?

4. Many commentators have suggested that firm size and motivation to succeed in international markets are closely correlated. Discuss. Is there a possible conflict in this relationship?

5. The process of internationalizing the firm can be seen as a sequential process of increasing knowledge and foreign market commitment. Discuss.

6. It is not sufficient to examine the firm alone; it is necessary to perform an integrated company, competitor and customer analysis to determine the firm's competitive position in international markets. Discuss.

7. Describe how an appropriate combination of a product-market and a business system analysis can assist the firm in developing a generic international marketing strategy.

References

Ayal, I. and Zif, J. (1979) 'Market expansion strategies in multinational markets', *Journal of Marketing*, **43** (Spring), 84–94.

Barney, J. B. (1991) 'Firm resources and sustained competitive advantage', *Journal of Management*, **17**, 99–120.

Bradley, M. F. (1984) 'Effects of cognitive style, attitude toward growth and motivation on the internationalization of the firm', *Research in Marketing*, **7**, 237–60.

Cunningham, M. T. and Spigel, R. I. (1971) 'A study in successful exporting', *British Journal of Marketing*, **5** (1), 2–12.

Eriksson, K. J., Johanson, J., Majkgard, A. and Sharma, D. (1997) 'Experiential knowledge and cost in the internationalization process', *Journal of International Business Studies*, **28** (2), 337–60.

Faschingbauer, T. R., Moore, C. D. and Stone, A. (1978) 'Cognitive style, dogmatism and creativity: some implications regarding cognitive development', *Psychological Reports*, **42**, 795–804.

Gilbert, X. and Strebel, P. (1988) 'Developing competitive advantage' in H. Mintzberg and J. B. Quinn, Eds, 2nd edn, *The Strategy Process*, New Jersey: Prentice Hall pp. 70–9.

Grant, R. M. (1991) 'The resource based theory of competitive advantage: implications for strategy formulation', *California Management Review*, Spring, 118.

Hunt, S. D. and Morgan, R. M. (1995) 'The comparative advantage theory of competition', *Journal of Marketing*, **59** (April), 1–15.

Johanson, J. and Vahlne, J.-E. (1977) 'The internationalisation process of the firm model of knowledge development and increasing foreign marketing commitments', *Journal of International Business Studies*, **8** (1), 23–30.

Kakabadse, A. (1993) 'Performing in style', *The Independent*, 7 April.

Liesch, P. W. and G. A. Knight (1999) 'Information internalization and hurdle rates in small and medium enterprise internationalization', *Journal of International Business Studies*, 30, 1 (First Quarter), 383–94.

Madhok, A. (1997) 'Cost, value and foreign market entry mode: the transaction and the firm', *Strategic Management Journal*, **18**, 39–61.

Penrose, E. (1959) *The Theory of the Growth of the Firm*, Oxford: Basil Blackwell.

Peteraf, M. A. (1993) 'The cornerstones of competitive advantage: a resource based view', *Strategic Management Journal*, **14**, 179–91.

Porter, M. E. (1986) 'Changing patterns of international competition', *California Management Review*, **2**, 9–37.

Prahalad, C. K. and Hamel, G. (1990) 'The core competence of the corporation', *Harvard Business Review*, **68**, 79–91.

Reid, S. D. (1981) 'The decision maker and export entry and expansion', *Journal of International Business Studies*, **12** (2), 101–12.

Simmonds, K. and Smith, H. (1968) 'The first export order: a marketing innovation', *British Journal of Marketing*, **2** (Summer), 93–100.

Teece, D. J., Pisano, G. and Shuen, A. (1996) 'Dynamic capabilities and strategic management', University of California, Berkeley, Working Paper, July, 53 pages.

Thompson, A. A. Jr. and Strickland, A. J. III (1996) *Strategic Management*, 9th edn, Chicago, IL: Irwin.

van Ittersum, K. and Candel, M. J. J. M. (1998) 'Development of experiential knowledge in internationalization through customer supplier relationships', in P. Andersson, Ed., *Track 6, Consumer Behaviour*, Proceedings, 27th, EMAC Conference, Stockholm, 20–23 May, pp. 297–308.

Welch, L. and Wiedersheim-Paul, F. (1980) 'Initial exports – a marketing failure', *Journal of Management Studies*, **9** (October), 333–44.

Wiedersheim-Paul, F., Olson, H. C. and Welch, L. (1978) 'Pre-export activity: the first step in internationalization', *Journal of International Business Studies*, **9** (1), 47–58.

4 Analysis of international competitors

The firm in international markets must deal with competitors in its own domestic market and in each international market it enters. Some of these competitors will be the same while others will be different and encountered for the first time. The number, size, quality and origin of competitors affect the firm's ability to enter and compete profitably in a particular market. Indeed, the fortunes of the firm are determined by a competitive and cooperative interplay of the firm, its customers and its competitors. It is not just a matter of only one or two of these elements; all three are involved.

In general it is difficult to determine the competitive structure of international markets. In the situation where the firm faces the same competitors in many markets it is clear that strategy must be integrated in some way, as a certain response in one market may have competitive repercussions in several. When there are several different competitors it is important to understand how each behaves so that appropriate initiatives and responses may be made.

After studying this chapter students should be able to:

- describe and explain how firms compete in international markets;
- develop a framework to measure competitiveness in the international firm;
- apply the industry structure analysis model in analyzing the international competitive environment;
- explain how firms develop successful competitive positions;
- identify and specify strategies used by firms to compete under different circumstances in international markets;
- determine competitive motives associated with the firm's unique capabilities.

Meaning of international competition

To be capable of competing in international markets the firm needs to have a complex mix of skills and accumulated knowledge which is mediated to customer groups through organizational processes that enables the firm to exploit its competitive advantage. The choice of which capability to nurture and where to commit resources must be guided by a shared understanding of multiple industry structures, the needs of customers, the positional advantages being sought and the trends in the environment.

The firm is competitive in international markets if it can sell its products and services and make a profit. Competitiveness is defined as 'the immediate and future ability of, and opportunities for, entrepreneurs to design, produce and market goods within their respective environments whose price and non-price qualities form a more attractive package than those of competitors abroad or in domestic markets' (European Management Forum, 1984).

When firms plan new ventures they seek significantly higher returns and that almost always means achieving some degree of monopoly power in economic terms either over resources or markets. In a sense marketing is about a search for some form of monopoly, however transient. The creation of brands and the control of access to customers confer on companies a limited form of monopoly power. The global success of R & A Bailey and Company Ltd is due almost entirely to the way it manages the Baileys brand through unique positioning and control of distribution in all major markets. Nestlé's success may be attributed to its powerful branding and competitive advertising while Procter & Gamble's success stems from continuously innovating mostly non-glamorous consumer products that perform better in areas of concern to consumers in global markets than competing products. Successful competitors therefore rely on, among other factors, branding, continuous product innovation and development and excellent customer relations through closely guarded channels of distribution.

In general, coping with international competition requires the firm to:

■ anticipate the challenge of innovative newcomers, especially with less costly, high-quality substitutes;

■ acknowledge the impact of an increasing number of new suppliers – a widening of the competitive cycle;

■ understand that technology allows cross-category competition (steel, aluminium, titanium, plastic, cork, copper and fibre optic cable);

■ access low-cost market information, outsource, reduce manufacturing intensity and avoid barriers to market entry; and

■ provide more customer information to reduce customer switching costs.

Competitor orientation in international markets

In a competitive world, it is difficult to create added value. Usually, added value arises by making better products, using resources more efficiently, listening to customers to determine how to make more attractive products and working with suppliers to discover more efficient ways of running the company's business, while being more effective for them. Companies which cannot produce an added value in the business system are not able to sustain a premium over cost; the company makes very little money.

A competitor orientation views customers as the ultimate prize to be won at the expense of rivals. Sources of competitive advantages are branding, a well-developed distribution system, preferential treatment by suppliers and lower costs. A competitor orientation implies that the firm attempts to capitalize on the weaknesses of vulnerable competitors to win market position and customers from them, which produces a high level of sales and long-run profits. At the same time, the firm attempts to remove its own weaknesses to defend market position and to minimize the loss of customers to competitors.

Traditionally competition for customers was defined as arising from other firms in the industry which make products or provide services similar to those of the company from a manufacturing point of view. This industry perspective is irrelevant when the focus in marketing is on solving customer problems in the context of a business system. Customers are interested in what they buy, not whether the provider belongs to a particular industry. Competitors should be determined, therefore, from the viewpoint of the customer. In this view of the business system, banks and software companies, although from separate traditional industries, could end up competing to supply customers with added value products and services such as e-money and smart cards.

A similar situation arises on the supply side; firms compete with the company in attracting the resources of suppliers. Competition for suppliers frequently crosses traditional industry and international boundaries. Listening to and working with suppliers is just as important as listening to customers (Brandenburger and Nalebuff, 1996). Many companies recognize the importance of working with suppliers, acknowledging that they are equal partners in the creation of value within the business system. In this view of the business system, supplier relations are just as important as customer relations. Both share the common goal of increasing wealth. Both create value and provide access to markets, technology and information.

Establishing competitive positions in international markets

The more similar competitors are to each other, the more intense their competition will be. This serves to underline the need for competitive analysis such as that performed by Airbus Industrie. The early Airbus A300 and A310 jets were mildly successful but as engineers at Airbus planned the A320, they wanted to make a major technological leap that would set their new plane apart, especially from Boeing. The search for such a competitive edge led Airbus to 'fly-by-wire' technology because it weighed less, which cut fuel consumption and so increased the plane's attractiveness to airlines. By adding a digital facility with computers, they introduced cockpit commonality, which brings airlines significant savings in pilot training and operating costs. In 1999 Airbus won significantly more orders than Boeing for the first time and continues to do so because of its focus on technology as a competitive weapon in the very competitive aircraft manufacturing industry.

To obtain such a sustainable competitive position managers try to understand the nature of the dynamics of the industry (Figure 4.1). To understand these dynamics the firm attempts to specify the underlying conditions of supply and demand. Included in an analysis of supply and demand conditions are factors such as management attitudes, public policy, raw material supplies, technology and product quality. An

Figure 4.1
Analysis of
industry
competition

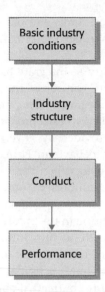

Source: adapted from Scherer, F. M. (1980), *Industry Market Structure and Economic Performance*,
second edition, Chicago, IL. Rand McNally, p. 4 © 1980 by Houghton Mifflin Company

understanding of demand conditions requires an examination of price elasticities, substitutes, sales trends, purchase patterns and competitor marketing programmes. Both
these factors influence industry structure.

An examination of the structure of the industry gives the firm much of the information it requires to understand the behaviour of its competitors. There are a number of
points to consider. First, it is necessary to specify the number of firms in the industry
and whether the product is standardized or highly differentiated. Second, firms desire
to enter industries that offer attractive profits. Some are easier to enter than others. The
major barriers to entry are brand strength, access to distribution, large capital requirements, scale economies, and international agreements. Some of these barriers are
intrinsic to certain industries such as petroleum, coffee and tin, while others are established by the actions of firms already in the industry, e.g. branded consumer products
firms. Third, in an ideal world firms should be able to exit an industry freely but frequently there are barriers to exit, such as obligations to customers and employees,
government restrictions and lack of alternatives.

The fourth consideration refers to cost structures which determine the strategic
behaviour of firms in the industry. Firms with large manufacturing and raw material
costs behave differently from firms with heavy distribution and marketing costs. Firms
tend to focus on activities associated with their greatest cost, which gives rise to competitive opportunities. Reducing costs to compete against Ford and Toyota was the
principal motivator for Volkswagen in deciding to reduce the number of floorplans,
the expensive structural basis of a car body, a decision, according to Volkswagen, that
enabled it to gain market share. During the early 1990s Volkswagen's strategy was to
develop a wide range of cars, all based on a few basic chassis and engine models, to
appeal to particular niche markets. The company had been making 30 different models
on no fewer than 16 floorplans – by 2000 it was selling 54 models based on only four

floorplans. Skodas, Audis and ordinary VW models may vary in looks, performance and pricing, but under the skin they share many parts, which produces large economies of scale.

Fifth, the ability to integrate backwards, forwards or horizontally can lower costs and provide more control of the market and the value-added chain. In industries which are thus integrated, some firms can manipulate their prices and costs in different country markets to earn profits where taxes are lowest. Transfer pricing to exploit the incentives provided by governments to attract foreign direct investment is an example of such behaviour. Firms that cannot integrate operate at a disadvantage. Lastly, the extent to which the industry has internationalized affects structure and competition in the industry. Some firms compete only in the domestic market while others have the choice of competing in many markets which affect the nature and extent of competition in the industry.

Industry structure in turn influences the conduct and behaviour of firms in the industry in regard to marketing and manufacturing strategies. The marketing behaviour of firms includes activities surrounding new product development, pricing, advertising and any contractual obligations established by the firm in the distribution channel. Manufacturing behaviour refers to R&D activities, investment in plant and equipment and supply chain contracts. Marketing and manufacturing strategies help determine industry performance such as the efficiency, growth, profitability and cash flows of firms. Also included are issues such as equity, technology and social progress.

Determinants of competitiveness in international markets

A great myth regarding competition in international markets, which must be dispelled, is that price explains all differences in competitiveness. While price is an important element in marketing strategy it is of course not the only element, as competitive advantage also may be gained in speed of delivery, design or service provided and brands developed, to name the more obvious.

A tendency to place too much emphasis on the importance of costs, inflation and exchange rates in international markets is tantamount to recognizing no other form of competition than price. So what does it take to compete internationally and be successful? Among a wide range of factors common across many industries are low costs; global sourcing; differentiation and branding. The continuous product innovation and designs in the Swiss watch industry allow it to sustain its strong competitive advantage. The competitive advantage depends on the technical competence and design of sophisticated products that are considered relevant to an exclusive global market segment. The combination of these factors with a strong focus on the relevant market appears to characterize the competitive positioning of the Swiss watch industry (Exhibit 4.1).

Measuring competitiveness in the firm

To assess the relative competitiveness of a firm three groups of factors dominate: the product; research and development; and marketing expenditure. In nearly all industries competitors can be usefully portrayed in terms of how intensely they

Exhibit 4.1   Complication and design are winners for the Swiss watch industry

In a global context, it is impossible to ignore the prime position of the Swiss watch industry. Company failures are few and triumphs are many and the industry enjoys a long national legacy. Switzerland was the country that produced the first ever series wristwatch, the first quartz watch (not in Japan), which in the 1970s established the standard quartz frequency at 36,769 Hertz, the first water-resistant wristwatch, the smallest and the most expensive watch and so on. The watch and clock industry is Switzerland's third largest exporter, after the machine tools and pharmaceutical industries. More than 95 per cent of its products were exported in 2003, valued at SFr10.2 billion according to the Swiss Watch Federation. In 2003 the US was the largest market, by value, for Swiss timepieces at SFr.1.67 billion. Hong Kong, Japan, Italy and France followed.

What are some of the possible reasons for Swiss dominance of the global watch industry? At the Geneva Watchmaking Grand Prix awards ceremony in November 2003, Patek Phillipe won the coveted Aiguille d'Or for its 10-day Tourbillon. The second prize went to Master Antoine LeCoultre, a platinum piece by Jaeger-LeCoultre, while the third prize, for technical innovations and complications, was awarded to Harry Winston for its Opus 3. That the first prize went to Patek Phillipe is indicative of a distinct trend among leading watchmakers for their ambitions for this most 'complicated' (a trade term) of wristwatches. A tourbillon is designed to overcome the effects of the earth's gravity by enclosing the escapement in a gyroscopic cage. Of course, Swiss watch companies also invest in branding and fashion design. At the Basel world trade show in April 2004 Omega demonstrated its design and fashion prowess with further original timepieces: the Aquarella Collection for ladies with a double row of diamonds around the dial, the monstrously large (49.2mm dial) Railmaster, and the Speedmaster Michael Schumacher, the legend watch.

Source: adapted from 'Business proceeds at jogging pace', Financial Times Special Report – Watches & Jewelry, *Financial Times*, Saturday 17 April 2004

compete with the business that is motivating the analysis. There are usually several very direct competitors, others that compete less intensely and still others that compete indirectly but are still relevant. A knowledge of this pattern can lead to a deeper understanding of the market structure. Those groups that compete most intensely may merit the most in-depth study, but others may still require analysis and close scrutiny.

Understanding competitors in international markets

Understanding the strategies of current and likely future competitors and their strengths and weaknesses may suggest opportunities and threats for the firm which allow it to identify an appropriate strategic position to adopt. From Porter (1980) and Aaker (1988) it is possible to identify six factors, an analysis of which allows the firm to understand its competitors (Figure 4.2).

Figure 4.2
Understanding
competitors

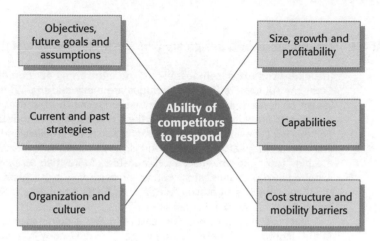

Source: adapted from Aaker, D. A. (1988), *Strategic Market Management*, 2nd edn, New York, NY: Wiley, p. 77; and Porter, M. E. (1980), *Competitive Strategy*, New York, NY: The Free Press

Competitor objectives, future goals and assumptions

Understanding the objectives that competitors set for themselves and the assumptions they make about the future provides the firm with a solid foundation in forming its own international strategy. Some firms, especially those in the United States, frequently operate on short-run financial objectives, whereas their Japanese competitors are known to operate on longer-term objectives. This also affects the market share objectives that a firm can set and how they are likely to respond when entering markets for the first time or when threatened by a competitor in an established market. Where the competitor is part of a larger organization it may also be important to understand the objectives held by the parent. The competitor may be seen by the parent as a growth unit or it may be expected to produce a cash flow to fund other areas of the business.

Competitors may have assumptions about themselves or their industry which may or may not be true but which can still influence their strategy. For example, competitors may perceive themselves as having a high-quality premium product which might lead them to ignore a price cut by others, or they may be overly optimistic about the competitive pressures in the industry and make decisions accordingly. Indeed most competitive moves can be interpreted as a statement about the future of a particular industry as the battle of words and actions between Airbus Industrie and Boeing are regarding the next generation of super-aircraft (Exhibit 4.2).

Review of competitor strategies

In general the firm monitors, at a minimum, competitors' approaches to new product development and the basis for competition. In particular an analysis of strategies which work and do not work in certain circumstances would seem valuable. On occasion firms compete on the basis of the portfolio of markets they serve. A firm can use its portfolio of markets to cross-subsidize competitive battles, but it can also cross-subsidize among

Exhibit 4.2   Airbus vs Boeing – different views of the future

The European aerospace industry's $12 billion gamble, backed by the governments of France, Germany, the UK and Spain, aimed at completing the overthrow of US domination of civil aerospace, is reaching its payoff, with the A380 due to make its maiden flight in less than a year. If it succeeds, the 555-passenger, double-decker airliner will cement Airbus's leadership over Boeing. Last year Airbus delivered more aircraft than Boeing for the first time.

Critics say the A380 is an overweight industrial dinosaur. 'Is there any question that the A380 is a very expensive airplane for a very small market?' says Randy Baseler, marketing vice-president of Boeing's commercial airplanes division. 'We predict that the world needs only 320 very large airplanes [during the next 20 years] and not the 1,138 airplanes that Airbus predicts.' In the meantime Boeing has opted for the 7E7 Dreamliner, a much smaller 200–250 passenger aircraft. The 7E7 is a replacement for the ageing Boeing 757 and 767 ranges, a segment where Airbus could be vulnerable as it only has its A330–200 to offer as competition.

The airlines also disagree on how airlines will accommodate growth in traffic. Boeing's vision is based on the 'fragmentation' of aviation markets, reflecting passengers' preferences for more point-to-point, non-stop services and more frequencies instead of being routed to their final destinations via multiple connecting hubs. For the present Airbus seems to have the market to itself, and it already has 129 firm orders from companies such as Singapore Airlines – which will fly the first A380 in 2006 – Emirates, Virgin Atlantic, Lufthansa, Air France and FedEx. Mr Baseler claims such orders came with discounts of up to 40 per cent off a list price of around $280 million. Not so, says Noël Forgeard, Airbus's chief executive.

Source: adapted from 'Europe's big hope for future of airline travel takes shape', *Financial Times*, Thursday 8 April 2004, p. 20

products within a market. The choices open to Ben & Jerry's, the super premium ice-cream niche producer in the US, were not so obvious before the company was taken over by Unilever. Faced from below with a challenge from premium ice-creams in its local market the company considered international markets but there it faced Häagen-Dazs entrenched in its product category. Given the entire marketing strategy and focus of Ben & Jerry's, a solution was not easy to find. One reason was that overseas expansion would not be easy. Häagen-Dazs was already present internationally. That brand had the advantage of the multinational marketing and distribution network of Grand Metropolitan. Häagen-Dazs was strong in several big markets outside America, including Japan.

Another difficulty with going international was that there was a risk that Ben & Jerry's idiosyncrasies would translate badly in different parts of the world. Proclaiming on ice-cream tubs that the ingredients come from Vermont may have been a selling point in New England but not in 'old' England nor Germany nor in many other markets of the world.

Lastly, locked into one corner of North America raised transport costs. Häagen-Dazs, by contrast, was made in two places in the United States, as well as in Canada, France and Japan and elsewhere. Nevertheless, Ben & Jerry's under Unilever tutelage and ownership has made it across the Atlantic and is now available in some countries of Europe.

Competitor organization and corporate culture

An understanding of the way in which managers in competing firms think and work together provides valuable information for the probable future activities of such firms. The choice of manager for a particular position can tell a great deal about the strategic thinking in the competitor firm. In addition, the way the firm organizes itself can give good clues as to its probable competitive behaviour and strategy.

A cost-oriented, highly structured organization that relies on tight controls to achieve objectives and to motivate employees may have difficulty innovating or shifting into an aggressive marketing-oriented strategy. A loose, flat organization that emphasizes innovation and risk taking may similarly have difficulty in pursuing disciplined product-refinement and cost-execution programmes. These two systems contrast markedly with a consensus-oriented company where the senior managers are leaders of closely knit teams that they coach rather than control. The organization culture, influenced by national cultures and the personal values of managers, tends, therefore, to influence the approach taken. An approach which works in Japan may not work in the United States; an approach which works in the Nordic countries may not serve in Latin countries. For example, sometimes the interaction of national culture and government policy creates a particular competitive environment in selected industries; the food industry in Japan illustrates this situation (Exhibit 4.3).

Exhibit 4.3 Competition, culture and consumer choice

The efficiency of the Japanese food producing industry is a mere 32 per cent of America's due to two factors: a Japanese cultural trait and government policies. The cultural trait is that Japanese are fanatics for the freshest possible food. In Japan a milk container bears three dates: the date of manufacture, the date it reached the supermarket, and the expiration date. Milk production in Japan starts at one minute past midnight so that milk reaching the market in the morning can be labelled as today's milk. If the milk were bottled at 23.59 hours no Japanese consumer would buy it as it would be yesterday's. As a result, a milk producer in northern Japan cannot compete in southern Japan because transportation delays would add one day to the date on the container, a curse of death for milk sales.

These local monopolies originating in a Japanese cultural preference are reinforced by the Japanese government, which penalizes competition from foreign producers by imposing arbitrary food-import restrictions such as a 10-day quarantine. Imagine the apoplectic reaction of a Japanese consumer, already skittish about one-day-old milk, on being offered month-old food shipped from overseas and then quarantined. Hence, Japanese food-producing companies are not exposed to competition with each other nor with foreign imports, don't acquire economies of scale, and don't learn the best international methods of food processing.

Similar organizational problems cripple the productivity of Japan's soap and beer industries – but not its differently organized steel, metal, car and electronics industries, which have higher productivity than their US counterparts and inspire well-earned envy in the US. Did you ever wonder why your TV and car, but not your soap, are Japanese made?

Source: adapted from *The Wall Street Journal Europe*, Wednesday 13 December 2000, p. 10

Size, growth and profitability of competitors

If there are many competitors in a market, it is usually necessary to identify the few most significant firms or strategic groups. One measure is their size and associated market share, both domestically and in each of the foreign markets under consideration. Firms that have achieved a recent and substantial increase in market share are also of interest even if they are relatively small. Growth rates, in addition to reflecting the success or failure of strategy, can suggest the possibility of organizational or financial strains that could affect future strategies. Profitability rates associated with competitors also may be relevant. A profitable firm generally has access to capital for investment.

Evaluating competitive strengths

International firms attempt to use their marketing skills to obtain competitive advantage in various international markets by meeting differentiated customer requirements more efficiently than other firms. Some firms compete on the basis of product superiority, innovation, prices, availability and delivery, image and reputation, and service. It is necessary to identify these customer advantages as well as determine competitor weaknesses on each.

Knowledge of a competitor's strengths and weaknesses can provide insights into how capable it is in pursuing various types of strategies. It also forms an important input into the process of identifying and selecting strategic alternatives. One approach is to attempt to exploit a competitor's weakness in an area where the firm has an existing or developing strength and then pit a strength against a competitor's weakness. Conversely, a knowledge of the competitor's strength is important so that it can be bypassed or neutralized. British Airways competes on service and a presence in all major markets. In terms of international market presence a number of US airline companies are attempting to catch up, especially American Airlines and Delta Airlines, which recently embarked on aggressive overseas campaigns with an emphasis on Europe.

Cost structure and mobility barriers

A knowledge of a competitor's cost structure, especially for a competitor that is relying on a low-cost strategy, can provide an indication of its probable future pricing strategy and its staying power (Aaker, 1988, p. 79). The goal should be to obtain information on both direct costs and fixed costs which will determine break-even levels. In some circumstances a high level of detail is required: labour and material costs, investment levels, and sales. In other circumstances, especially for international labour cost comparisons, it may not be necessary to carry out such an exhaustive analysis for many countries. Because of economies of scale, superior technology and lower wage rates, the cost advantages of certain countries, e.g. Japan, South Korea and Taiwan, may be quite evident. Cost advantages and creative freedom have supported the Chinese firm, Haier's, global ambitions but a shortage of capability may constrain the overseas march of the company (Exhibit 4.4).

High mobility barriers, especially if they are exit barriers, experienced in a few countries, tend to increase competitive pressures within an industry. These barriers include specialized assets, fixed costs such as labour agreements and leases, relationships to other parts of the firm due to shared facilities, distribution channels or a sales force, government policies and managerial pride.

Exhibit 4.4   Haier's purpose

At first glance, Haier, China's leading white goods manufacturer, looks like a potentially global firm. It has factories in more than 100 countries and HQ in China and New York and is about to invest in a small Hong Kong firm to springboard Haier on its foreign acquisitions drive. Sales have grown by 70 per cent a year over the past two decades with $9.7 billion in 2003. Its chief executive, Mr Zhang, turned a loss-making refrigerator firm into a national brand, returning the firm to profitability within one year of starting. Now it enjoys moderate overseas success with sales totalling $1 billion, claiming 30 per cent of the American market for mini-fridges and 10 per cent of the European air-conditioner market, placing it fourth behind Whirlpool, Electrolux and Bosch-Siemens. However, this is mainly due to its voluminous domestic productions, as Haier pushes into new domestic markets, opportunistically rather than strategically.

As the presence of multinational companies competing in China drives margins down, Haier must look abroad, but it lacks the R&D capabilities and the design discipline to focus on core competencies. Haier has 96 product categories with 15,100 different specifications, including a washing machine that also cleans sweet potatoes. This creative freedom combined with Mr Zhang's willingness to exploit opportunities as diverse as computers and mobile phones produces a firm that is broad but thin on resources and capabilities.

Source: adapted from *The Economist*, 20 March 2004, p. 72.
The Economist © The Economist Newspaper Limited, London (20 March 2004)

Motives associated with unique capabilities

All companies that compete successfully in international markets rely on some combination of capabilities (Figure 4.3). Such capability may be related to the unique way that the company integrates markets by being able to:

■ understand and integrate customer tastes across international markets;

■ cope with global branding if it is a feature of the market; and

■ serve customers who may be located in diverse countries and influenced by diverse cultures.

Integration also means attempting to gain marketing and manufacturing scale benefits if they exist while defining the scope of the firm to compete effectively.

Besides being able to integrate markets, the company must also be an innovator which means converting new product ideas into profit, establishing and maintaining facilitating mechanisms in the company and obtaining senior management commitment and leadership for the endeavour.

Figure 4.3
Company
competitive
capability

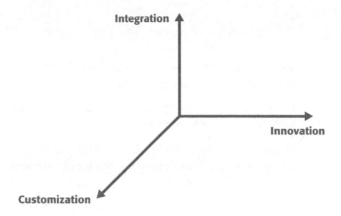

Lastly, it is necessary to customize the company's endeavours for different customer tastes, to select the most appropriate distribution channels and to cope with market regulations and protection so that country or segment market programmes may be developed. Customization refers to the ability of the firm to understand:

- customer tastes in different markets;
- new and evolving international distribution channels;
- market regulations and consumer protection legislation; and
- how to design and implement a marketing programme in different national markets while allowing for spill-over effects, especially if the markets served are contiguous.

Summary

In this chapter we noted that success in international markets depends on a detailed analysis of the competitive environment and a recognition that firms adopt different positions in the business system in order to compete. A hierarchy exists in the levels at which competition takes place – some firms deliberately select positions in the hierarchy in order to compete while ignoring others. Competition allows the firm to improve its own competitive advantage by focusing on strong and weak points. Many factors contribute to competitiveness in firms; costs and prices but also the other elements of the marketing programme including product quality, delivery and reputation. A number of ways of measuring competitiveness for the firm in international markets were identified. Various criteria to help in understanding competitors were identified including size, competitor objectives, strategies, organization, cost structure and general capability. In examining potential competitors the firm should understand their motives for product-market expansion, for integration with suppliers and customers, and should assess their ability to compete. The firm should decide on ways of competing in a structured and controlled fashion in areas such as quality, manufacturing, flexible systems, innovation and organization.

Questions

1. What are the principal influences on a firm's competitive position? Do they differ between domestic and international markets?

2. To what extent is the structure, conduct and performance framework useful in analyzing international competition?

3. Identify the factors which must be examined in detail in order to give the firm an understanding of the structure of the industry in which it operates. Explain why each factor identified merits attention.

4. Sometimes the presence of competitors in the market can have favourable consequences for the international firm. Discuss.

5. Discuss how you would evaluate competitiveness in a market. Distinguish between price competitiveness and cost competitiveness. What other variables are used to compete?

6. In order to understand thoroughly competitors in international markets, the firm must understand current and future strategies of existing competitors and also their strengths and weaknesses. The firm must also examine potential competitors. Outline an approach to such an analysis.

7. Company competitive capability may be judged on how the company innovates, integrates markets and customizes its products and services for its customers. Discuss.

References

Aaker, D. A. (1988) *Strategic Market Management*, 2nd edn, New York, NY: Wiley.

Brandenburger, A. and Nalebuff, B. J. (1996): *Co-opetition*, New York: Currency-Doubleday.

European Management Forum (1984) *Report on International Industrial Competitiveness*, Geneva.

Porter, M. E. (1980) *Competitive Strategy*, New York, NY: The Free Press.

Scherer, F. M. (1980) *Industry Market Structure and Economic Performance*, Chicago, IL: Rand McNally, p. 4.

5 Culture, values and technology

International marketing is a cultural as well as an economic phenomenon. The growing reference to anthropology, sociology and psychology is an explicit recognition of the non-economic bases of international marketing behaviour.

After studying this chapter, the student should be able to:

- evaluate the role of culture in international marketing;
- list the key characteristics and elements of culture;
- outline the role of language and communication for the company;
- recognize the influence of religion and values in different countries;
- describe the impact that different social structures can have on internationalization; and
- discuss the phenomenon of socio-cultural distance as a barrier to internationalization.

Influence of culture in international marketing

Many writers claim that modern communications and rising income levels promote a common culture worldwide. If there were a common culture the international marketing task would be much easier. When people write about a convergence of cultures the evidence cited is usually taken from people's behaviour and practices with regard to the products they wear and the food they eat. However, these 'rather superficial manifestations of culture are sometimes mistaken for all there is; the deeper, underlying level of values, which moreover determine the meaning for people of their practices, is overlooked' (Hofstede, 1991, p. 181). Just because there are many branded products and services which are available throughout the world does not mean that these brands have the same meaning in different cultures. Brands such as Coca-Cola, Sony, McDonald's, British Airways and Singapore Airlines are available worldwide but do they have the same meaning in different countries? The fact of their ubiquitous availability 'only tells us that there are some novel products that can be sold on a universal message. It does not tell us what they mean in the different cultures where they are visible' (Hoecklin, 1995, p. 2). A deep appreciation of culture is essential for an understanding of the meaning attributed by recipients to the firm's international efforts.

Sensitivity of a particular business activity to cultural influence depends on the level of direct exchange between that activity and the cultural environment. Activities such as marketing and public relations generally demand more interaction with local culture than, for example, do finance or production. The firm's capability in dealing with international markets is based on three different but related abilities (Langhoff, 1977, p. 159); the ability to:

■ cope with cultural heterogeneity in different international markets;

■ harmonize marketing endeavours with their symbolic meaning among customers in different cultures; and

■ identify new business opportunities in foreign cultural contexts.

Culture is so pervasive yet complex that it is difficult to define: each scholar seems to have a separate definition. Culture has been called 'the integrated sum total of learned behavioural traits that are manifest and shared by members of a society' (Hoebel, 1960, p. 168). Culture includes both conscious and unconscious values, ideas, attitudes and symbols which shape human behaviour and are transmitted from one generation to the next. 'Culture is a mental map which guides us in our relations to our surroundings and to other people' (Downs, 1971, p. 35). In this sense culture does not refer to the instinctive responses of people, nor does it include one-time solutions to unique problems but rather it refers to values understood at the higher level of knowledge. Hall (1960) states that:

> culture is man's medium; there is not one aspect of human life that is not touched and altered by culture. This means personalities, how people express themselves (including shows of emotion), the way they think, how they move, how problems are solved, how their cities are planned and laid out, how transportation systems function and are organized, as well as how economic and government systems are put together and function.

An alternative view of culture (Kroeber, 1951, p. 19) is that it:

> is a way of habitual acting, feeling and thinking, channelled by a society out of an infinite number of variety of potential ways of living.

That which gives humans their identity no matter where they were born is their culture – the total communication framework of words, actions, posture, gestures, tones of voice, facial expressions, the way they handle time, space and materials and the way they work, play, make love and defend themselves and their property (Hall, 1960). All human actions are modified by learning. Once learned, habitual responses and ways of interacting gradually sink below the surface of the mind and operate from the unconscious. Culture encompasses the knowledge, language, values, customs and material objects that are passed from person to person and from generation to generation

(Funakawa, 1997, p. 15). Different cultures vary greatly on how they conceptualize, classify and order their everyday experiences. Westerners organize their experience and make sense of it by means of categories of space, time, causation, numbers, agency and persons. These are most certainly not universal classifications. Other cultures do not have westerners' notion of the self and some seem to have no idea of personal identity at all. Even with a single culture deep conceptual divergences are quite common (Hollis, 1994, p. 237).

Cultural determinants of marketing behaviour in the international firm

Managers require a great deal of knowledge to work within their own cultural context but in international markets they must be able to work with a culturally diverse population which requires a different managerial competence. The analysis of the cultural environment of international marketing is facilitated with the help of anthropological, sociological and psychological frameworks. The cultural environment consists of:

■ the learned behavioural features shared by people of the same culture;

■ real physical attributes or appearances;

■ physical idealized traits, i.e. advertisement stereotypes;

■ demographic characteristics such as population size, age distribution.

Culture is a complex concept which includes specific knowledge, beliefs, morals, laws and customs shared by a society. Culture is how we behave; there is a pattern that all people belonging to the same group share. People of the same group all know the rules even if they cannot articulate them. They have learnt these rules by watching and copying the behaviours of other group members. Culture encompasses the values shared by all the members of the group where values are the criteria by which we judge ourselves and others. It provides the rules, the morality, the values, and the ethics of the group; what binds people together. Without such rules and values we could not stay together nor belong to a group.

The international marketing implications of the cultural environment may be discovered by assessing the influence of a number of elements on marketing behaviour in the firm. In particular the firm must determine the impact of norms, values and attitudes on the behaviour of potential customers, their demographic profile, the specific characteristics of culture including the special position of language, the influence of ethnic factors and the role of material culture (Figure 5.1).

Behavioural attributes

Behavioural attributes derive from societal norms, personal values and attitudes (Figure 5.2). Societal norms are standards shared by a society to which members are expected to conform. They are rules that specify appropriate and inappropriate behaviour. For the international firm it is important to note that some norms are more important

Figure 5.1
Cultural
determinants
of marketing
behaviour in the
international
firm

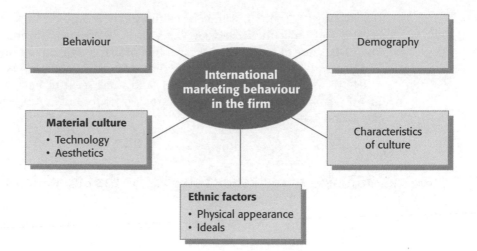

than others. Some norms in a society, referred to as 'folkways', are considered by its members as not being extremely important and, therefore, may be violated without severe reprimand or punishment. These folkways may be the target for innovative marketing campaigns by international firms. For example, Sunday opening of shopping centres in different traditionalist society contravenes folkways but is welcomed by a growing number of families where both partners share work and family responsibilities and find that Sunday is the only time they can shop. Horse racing on Sunday, welcomed by a large section of the population in Northern Ireland, is, because of its strong association with gambling, considered to contravene important folkways among some Christian faiths.

Other norms of society, referred to as mores, are those that are seen as extremely important to the welfare of society and whose violation reaps severe punishment. A marketing practice which contravenes the mores of a society would be met by product failure, withdrawal from the market and even forced closure. The use of certain ingredients in foods and beverages, the promotion of some medical devices and forms of clothing may easily cause difficulty for the unwary firm. An understanding of the distinction for each international market between its folkways and mores is an important managerial responsibility for the international firm.

Figure 5.2
Behavioural
attributes

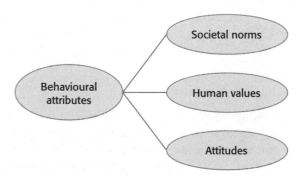

A behaviour pattern, in contrast, is a uniformity of acting and thinking that regularly recurs among a plurality of people. The behaviour pattern, besides being a form of conduct, is also a norm of conduct. The international firm must make a distinction here; this time between ideal norms, those to which people give their verbal allegiance, and real norms, those with which people comply.

The manager of the international firm must realize that ideal norms are what the individual says or believes he would like to do which may coincide with the real norms, but which may at times have only an indirect and remote relationship to actual behaviour. Even when ideal norms do not coincide with real norms, they provide guides to behaviour in the sense of being remote goals which are to be reached indirectly.

Role of human values and attitudes

People generally and consumers and managers in particular are motivated by constrained self-interest seeking that depends on two irreducible sources of valuation: pleasure and morality (Etzioni, 1988). People pursue pleasure and avoid pain but they are constrained in their self-interest seeking by considerations of what is right, proper, ethical, moral and appropriate. Different cultures and value systems directly and purposefully influence the behaviour of consumers and managers. While opportunistic behaviour may occur it does not prevail in all circumstances in different countries and cultures.

Much of human behaviour depends on values and attitudes. Our values and attitudes help to determine what we think is right and wrong, what is important and what is desirable. A value, a criterion by which we judge ourselves and others, is an enduring prescriptive or prospective belief that a specific mode of behaviour is preferred to an opposite mode of behaviour – this belief transcends attitudes towards objects and situations (Rokeach, 1968, p. 25). Schwartz (1994) attempts to answer questions such as: 'how are the value priorities of individuals affected by their social experience and how do the value priorities held by individuals affect their behavioural orientations and choices'. Using the work of Rokeach (1968) in an attempt to answer these questions, Schwartz and Bilsky (1987, p. 551) derive seven distinct value domains which are predicated on three universal human needs: the biological needs of the individual, the individual's social interaction needs and the individual's social institutional needs (Figure 5.3).

Some of the value domains are highly culture-bound while others are universal values, indicating that the international firm must ensure that the standardized components of its strategies appeal to universal human values while being careful to ensure that values that are culture-bound are addressed in a customized manner. As a biological need, the human value enjoyment addresses the individual's need for physiological satisfaction, pleasure, sensuousness and emotional gratification. The relevant values focus on pleasure, a comfortable life and happiness. The value maturity informs the individual how to appreciate, understand and accept oneself, other people, and the world. The relevant values focus on wisdom, open-mindedness, a world of beauty and courage.

Social interaction needs reflect the three values of self-direction, achievement and social concerns where self-direction refers to the individual's reliance on a capacity for

Figure 5.3
Seven value
domains

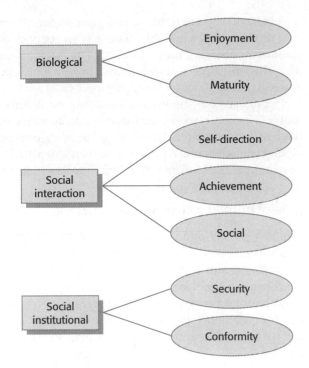

independent thought and action. The relevant values focus on imagination, logical thought, independence and intellect. Achievement is the value possessed by the individual that reflects the skills and competences that allow personal growth and improvement. Relevant values focus on ambition, capability and social recognition. The social value refers to a concern for the welfare of others to ensure group survival. Relevant values focus on being helpful, forgiving and loving and on equality.

Lastly, social institutional needs refer to security and conformity where security refers to physical survival, mental well-being and threat avoidance. Relevant values focus on inner harmony, family security, national security and world peace. The value conformity refers to a restriction of behaviour which impedes others. Relevant values focus on preventing harm to others, being obedient, polite, clean and self-controlled.

A subset of values constitutes a person's religious beliefs. Understanding the role of religion in society means examining our deepest value convictions. A person's religious beliefs influence consumption behaviour, social behaviour, manner of dress, ways of doing business, general societal values and harmony and conflict in society. Religion also affects our attitudes toward time, wealth, change and risk.

Not only does religion establish taboos and moral standards and norms within a culture affecting behaviour, it also reflects the principal values of different people in very observable ways. Social mobility and the achievement ethic in the West are supported by Christian values of self-determination and the importance of work. The Hindu religion emphasizes reaching Nirvana through a combination of inherited status and a contemplative life. Where religion is important in a society, the religious institutions usually play an important role in either promoting or discouraging change.

Attitudes, particularly attitudes toward time, express important values in society and they are also culturally distinctive in that they vary from culture to culture and occasionally within the same culture. In some countries, for instance, an executive knows what is meant when a client lets a month go by before replying to a business proposal. In other societies such delays would not be acceptable.

In Arab countries time does not generally include schedules as they are known and used in western countries. The time required to get something accomplished depends upon relationships. In Latin America, to be kept waiting does not necessarily mean a lack of attention. Even in neighbouring European countries attitudes to time can be very different, causing conflict in management relations. In international marketing it is necessary to understand attitudes to time in different cultures; attitudes to time are a manifestation of some latent values of society.

Consumption and business behaviour is directly related to the broader set of human values. For instance, achievement and success are regarded as being very important in some countries which can act as a justification for the acquisition of material wealth. These factors are fundamental to an understanding of the international marketing environment and an understanding of consumer and buyer behaviour in different cultures.

Demographic factors

Demographic changes also influence the international firm (Figure 5.4). For many products, population size may be used as a broad preliminary indicator of market potential. However, population size should only be used in conjunction with income levels and other measures, as a large population may represent little potential where income levels are quite low.

Population growth rates should also be considered: low population growth rates are more typical of countries generally regarded as more highly developed economically. This arises from an historical tendency of both birth and death rates to decrease following, rather than preceding, economic development. In most developing countries in recent years, the death rate has fallen markedly because of medical advances while the birth rate has remained high. This has caused an unprecedented population explosion that has hampered efforts to raise living standards.

Figure 5.4
Demographic factors

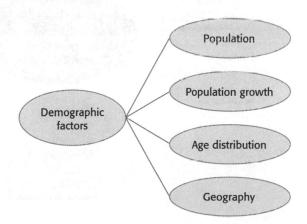

Not only is the world's population growing rapidly, but the population density is shifting from the industrial countries of the North to the developing countries of the South. By the year 2050, population in the developed world is expected to increase by somewhat less than 200 million, whereas the developing areas of Africa, Asia and Latin America are expected to increase by two billion. The World Bank predicts that over four-fifths of the world's population will be concentrated in developing countries.

Age distribution in a foreign country is yet another factor which affects both sales and investment opportunities. A country with a larger proportion of people in the older age brackets would have a smaller market for items such as maternity and infant goods, and school equipment. Conversely, a more elderly population would represent a larger market for healthcare products. Hence, it is important to understand the impact of the age distribution in different international markets.

The age distribution of the population has important consequences for the size of the labour force and its productivity. If a population has a higher than normal proportion of very old or very young people, as may be found in France, Germany, parts of the US, and many developing countries due to wars, illness such as AIDS, and other disasters, then fewer people, proportionally, will be available to do productive work. This may lead to a shortage of skilled or manual labour and in some cases greatly increased wage rates.

Overall, country data obscure differences that exist within individual nations. Within developing countries there are, typically, fairly substantial groups that have the characteristics of advanced countries. Of course, it is also possible to find backward areas or groups within the most developed countries.

Characteristics of culture

For the firm in international markets there are four major characteristics of culture: a) it is learned, b) interrelated, c) adaptive and d) may operate at times as subcultures (Figure 5.5). The two ways in which a person develops cultural norms and values are learning by socialization and learning through acculturation. By socialization a person

Figure 5.5
Characteristics and elements of culture

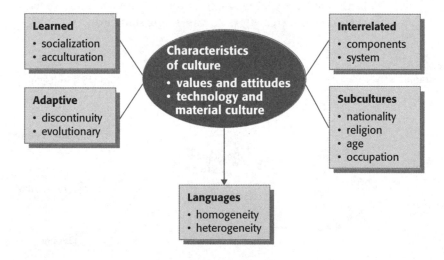

learns a culture when very young from two sources of values, referred to as a) the institutional triad – families, religious and educational institutions and b) early lifetime experiences which may include war, social disturbances and family upheavals. Values and norms formed at this stage lead to differences between the generations, when the population as a whole is being considered. Learning through acculturation in contrast is the process of learning a culture of which one is not native. For example, if a firm wishes to invest in, or to sell to, another country, it must learn the culture of that country.

The various parts of culture are interrelated. Cultural systems have a unity which, as a result of the interaction among the parts, is different from a simple sum of the parts. To achieve understanding of any culture, one must not only understand the content, but also how the system is put together and how its parts are interrelated. Culture is also adaptive and may change rapidly or slowly, through either a discontinuous or an evolutionary process (Engel *et al.*, 1993). Changes occurring in the Hispanic population in the US illustrate how the various parts of culture are interrelated and how different generations are socialized and acculturated. As the Hispanic American population approaches 40 million in that country, companies are taking notice and delivering value to a segment whose spending power is swelling accordingly. Procter & Gamble's Tide Tropical Clean – a Tide washing detergent brand extension – is a product developed with the Latino market in mind, recognizing the importance of smell to Latinos: '57 per cent of Hispanics describe themselves as avid scent seekers' according to P&G's Mauricio Troncoso. Nevertheless, this is not a uniform market segment (Exhibit 5.1).

A very sharp discontinuity occurs in the pattern of cultural change, for example, when the value system of a culture becomes associated with the gratification of only one class. Other classes reject the logic of the value system and replace it with a new value system. In an evolutionary process change comes but is a process of modification and adaptation. The adaptive nature of culture is an important consideration in developing an understanding of behaviour in that culture. In the past cultural change was usually slow and gradual. The accelerated technological changes that characterize contemporary society, together with rapid changes in the institutional triad mentioned above, have created a situation where change is now quicker and more unpredictable.

Most cultures are also characterized by a series of subcultures which involve sets of learned beliefs, values, attitudes, habits and forms of behaviour which are shared by subjects of a society and are transmitted from generation to generation within each subset (Bennett and Kassarjan, 1972). Members of subcultures typically conform to many of the norms of the dominant culture and deviate from others which are not compatible with the norms of their subculture.

There are a number of variables on which subcultures are based. Some are based on nationality, such as the Turkish immigrants in Germany, who represent about 5 per cent of the total population. Race is an important base of subculture in the United States while religion is the base for subcultures in Northern Ireland. Indeed, the influence of religion on business through company regulations and restraints on consumer behaviour in some societies is all-pervasive. Age can also represent an important basis for recognizing subcultures with, for example, teenagers and older age groups exhibiting quite different patterns of consumption. Often the values of a subculture are passed on to the dominant culture. For example, denim jeans, originally designed for miners in the American west, soon became popular among farm people and ranchers and decades later began to be worn by the youth subculture; they are now worn by all age groups.

Exhibit 5.1   The American dream gets a Latino beat

'Hispanic' is an ethnic term that encompasses all Latino peoples from Mexico to Argentina. And what is more, companies must take into account the various levels of acculturation among differing generations of the Hispanic community. It seems younger Hispanic consumers, the 18–34 age group, are more persuaded by advertisements in Spanish, while the 12.5 million Hispanic-American web users are split approximately fifty-fifty as regards their preferred language, English or Spanish.

Biculturalism is emerging as a fine but important balance for companies targeting Hispanic segments, so that while an advertisement may be produced in Spanish, the backdrop may be New York rather than Mexico City. Indeed companies are learning much about how to tap into the Latino mindset, where community involvement is a gold star for a company, something adopted by P&G in their 'Avanzando Con Tu Familia' (getting ahead with your family) offering community advice and support through a magazine which enjoys a reach of four million households. While P&G may have spent $90 million on Hispanic advertising and established a separate multicultural marketing department, stereotypes remain of Hispanics as less sophisticated consumers, many lacking health insurance and credit cards. However, the growth in their spending power from 1990 to 2008 at 8.8 per cent compared with 4.9 per cent for non-Hispanics, translates into a projected $1,000 billion which cannot be ignored as a significant demographic shift for US companies to rise to.

Source: adapted from Murray, S., 'The American dream gets a Latino beat', *Financial Times*, Thursday 25 March 2004, p. 9

Special position of languages

Language is perhaps the most obvious difference between cultures and has been described as a cultural mirror which reflects the content and nature of the culture it represents. Language is human behaviour, not just a collection of words and sounds. It is the spoken and not the written language which most accurately describes and reflects the contemporary behaviour and values of members of a culture. Language is probably the most important of all human skills since it is by means of language that humans are able to exchange ideas which makes organized social life possible.

Language is a primary way of separating cultural groups (Griffin and Pustay, 1996). It establishes the categories on which our perceptions of the world are organized. Our perceptions of the world depend on how language influences the way we think: thus 'speakers of any two languages will not perceive reality in exactly the same way; language is not merely a mechanism for communicating ideas, but also a shaper of ideas' (Ueltschy and Ryans, 1997, p. 482). In a study of the possibility of standardizing advertising in the US and in Mexico, these authors state that any advertising campaign using an emotional appeal may be difficult to standardize, since the success of an emotional appeal depends on viewers bringing similar cultural values to the situation (p. 491), but where advertisements are cognitively based the possibility of standardization exists but viewers prefer customized advertisements. In this context language and perception are intimately intertwined. Culture influences what we perceive: we never really see the physical world around us. The world we perceive is a product of the interaction between the physical aspects of the universe and what we have learned from previous experience. It is particularly difficult to obtain agreement on perception and meaning when cultures as different as the French and Japanese are involved as Renault and Nissan discovered when they merged (Exhibit 5.2).

Exhibit 5.2   A common language to communicate across cultures

When Renault and Nissan joined together both companies decided the common language between them should be English. Louis Schweitzer, chairman of Renault, later recalled that [English] 'is not a familiar language either in Renault or in Nissan. Some are fluent in English, a lot are not. We have put in intensive English training. The risk is that people who speak English have an undue advantage over those who don't speak it well. But we have found that in a number of meetings that it is better to communicate through a translator than by speaking English. Translators can be the best way to get the message across. Over time it will improve. But the language barrier was what we expected to be the most difficult barrier, and it has been.'

Source: adapted from *The Wall Street Journal Europe*, Thursday 15 February 2001, p. 38

Language heterogeneity

Some countries are linguistically homogeneous while others are heterogeneous. The degree of linguistic heterogeneity varies greatly between countries. Some countries are almost 'pure' linguistically, with nearly all the citizens speaking the same native tongue. Most countries in Asia and Africa are linguistically heterogeneous. Europe and the Middle East are about evenly balanced, while Latin America, except for Brazil, is almost homogeneous linguistically.

In addition to differences in official languages, nations also differ in the number of languages used within their boundaries. Examining national official languages alone can give a misleading picture of the linguistic uniformity within countries. There are only about 100 official languages for all countries in the world, whereas there are at least 3,000 languages currently spoken throughout the world. Well under half of the countries of the world are linguistically homogeneous in the sense that 85 per cent or more of the population speaks the same native tongue.

A complicating factor in most countries is the issue of dialects. In countries where more than one language is spoken widely the issue of dialects is, of course, much more complicated. Switzerland is a good example of a small country in which there are a number of official languages but a range of dialects based on these languages.

Ethnic factors

Among human variations, the most noticeable are physical attributes or appearance. While most differences in appearance are readily apparent, there are a host of subtle variations that, although important to people within a given society, may be easily overlooked by non-discriminating outsiders. Size of individuals would seem to be one of the most noticeable differences, but many firms make mistakes in this respect. For example, the well-known UK retailer Marks and Spencer attempted to sell men's suits in China based on UK patterns for tailoring, only to realize that they fitted few Chinese men because of their narrower hips and shoulders.

Not only must actual physical differences be taken into account, so also must traits that a country has idealized. Various populations have created wishful stereotypes of themselves that must be considered when creating imagery. For this reason, advertisements in the United States typically depict individuals who are somewhat younger and thinner than the majority of the people toward whom the product is aimed. In Germany there has been an idealization of the tall Nordic type, who is actually no taller than the average Pole, Frenchman or Dutchman.

Material culture and the international firm

Material culture, material things which humans create and use, e.g. buildings, works of art, tools, machinery and transportation equipment, constitutes a human-created environment interposed between people and the material environment and greatly influences human behaviour. Material culture is influenced by technology and aesthetics in a society (Figure 5.6). Technology includes the techniques used in the creation of material goods and the educational and technical know-how possessed by the people of a society. Both of these affect the level of demand, the quality and types of products demanded, the means of producing goods and services and the means of distributing goods and services.

The marketing implications of the material culture of a country are many. Electrical toothbrushes, for example, which are acceptable in the West, would be considered a waste of money in countries where income could be better spent on clothing or food.

Closely related to a country's material culture are its aesthetic values or preferences in the arts, music and design. For example, Americans often feel that Japanese homes are barren while the Japanese comment on the sterility of the American home. Similarly Hoover, the large washing machine manufacturer, found that the generally accepted ideas about what constitutes good design were different in the French and German markets. The German homemaker preferred a design that was larger and more sturdy in appearance, that gave a feeling of sound engineering and durability, while

Figure 5.6
Influence of
material culture

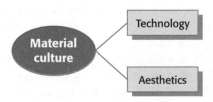

the French homemaker preferred a smaller, lighter machine that did not overly dominate a small kitchen. No single compromise design would allow maximum penetration in both markets.

In the same way a visual advertising appeal that may seem attractive to potential buyers in some countries, may seem dull or incomprehensible in others. When advertising in Germany a few years ago, Guinness used the same press media advertising copy as in Ireland and Britain. The commercial consisted of a small humorous story involving Guinness. It was not successful because Germans do not read the small print in advertising, considering it as a waste of time. If they need to read details about a product they expect to find them in a technical magazine or journal.

Analysis of culture influence

We usually attempt to understand other cultures in terms of how they are similar to or different from our own but attributions reflecting our culture frequently interfere with our understanding. Misunderstandings that arise are due to the influence of the self-reference criterion (Lee, 1966) and can lead to mis-judgements of a marketing situation. The firm must also acknowledge that cultural differences tend to stand out more than similarities, yet it is the similarities that may be more important. Similarities may be analyzed across factors referred to as cultural universals (Table 5.1).

While these phenomena are found in most cultures and are considered as universals, a similar mode of behaviour existing in all countries should not be presumed. For example, humour is not something that travels well even though joking is a universal phenomenon. Companies pursuing a global strategy for their products attempt to discover cultural universals since 'universal aspects of the cultural environment represent opportunities for global marketers to standardize some or all of the marketing programme' (Keegan and Green, 1997, p. 84). Analyses of business structure and behaviour should include, therefore, consideration of institutions, ideas and beliefs but they should be treated with caution since it is so easy to attempt to draw causal links

Table 5.1 Phenomena considered as cultural universals

athletic sports	games	modesty
cleanliness	gestures	mourning
courtship	gift giving	music/dancing
decorative arts	greeting	personal names
education	hair styles	property rights
ethics	hospitality	religious rituals
etiquette	joking	status
folklore	marriage	trade
food taboos	medicine	visiting

Source: Murdock, G. P. (1945) 'The common denominator of cultures', in R. Linton, Ed., *The Science of Man in the World Crises*, New York, NY: Columbia University Press, pp. 123–42

between culture and modern business practice where they do not exist (Wilkinson, 1996, p. 442).

A cultural study for international marketing decisions may be carried out at the macro and micro levels (Cundiff and Tharp Higler, 1984; Terpstra, 1978). The purpose of the macro or cultural level study is to examine the general influence of the cultural environment on business in a country, its attitudes towards foreigners and new products. The micro or firm level study is concerned with interpreting culture's impact upon a specific group of people in a country (Cundiff and Tharp Higler, 1984) who may be potential customers. The analysis of cultural influence takes place first at the cultural level and then proceeds to the firm level. Both levels of cross-cultural analysis are concerned with a search for cultural universals that may be used in a marketing campaign. To the extent that aspects of the cultural environment are universal as opposed to unique, it is possible for the international firm to standardize some aspects of the marketing programme such as product design and communications, two of the major elements. Firms must be careful, however, in deciding what is universal and what is unique in a specific culture. Attempts are often made, for example, to indicate that relationship marketing, a western concept, is a universal and very similar to *guanxi*, a Chinese phenomena, whereas in practice while there may be similarities, the provenance of the two concepts is completely different and requires careful consideration by the international firm (Exhibit 5.3).

Exhibit 5.3   Culture is of the essence – guanxi and relationship marketing

In China, people are viewed as relation-oriented beings, regulated by cardinal relationships that dictate an individual's obligations toward other people. A special relationship, guanxi, governs the exchange of favours. It is similar to insurance in that favours are registered (like premiums) so that benefits may be obtained if and when required. Guanxi involves building a long-term relationship, based on trust and mutual exchange, to secure customer relations. Guanxi forms a bond among buyers and sellers and between suppliers and producers.

When a relationship is more valuable than a transaction, then it is likely that the transaction will be smooth. The sense of obligation would come from the relationship, rather than a piece of paper. In the absence of a strong relationship, however, there exists the possibility that one of the parties might ignore a contract. The West has known contract law since the 1700s; the purpose of such legislation is to give business an assurance that deals will be honoured. In the absence of an elaborate contract law, the Chinese have relied on guanxi for the same assurance.

It may be argued that firms in the West also value relationships and that these hold mutual obligations. In the West, relationship marketing, the pursuit of customer loyalty, involves the fostering of long-term alliances with customers. There is, however, an important difference between Chinese and western views of relationships. In the West, successful transactions lead to good relationships. In Chinese circles, one builds relationships to initiate transactions; the common belief is that if a relationship is well built, then transactions will follow.

Source: adapted from Dana, L., 'Culture is of the essence in Asia, even global companies can make major mistakes when dealing with Asian cultures', *Financial Times*, Monday 27 November 2000 – Supplement: Mastering Management, p. 12

Figure 5.7
Cultural-level
analysis

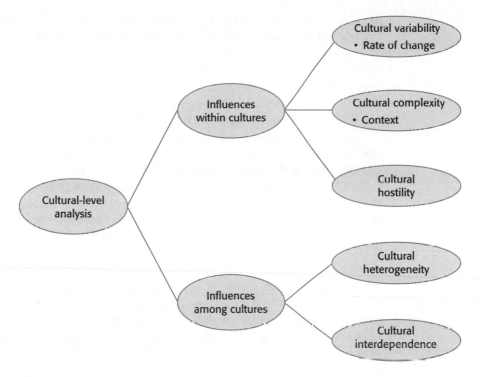

Source: adapted from Terpstra, V. (1978) *The Cultural Environment of International Business*, Southwestern Publishing Company

Cultural-level analysis

The elements of a cultural-level analysis of the cultural environment include an examination of variability, complexity, cultural hostility, heterogeneity and interdependence (Terpstra, 1978). By proceeding in this way the key influences within cultures and among cultures are identified (Figure 5.7).

Influences within cultures

Factors that have a pronounced influence within cultures include cultural variability, cultural complexity and cultural hostility.

Cultural variability

Cultural variability refers to matters of social organization and concerns the ways in which people relate to one another and organize their activities in order to live in harmony. Social classes, the family, positions of men and women, group behaviour and age groups are interpreted differently within different cultures.

Social classes tend to have quite different consumption patterns which affect, among other things, the purchase of housing and home furnishings, food and alcoholic beverages. The degree of social mobility is also an important dimension of class structure, as is the relative size and number of distinct classes within a society.

As a general rule upper classes in different countries are more similar to each other than to the rest of their society while middle classes are more apt to engage in 'cultural borrowing' and lower classes are more likely to be culture-bound, i.e. are less aware of other cultures. Therefore, the larger the upper and middle classes, the more likely a market is to buy imported products and services that are not culturally constrained.

The role of the family may also vary among cultures. In primitive and rural societies the family is the all-important social focal point, providing food, clothing, shelter, education, acculturation and a social centre.

In some of the more sophisticated urban societies the family may provide little more than food and basic acculturation. All other activities are partially or totally transferred to other groups, especially peers and educational institutions.

The role of women varies widely from society to society. In many societies women do not enjoy parity with men as participants in the economy. The extent to which they participate affects their role as consumers, consumption influencers and workers in the money economy.

In the industrialized world the educational system is synonymous with schools and these play a major role in passing on cultural values to the individual. In many developing countries, however, elders and oral historians play a greater role in the transmission of cultural traditions and values to young people. Formal education through schools has a strong relationship to literacy levels within a society. In those countries where schools are provided for the broadest possible group, literacy levels tend to be highest. Well-educated people tend to want more sophisticated information about products and tend to use more sources of information when making purchase decisions. Successful international firms attempt to understand the nature of the formal educational system, to whom it is available, and its relative importance in transmitting cultural values compared with other institutions.

Within cultures variability refers to the degree to which the above social organization and educational conditions within a culture change at a low or high rate or do not change at all. As cultural environments become more turbulent, i.e. more variable, the unpredictability of operations increases. Facing unpredictability, the firm needs to become more receptive to change. Internal structures and processes need to be altered in order to cope with change. Open channels of communication, decentralized decision-making and predominance of local expertise help improve the firm's capacity for perceiving and adjusting to rapid change.

Cultural complexity and context

Cultural complexity refers to the degree to which understanding of conditions within a culture is dependent on the possession of background data which place it in its proper context. Cultures, according to Hall (1960), differ widely in the extent to which unspoken, unformulated, and unexplicit rules govern how information is handled and how people interact and relate to each other. In 'high-context' cultures much of human behaviour is covert or implicit, whereas in 'low-context' cultures much is overt or explicit. For a foreigner, ease of understanding and communication in a culture is inversely related to the importance that culture places on 'silent language' and 'hidden dimensions'. The extent of contexting required, therefore, extends from low in some cultures to high in others. Hall places Germany, Switzerland, Scandinavia and the United States at the lower end of the continuum, France in the middle and China and Japan at the high end of the scale.

In low-context cultures, according to Hall (1960), much information is contained in coded, explicit, transmitted messages. There are fragile bonds and low involvement between people and there are fewer distinctions made between insiders and outsiders and change is easy and rapid. In high-context cultures the opposite is true. Much information is implicit in the physical context or internalized within people. There are strong bonds and high involvement among people. In such cultures there are greater distinctions between insiders and outsiders and cultural patterns are long lived and slow to change.

Context of cross-cultural relationships

Cultures vary in the extent to which communication is influenced by context. In high-context communication, much of the meaning is internalized by the individual whereas in low-context communication, meaning is derived from the coded explicit part of the message (Hall, 1976). Using context as the foundation Bush and Ingram (1996) develop a framework that captures the general comparative characteristics of culture which may be applied to international marketing phenomena (Table 5.2). The concept of context is valid in understanding the behaviour of customers in different countries and in dealing with all forms of negotiation involving companies in these countries.

At a more general level it is accepted that there are pronounced differences in cognitive structures or intellectual styles which influence international communications. For example, it is generally believed that there is a wide gulf between the ways in which people in the West and East think. Western cognition tends to be logical and uses sequential connections and abstract notions of reality to represent universals. The emphasis is on causes rather than outcomes and provides an incremental understanding.

Oriental cognition, on the other hand, tends to be intuitive with more reliance on sense data. It is concrete, with emphasis on the particular rather than the universal, and highly sensitive to context and relationships and expresses a concern for harmony, reconciliation and balance in relationships and provides understanding in intuitive lumps or systems. Oriental cognition is influenced by Confucianism and Buddhism, which leads to an emphasis on loyalty and harmony and an adherence to group norms whereby the individual is subordinated to the welfare of the group (Dubinsky *et al.*, 1997, p. 196). The converse is true in the West where culture reflects a Judeo-Christian value system where people have an individualistic approach towards everything that affects them leading them to place their own self-interest ahead of the organization or group.

Culture also influences the way people in different countries think, understand phenomena and express themselves which is likely to affect the way companies should develop their marketing strategies. The influence of 'Mad Cow Disease' on beef

Table 5.2 Comparative characteristics of culture

Characteristic	Low-context	High-context
Communication and language	Explicit, direct	Implicit, indirect
Sense of self and space	Informal handshakes	Formal hugs, bows and handshakes
Dress and appearance	Dress for individual success, wide variety	Indication of position in society, religious rule
Food and eating habits	Eating is a necessity, fast food	Eating is a social event
Time consciousness	Linear, exact, promptness is valued, time = money	Elastic, relative, time spent on enjoyment, time = relationships
Family and friends	Nuclear family, self-oriented, value youth	Extended family, other oriented, loyalty and responsibility, respect for old age
Values and norms	Independence, confrontation and conflict	Group conformity, harmony
Beliefs and attitudes	Egalitarian, challenge authority, individuals control destiny, gender equality	Hierarchical, respect for authority, individuals accept destiny, gender roles
Cognitive style	Linear, logical, sequential, problem-solving	Lateral, holistic, simultaneous, accepting life's difficulties
Work habits	Task-oriented, rewards based on achievement, work has value	Relationship-oriented, rewards based on seniority, work is a necessity

Source: adapted from Bush, V. D. and Ingram, T. (1996) 'Adapting to diverse customers: a training matrix for international marketers', *Industrial Marketing Management*, **25**, 373–83

consumption in different countries depends on the consumer trust and perception and the way governments manage the information about the disease. Consumers in the US trust their government to look after them in all respects and believe what is said about Mad Cow Disease whereas Europeans are less trusting of politicians and are more sceptical of public statements about such matters (Exhibit 5.4).

These examples demonstrate for the firm the importance of noting the way people in different cultures think when it attempts to develop a sales or negotiation strategy for various markets. A sequential sales approach based on obtaining agreement from customers for each individual aspect of the offer, for example, may be appropriate in western countries accustomed to thinking in a logical step-by-step fashion but is unlikely to work in eastern countries where buyers are likely to wait until the full proposition is clear and understood before giving a meaningful commitment.

Exhibit 5.4   Mad Cow fallout differs in the US, Europe and Japan

Mad Cow Disease or Bovine Spongiform Encephalopathy (BSE) affects all cows similarly. From Japan, to Europe and the States, cases have been reported, yet while the dangers to humans may remain consistent across borders, consumer response has not. A month after the first case of mad cow disease was uncovered in the US, beef sales have stood firm. McDonald's, the number one hamburger franchise in the US, has ensured the beef it uses would be safe from BSE contamination. As such it has reported no significant impact on its US sales while suffering double figure fall-offs in European and Japanese sales.

Back in 2000, within Europe, reactions differed to the outbreak; Germany cut back 70 per cent in beef consumption over five months while Holland only suffered a 25 per cent drop-off. Across the Atlantic, Canadian restaurant beef sales have increased beef by 5–10 per cent and even home-cooked meals feature beef more often since 2002. There was a little bit of patriotism according to market research firm NPD Canada. In Japan consumers lost confidence in government reassurances when a second case of BSE was discovered within a month of the first, slicing beef sales in half according to Thomas Wahl's study of Japanese reactions to mad cow disease.

The disparity is in no small part due to the level of trust consumers place in their government, according Professor Wansink's research of consumer reaction to mad cow disease in Europe, something echoed by Jim Cantalupo, McDonald's CEO, 'the US has one of the best if not the best systems in the world in regards to food safety . . . the consumer recognises that'. While consumer confidence is a significant factor, the media role is another. According to Daniel Laufer, assistant professor of marketing at the University of Cincinatti, Europeans responded to images of infected people succumbing to the disease, while Americans and Canadians were only shown cows, 'if people only see cows on the news people don't feel personally vulnerable' he explained.

Source: adapted from *The Wall Street Journal* (Eastern Edition), Wednesday 21 January 2004, p. 12

Cultural hostility

A culture may be munificent or benign on the one hand or malevolent or illiberal on the other. In the latter situation cultural hostility prevails. Cultural hostility refers to the degree to which conditions in a culture threaten company goals. The extent of hostility depends on the perceived acceptability and legitimacy of the firm. Hostility means that the firm is less able to acquire raw materials, capital, personnel, information, goodwill, political favours and other resources. Hostility may also reduce the firm's ability to sell its products and services.

Influences among cultures

In examining influences among cultures, the manager must determine the extent of cultural heterogeneity and the degree of cultural similarity that exists in different markets. The manager must also assess interdependence among markets – the degree to which conditions in one culture are sensitive to developments in other cultures.

Cultural heterogeneity and interdependence

Among cultures heterogeneity refers to the degree to which separate cultures are similar or dissimilar. The cultures in which a firm operates can range from relatively homogeneous to extremely heterogeneous. Increasing heterogeneity means that there is greater variety that the firm must take into consideration in decision-making.

Cultural interdependence refers to the degree to which conditions in one culture are sensitive to developments in other cultures. Interdependence of cultures operates by way of contact. Advances in communication and transportation, growth or cross-border economic exchange, expansion of regional and international institutions and the emergence of transcultural interest groups all serve to increase the volume of transactions between different cultures. Given increasing cultural interdependence, the actions of the firm in one culture are likely to be exposed to the scrutiny of governments and interested groups in others. For example, in cases as diverse as bribery, sale of powdered infant milk in developing countries, ecological destruction and food safety, international firms have been faced with transcultural interest groups and demands. Each of the above factors is best interpreted as part of a continuum from low to high. Within and among cultures it is possible to find high and low expressions of each of the dimensions of culture discussed above.

Firm-level analysis

We now turn to an examination of the patterns of cultural influence at the level of the firm. The impact of culture at the level of the firm depends on the pattern of cultural influence and the cultural barriers that arise there. The patterns of cultural influence are in turn influenced by national ideology which represents the way the citizens of a particular country think about and react to various stimuli and their attitudes toward foreign people, products and services (Figure 5.8).

Figure 5.8
Firm-level
analysis of
culture

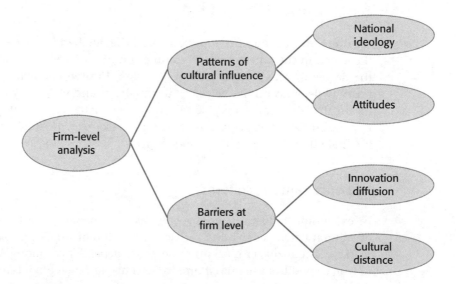

Patterns of cultural influence

Frequently we wish to predict how the typical French, Italian or Portuguese person would act in certain defined situations. Even though all three of these countries are predominantly of the same religion, the Portuguese is likely to react more strongly to infringements of its rules than the French or Italians. The French have a much stronger sense of national pride and unity than the Italians or the Portuguese. As a consequence they tend to be less willing to substitute a foreign-made product for a French product, at least in areas that reflect national expertise. Sometimes such stereotyping is valuable; sometimes it is a hindrance to understanding the micro cultural environment.

Economic philosophy is an important element in national ideology. Sweden had a strong national commitment to socialism and for several decades permitted extensive government involvement in business and economic affairs. This contrasts with the United States and other countries operating under a capitalistic ideology, where massive government involvement in economic affairs has been strongly resisted.

National ideology is strongest and most consistent in countries that have a long cultural identity. For example, there is a strong, easily identifiable national ideology in a country such as Egypt which, even though it has not consistently had political independence in recent centuries, possesses a long and consistent cultural history. However, some of the newer nations in Africa have not had separate identities long enough to have developed strong national ideologies. Instead, different subgroups within these nations reflect the ideologies of the subgroups or tribes from which they descend.

Even in countries with strong national ideologies, however, these ideologies often represent a general cross-section or average. Not all individuals fit the pattern. Nevertheless, it is important for the international firm to know the general national ideology so that it can fit the product and its marketing strategy into the local environment.

Attitudes to people and products

Allied to the preceding point is the observation that people may view that which is foreign as different and potentially threatening to existing patterns of action and behaviour. In some countries this reaction toward foreign peoples and ways is reflected in a fear of contamination or change from outside. An extreme example of this fear is the policy of the Chinese government in early years when foreigners and foreign products were not welcome. Yet even when foreigners and foreign products are not perceived as a threat to the local economy, they may still be perceived as different and/or inferior. It is for this reason that international firms often play down their foreignness and try to blend in with the local scene.

Not all attitudes toward foreigners and foreign products are negative, however. Highly sophisticated and talented individuals may be perceived as interesting rather than just 'different' by nationals of other countries. Foreign products of high quality are often viewed in the same light. Belgian lace, French wine, Japanese cameras and German microscopes are all viewed as distinctive and of extra high quality in world markets. In these instances, the foreign identification actually provides an advantage in the marketplace. Success in a foreign market, then, may depend on the firm's ability to blend in with the local scene and to develop a domestic identity, or it may depend on the firm's ability to convince local buyers that foreign means better. In contrast to values, discussed earlier, which are difficult to influence and slow to change, attitudes may be influenced and may change in the shorter term, hence the role of a marketing communications package if appropriately designed and properly executed.

Barriers at firm level

Patterns of cultural influence may affect the number and impact of cultural barriers at the level of the firm. In general, national ideology together with the attitudes formed toward foreign products influences the level of innovation and the rate of diffusion in a country.

Innovation and diffusion

Attitudes toward innovation diffusion influence the success or otherwise of the international firm. There are a number of factors which influence the diffusion of an innovation. Frequently, when a foreign firm enters a market, it is introducing a product or service that represents an 'innovation' in that market. If a product is sufficiently different from others in a market, local consumers may see it as something entirely new. Hence, the firm must try to anticipate how consumers in that market will react to change. If local people show a strong resistance to change, some other less resistant market may prove to be more fruitful. Even where the introduction of a new product seems promising, it is important to understand the process through which changes are introduced and accepted. Many well-known international brand companies fail to appreciate the significance of this lesson.

A consumer's perception of an innovation may have a strong impact on how quickly it is adopted. An innovation that consumers perceive as being clearly superior to other ways of meeting their needs will be adopted faster than those products or services which do not have such relative advantages. If it is easy for consumers to understand the functions of an innovation and it can be 'tried' or 'explained', this product or service will also be adopted quickly. It follows that products or services that are less costly and more compatible with cultural values and traditional ways of doing things will be adopted faster than others. International firms need to be aware that they must communicate these qualities to markets when the product or service is seen as new.

Cultural distance

Normally, distance is thought of as the spatial difference between two or more points. Distance in this sense, which takes account only of physical or geographic characteristics, is a unidimensional concept and limiting when attempting to understand the internationalization process of business. In the present context, distance is also taken to include economic and cultural distance. It is possible to measure the separation of countries in terms of all three distance concepts to derive a separation of markets based on what is referred to in the literature as business distance (Luostarinen, 1980, pp. 124–52).

The importance of distance may be gauged by observing that companies tend to be more knowledgeable and to have more information about foreign markets that are culturally near to them than for more culturally distant markets and so they favour markets that are culturally close and which are known to them. Companies new to the internationalization process tend to avoid those markets which are unfamiliar. So far the discussion has only considered the flow of information or knowledge. The same argument holds for the movement of products and people. For all three flows, therefore, cultural distance is an impediment and restricting force which predisposes the company to closer markets.

An analysis based on cultural distance normally suggests that experience in international marketing, tourism, education and television and increases in the number of foreign-owned companies constitute the principal explanatory factors in encouraging an openness of attitudes toward international business. In a direct business context, of course, international marketing and tourism are probably the most directly affected.

Influence of culture on consumer behaviour – an application

The rate of innovation diffusion itself varies between markets and different parts of the world. In the West, particularly in the United States, diffusion of new products and ideas is thought to follow the traditional normal bell-shaped curve, rising slowly at first, maturing and then declining in a predictable way (Figure 5.9a). By adopting the dictates of this curve, analysts have been able to categorize consumers according to their responses, fast or slow, to innovations. Consumer behaviour in western countries, for example, is thought to be different in a number of respects to behaviour in eastern countries. This may not be the universal situation.

Consumer behaviour is strongly influenced by culture and is not universal; the different tastes, habits and customs may prevent consumers from universally preferring

Figure 5.9
Innovation
diffusion in the
East and West

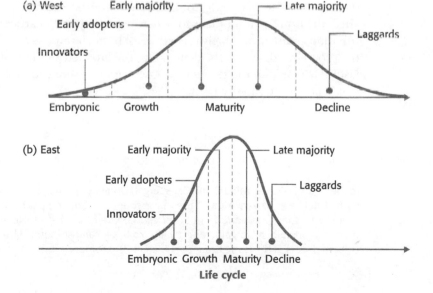

the same marketing mix. As a result some western firms may be using a 'push' strategy in the East with their brands in order to capture savings through standardization rather than being 'pulled' by eastern consumers. The popularity of western luxury products among high income earners and young people in Asia, therefore, may not be proof that they are 'global' consumers – they may try the same products but for different reasons. Branded clothing products such as Yves St Laurent and Burberry may be bought more for 'face' reasons and regard for others in the group than because of an individual preference for the product. Furthermore, J & B Rare Whisky and Baileys Original Irish Cream may not be purchased because consumers prefer them over local beverages but because of peer pressure.

In the East, because of peer pressure among groups of consumers the response pattern may be quite different (Figure 5.9b). After a relatively cautious start, groups tend to rush to buy the innovation and later, on reaching maturity in the market, these same groups desert the product or service just as rapidly in great numbers, causing pronounced changes in the shape of the innovation diffusion curve thought to apply to consumers in the East. The reasons why the rate and patterns of diffusion are different in the East and the West may be attributed to:

■ attempts to avoid uncertainty in Asia;

■ shopping is done in groups, hence the role of peer pressure;

■ for Asians the social risk of trying a new product first is high;

■ the proportion of innovators and laggards is much lower among Asians;

■ referral is a very powerful way of expanding product trials by the first wave of consumers in Asia.

Presumably it was a recognition of the differences in innovation diffusion between East and West that led Heineken to use an innovative marketing approach based on the 'perceived popularity' of the brand in their initial exporting efforts in Hong Kong (Exhibit 5.5). The very different innovation diffusion curves for East and West greatly affect the firm's roll-out plans for a new product and, in particular, the impact on distribution channels and logistics in the East is much more severe than in the West given the pronounced peak in the demand for the product. Similarly, there may be a shorter fashion element in the reaction to a new product resulting is a shorter life cycle than would be expected in the West.

Exhibit 5.5 Heineken's perceived popularity in Hong Kong

In the mid-1990s San Miguel and Carlsberg in Hong Kong together accounted for 70 per cent of the total beer market. Today, they only account for about 45 per cent of total volume while Heineken's share has gone from 5 per cent to over 20 per cent. Heineken did not achieve these remarkable share gains directly. It was the local distributor who truly understood the cultural drivers of the Hong Kong beer market. The company knew that they were challenging brands with large market shares and effective advertising. To spend millions of advertising dollars to achieve anything against two major and entrenched brands was considered unrealistic. Instead the distributor tapped a key Asian value – make people truly believe the beer is popular.

The Heineken distributor in Hong Kong pushed the product first in aspirational, on-premises outlets where it might develop an up-market niche; also, perhaps most importantly, they asked on-premises staff to leave the bottles on the table, either by not pouring full beers or by not collecting the empties. Suddenly, the little green bottles were seen everywhere, being drunk by white collar, up-market types in expensive, trendy outlets. This evolved until suddenly more and more people were drinking the beer and it eventually took on its own momentum, the biggest key to marketing to Asians – perceived popularity. If you can convince Asians that many of their colleagues are buying your brand and you can make it highly visible, you may have a winner.

Source: adapted from Robinson, C. (1996) 'Asian culture – the marketing consequences', *Journal of the Marketing Research Society*, **38** (1), 58–9

Synthesis of cultural influence on buyer behaviour

In this chapter we have noted how the role of the family, the group, education and other factors influence culture in every country. Cultural messages which manifest themselves through ethical standards and morality norms, behaviour and roles for people affect designs, shapes and colours chosen for products and other manifestations of material culture. Culture is also influenced by the universal needs and wants in society, consumer trends and consumer behaviour. Culture in a country is mediated through each of these three sets of factors: cultural forces; cultural messages and consumer decision processes (Figure 5.10). This process gives rise to different cultures in different countries that may be in conflict. International marketing managers must cope with these differences to reduce potential conflict and harness the tension to bring about a reconciliation among the different cultures. By synthesizing cultural

Figure 5.10
A synthesis of cultural influences in international marketing

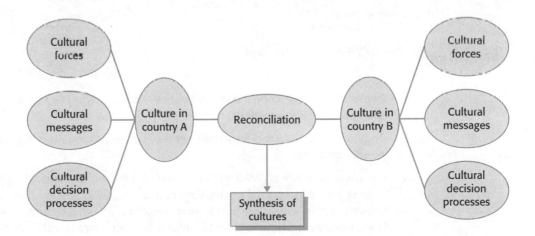

influences in this way the international marketing company integrates different cultural perspectives and seeks a dynamic solution to cultural problems that the firm may face.

Summary

Cultural influences have been identified as critical determinants of international management behaviour. International business and especially marketing is seen as a cultural as well as an economic phenomenon. The basic argument behind the need to examine the cultural dimension in the internationalization of the firm is that management is sometimes culture-bound and therefore inward looking and subject to the dictates of self-reference criterion. The elements which go to make up culture in the international marketing environment include the following: language, religion, varying attitudes towards time, wealth acquisition and risk taking, organization of relationships in the form of social and cultural stratification, family units; level of education; technology and material culture development in general and aesthetic values. Through the analysis of cultural influences, an attempt has been made to determine international modes of behaviour.

At the macro level the elements of the cultural environment involve the following: cultural variability, complexity, hostility, heterogeneity and interdependence. At the micro level, the main patterns of specific cultural attitudes include the following: national pride, economic philosophy, national identity and fear of foreign influences and attitude toward innovation. Cultural distance as a barrier to internationalization involves the notion of business distance which is multidimensional in nature. Cultural distance takes into account not only the geographical distance and physical characteristics but also economic and cultural differences. The greater the business distance and subsequent weaker information flow from the market, the fewer movements of products and people. This business distance has to a certain extent been diminished in recent years as a result of increased use of the media as a means of communication and increased travel. Cultural analysis can only be made in reference to one's own situation and thus tends to be subjective in nature. Despite these restrictions it is essential for a firm to fully understand the cultural environment in which it operates in order for it to succeed. This may mean synthesizing similarities and differences between markets.

Questions

1. What is culture? Describe the characteristics of culture. Why is an understanding of culture important in international marketing?

2. Outline and discuss the principal elements of culture as they affect the behaviour of the international firm.

3. The scope of culture is very broad and covers many aspects of behaviour within a country or culture. Describe the implications of this observation for the firm in international markets. In this context describe how you would carry out a cultural-level analysis of a foreign market and how you would perform the same analysis at the level of the firm.

4. It is not possible to understand how markets evolve and how buyers react to marketing programmes developed by the firm without accepting that markets are based on individual and group behaviour determined by cultural-level and human values. Discuss.

5. What role has the firm in international markets as an agent of cultural change? Is the role different in different countries?

6. Patterns of innovation are different in western-style markets than they are in the East. Can you explain how these differences arise and indicate the impact such differences can have on the firm's international marketing activities?

7. Describe the importance of synthesizing cultural influences between markets and show how this might be done.

References

Bennett, P. and Kassarjan, H. (1972) *Consumer Behaviour*, Englewood Cliffs, NJ: Prentice Hall.

Bush, V. D. and Ingram, T. (1996) 'Adapting to diverse customers: a training matrix for international marketers', *Industrial Marketing Management*, **25**, 373–83.

Cundiff, E. A. and Tharp Higler, M. E. (1984) *Marketing in the International Environment*, Englewood Cliffs, NJ: Prentice Hall.

Downs, J. F. (1971) *Cultures in Crisis*, Beverly Hills, CA: Glencoe Press.

Dubinsky, A. J., Kotabe, M., Lim, C. U. and Wagner, W. (1997) 'The impact of values on salespeople's job responses: a cross-national investigation', *Journal of Business Research*, **39**, 195–208.

Engel, J. F., Blackwell, R. D. and Miniard, P. W. (1993) *Consumer Behaviour*, 7th edn, New York, NY: Dryden Press.

Etzioni, A. (1988) *The Moral Dimension: Towards a New Economics*, New York, NY: The Free Press.

Funakawa, A. (1997) *Transcultural Management*, San Francisco, CA: Jossey-Bass.

Griffin, R. W. and Pustay, M. W. (1996) *International Business*, Reading, MA: Addison-Wesley.

Hall, E. T. (1960) 'The silent language of overseas business', *Harvard Business Review*, **38** (May–June), 88–96.

Hall, E. T. (1976) *Beyond Culture*, New York, NY: Anchor Press/Doubleday.

Hoebel, A. (1960) *Man, Culture and Society*, New York, NY: Oxford University Press.

Hoecklin, L. (1995) *Managing Cultural Differences*, Wokingham: Addison-Wesley.

Hofstede, G. (1991) *Culture and Organizations: Software of the Mind*, Maidenhead: McGraw Hill.

Hollis, M. (1994) *The Philosophy of Social Science*, Cambridge, England: Cambridge University Press.

Keegan, W. J. and Green, M. C. (1997) *Principles of Global Marketing*, Upper Saddle River, NJ: Prentice Hall.

Kroeber, A. L. (1951) 'The nature of culture' in A. L. Kroeber, *The Ancient Oikoumené, as a Historic Cultural Aggregate (a compendium of essays by A. L. Kroeber 1909–1951)*, Chicago, IL: University of Chicago Press.

Langhoff, T. (1977) 'The influence of cultural differences on internationalization processes of firms' in I. Björkman and M. Forsgren, Eds, *The Nature of the International Firm*, pp. 135–64, Copenhagen: Handelshøjskolens Forlag.

Lee, J. A. (1966) 'Cultural analysis in overseas operations', *Harvard Business Review*, **44** (March–April), 106–14.

Luostarinen, R. (1980) *Internationalization of the Firm, Acta Academiae Series A*, Vol. 30, p. 260, Helsinki: The Helsinki School of Economics.

Murdock, G. P. (1945) 'The common denominator of cultures' in R. Linton, Ed., *The Science of Man in the World Crisis*, Columbia University Press, New York, pp. 123–42.

Robinson, C. (1996) 'Asian culture – the marketing consequences', *Journal of the Marketing Research Society*, 38 (1), 58–9.

Rokeach, M. (1968) *Beliefs, Attitudes and Values*, San Francisco, CA: Jossey-Bass.

Schwartz, S. H. (1994) 'Beyond individualism/collectivism new cultural dimension of values', in U. Kim, H. C. Triandis, C. Kagitcibasi, S. Choi and J. Yoon, Eds, *Individualism and Collectivism – Theory, Methods and Applications*, Cross Cultural Research and Methodology series, **18**, pp. 85–119, Sage Publications.

Schwartz, S. H. and Bilsky, W. (1987) 'Towards a psychological structure of human values', *Journal of Personality and Social Psychology*, **53**, 550–62.

Terpstra, V. (1978) *The Cultural Environment of International Business*, South-Western Publishing Company.

Ueltschy, L. C. and Ryans, J. K. Jr. (1997) 'Employing standardised promotion strategies in Mexico: the impact of language and cultural differences', *International Executive*, **39** (4), 479–95.

Wilkinson, B. (1996) 'Culture, institutions and business in East Asia', *Organization Studies*, **17** (3), 421–47.

6 Political economy and created advantage

There have been very many changes in the international competitive environment in recent years. Competition for US, European and other western-style economies such as Japan now comes from what were traditionally considered as resource-poor countries especially Hong Kong, Korea, Singapore and many other countries in south-east Asia. These countries have consistently achieved more rapid increases in productivity, output and exports than the more established countries by deepening their knowledge base and concentrating on advanced and sophisticated products. Many of them also have large populations and avid consumers on which to test-market their products before going abroad. Such changes have forced the older competitors to question their approach to competing internationally and to examine the role of advanced technology developed through creative industrial and commercial policies. The critical element of the response by some older economies has been to seek effective participation by national governments in shaping the business environments in which their companies compete.

After studying this chapter, students should be able to:

- recognize the significance of market integration and global trade;
- outline the regional approaches toward market integration, such as the European Union, NAFTA and Mercosur;
- evaluate the contributions of the World Trade Organization to the development of markets and world trade;
- specify the appropriate role for marketing within economic development;
- define competitiveness and the different competitive situations evident in the world today;
- distinguish between country-level and company-level competition;
- explain what is meant by industrial targeting and evaluate the role of public policy in international markets.

Impact of market integration

The world economy is now more integrated than it has been for many years as a result of the many trade agreements and market integration mechanisms that exist. The success of trading blocs in the world economy depends on members having similar economic structures, being geographically close to each other, experiencing a political commitment and showing evidence of trade compatibility. The first criterion refers to the need to accommodate the redistribution of trade flows, employment and income which would necessarily arise from the integration of the economies.

Many successful trade blocs exhibit geographic proximity. Rarely do we see free trade arrangements being formed between countries great distances apart. Generally, meeting the geographic criterion means having contiguous borders or non-contiguous borders separated only by water. For trade agreements to be successful they should create more trade than they divert. Regarding political commitment, for success it is generally necessary to witness a convergence of national trade laws and a commitment to establish regional institutions and an equitable division of gains between less advanced countries and highly developed economies.

Influence on the international firm

Arising out of the globalization debate there are two important sets of factors which influence the performance of the international firm. First are the geopolitical influences which refer to technology advances and the emergence of new markets. These geopolitical forces are now all-pervasive. Open markets and liberalization of industry and trade have fostered innovation and technological advances in western-style economies. The increased wealth and improved human development conditions associated with these new technologies have encouraged former closed and less developed countries to seek to share these benefits. Second are the international trade and investment influences, which refer to the liberalization of international markets, the integration of regional markets throughout the world and the growth in foreign direct investment. While deregulation and liberalization of markets is widespread, a number of key industry market sectors that are politically sensitive in the US and the EU particularly, have yet to be opened. For example, an 'open skies' agreement has yet to be signed between these economic powers (Exhibit 6.1).

Exhibit 6.1   US damps European hopes for 'open skies' agreement

The skies above us aren't as open as they seem to be. That is not for want of trying as the EU Commission and US negotiate an open skies treaty that should dismantle much of the existing regulatory framework, which clogs up the international flight paths. However, US political considerations seem to be slowing progress as American negotiators withhold the right to cabotage, which would permit a European carrier to pick up passengers from one US airport and transfer them to another. Totally open skies would threaten US airline profitability and as such US jobs which would antagonize the unions. Secondly, while the EU and the Bush administration would like to see an increase in the foreign ownership limit from 25 per cent to 49 per cent, US carriers fear their lack of profitability may repel any foreign investment. While these and the Fly America programme, which guarantees that US carriers win all government-related travel, may take time to resolve, the nationality clause which restricts EU airlines flying to the US from countries other than their home is likely to be lifted. All in all, these negotiations are something the EU for its part is not rushing into.

Source: based upon an article by Sevastopulo, D. and Buck T., 'US damps European hopes for 'Open Skies' agreement', *Financial Times*, Thursday 5 February 2004, p. 9

Concept of free trade

Free trade is traditionally promoted by the world's most advanced economic power. It was Britain in the nineteenth century and the US after World War II. Now there is no clear leader. Instead we have a triad of economic powers: the United States, the EU and Japan with China rapidly catching up and likely to replace Japan as a manufacturing powerhouse in the near future. It is the imbalances in world trade which have given rise to sharp debates in recent years, particularly in the United States. The argument has centred on issues such as 'free trade', the emotive 'fair trade' and the need to 'integrate and manage' regional markets in order to survive in the global economy.

The theoretical justification for free trade derives from the work of Ricardo in the nineteenth century who argued that free trade was beneficial based on the notion of comparative advantage; countries specialize in certain goods rather than aim for self-sufficiency. This applied even if a country could produce everything more cheaply than others, because there would be activities where this country would enjoy a relative cost advantage. This theory has applicability in a world where there are no transport costs and where productive factors are not mobile. Multinational companies use the opportunities of free trade to become the cheapest producers of goods. This search for absolute advantage keeps wage rates down, promotes unattractive working conditions and can be unfriendly to the environment. Competition becomes the key phrase in the argument.

In recent years European countries have not been able to compete with regard to labour costs with Thailand, Sri Lanka, Indonesia, Taiwan and Hong Kong. There is political pressure to protect jobs through trade measures and social provisions. The idea of free trade is also under attack by environmentalists, who see unrestrained growth through free trade as contrary to sustainable use of the world's resources in the future.

Developments in industrial markets

In responding to this changing marketing environment firms have put pressure on governments to establish economic and political structures which would allow business to revitalize and flourish. This has been a major objective of the General

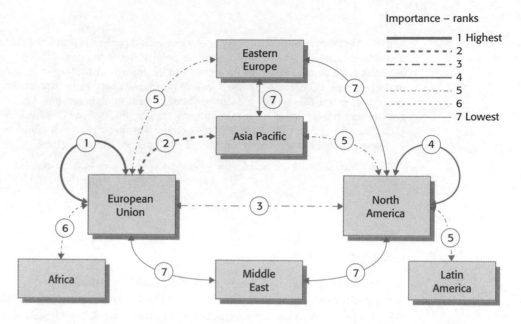

Figure 6.1
Indicative trade
flows among
different regions
of the world

Agreement on Tariffs and Trade and the Uruguay round of trade discussions. As a result there has been harmonization and convergence in the political, technical, legal and fiscal environments. This is especially true in Europe with the establishment of the Economic Union. Other regions of the world are following similar paths of development; in North America there is NAFTA, in Latin America there are a number of groups, especially Mercosur. The various approaches to market integration have been influenced by politics and the stage of economic development reached in the various regions. As a result of free trade agreements and the formation of large formal and informal trading blocs, trade flows are heaviest within these groups and also among the triad of regional economies of the EU, North America and the Asia Pacific region (Figure 6.1). Intra-EU trade is the highest followed by EU-Asia Pacific and EU-North America trade. Trade between the EU and North America and the Middle East and between Eastern Europe and Asia Pacific and North America is the lowest.

Position of developing countries

The pressure to open markets and to develop economies recognizes that poverty in the world should be eliminated and that trade and marketing have a role to play in that process. Economic disparities are believed to give rise to political unrest and social disruption. Implementing the recommendations of the GATT may be seen as an endeavour to reduce economic disparities. Countries representing the richest fifth in the world are responsible for over four-fifths of the world's GNP, world trade, domestic savings and domestic investment. The poorest fifth barely register on these scales (Figure 6.2). Future GATT talks are expected to reduce some of these disparities, though it is a long process.

Many types of macro economic trade policies can be prejudicial to the alleviation of poverty in developing countries which, if not removed, can make it very difficult for

Figure 6.2
Global economic
disparities

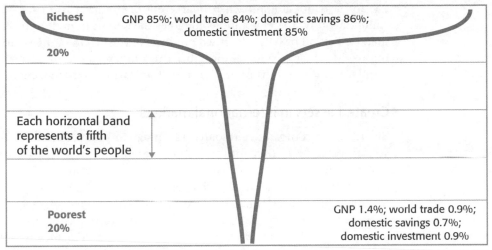

Distribution of economic activity (% of world total)

Richest

GNP 85%; world trade 84%; domestic savings 86%; domestic investment 85%

20%

Each horizontal band represents a fifth of the world's people

Poorest
20%

GNP 1.4%; world trade 0.9%; domestic savings 0.7%; domestic investment 0.9%

Source: adapted from United Nations Development Programme (1994), *Human Development Report*, Oxford: Oxford University Press, p. 63

people there: trade policies which provide effective protection to import competing manufacturing; overvaluation of exchange rates which lowers returns to agricultural exports; making imported food cheaper relative to domestic substitutes; high margins to government-sponsored commodity boards. At the same time subsidies for inputs and other non-price measures are often not sufficient to offset taxation and low product prices. Such policies tend to reduce or stop the flow of resources and to discourage investments in the developing countries.

Closer trade links between developing and developed countries are expected to produce benefits for developed countries at two levels. First, there are gains from efficiency and specialization which arise from the traditional comparative advantages of trading partners. These include the benefits of the availability of greater variety of goods and possible benefits from scale economies and increased competition. Second, the benefits of efficiency and specialization themselves create more wealth for investment leading to greater growth rates. This endogenous growth may arise from the possibility of spreading product research and development costs over a larger market, thus reducing unit costs and encouraging more innovation and technical progress.

Challenge of open markets

Two major factors are at play in the international marketing environment. First, markets are fragmenting due to the combination of participation by a greater number of smaller countries in the international arena and the growing importance and recognition of regional markets. Regional markets are a relatively new feature of what were once large homogeneous markets such as the US and China where local tastes dominate and a national approach to marketing of products is on the wane. Second and simultaneously, the big-brand companies have been investing heavily to consolidate markets behind heavily advertised products in the EU, the Far East and in the developing world. These two forces are subject to numerous pressures, market deregulation, standardization and customization and other barriers to homogeneity of markets.

Created assets in international markets

By creating a comparative resource advantage in production and trade, governments seek to promote a competitive advantage among firms in their jurisdiction. Usually governments attempt to create an assortment of resources. For example, country-specific endowments in areas such as electronic design skills, design and weaving skills for the fashion industry and other 'economic cluster' benefits help to create an environment in which companies are established and learn to compete effectively in certain areas and, as such, provide the essential ingredients for achieving international competitive success. Creating competitive advantage at firm level in this way raises productivity and the incomes of people which allows a higher standard of living through international marketing and trade with other countries.

Most countries and governments actively support the creation of competitive advantage for enterprises located within their borders (Bradley, 1985). Some do it explicitly: Japan, Korea, Taiwan, Singapore, Ireland and Portugal are examples. In many other countries the support is less explicit but, nevertheless, effective: the United Kingdom, Germany and the United States.

Comparative advantage and competitive advantage

A fundamental economic principle is that any country's standard of living depends almost entirely on its own domestic economic performance and not on how it performs relative to other countries. Failing to appreciate this principle leads to trade wars.

Frequently, there are politicians who state that a country should be more productive to compete internationally. The reason a country should try to be more productive is to produce more and thereby to raise the standard of living. A country that is not productive has a low standard of living. Such a country still has the option of exporting to superior rivals those products that it does not make too badly and import from them the things which it makes badly. Doing so delivers a somewhat higher standard of living than a country with a very low domestic productivity might enjoy. This is why we focus on imports – the purpose of international trade is to import products and services the country wants; exports are the prices paid for the imports demanded by the citizens of a country.

Countries, however, do not compete with each other in the same way that Toyota competes with Volkswagen. Trade between countries can be win–win, whereas companies such as Toyota and Volkswagen are almost pure rivals – the success of one tends to be at the other's expense. A country, therefore, is not the same as a large company.

The distinction made above raises the need to separate two important concepts which are often confused – comparative advantage, which deals with countries and competitive advantage, which deals with companies. Germany and Japan would experience certain comparative advantages, whereas Volkswagen and Toyota seek competitive advantages. By concentrating on improving productivity in a country and providing R&D and other assistance, the country lowers the price of imports which may indirectly feed into the competitive advantage of companies. Comparative advantage focuses on efficiency of national production, whereas competitive advantage emphasizes effectiveness of the company. While comparative advantage concentrates on lower costs and prices, competitive advantage stresses superior management polices aimed at providing consumers with products and services required (Samli and Jacobs, 1995, p. 24). The critical issue for society is that it is necessary to seek congruence between the international trade and investment policies of the governments and the strategies of firms and industries.

Country and company competitiveness

Competitiveness for the firm refers to its ability to increase earnings by expanding sales and/or profit margins in the market in which it competes so that it defends market position in a subsequent round of competition as products and processes evolve. Competitiveness in this sense is almost synonymous with the firm's long-run profit performance relative to its rivals. An analogue exists at the national level, but it is much more complicated (Cohen *et al.*, 1984). A country's competitiveness is the degree to which it can produce goods and services that meet the test of international markets while simultaneously expanding the real incomes of its people.

International competitiveness at national level is based on superior productivity performance and the economy's ability to shift to high-productivity activities, which in turn can generate high levels of real wages. Competitiveness is associated with rising living standards, wealth, expanding employment opportunities and the ability of a country to maintain its international obligations. The key consideration is the country's ability to stay ahead technologically and commercially in those product markets likely to constitute a larger share of world consumption and value added in the future and not just the ability to sell abroad to maintain a trade equilibrium.

In an analysis of the dynamics of competition in international markets three different competitive situations are encountered:

■ newly industrialized countries focus on low-cost labour, government promotion and standard mature technologies;

■ advanced industrialized countries rely on complex manufacturing processes to increase quality and reduce costs;

■ high-technology industries usually located in developed countries concentrate on R&D to achieve advances in product performance.

The newly industrializing countries, e.g. South Korea, Taiwan, Malaysia, Thailand and Mexico, have entered western markets by combining, in varied formulas, low-cost labour, government promotion and standard mature technologies. Western firms, especially EU and US firms, have responded to such competition by moving production to low-cost locations to match foreign labour costs; by concentrating on speciality products to move competition away from price; and by innovative automation to reduce the labour content in manufacturing to become low-cost producers. The second competitive situation arises in industries where product quality and costs depend on dominating complex manufacturing processes. Here success depends on factors such as the quality and speed of product design, the organization of production and services, e.g. Ford cars and Sony and Philips consumer electronic products. Competition in such industries tends to be concentrated among the advanced industrial countries of Europe, North America and Japan and increasing in some of the newer economies such as South Korea and Malaysia.

In the third situation are high-technology industries where advances in product performance based on research and development are critical, e.g. Alltech Inc's advanced fermentation in the natural feed additives business. As advanced products are copied, however, holding markets in high-technology competition depends on sophisticated manufacturing and marketing skills since the pace of imitation is faster. Competitors are closer to the same technology frontier and design processes can be accelerated. Even in the so-called haven of high technology, long-run competitiveness rests on the firm's ability to translate product advantage into enduring market position through the application of sophisticated marketing expertise.

Labour productivity and wealth

Because many countries produce most of their goods and services for domestic consumption it is not necessary that all countries be internationally competitive: an uncompetitive country, unless it is very small and open, continues regardless, however, the standard of living of its people falls. When countries trade the gain can benefit all owing to the law of comparative advantage, irrespective of their ability to compete. Eventually an uncompetitive country must lower its costs to restore competitiveness. This may occur as a result of low inflation or depreciation of the currency. For a country what matters, therefore, is productivity, not competition, since productivity is directly related to economic performance. Internationally, productivity growth rates serve as a competitive benchmark.

Productivity growth means higher living standards. The faster the rate of productivity growth, the faster the country can grow without inflation. Changes in relative productivity growth affect a country's standard of living. A country which lags in productivity will also lag in incomes and eventually become a low-wage economy, which will tend to shift the pattern of comparative advantage away from capital- and knowledge-intensive to labour-intensive businesses.

Vicious circle of poverty

Market imperfections in developing countries lead to a vicious circle of low efficiency in production and marketing, leading to underemployed people and a misallocation of resources. The vicious circle of poverty derives from:

- a weak economic structure;
- inadequate social structure, leading to;
- market imperfections.

In attempting to improve the marketing system it is necessary to consider a number of elements of the vicious circle (Figure 6.3). The result of a weak economic structure and an inadequate social structure is a series of market imperfections which means that prices vary greatly for homogeneous products and are inflexible, markets are not cleared and participants in the markets lack knowledge concerning actual transactions and lack free access to markets. In addition, there are often price and quantity restrictions and individuals control the market, thereby exerting undue power. The final outcome of such a situation is underused resources, unemployment and poverty.

Figure 6.3
Marketing imperfections – vicious circle of poverty

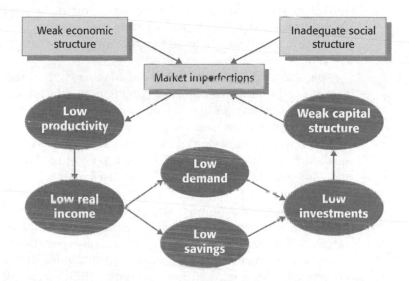

Market imperfections in turn lead to the vicious circle of low productivity leading to low real incomes, leading to low investment through low savings and low demand and finally, a weak or inadequate capital structure, which contributes further to market imperfections thereby ensuring that poverty continues. Intervention to promote development means breaking this vicious circle in a number of places to reduce market imperfections. By changing the demand constraint through the introduction of foreign buying power emanating from international markets, investment in local productive enterprise may arise, thereby improving the weak capital structure and so alleviating the poverty cycle. It is not a simple matter, however, as policy issues related to the weak economic and inadequate social structure also need to be addressed. Much international assistance is frequently used to address these problems. Furthermore, to remove the demand constraint industrialized countries are frequently requested to adopt a policy of duty- and quota-free access for exports from the least developed countries. Communities in developing countries usually require special:

- access to resources and markets;
- access to credit and business services;
- access to export markets;
- access for women in the least developed countries, especially to resources and markets, and the freedom to make independent decisions.

Relevance of marketing in developing countries

There are two opposing views on the relevance of basic marketing principles to developing countries. The first suggests that environmental factors prevent the straight transfer of marketing principles and concepts. Conditions of a strong market, increasing competition based on innovative products and services, better education and consumerism, all of which led to the acceptance of the marketing concept in the advanced world, are usually missing in developing countries. In addition, state planning frequently means that supply and demand are centrally controlled, which interferes with free market forces. Cultural factors often prevent the application of the marketing concept.

The second view accepts that the marketing concept should be modified to take account of different environmental conditions but the principles and concepts should, nevertheless, be applied in developing country markets. While the marketing sophistication found in developed country markets may not be required, the basic functions and objectives of marketing remain relevant. The process is the same but there may be qualitative and quantitative differences, e.g. fewer products moving through the system, different kinds of products and a smaller variety.

The relevance of marketing in the development of a country may be seen as part of a simple stage model of marketing development. By relating different approaches to marketing and the different levels of economic development experienced, different international marketing outcomes may be observed (Figure 6.4). In poor stagnant countries, exchange, where it occurs, is usually through barter. Marketing activities are limited in such self-sufficient economies. In the second stage of development the

Figure 6.4
Marketing and economic development

economy is beginning to emerge and develop and the emphasis is on trade, production, distribution, storage and transport, the appearance of trade specialists and other intermediaries. Barter is replaced by money. The emphasis is still very production-oriented. By this stage local producers will have begun to sell to expanded markets nearby. The third stage, referred here to the industrial market economy, arises when modern technology extends to most areas of economic activity. Trade with other countries and regional markets may occur as production and distribution are now well established and marketing shifts from an institutional focus to a more sophisticated form of consumer satisfaction, based on extended products and brands. The final stage of mass consumption arises when advanced technology spreads to all economic activity. The society has considerable discretionary income and manufacturing capacity strains the distribution system, which increases the level of competition. Trade with numerous foreign countries is now essential for continued growth and prosperity to satisfy highly developed consumer and society values.

The developed markets are increasingly dependent on emerging markets in the developing world. The continued expansion of developed economies depends on investment in and trade with the developing world. Emerging developing country markets are responsible for an increasing proportion of the exports from developed countries. The ability to increase exports to new markets is also important because these countries are selling so much to the developed world. The enhanced competitiveness of emerging markets derives from the economic reforms, low wage rates and increased productivity (Garten, 1997, p. 47). There are two additional reasons for mutual dependence between developed and developing markets. First, changing market conditions and ageing demographic profiles in developed markets have made developing markets attractive. Second, any decline in the size or growth of developing country markets would lead to more severe rivalry among developed country governments as they attempt to protect their economies.

Phenomenon of emerging markets

Developing country markets are different from those in the developed world, often because of poor access to information. In developing countries, buyers and sellers do not have the same access to information for three reasons (Khanna and Palepu, 1997, p. 42):

- the communications infrastructure is not sufficiently developed;
- there are no mechanisms to corroborate the claims made by sellers;
- consumers have no redress mechanisms if a product does not deliver on its promise.

In developed markets, and increasingly in new emerging markets, information is often part of a product's brand equity. A company with a reputation for quality products and services may use its brand name to enter new international product markets. In many instances, successful brand companies can diversify into unrelated businesses using the company brand. Samsung has used its brand name to diversify into a range of products from televisions to microwave ovens. Where information is not accessible, companies face much greater costs in building credible brands than do companies in developed markets.

Radical changes are, however, taking place in consumer tastes and preferences, consumer information seeking and purchase behaviour and the diffusion of new products and ideas. Consumers are becoming more mobile and travelling more both for pleasure and for business and as a result are becoming more exposed to new products, different lifestyles and behaviour patterns of consumers in other countries (Douglas and Craig, 1997, p. 380). These patterns have generated an increasingly complex pattern of consumer behaviour in which companies and countries can no longer be viewed as a set of distinctive value systems. Rather, a complex collage of culture is emerging in which no clear demarcation line identifies where one culture begins and another ends.

Industrial and commercial policy

It is increasingly being recognized by governments that, for a wide range of manufacturers, competitive advantage may be relatively malleable instead of rigidly predetermined by national endowments of resources. Governments use a range of public policy initiatives to promote growth and productivity to support the internationalization of firms in their jurisdictions (Figure 6.5). Public policy operating through the establishment of standards and industry deregulation, a benign economics and finance regime, heavy investment in education and industrial sponsorship of large technological projects assists firms in becoming more competitive. Government policies can alter the process of physical and human capital accumulation over time to improve the country's strategic position in international competition. According to Enright (1995, p. 2):

> The key to developing competitive advantage in modern economic competition . . . is to have an environment that creates processes, market incentives and capabilities to innovate and to improve. . . . All three are often necessary. Processes and incentives result in competitive failures. Incentives and capabilities without processes result in inefficiencies. Processes and capabilities without incentives result in emigration.

Figure 6.5
Creating competitive advantage in integrated markets

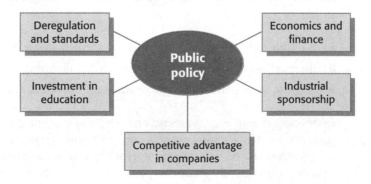

Invisible hand or direct intervention

Countries which are resource-oriented tend to see markets and competition guided by the invisible hand as the most effective way to develop those resources. Governments in such countries are expected to play the role of benign regulators and observers, entering the fray only when state security or the national currency is threatened. The threat of a bio-terrorism attack on France justified French government intervention in the possible indirect attempt by the Swiss company, Novartis, to take over the French company, Aventis, though some people suspect that while security may be an issue other more patently political reasons were behind the intervention (Exhibit 6.2). Commenting on the proposal a French government minister, according to the *Financial Times* (Tuesday 29 April 2004, p. 20) said, 'Legally we might be neutral, but there are political concerns relating to health and national security that require public authorities to be able to act. Vaccines are extremely important to the national interest. Aventis has been built along Franco-German lines and a merger with Sanofi-Synthélabo (a smaller French rival) is an extension of that logic.' Meanwhile in the same source Henri de Castries, chief executive of Axa, France's largest insurer said, 'You cannot promote foreign investment in general, because it is good for employment and growth in France, and at the same time refuse it in certain cases.'

In contrast, countries that are market-led acknowledge a role for the visible hand of government in supplementing market forces. Such countries provide incentives to promote savings and investment in certain kinds of industries. They discourage consumption through heavy sales taxes, promote the mobility of resources and alter the risk–reward relationships. Many such countries actively promote the establishment of new industries and the attraction of foreign-owned industry through well-funded inward investment agencies.

Exhibit 6.2   Sanofi Aventis

It seems laissez faire is not so free and easy after all. Jean-Pierre Raffarin, French prime minister, announced on television that the threat of a bio-terrorism attack justifies keeping Aventis, famous for mumps and measles vaccines, a purely French concern. As pharmaceutical companies go, Aventis is small, one quarter the market capitalization of Pfizer, the world leader with €210 billion. It may be the biggest French company in the industry and the jewel in the French government's strategic national development plan. However, it was also a target for Sanofi, ranked 15th worldwide, in a €46 billion hostile takeover bid, applauded by the same government. The twist lies in the fact that Novartis, a Swiss based drugs company, had launched its own counter attack bid for Aventis, which would also have left Sanofi vulnerable to takeover, and ultimately reallocate ownership of these knowledge based businesses which represent 8 per cent of GDP to a foreign company. Paris based Sanofi won the three-month campaign for its Franco-German rival, however, by raising the premium – 'He who pays the premium controls the company' says Jean-Francois Dehecq, chief executive of Sanofi-Synthélabo. Novartis had a different view – 'I think it is, in the short term, a big win for [French finance minister Nicholas] Sarkozy but in the longer term it is a setback for the country in

▶

terms of foreign investment.' Mr Raffarin countered that, 'This does not mean France will be nationalistic, individualistic and egotistical, but that it will open to projects with our European and other partners.' In approving the planned acquisition of Aventis on 26 April 2004, the European Commission commented that the French government's statements opposing a Novartis bid were not sufficient grounds for legal action against France. The French government's interests, however, in intervening in sectors of its laissez-faire economy, which it regards as strategically vital, may tarnish their liberal image. The uncertainty as to intervention may adversely affect foreign investment and even ironically increase vulnerability to foreign buyers for companies sold under Mr Raffarin's privatization programme by raising the cost of capital for French private sector business. Jean-Francois Dehecq believes that the acquisition represented the last opportunity for Sanofi to expand in continental Europe – 'I had a very strong feeling that if we didn't do this deal now then one of our international competitors would have bought either Aventis or Sanofi.'

Source: based upon articles from the *Financial Times*, 27–28 March 2004, p. 7;
The Irish Times, Tuesday 27 April 2004, p. 19

Public policy is increasingly designed to produce various forms of actions directed towards specific companies or industrial groups. Such micro level policies are now common in Europe, particularly in the newly emerging economies that joined the EU in 2004. Policies aimed at attracting foreign firms or developing small indigenous businesses are a clear illustration of this type of industrial policy. There are many instances of direct intervention by governments in the operational and strategic affairs of specific firms.

Many countries in the early stages of development start out with few policies directed toward development or investment on the one hand or income distribution and consumption on the other (Figure 6.6). Most countries start with low levels of investment and development and low levels of distribution and consumption. Strong intervention by governments can lead to a rapidly growing productive and innovative industrial base, provided distribution and consumption is strictly controlled. Here the economy achieves rapid growth. Thereafter, two sets of pressures appear – pressure to continue with balanced investment-consumption policies (the route followed by Japan in the period 1960–1990). Balanced investment and consumption policies lead to a situation of dynamic high investment and high consumption. Alternatively there may be political and societal pressures for consumption-dominated policies (the route currently favoured by Japan). Consumption dominated policies lead to stagnant high consumption and low investment economies. Inevitably, a trade-off arises between situations reflecting dynamic investment and high consumption on the one hand and stagnant high consumption and low investment policies on the other.

Dynamic comparative advantage

Some of the successful Asian countries such as Taiwan, South Korea, Singapore and Hong Kong and 'western' countries such as Finland, Ireland and New Zealand have

Figure 6.6
Alternative
routes to country
development

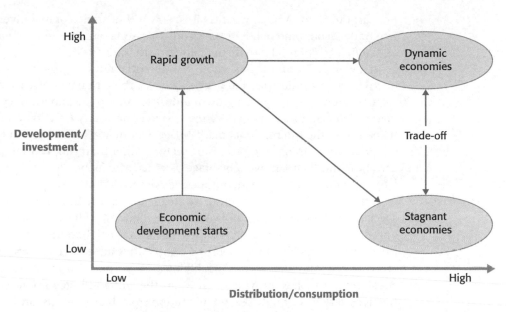

operated on the principle of dynamic comparative advantage. Instead of focusing on static factor endowments and rising short-run costs these economies have focused on factor mobility and the possibility of declining long-run costs based on the learning curve and scale economies. This is a dynamic view of comparative advantage that focuses on the opportunities for change through time. Indeed, the whole thrust of the concept of dynamic comparative advantage is: 'that the competitive challenge comes from well-managed companies based in countries characterized by developmentally oriented national strategies. How one views this challenge frequently tends to be influenced by whether one is positioned with the challengers or the challenged' (Scott, 1985, p. 138).

International competition is now influenced by national strategies as well as by the strategies of firms. A developmental strategy based on mobilizing the resources of a country to create comparative advantage in growth industries and industries in which technological change is rapid has been shown to yield higher growth over the medium term than simply accepting advantages as 'given'.

To place the issue of dynamic comparative advantage in context let us assume that we are dealing with a small open country such as New Zealand or Denmark or called Country X for illustration. The short-run advantage for Country X might arise from specializing in producing commodity foods; the long-run advantage might arise from making a success of biotechnology, a high-technology, high-growth rapidly changing industry. If Country X follows the theory of comparative advantage it sacrifices long-term growth for short-term gains and implicitly accepts a lower standard of living than its neighbours. Concluding otherwise implies that for some reason Country X is unable to compete in biotechnology, a proposition much like the once popular notion that it was not possible to sell coals to Newcastle, the centre of the UK coal industry, nor sand to Saudi Arabia, whereas it is. A world of static comparative advantage and free trade favours the rich and the strong. It also favours those with natural resources and high levels of productivity in major growth industries.

In a world of technological change, differential rates of growth in volume and productivity across industries and declining costs, the rational choice for a small country such as Country X is to select growth industries and to use public policy to supplement market forces in order to organize the resources necessary for entry and successful participation in the international marketplace. Country X must think in terms of acquiring or creating strength in promising sectors rather than simply attempting to exploit the short-run comparative advantage as efficiently as possible. The relevance of the labour productivity argument outlined above should now be apparent.

Following this line of reasoning we are led to the conclusion that Country X should specialize in biotechnology, not commodity foods, regardless of whether their costs are lower or higher than those prevailing in its rich neighbouring countries. Following the dictates of the dynamic theory of comparative advantage Country X, or any other growing economy, has a considerable measure of freedom to create the comparative advantages it wishes, provided that it has the will and ingenuity to create or borrow the necessary mix of policies and institutions to achieve the cost and quality positions required for success. The freedom is constrained by the need to meet international competitive standards.

The criterion used by the Japanese in selecting which industries to promote is often described as higher value added. However, as Scott (1985) suggests, their selection criteria appear to have been more subtle and less mechanical and above all appear to require sophisticated judgements about the future. In this respect the Ministry of

Figure 6.7
Dynamic
evolution of
international
competition

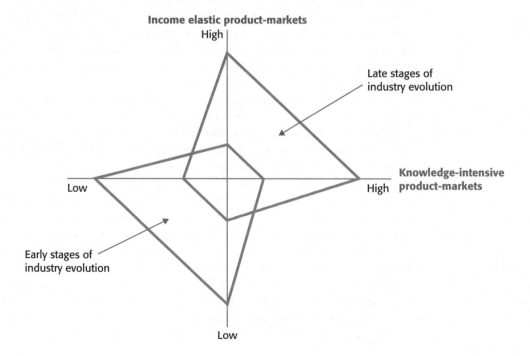

International Trade and Industry (MITI) has relied on two basic criteria: an income elasticity criterion and a comparative technical progress criterion. The income elasticity criterion suggests that industries with comparatively high demand elasticities with respect to world real income should be developed as export industries. The comparative technical progress criterion attempts to ensure that technical progress in the future of the selected industry is guaranteed, even though this may mean relatively high investment costs (Shinohara, 1982, pp. 24–5).

Many 'direct intervention' countries have followed similar approaches to exploiting dynamic comparative advantage, focusing development policies on income elastic and knowledge-intensive products. In these countries the envelope of international competition has shifted from being predominantly dependent on low income elastic and low knowledge-intensive product markets, the situation facing the Tiger Economies of Asia in the late 1960s and early 1970s, to high income elastic and knowledge-intensive product-markets, the situation faced by these economies today (Figure 6.7).

Summary

The international competitive environment has changed enormously over recent decades. Consequently, both government and firms have had to adapt their policies so as to ensure survival and growth through internationalization. National competitiveness is essential to enable the firm to stay ahead both technologically and commercially in important market segments. Three competitive situations are evident in the world today: a) newly industrialized countries which focus on low-cost labour, government promotion and standard mature technologies; b) advanced industrial countries which rely on complex manufacturing processes to increase quality and reduce costs; and c) high-technology industries which concentrate on R&D in order to achieve advances in product performance. Industrial and commercial policies are used to influence the allocation of resources in industrial sectors so as to achieve structural changes in capital, labour and product markets and to help domestic industries to respond to international challenges by addressing economic and political issues. Different government policies exist – the invisible hand versus heavy interventionist role of government. In the former approach governments play the role of benign regulators and observers; in the latter the government supplements market forces. Three outcomes are likely for the future: a) welfare states may realign their priorities and become more competitive; b) development-oriented countries may become more security oriented and less competitive; and c) welfare states might take the lead in restricting access to their markets. Evidence to date supports these outcomes, e.g. the Japanese are showing signs of being more distribution conscious, while the Europeans are beginning to become more developmental in thinking and practice. Comparative advantage is dynamic and can be created. Belief in such creation has encouraged many countries to play an active role in the development of local firms. Increases in trade has internationalized the economies of many countries. Traditional models of economic growth based on mercantilism and protected markets do not give the desired result, especially to businesses that see the benefits of open international markets. Because of the benefits involved there has been a great deal of political interest in reducing barriers to trade.

Questions

1. Industrial and commercial policies can provide the framework in which the firm in international markets operates. Public policies cannot be used to pick winners but to create comparative advantage. Discuss.

2. Judging from the success of Korea and the Tiger Economies there is much to recommend in a policy of industrial targeting. What would be your advice to policy-makers in your own country? Provide a reasoned answer.

3. For firms located in resource-rich countries public policy is likely to take the form of the invisible hand strategy, with government providing little support to supplement market forces. Discuss.

4. Now that the EU is beginning to formulate and implement industrial policies which affect the firm in international markets is there any value in individual EU countries pursuing their own individual country policies?

5. Does your town or region benefit from your country's participation in a trade agreement or economic–political union such as may be found in the EU?

6. Describe the vicious circle of poverty found in developing countries; how may open markets alleviate some of the problems associated with underdevelopment?

7. How relevant is international marketing to firms in developing countries?

References

Bradley, M. F. (1985) 'Key factors influencing international competitiveness', *Journal of Irish Business and Administrative Research*, **7** (2), 3–14.

Cohen, S., Teece, D. J., Tyson, L. and Zysman, J. (1984) 'Global competition: the new reality', *Working Paper of the President's Commission on Industrial Competitiveness*, Vol. 3.

Douglas, S. P. and Craig, C. S. (1997) 'The changing dynamic of consumer behavior: implications for cross-cultural research', *International Journal of Research in Marketing*, **14**, 379–95.

Enright, M. J. (1995) 'Creating national and regional strategies for competitive advantage', *The Island of Ireland Conference*, Irish Management Institute, Dublin, 13 December.

Garten, J. E. (1997), 'Troubles ahead in emerging markets', *Harvard Business Review*, **75** (3), 38–50.

Khanna, T. and Palepu, K. (1997) 'Why focused strategies may be wrong for emerging markets', *Harvard Business Review*, **75** (July–August), 41–51.

Samli, A. C. and Jacobs, L. (1995) 'Achieving congruence between macro and micro generic strategies: a framework to create international competitive advantage', *Journal of Macromarketing*, **19** (Fall), 23–32.

Scott, B. R. (1985) 'National strategies: key to international competition', in B. R. Scott and G. C. Lodge, Eds, *US Competitiveness in the World Economy*, Boston, MA: Harvard Business School Press, pp. 71–143.

Shinohara, M. (1982) *Industrial Growth, Trade and Dynamic Patterns in the Japanese Economy*, Tokyo: University of Tokyo Press.

7 Public policy risk and regulation

In this chapter we discuss the political environment facing the international firm. Political policies are manifested through public policy laws and regulations which affect the flows of products, services, people, technology, investment and money. The management issues which arise are examined from the points of view of the firm in the source country involved in the transfer and the recipient firm in the host country. Circumstances arise occasionally in which firms in international marketing find themselves in dispute over some aspect of marketing. In such situations arbitration is frequently used but the law is referred to quite frequently. For this reason the legal framework in which disputes may be settled is also examined.

After studying this chapter students should be able to:

1. recognize how political instability can affect international competition;
2. analyze political stability in various countries to determine the likely impact on the international marketing firm;
3. understand how regulation affects international business and how to cope with it;
4. discuss the mechanisms used to restrict international transfer of products and services

Public policy environment of international marketing

A crucial aspect of doing business in a foreign country is that the host government controls and restricts a foreign company's activities by encouraging and offering support or by discouraging and banning its activities, depending upon the interests of the host. Reflected in its policies and attitudes toward foreign business are a government's ideas of how best to promote the national interest considering its own resources and political philosophy. In analyzing the political environment international managers include a number of factors: the type of government in the host country; its philosophy; its stability over time; its attitude to international business.

The philosophy of the government toward foreign business should specifically be taken into account. Conservative governments usually promote a broad role for private business with a minimum of restrictions. Socialist governments, on the other hand, may encourage public ownership of business with an emphasis on restrictions and a more comprehensive regulatory environment.

Because of different political viewpoints, international firms are often treated in a very different way to local businesses. Within the EU, however, it is not permissible to discriminate in favour of local business. In some countries the prevailing philosophy is that imports are to be discouraged but foreign investment in manufacturing encouraged. In other countries, only joint ventures find government support. The international firm must discover the perceived role for foreign business activity in a country.

Role of government

In recent years, there has been a revitalized discussion on the appropriate role for government in business and in international business in particular. Too much government is not a good thing, yet too little government perhaps even less so. Governments cannot provide growth, but they can provide an institutional framework to support the markets that are concerned with growth. For speedy growth and development governments cannot afford to be capricious. The application of predictable rules and policies reflects how credible the state is as a source of exports or as an attraction for investors. Poor state credibility results in lower investment and growth and undermines development. There are a number of acceptable roles for government in modern societies:

■ establish a legal foundation in society;

■ maintain an effective and stable macro economic policy;

■ invest in basic social services;

■ protect vulnerable members of society;

■ protect the environment.

With increased international competition between companies and industries, there are likely to be winners and losers, especially in the short and medium term. Many sectors of society thrive and grow in a world of dynamic growth, but others suffer. The challenge for governments is to take advantage of international business growth, while ensuring that vulnerable groups are not marginalized. There are three sources of tension between economic growth and social stability (Rodrick, 1997):

■ lower trade barriers mean greater freedom to move capital and skills;

■ diffusion of technology and skills places people in different countries as competitive adversaries;

■ social insurance and other protection schemes come under threat owing to funding difficulties.

With regard to the first point, people at the upper end of the skills spectrum are more mobile. People at the lower end are least mobile, so their jobs can be outsourced to international workers, who are cheaper, more mobile or more flexible. With regard to the second point, technology transfer may have an adverse effect on the relationships between countries which have very different sets of values and norms. Competition can lead to a weakening of these values in individual countries. With regard to the last point, because capital is mobile, it is difficult to tax, so taxes fall disproportionately on income which adversely affects the less mobile and the poorer in society.

Risk and uncertainty in international markets

Stable governments are more likely to ensure continuity in government policy which allows firms to plan their affairs with some degree of certainty. Political instability arises from political risks of doing business in a foreign market, political harassment and excessive nationalism. Change is the main source of political risk, and radical change causes the most difficulty for business adjustment. Because change in a government or its political philosophy can lead to unknown consequences for business, it is more disruptive than other business constraints.

Political risk in international business exists when discontinuities occur in the business environment, when they are difficult to anticipate and when they result from political change (Robock, 1971, p. 7). To constitute a risk, these changes in the business environment must be capable of adversely affecting the profits or other goals of the firm.

Risk refers to general environmental risk, industry risk and firm-specific risks (Miller, 1992). The first refers to those variables that are constant across all industries within a given country, e.g. political risk, government policy uncertainty, economic, social or physical environmental uncertainty. Industry uncertainty refers to risks associated with differences in industry-specific variables, e.g. materials or labour supply, quality and availability. These uncertainties also include product-market uncertainties, such as changes in consumer tastes and the availability of substitutes and complements. Competitive uncertainty is also part of industry risk and refers to the firm's ability to predict accurately the amount and type of goods available in the market, which varies due to competitive rivalries among firms, entrance of new firms and technological change. Firm-specific risk arises from such things as product liability issues, credit uncertainties, behavioural uncertainty among employees and customers, and R&D uncertainty. International markets exacerbate these uncertainties because the firm operates in different cultures and because international operations are, by their nature, difficult to control and manage (Brouthers, 1995, p. 10).

Firms in international markets face all three types of risk, environmental, industry and firm-specific risks, simultaneously, so decisions in one risk area affect the magnitude of risks and decisions in other risk areas. Management must be cognisant of the overall risk management package, as studies that examine only an element of international risk, e.g. political risk or financial risk, may lead to incorrect entry mode decisions because other related risks, such as social or product-market uncertainties, have been ignored (Brouthers, 1995, p. 10). Assessing and quantifying political risk in international markets is especially difficult. In a political risk analysis the firm first

Figure 7.1
Risk reduction
process in
international
marketing

examines relevant home and host country factors in addition to international legal issues stemming from the World Trade Organization and other bodies (Figure 7.1). The components of political risk should then be apparent. The firm may reduce its political vulnerability by having recourse to strategies to establish corporate citizenship, external affairs and public relations programmes.

In regard to home country factors it is necessary to consider reciprocal agreements, legal restrictions, sanctions and current or unresolved disputes. International legal factors take into account the deliberations and functions of the World Trade Organization and also include a consideration of sanctions and restrictions. Host country factors include a determination of the political stability, legal restrictions, the development of infrastructure and, again, sanctions and disputes. Political risk analysis, discussed below, considers economic risk, local content regulations, political vulnerability in the foreign country, import-export regulations and attitudes to the participation by foreign companies in local investment projects. In attempting to reduce political vulnerability the firm attempts to be a good corporate citizen, manage its public affairs and develop a good local image through public relations and other marketing strategies.

Common political risks

The list of risks an international firm faces from the political environment is extensive – loss of ownership, political harassment and nationalism (Figure 7.2). The range

Figure 7.2
Analyzing
political risk in
the host country

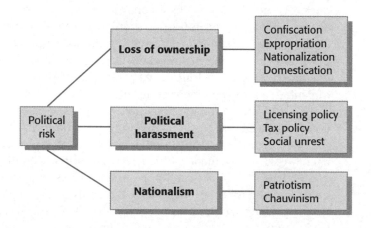

of political risks depends on the country in question, the firm and the nature of its business. At one extreme the firm may lose all control, ownership of assets and market access; at the other extreme, it may simply face customs delays or problems in obtaining working visas for headquarters staff.

A firm can lose ownership of foreign assets in one of four ways: confiscation, expropriation, nationalization, domestication. Confiscation requires nothing more than a government decision to take control of a foreign firm's assets in its country: no payment is made to compensate the firm for its loss. Expropriation differs only in that some compensation is given for the firm's assets. Both forms of risk are higher in poorer developing countries and in resource-based industries such as oil exploration and refining and in the extractive industries. With the rise of industry and trade agreements, confiscation and expropriation are on the decline.

Nationalization is the process whereby a government decides to take over ownership of an industry for its own control. Both local and foreign-owned firms may be affected. Government ownership and management of an industry may give it more control over the country's economic life and are usually tied to issues of economic sovereignty, national defence or control of strategic industries.

Domestication represents a variety of pressures that can be placed on a foreign-owned firm to transfer ownership and/or control to local citizens. At one extreme, a foreign investor may be forced to sell shares of stock to local investors at a predetermined price. Alternatively, the firm may be asked to develop a plant for sale to locals over a certain time period, but the business is allowed to determine how the transfer of ownership will occur. Other examples of domestication policies include pressure to employ nationals at top decision-making levels, permits required for importing equipment, parts, personnel or technology.

Political harassment can take many forms and can affect all areas of business operations, from labour relations to customer relations, product design or pricing. The foreign firm may be singled out for harassment, or an entire industry may be the target of new, restrictive regulations. A government's power to license may be used to harass. A licence may be required to establish a business, acquire foreign exchange, purchase imports, change prices, hire or fire personnel or sell to government agencies. Changes in tax policy can also be used to capture more revenue and penalize businesses.

Another form of harassment for the foreign firm is social unrest. Political terrorists in many parts of the world, especially in Latin America and the Middle East, have increasingly used kidnappings of business executives to publicize their demands and to fund their causes. Damage to property from riots and insurrections can also be significant.

Nationalism can have similar effects to those discussed above. Citizens of every nation typically have some sense of national identity, which manifests itself in national feelings, pride and attitudes towards foreign firms and products: patriotism. The excessive form of this is chauvinism. Today, nationalism is considered a divisive force, hindering regional and international cooperation.

Firms attempt to reduce political risks by identifying points of political vulnerability which they attempt to manage. They also attempt to establish positive relationships between themselves and the political institutions in the host country.

Analysis of political environment

Favourable political attention can mean protection, reduced tax rates, exemption from quotas, control of competition and other concessions. Some products, however, appear to be more politically vulnerable than others. Political vulnerability can lead to labour agitation, public regulations, price-fixing, quotas and other forms of government harassment if, for any reason, the product is considered to be undesirable. A concentration on commodity exports can raise political risk and even contribute to the risk of civil war in a country (Exhibit 7.1).

A change in attitudes toward politically vulnerable products does not always come from obvious instability in the political system. Even an orderly change of government, or a change in existing government attitudes, can lead to a drastic change in public policy toward certain products.

The safest long-term strategy for minimizing political risk is to acknowledge the importance of positive interaction with host governments. Some firms implement this by reminding personnel that they are 'guests' in foreign markets and that continued permission to operate is contingent on showing the benefits brought to host countries.

International firms use a variety of techniques to ensure a supportive political environment. In spite of efforts at being a 'good citizen', however, different modes of entry or investment which render the venture less risky may be the only long-run solution to hostile political environments, e.g. joint ventures and licensing where the technology used is unique and the risk is high.

Exhibit 7.1 **Concentration on commodity exports raises political risk**

Political instability may only hurt economic growth in commodity-dependent developing countries according to a study by the World Bank. The risk of civil war is highest when a country is dependent on commodity exports. This is not because of greater inequality or ethnic differences, but because commodities provide a source of financing for opposition groups. 'The risk of civil war has been systematically related to a few economic conditions such as dependence on primary commodity exports,' the World Bank study states. 'This is because civil wars occur where rebel organizations are financially viable,' says the author, Paul Collier.

The World Bank report calculated that if a country derives 26 per cent or more of its gross domestic product from exports of a primary commodity, it has a 23 per cent risk of falling into civil war. Another country with exactly the same statistical profile, but without any primary commodity exports, would have a risk of civil war of 0.5 per cent. Without primary commodities, ordinary countries are pretty safe from internal conflict but when such exports are substantial, the society is highly dangerous, according to the report.

Because production cannot relocate (it is not mobile) and once the initial, usually heavy, investment has been made, it makes sense to continue to produce even if rebels are taking a large share of the product or revenue. 'Once a mine shaft has been sunk, it is worth exploiting it even if much of the anticipated profits are lost to rebels,' Mr Collier says. 'Once coffee beans have been planted, it is worth harvesting them even if much of the coffee has to be surrendered.'

Source: adapted from *The Wall Street Journal Europe*, Friday/Saturday 6–7 October 2000, p. 15

Regulating international transfers

The issue of international transfers covers the physical transfer of products through importing and exporting, financial flows, the transfer of people, technology and data. The question arises as to why, in view of the widely espoused benefits of free trade, countries sometimes attempt to control such international transfers. Political restraints are used to control transfers associated with four distinct phenomena:

■ products and services;

■ money;

■ people; and

■ technology.

Regulating transfers of products and services

The most common type of trade control is the tariff or duty, a government tax levied on goods shipped internationally, usually in the form of an import tariff, but there are numerous others which can be equally effective (Table 7.1). Import duties serve primarily as a means of raising the price of imported products so that domestic products gain a relative price advantage. The government may impose a tariff in order to curtail consumption. In developing countries tariffs are often a major source of revenue.

Sometimes a country holds the value of its currency so that it buys less of a foreign currency than might be the case in a free market. This is referred to as exchange rate manipulation. In such circumstances, domestically produced products have a relative cost advantage over the imported product. There is evidence that artificially maintained exchange rates have influenced world trade patterns in the past. US government officials and business commentators have frequently accused Japan of manipulating the exchange rate. In early 2004 it was believed that China was following a similar policy to ensure its products were cheaper and, therefore, more attractive on world markets.

The most common form of quantity control is the quota. A quota most frequently sets a limit on the quantitative amount of a product allowed to be imported in a given year but it may also apply to monetary values or market share. The amount frequently reflects a guarantee that domestic producers have access to a certain percentage of the domestic market. Controlling the international transfer of products and services may

Table 7.1   Mechanisms used to restrict international transfer of products and services

- Tariffs and duties on imports
- Exchange rate manipulation
- Quotas – quantity controls
- Buy local legislation, standards and licences
- Restrictions on services

be by way of quotas which set a limit on the quantitative amount of a product allowed to be imported in a given year. Import quotas are used to:

■ protect domestic producers;
■ increase bargaining power of exporters;
■ avoid excess dependence on any one source.

Export quotas may be established:

■ to ensure that domestic consumers have sufficient supplies at a low price;
■ to prevent depletion of natural resources; or
■ to attempt to raise an export price by restricting supply in foreign markets, e.g. OPEC restrictions on oil output. Quotas can create inefficiencies and the allocation of quotas is often quite arbitrary and open to abuse since they are based on an administrative rather than a market system.

'Buy local' legislation may restrict purchases by government agencies to local suppliers or ensure that a certain percentage of the product for governmental purchase must be sourced locally. Aside from direct legislation, campaigns are sometimes conducted by governments to persuade their nationals to buy locally made products and services rather than those of foreign origin. Indeed, in some countries government agencies have been established to promote such campaigns, many of which are increasingly being questioned. The EU Commission takes a keen interest in such campaigns and seeks to limit their application.

It has not been uncommon for countries to set classifications, labelling and testing standards in such a manner as to allow the sale of domestic products but to inhibit the sale of foreign-made products. These are sometimes ostensibly for the purpose of protecting the safety and health of domestic consumers; however, imports are often tested under more onerous conditions than are domestic products. Within the EU such practices are being eliminated.

Internationally traded services have not been exempt from restrictions. There are reported incidents of widespread discrimination by countries which favour their own firms. Among the complaints have been that Japanese airlines obtain cargo clearance more quickly in Tokyo than do foreign airlines, that Argentina requires car imports to be insured with Argentine firms and that Germany requires models for advertisements in German magazines to be hired through a German agency, even if the advertisement is made abroad. Similar restrictions face international advertising agencies attempting to extend their services in the Australian market.

Regulating money transfers

Countries influence international transfers of money through foreign exchange controls, capital controls, policies of tied aid, supervision of the foreign operations of domestic banks and other financial institutions and taxation.

Taxation laws are used in many ways to influence international financial transfers. Taxation levied on remittances of profits, for example, encourages re-investment and discourages remittance back to the tax jurisdiction. In both the United States and the United Kingdom, the policy has shifted from taxation on remittances towards taxation on income, whether or not remitted.

Control over funds granted for foreign aid has at times been attempted through tied aid or tied loans. The granting country sometimes requires that funds be utilized in purchasing goods or services from the granting country, hoping to avoid balance of payments problems from the outflow of funds. An increasing number of countries are beginning to tie their aid in this fashion.

Regulating people transfers

National policies controlling the entry and exit of people from a country are generally not motivated primarily by international business considerations. Broader political, economic and social considerations invariably underlie such policies, which generally distinguish between people entering a country for a temporary stay, such as tourists, and, at the other end of the spectrum, people who want to enter a country on a permanent basis. Passports and visas are the basic means of controlling this form of international movement.

Most countries, anxious to expand their tourist industry, impose few restrictions on the entry of persons on temporary visits. The most restrictive policies are applied to persons who wish to seek employment in a foreign country or to become permanent residents. For most countries the basis for admitting immigrants has increasingly favoured those professionally trained or highly skilled, with resources and able to join the workforce so that they do not create a burden on social welfare systems. Labour shortages often occur with rising incomes and rapidly growing economies. Such circumstances encourage countries to relax entry restrictions to ensure sufficient labour, especially for service industries.

Regulating technology transfers

The concept of technology encompasses technical and managerial know-how that is embodied in physical and human capital and in published documents and is transmitted across national boundaries in various ways. In recent years governments, especially those in developing countries, have encouraged inflows of technology as a major means of achieving national development goals.

In industrially advanced countries few controls exist over the international transfer of technology or even the price received for such transfers. This is so even when the international sale of technology can produce major social costs in the shape of unemployment and redundant production facilities. Even taxation authorities have little say on transfer prices as long as they are determined at arm's length. Attitudes in the developing countries differ markedly. They are predominantly buyers rather than sellers of technology. The objectives of the developing countries are ambitious. They want to ensure that imported technology is appropriate to their needs, which generally means smaller-scale and labour-intensive technology, and that it is actually transferred to local nationals.

Importance of exchange rate stability

Companies tend to be risk averse, especially with regard to international markets, which means that exchange rate instability tends to lead to lower levels of exports (Viaene and Vries, 1992). The currency stability provided by the euro has contributed to higher levels of intra-EU trade. It is expected that an extended European Monetary Union (EMU), when fully operational, will provide a still greater incentive for such trade.

The euro represents the advent of exchange rate stability in Europe that is essential in promoting a stable and efficiently managed economic framework for the region. The euro is the most visible proof yet that people of Europe are part of a wider European Union. Of the EU's 15 member states 12 joined the EMU and use the euro; Britain, Denmark and Sweden have remained outside the system by choice. The euro is now the recognized currency in these 12 members of the EU. The major benefits of the euro are:

- more transparent prices;
- lower transaction costs;
- reduced uncertainty for investors;
- greater competition;
- end of exchange rate fluctuations between EMU members; and
- price stability as EU monetary policy is maintained by an independent European Central Bank.

With prices in the EU denominated in euros instead of francs or pounds or pesetas, price comparisons are immediate and retail and wholesale competition is more pronounced. With the euro established, large consumer products companies, such as firms producing cars and pharmaceuticals, have cut costs and formed strategic alliances to defend their position in a regime of greater competition and lower margins.

Consumers stand to gain from this competition provided that industries do not concentrate in particular locations within the EU. Countries on the periphery, especially, fear that the single currency may have such an effect since it encourages specialization, which may result in concentration of certain industries near the centre of the enlarged single market.

World Trade Organization

The stated goal of the World Trade Organization (WTO) is to improve the welfare of the peoples of the member countries. Established in 1995, it succeeds the General Agreement on Tariffs and Trade, which came into being after World War II. To achieve this goal, the WTO performs several functions:

1. Administration of WTO trade agreements;
2. Settling trade disputes;

3. Acting as a forum for trade disputes;
4. Review of national trade policies;
5. Assistance to developing countries in trade policy issues, through technical assistance and training programmes;
6. Cooperating with other international organizations.

With 146 members who account for 97 per cent of world trade, decisions are made by consensus. The WTO came into being as the result of a series of negotiations from 1986–1994 concerned with the reduction of tariffs, the Uruguay round. With a staff of nearly 600 the WTO's main duties are those of legal assistance in dispute settlement and technical support to countries and to act as the WTO's spokesperson to the media. It is not involved in decision-making.

The primary decision-making body is the Ministerial Conference which meets at least once every two years. The most recent meeting took place at Cancun, Mexico, in September 2003. Next comes the General Council, which meets in Geneva several times a year. It also acts as the Trade Policy Review Body and the Dispute Settlement Body. Reporting to the General Council are the Goods Council, Services Council and Intellectual Property Council (TRIPS). The final level of administration are the numerous working groups and committees focusing on individual agreements in areas like the environment, membership applications, regional trade agreements, and development.

Through agreements in trade, WTO members operate a non-discriminatory system that makes explicit their rights and obligations. Each country guarantees that imports into its market will be treated fairly and consequently exports receive the same guarantee, while there is some leeway in participation for developing countries. Differential taxation systems sometimes make it difficult to agree a transparently equitable treatment of trade and production in different countries, often with the effect of industry associations seeking protection from the WTO (Exhibit 7.2). If at any time there is a dispute, resolution may be sought through the Dispute Settlement Understanding. This follows a step-by-step process, which may culminate in a ruling by a panel of experts that is open to appeal on legal grounds. In the eight years of existence to 2003 the WTO has considered about 300 disputes compared with 300 dealt with by GATT in its 47-year existence to 1994.

In the special case of developing countries the Ministerial Conference in Doha, 2001, referred to as the Doha Development Round, laid out tasks including negotiations concerning developing countries. In all, over three-quarters of WTO members are developing or lesser-developed countries. All WTO agreements maintain a special provision for these countries like longer time periods for the implementation process, while a WTO committee on trade and development supported by a sub-committee specializing in least-developed countries' needs offers technical assistance. In this respect the WTO organizes technical cooperation missions to developing countries, trade policy courses at the Secretariat for government officials, training for coping with the transition to market economies, and regular seminars in all regions of the world with special emphasis on Africa.

Exhibit 7.2   America's semiconductor lobby picks a fight with China

China's sales taxation policy on semiconductor chips could be the subject matter of its first appearance before the WTO since joining in 2001. The plaintiff, the American Semiconductor Industry Association (SIA), says that by taxing imports heavily, China ultimately gains from the resulting favourable decisions regarding the location of semiconductor chip fabrication plants, or 'fabs', which threatens American exports. With approximately €15 billion sales per annum, China is the third largest consumer of chips and the fastest growing market in the world.

More capital than labour is used in chip production, which means that since American overheads are only about 10 per cent higher than those in China, there is little native advantage to be gained by Chinese producers. Imports are subject to VAT rates of 17 per cent, and while tax rebates for chips made in China lower the rate to 6 per cent, chips designed and made in China are charged at 3 per cent. Since the inception of the tax rebate policy, eight Taiwanese firms have built 'fabs' there and there are plans to build 11 more.

Source: adapted from *The Economist*, 10 January 2004, p. 49.
The Economist © The Economist Newspaper Limited, London (10 January 2004)

International legal framework

In the international economy there is nothing equivalent to national legislation ensuring an equitable taxation system, environmental management and labour rights, and protection against large monopolies. Efforts have been made to regulate the global economy, but with little effect.

The legal environment for international business consists principally of the laws and courts of the individual nation states. Increasingly, international firms, especially high-technology firms, are going to court or using political influence to resolve claimed infringement of patents and other similar intellectual property. Since no single international commercial legal system exists, the international firm is confronted with as many legal environments as there are countries. The national systems differ significantly in philosophy and practice, and each nation state maintains its own set of courts in complete independence of every other nation. The closest approximation to an international legal framework is a patchwork system of treaties, codes and agreements among certain nations that apply to selected areas of international business activity.

What is normally called international law is more accurately described as international public law or the law of nations. It consists of a body of rules and principles that nation-states consider legally binding. It can be enforced through the International Court of Justice, international arbitration or the internal courts of the nation states. It is mainly concerned with the relationship between states, the delimitation of their jurisdictions and control of war. In recent years, international law has also emphasized the protection of individual human rights, even against the individual's own state.

Apart from EU institutions, the only international court is the International Court of Justice at The Hague. It is the principal legal organ of the UN, and all members of the UN are parties to the statute establishing the court. The function of the court is to pass judgement on disputes between states. Private individuals or corporations do not have direct access to the International Court.

From the standpoint of international business, an approximation to international law is the growing number of treaties and conventions covering commercial and economic matters. The more important international agreements are referred to as treaties. Those of lesser importance are called conventions, agreements, protocols or acts. All these forms are agreements between two or more nation states which normally become legally enforceable through the municipal courts of the participating countries and an international court is not essential. Very frequently such agreements, enshrined in the laws of one of the countries, are bilateral and result from political pressure.

EU laws and directives

Business is subject to the requirements of the law whether in the domestic market or in the foreign market. For most businesses it is a relatively easy matter to comply with the law because of familiarity and a homogeneous culture. In dealing in foreign markets, however, different local laws apply. In the EU a process of ensuring commonality in the application of laws is already at an advanced stage. From a series of national laws, all different in many respects, there is now agreement that a common law should apply throughout the EU.

The most significant EU laws which affect the firm international markets are the rules governing competition. While most firms are too small in an EU context to be affected by these laws it is, nevertheless, as well to know that they exist and to understand what is implied. EU competition laws prohibit, under heavy penalties, any agreements between companies which may affect trade between member states of the EU by preventing or distorting competition. Such agreements might be those fixing prices, or offering unequal conditions between equivalent customers or limiting markets by preventing a distributor to sell in response to unsolicited enquiries from outside an allotted territory. Awarding contracts without a proper tendering procedure especially if large infrastructural development is involved usually result in very prompt intervention by the EU Commission where it is appropriate (Exhibit 7.3).

Drawing on these legal principles the French government prevented Pernod-Ricard from selling Orangina to Coca-Cola on the basis that it would reduce competition among firms selling soft drinks. 'Pernod-Ricard is the victim of a planetary conflict between Pepsi and Coca-Cola,' said Thierry Jacquillat, Pernod-Ricard's managing director at the time. 'We have lost two years in implementing the strategy we have defined' (*The Wall Street Journal Europe*, Thursday 25 November 1999, p. 1). The French government blocked Coca-Cola's original $820 million bid for Orangina on the grounds it would leave other soft drink companies – PepsiCo Inc – without a distributor in the French on-premises market. PepsiCo used Orangina's distribution network to get its drinks into French bars, cafés, hotels and restaurants, and had lobbied fiercely against the deal. For the French Competition Council, Orangina's purchase by Coca-Cola would not 'make enough of a contribution to economic progress to compensate for the risks of distortion of competition in the carbonated, non-cola, on-premise soft drinks market'. In France, Coca-Cola's soft drinks hold a 60 per cent market share; with the purchase of Orangina, that figure would have reached 70 per cent. At the same time when Pernod-Ricard decided to sell what it considered a non-strategic business, it had only two potential buyers: Coca-Cola and PepsiCo. Pernod-Ricard first offered Orangina to Pepsi, since they already shared distribution, but Pepsi declined to make an offer, so the French group turned to Coca-Cola, according to Thierry Jacquillat. It is important, therefore, that any agreements the company makes with agents or distributors are not anti-competitive, especially where there is any element of resale price control or exclusivity in sales territories.

In many EU countries there are local competition rules in addition to the EU laws. Many of these refer to the prohibition of resale price maintenance and in most cases the authorities have the power to impose maximum prices. Similarly, the protection of copyright, patents, trade marks and designs varies from country to country and it is important to ascertain before entering the market whether the enforcement of the company's rights in these matters is likely to be a problem in the target country market.

Exhibit 7.3   Commission probes how Bechtel won Romania job

Infrastructure development is big business and how that business is brokered matters. The award of a €2 billion, 450km Romanian motorway contract – without a tender – to an American company, Bechtel, is under investigation. Negotiated sole contracts may be in keeping with Romanian law, and may be faster than inviting companies to tender, but EU officials maintain this incident smacks of corruption and lacks the transparency necessary in such projects. It is this politicization of a commercial process which Brussels fears will inhibit Romania's EU accession in 2007, because the country may fail to win market economy status, a vital prerequisite to union entry. What is more, the contract clashes with existing proposals to build an EU-funded motorway connecting Romania with its western neighbours, creating doubts that the two projects will be simultaneously viable. Even if traffic demands would warrant such capacity, the Romanian transport ministry's proposed funding needs further clarification at a time when it will be doubly stretched, especially when it is similarly trying to balance its budget to finance EU accession.

Source: based upon an article by McAleer, P., 'Commission probes how Bechtel won Romania job', *Financial Times*, Thursday 5 February 2004, p. 6

Product quality standards

Quality leadership is considered essential if the firm wishes to assure itself of long-term product supremacy, at home and abroad. Many product standards have been harmonized across EU member countries. This has been done by setting minimum product safety standards which must be accepted by all member countries. In many cases these standards have become acceptable throughout the world. As these standards refer to minimum levels of attainment, competitive pressure tends to push the market standard very much higher. Herein lies the risk for smaller firms; they may become trapped between the minimum and the competitive quality standards without any of the scale effects. Many such firms are forced out of the market. This shake-out normally occurs when markets and industries begin to mature, as has happened in the personal computer and mobile telephone businesses. Many of these companies suddenly found themselves with products which were less advanced and less reliable than those of their competitors but did not have sufficient resources to overcome the disadvantage. Many withdrew from the market, leaving it to the now dominant brands such as Dell, Apple, Toshiba, Nokia, Samsung and Motorola.

Major world legal systems

Two major structures have guided the development of legal systems in most countries of the world. Common law is the basis of law in countries that have been at some time under British influence. Common law countries do not attempt to anticipate all areas in the application of a law by writing it to cover every foreseeable situation. Instead, cases in common law countries are decided on the basis of tradition, common practice and interpretation of statutes. Civil or code law countries have as their premise the writing of codes of conduct that are inclusive of all foreseeable applications of law. Codes of law are then developed for commercial, civil and criminal applications. Precedents are important in understanding common law as it is or has been interpreted. The laws themselves are the key to understanding the legal environment in civil or code law countries.

Perhaps the best example of how common and code law differ is in the recognition of industrial property rights. These include trademarks, logos, brand names, production processes, patents, even managerial know-how. In common law countries, ownership of industrial property rights comes from use. In code or civil law countries, ownership comes from registering the name or process. The implications of this difference are obvious; a company may find itself in litigation in a code law country to gain the rights to use its own names or logos, and it may not win. The EU Commission takes a keen interest in developing directives regarding such property rights which have applicability throughout the community and also affect firms outside the EU. While interest may be there, a simple cost-effective EU patent system is still at the planning stage due to technical and legal difficulties (Exhibit 7.4).

Exhibit 7.4   Plan to set up EU-wide patents regime

Applying for a patent in the EU costs double that in the US. A new proposal aims to simplify matters by reducing the existing tedious translation process. Whereas previously a patent would be translated into the language of each country in which a patent was sought, the leaner system only demands one copy that would be printed in English, French and German, and only the initial claim be translated into the 19 official EU languages; halving the translation costs. If accepted, the community patent as it is called, would help stimulate investment and innovation by supporting a single market. To some this community patent makes the system more user-friendly, with centralized litigation at a proposed EU patent court in Luxembourg. This court may adopt a more lenient stance in the case of infringers found to be acting originally in good faith with respect to their unwitting use of an existing patent. However, to others, notably Germany and Unice, the European Business Group, the community patent may undermine the existing common EU patent and so the vision of a single market.

Source: based upon an article by Murray Brown, J. and Levitt, J., 'Irish presidency to put forward plan to set up EU-wide patents regime', *Financial Times*, Thursday 11 March, 2004, p. 12

Intellectual property rights in international markets

A very large proportion of world business is now regulated by intellectual property rights. Counterfeiting, copying and 'piracy' are now very common and present obstacles to fair trade and a fair return to the owners of the intellectual property. The industries worst affected are chemicals and pharmaceuticals, books, software and music. To this list must be added the appropriation of brand names. In this regard the offending parties are usually companies in developing countries, where such practices are not illegal. To add insult to injury, the poor quality of the 'copy-product' damages the distribution and reputation of the genuine articles (Exhibit 7.5).

As a result of these trends, intellectual property rights were included within the Uruguay Round of GATT negotiations and there has been a considerable strengthening of those property rights in the following areas:

- stronger protection of trademarks, especially with regard to EU brands;
- industrial designs receive greater protection, especially for textiles and clothing;
- patent protection for pharmaceuticals and chemicals is being introduced in all countries, members of the WTO;
- the EU semiconductor design protection extended internationally;
- future appropriation and misuse of geographic 'appellations' for food and beverages to be prohibited.

Exhibit 7.5 Unilever and counterfeiting in China

A senior manager of Unilever's China operations has been accused of helping a local firm to produce fake Unilever products. The situation underlines the flagrant abuse of trade marks by local manufacturers in China, many of whom are turning to company insiders to help produce fake famous-name products, sometimes even using genuine packaging.

Manufacturers of large-volume consumer goods such as Unilever are particularly vulnerable to counterfeiters, experts say. The former Unilever employee was arrested and the counterfeiting operations were closed down. The former manager allegedly used his knowledge of the detergent market in China to help sell fake Unilever and other brand products.

Source: adapted from *The Wall Street Journal Europe*, Tuesday 20 March 2001, p. 6

Legal aspects of marketing claims

The development and introduction of new products must conform to laws that regulate units of measurement, quality or ingredient requirements, safety or pollution restrictions and industry standards. This may force the firm to modify its products in every national market in order to meet varying legal rules. Labelling and branding also face many laws regulating their use. Product liability is yet another area of concern; the differences in interpreting implied and explicit warranties and product returns are special areas of concern to the international firm.

The use of specific terms which are not bound to one culture is most important for the international firm when writing a contract for business in a foreign market. Consider the problems that might be caused by terms such as 'premium', 'first rate quality' and 'commercial grade' when a different country's cultural and legal perspectives are used to interpret such terms.

Conflicts can also arise when units of measurement such as weight and length are not sufficiently clear. Standard contracts used in domestic markets are often inadequate in international markets because they make too many assumptions about the interpretation of terminology, e.g. garment sizes as small, medium or large. Another example which caused considerable difficulty for a bread-mix exporter to the United States was liquid measure instructions based on the Imperial measure of the pint; in the UK a pint contains 20 fluid ounces of liquid, whereas in the United States it contains 16 fluid ounces. As the US pint is smaller, instructions to add a certain quantity of liquid based on the Imperial pint measure caused failure in food preparation.

Promotion is another area of marketing strategy where the impact of varying legal rules is particularly contentious. In Germany, for example, advertisements cannot claim that the firm's products are the 'best', since that is interpreted as violating a law that forbids disparaging competitors, whereas such practice has been quite common in the United States but is now on the wane. In Austria, premium offers to consumers come under the discount law which prohibits any cash reductions that give preferential treatment to different groups of customers. In France it is illegal to offer a customer a gift or premium conditional on the purchase of another product. Furthermore, a manufacturer or retailer cannot offer products that are different from the kind regularly offered. For example, a detergent manufacturer cannot offer clothing or cooking utensils. The typical premiums or prizes offered by cereal manufacturers would be completely illegal under this law. The idiosyncratic nature of these laws and regulations continues to provide concern among firms active in international markets.

Summary

In this chapter concern has rested on analyzing the political environment as it affects the firm in international markets. The importance of political stability in providing a basis for international marketing activities was examined. The recognition that the political risks of operating abroad are much greater than those of operating in the familiar domestic market: political philosophics, cultures and laws are different, which affects the way business is done; attitudes to property and contracts are therefore also very different. In some markets the political–business interface is quite strong and positive, whereas in other countries business is seen as a basis for taxation and control. For these reasons some markets are more open and dynamic than others. Governments in all countries, however, attempt to regulate cross-border flows of products, services, people, money and other assets; the regulation of technology transfers also is of increasing interest in recent years.

Regulations provide a source of anxiety to some firms, especially those seeking open markets and freer competition. To other firms regulation is seen as a source of protection and monopoly power. Countries, separately and together, attempt to coordinate regulation and controls through a legal framework. To date, the legal framework which applies to business transactions tends to vary from country to country. The code of law which applies in an individual country can complicate matters. Increasingly, transnational bodies, including the EU, are taking a greater interest in providing a coordinated legal framework within which the firm in international markets can operate. Because of cost and the time factor involved, international firms prefer arbitration as a means of settling disputes.

Questions

1. What aspects of international marketing are most affected by political instability in a country? Describe the risk reduction process that some firms follow.

2. How can you measure political risk and instability? Are they also a matter of perception?

3. Some countries have been more successful than others in developing a positive political–business interface. Discuss. Evaluate the situation in your own country.

4. Regulation of international transfers of any kind is invidious and should be banned by the recognized international authorities. Discuss.

5. The manager of the international firm can cope with regulations once they are clear and unambiguous. Do you agree?

6. Regulations which remove restrictive business practices in major world markets should be favoured. Discuss.

7. How do firms minimize international legal problems?

8. All firms are increasingly faced with EU directives, laws and regulations and WTO regulations. How will this affect the international marketing of products and services?

References

Brouthers, K. D. (1995) 'The influence of international risk on entry mode strategy in the computer software industry', *Management International Review*, **35** (1), 7–28.

Miller, K. D. (1992) 'A framework for integrated risk management in international business', *Journal of International Business Studies*, **23** (Second Quarter), 311–31.

Robock, S. H. (1971) 'Political risk: identification and assessment', *Columbia Journal of World Business* (July–August), 6–20.

Rodrick, D. (1997) 'Has globalization gone too far?', *California Management Review*, **39** (3), 29–53.

Viaene, J. M. and Vries, C. G. (1992) 'International trade and exchange rate volatility', *European Economic Review*, **36**, 1311–21.

Part II Product and brand strategies in international markets

There are five chapters in this section. Depending on circumstances the firm is likely to be initially concerned with three different situations. If it is a consumer products firm, the issues examined in Chapter 8 should be considered. If the firm produces high technology or industrial products interest will focus on the discussion in Chapter 9. Chapter 10 is devoted to examining the issues faced by services firms in international markets. In many circumstances firms deal with consumer products, high technology and industrial products and services simultaneously or on different occasions, in which case the material in all three chapters is relevant. Chapter 11 is devoted to ways of building the global brand irrespective of the underlying nature of the company. All companies attempt to promote themselves through some form of branding so it is important to understand approaches to product and corporate branding in international markets. These issues and the special difficulties faced by the firm in transferring brands to markets with different cultural backgrounds are also discussed in this chapter. At this point the firm is in a position to select the markets it intends to evaluate for possible entry. International market segmentation and the criteria for selecting international markets are discussed in Chapter 12.

8 The consumer products firm

In this chapter the development and management of consumer products in international markets are examined. The chapter is divided into two sections. In the first section the nature of consumer products in international markets is examined and in particular the role of product innovation and differentiation is discussed. Of particular interest is the need to understand how manufacturers use product platforms to compete in rapidly changing markets. The second section deals with the relevance of product platforms and product standardization in consolidating international markets. Within this section the special position of prime mover markets in launching and testing new products is examined. Lastly, product category life cycles are examined to determine appropriate changes required in the marketing mix at the different stages.

After studying this chapter students should be able to:

- specify product innovation and differentiation requirements for foreign markets and specify the approach the firm should adopt to ensure success at varying stages of the new product development process;
- determine the conditions in which it is necessary to adapt a product for possible sale in international markets;
- evaluate the role of product leadership to determine how fragile this leadership may be in an environment where competitors can leap-frog the leader's technology;
- acknowledge the role of product design in the firm's attempts to dominate the market;
- determine the appropriate role of prime mover markets in new product development among multinational companies;
- evaluate the role of product platforms in consolidating and standardizing product requirements in consumer markets;
- recognize the differential evolution of product categories in international markets and specify how the marketing mix may have to be varied accordingly.

Figure 8.1
Extending the
product life cycle
internationally

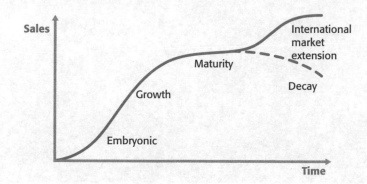

Consumer products in international markets

For centuries consumers have sought choice in the things they buy. The growth in consumer products markets is related to the general increase in living standards which fuels the demand for choice. As more products are produced better, faster and in greater quantities, and as the consumer is willing and able to pay for them, consumer demand continues to grow.

Consumer products are usually associated with developed countries. Food, clothing, toys, cars, beer and magazines may be cited as examples. Most developing countries also have a very high demand for the products mentioned, and the growth in many of these markets is faster than growth in developed country markets. Nevertheless, many consumer products are developed first in western-style developed country markets and rapidly transferred to developing country markets. Large multinational companies are usually at the centre of such activity. International consumer products are usually introduced sequentially from market to market or region to region, leading to the same products and services being available in many countries and even worldwide.

This process may be described as a market life cycle in which the firm extends the product into selected international markets (Figure 8.1). By the time the domestic market matures it becomes necessary to consider geographic expansion into new foreign markets that tend to be of close business distance. While this approach may be successful in some situations it is not always the best approach. Just as with any extension there should be synergies between the domestic and foreign markets. The firm should be able to transfer product equity benefits to the foreign market and in return receive similar benefits from those markets. In many cases the firm obtains such benefits and the international market extension strategy works well. There are many circumstances, however, where such an international product strategy results in failure.

The presumption that products can easily be transferred between markets without adaptation and, in some cases, a complete re-design, is a myth and demonstrates a complete misunderstanding of the nature of the product and its role in international marketing. A consumer product is a physical item that provides satisfaction to the buyer, including colour, form, function, ingredients, packaging, service, smell, taste, texture and warranty. Other factors, discussed in later chapters, such as branding and distribution also influence the buyer. Physical attributes are required to create the

Figure 8.2
Core product, packaging and service adaptation for international markets

product's core or primary function. The core product is supported by packaging and service (Figure 8.2).

The primary function or core product associated with toothpaste, for example, is to clean teeth. This ability requires the paste to be somehow spreadable and contained in a package sufficiently flexible to protect the product but also to dispense it when required. The physical features and core functions of toothpaste are generally in demand by people in all countries that clean their teeth using some form of paste. Few changes to the two physical attributes outlined are required when manufacturing toothpaste for different international markets. There are, however, a number of product attributes that may have to be adapted – taste, texture and ingredients. Each of these core product attributes may not be sought in precisely the same form in different markets and may require adaptation. In addition to these physical aspects, other psychological aspects usually associated with packaging must also be considered – colour, design, pack size and brand name. Lastly the support services provided with the product must also be considered, e.g. repair, installation, warranty and delivery.

While it is unlikely that such services would be required for toothpaste there may be special circumstances when support services would be advisable. A few years ago a US company launched a new dental hygiene product to be used in conjunction with a new brand of toothpaste in the Hong Kong market. The company took the innovative step of being the first to use television advertising to launch the product. Because Hong Kong dentists had been focused on extraction as a solution to dental problems rather than on preventive dentistry, the company decided to provide an educational service aimed at dentists to obtain their cooperation in promoting the new product. In general, therefore, the firm must consider the product adaptation issue at three levels – the level of the core product itself, at the level of product packaging, and at the service level.

When evaluating a product developed for one market for possible sale in another foreign market the extent of the adaptation required depends on cultural differences in product use and different product perceptions. The greater these differences the greater the extent of the adaptation required.

Product innovation and differentiation

Successful international companies constantly innovate to stay ahead of the competition and to meet the needs of increasingly demanding consumers. The strength of a consumer product depends on real differentiation and genuine innovation that meets consumer needs while providing value for money that usually means a reasonable price for a superior product. In developing and implementing an international product strategy the company must, therefore, be concerned with product innovation as it may be necessary to develop new products and most likely it will be necessary to modify existing products if they are to be successful in international markets.

Product platforms in new product development

In new product development or modifying existing products for international markets the initiation phase when the firm attempts to understand the new product development process for international markets is crucial. Firms intent on developing successful products for sale abroad should keep an open mind and follow a reasonably unstructured approach at the initiation stage since it is unlikely that what works in the domestic market will, without adaptation, successfully work elsewhere. Thus firms should be especially diligent about conducting marketing research, opportunity identification, concept generation and idea screening. In the implementation stage of new product development, however, it is usually necessary to be highly integrated across all functions in the firm and to be more focused on achieving technical targets. In a study of new product development among Korean and Japanese firms, it was discovered that close-knit teams are helpful in implementing new product development but less so at the initiation stages: 'Insisting on intensive communications and agreement before actions are taken during this open fluid phase may be costly in terms of time effort and even in the quality of ideas forwarded' (Im *et al.*, 2003, p. 105). As a general statement regarding new product development, especially when firms in different countries collaborate in the manufacturing process, cultural issues may dominate the consideration of how to cooperate. A loosely structured interfacing among functions across cultures may be appropriate during the early stages of the process. More tightly controlled procedures may be more appropriate during the stages when the new products are being designed and manufactured.

Technological leap-frogging

To be innovative means creating a stream of new products in new product categories using new technologies, perhaps taking account of different systems of the new product development process and the performance impact on that process of different cultures. Innovation is particularly important in mature markets, where product extensions are the norm and it is essential to stay ahead of low-cost competitors who may be able to leap-frog the market leader with a new technology or design, a challenge Nokia faced as 'clamshell' mobile phone handsets crowded the market (Exhibit 8.1). Samsung has became a threat to Nokia and Motorola with its trendy clamshell handset and sophisticated camera phones, with twisting flip-up screens that allow the user to take, send and show photos, aimed at the top end of the market. In this market Samsung has a number of advantages not immediately apparent. Besides being the third largest mobile phone producer in the world after Nokia and Motorola, Samsung is the second largest chipmaker after Intel and the second largest LCD manufacturer after LG Philips. It has positioned itself in the fastest growing and highest value segments of its markets. Samsung's ability to blend design and technology, where design expresses the performance of the phone to ensure product relevance to consumers, has challenged Nokia just as Nokia originally displaced Motorola and others by producing mobile handsets as attractive and desirable consumer goods. Another advantage, not available to Nokia in Europe, is the willingness of young Korean consumers to pay premium prices for new electronic devices and the much easier access to high-speed broadband telecommunications services. Furthermore, Samsung uses its own relatively large domestic market to develop the required critical mass to launch successful global products. This demographic advantage possessed by Korea is not available in European countries.

Analysts are divided as to whether Nokia can stage a comeback as it faces renewed competition from Asian manufacturers that are launching models with more sophisticated features. With its large financial muscle Nokia could possibly win back market share in the short term by cutting prices and increasing marketing expenditure, although this will hit its margins. At the same time its rivals, Samsung, Siemens and Sony Ericsson in the EU and Motorola in the US, are unlikely to give up their newly won ground. Nokia is feeling the brunt of intense competition; it acknowledges that while design skills are transferable, other more fundamental factors such as continuous innovation and demographic trends are not.

Exhibit 8.1 Nokia's dominance questioned　　　　　　　　　　　　　　　　　**FT**

The allure of 'clamshell' handsets is clear from the customers flicking them open and closed in retail outlets. 'For the past two years Nokia has had the best designed phones, but you simply can't say that any more,' says Andreas Dolonossos, manager of the Phone House in Stockholm. 'People are much more open to try new stuff – they are not as loyal to Nokia as they have been,' he adds. Nokia, with only one clamshell model available and in short supply, was forced to admit that this gap in its product range had hit results. The question is whether the sales decline is a temporary blip caused by misjudging the trend, or whether its overwhelming dominance of the market may at last be under serious challenge.

Nokia has remained with the candy-bar design format because it is reluctant to introduce a new platform when its economies of scale on the single format are so large. There is also a branding issue. 'Clamshells are a problem for Nokia's branding strategy. If you lay 10 clamshells on a table together it's difficult to tell one from another. With the candy-bar design you can spot a Nokia immediately,' says Niclas Isaksson, an analyst with Enskilda in Stockholm. 'Customers are quite promiscuous about brands. If there are other models with superior specifications, customers will go to them,' says Charles Dunstone, chief executive of Carphone Warehouse, Europe's largest mobile phone retailer.

Source: adapted from Budden, R. and George, N., 'Nokia's dominance in question after wrong call on handsets', *Financial Times*, Thursday 8 April 2004, p. 25

For some consumer products companies being innovative and creative in new product development is not an easy task as Procter & Gamble discovers on a regular basis. P&G does not have the luxury of universally sought-after brands. It has to battle for every extra sale by inventing 'new improved' products – striving to make household goods that genuinely do the job better than those of its rivals, then charging a premium price for them. Unlike Coca-Cola, for example, which has hardly changed Coke's formula in more than a century, P&G has changed its Tide detergent 30 times in the past 50 years. 'We live or die by product innovation and technology,' John Pepper, P&G chief executive, says, 'we know that if we don't have it, we can't grow the business in North America. Nor can we succeed in China or Russia the way we need to' (*Financial Times*, Thursday 21 May 1998, p. 24). For this reason it is possible to witness generations in soap and detergent product versions that have evolved over time and have crossed international borders at different rates depending on consumer readiness in different countries to use them, for example, conventional soap powder; simple synthetic detergents; synthetic detergents with bleaching and blueing additives; low sudsing detergents for use in washing machines; hot and cold water synthetic detergents required in different countries; bio-degradable detergents and bio-active synthetic detergents. Even within a large market such as China Procter & Gamble take great care to adapt their products to fit local market requirements (Exhibit 8.2).

Exhibit 8.2   P&G takes China personally

According to Austin Lally of Procter & Gamble, 'the strategy that is guaranteed to fail in China is the one size fits all approach.' For their part, recognizing and delivering on this is why China has jumped from being P&G's tenth biggest market to its sixth in only three years. Adapting to the diverse nature of the Chinese market, and hence customer preferences, is crucial to long-term success. For example, with varying geographies, water hardness, water quality and types of soiling, a standard Tide detergent could not cope with all these washing conditions. Faced with considerable local brand competition mainly based on price, Lally welcomes the stimulus despite the nationalist pride that may develop with the run-up to the 2008 Olympics. TV advertising has been the means for P&G to build their brands, communicating those brand values to consumers: 'the truly great brands go beyond the respect that comes with functional performance and move to love and emotional connection.'

Source: adapted from *The Wall Street Journal Europe*, Tuesday 20 January 2004, p. A8

Competing on innovation and design

Other companies are very adept at using innovation and design to enter and compete in foreign markets. The watch industry is famous for its innovation and design and Tissot is a significant contributing firm. Ronald Carrera, a distinguished watch industry commentator, in 1994 wrote: 'In over a century, which has seen the entire history of low-cost watches, there have been just three truly significant inventions: the Roskopf watch, the Astrolon by Tissot, 90 years later, and the Swatch.' The inclusion of Tissot might come as a surprise to some watch industry participants but throughout its

Table 8.1   Evolution of the watch at Tissot

1917	Curved Banana Watch
1930	First of a kind anti-magnetic wristwatch
1953	The Tissot Navigator – self-winding automatic with a universal calendar
1950s	Tissot 12 – a water-resistant product
	Tissot PR Sonor – enshrined a miniscule microprocessor which changed time zones
1960s	Carrousel – with interchangeable coloured bezels
	Sideral – combined high-tech fibreglass with a trendy design
1971	Astrolon otherwise known as the Idea 2001 – with movement made in plastic which had only 52 parts (more than 90 in metal movements); a precursor to the Swatch
1985	Rock Watch – the case was made of Swiss granite
1986	The Two-Timer – combined both analogue and digital time displays
1987	The Pearl – first ever wristwatch to be entirely encased in mother-of-pearl
1988	The Wood Watch
2000	T-Touch, a product range controlled by the pressure of a finger on the sensitive dial offering the time and date; altimeter, chronograph, alarm, barometer, thermometer, and compass, both magnetic and geographic north
2004	T-Win – choice of two dials with a twist of the wrist
	Silen T – the first watch with which the wearer can 'feel' the time and sense the vibrations of the alarm

Source: 'A history of innovation', *Financial Times*, Saturday 17 April 2004

history the Le Locle company in the Jura mountains of Switzerland has been consistently innovative in its approach to the global needs of the wristwatch market as the evolution of its wristwatch products demonstrates (Table 8.1).

Product design in any industry is an attractive way of taking standard products sold almost as commodities and turning them into popular consumer products as IKEA discovered when it started out with a modification to the design of the simple kitchen chair. As already well known, very often the appearance of IKEA furniture hints at a design classic, such as Alvar Aalto's bent plywood arm chair. 'There are no more than ten completely new, independent products in the world every year,' says Ingvar Kamprad, IKEA's founder, by way of justification. 'We found ideas on the market and translated them; we did not copy them but rationalized them, we simplified and added.' Those traces of famous designs go a long way to explaining how IKEA products can become desirable without being unattainable.

Consumer products as competitive platforms

International competition in consumer products markets has moved companies beyond the business of supplying products alone. Increasingly, successful companies treat products and services as platforms on which to add information, and additional technology and services. A product platform refers to the development of a set of sub-systems and interfaces that form a common product structure. From this common structure a stream of product derivatives can be efficiently developed and produced (Meyer and Selinger, 1998). In this world products and services have changed from being a goal in themselves to being a means to establish close, long-term, interactive customer relationships, almost on a customized basis.

The car industry illustrates the point. Cars are being transformed from being a wheels and boxes industry to a consumer industry and from a transaction industry into a relationship business. The traditional approach in the automotive industry had been to design a good product, manufacture it defect-free, send it to a dealer, expect the customer to buy it and to enjoy it for a period of three years or more. This is an old fashioned idea; most firms in the motor industry now want to participate not only in the transaction but in a long-term relationship with the customer.

Product platforms in the car industry are typically designed with the idea of compon-ent modularity as the key driver. Modularity relies on standardized component inter-faces that allow the manufacturer to mix and match the desired components. For the car manufacturer the advantage is that the design process modularity allows the devel-opment of individual components, e.g. the transmission or the suspension systems, to be isolated from one another. Modularity is a necessity with a diversity of technologies in a given market (Mohr, 2001). Advances in one aspect of the product, say software, used to control the electronic features of the car, can be accommodated without changing the entire system (Grenadier and Weiss, 1997). Designed around a common platform and system interface both designers and manufacturers gain flexibility.

There is a difficulty with this process, however, as the customer may be taken for granted in what is essentially a production-driven process. Rather than differentiating the product to heighten its uniqueness and, hence, its value to the customer, modular design directly invites manufacturers to become the providers of assembly kits, the final product of which may be little different in the eyes of the customer. In such a world it is possible to envisage new cars being made available as 'flat-packs' in shop-ping centres, rather like IKEA products, for local assembly and delivery. Recognizing the production focus of this approach to product development, many car manufac-turers have concomitantly exploited new information technologies in an effort, in effect, to customize cars for discerning customers by allowing them to influence the design of the final assembled product.

Impact of information technology

Through the Internet and websites car firms now obtain 'unfiltered relationships' with customers which are integrated into the product design and creation process. This is a new approach to dealing with customers in various international markets. Under the older regime mass production techniques resulted in the rise of mass marketing tech-niques as firms communicated with millions of customers using a single message. With the arrival of the Internet the way firms deal with customers has been transformed by giving them the ability to instantaneously interact with millions of customers on an individual basis. This is customer relationship management supported by modern technology with a strong international dimension. Successful firms place the customer at the centre of their thinking and integrate their product and service provision, communication and delivery processes around a single view of the customer.

Modern information technologies are not the sole preserve of sophisticated high-technology products and consumer durables such as cars. Even in fast-moving consumer goods businesses many companies exploit the new information technologies to identify customers and determine their motivation. Recognizing that women in seeking products and services on the Internet use it in the same way as they structure their daily lives, around efficiency in shopping, Unilever concentrates on using portals rather than exclusive websites in trying to reach them. 'Companies have to go out and engage consumers in environments to which they naturally gravitate, such as women's and children's portals,' according to Arjan Korstjens, consultant to Unilever, 'contrary to men who visit car, sport, computer and sex sites, women look for quick answers to their questions and chat. They don't go looking for products in ten supermarkets, they go to one and then they have the rest of the day free. They approach the Internet in the same way' (*The Wall Street Journal Europe*, Thursday 21 September 2000, p. 8). Targeted media are being used to reach these emerging target segments: direct mail; cable TV; the Internet; advertisements displayed in areas frequented by the targeted customer segment.

Market consolidation and product standardization

Many international consumer markets are fragmented due to differences in tastes, culture and other factors which encourage differentiation and a recognition of local preferences, an issue referred to in Chapter 1. In such an environment large consumer products companies cannot achieve cost competitive advantages and so try other ways of dealing with fragmented markets. In an industry where sales are stagnating, Nestlé, with a long history of blending food with science, believes there is a possibility of combining food science and pharmaceutical discoveries to produce new food products that customers will buy (Exhibit 8.3).

Exhibit 8.3 Nestlé puts food and science on same plate

Nestlé sees a niche in nutritionally enhanced products, 'phood' that is, according to Peter Brabeck of Nestlé who goes on to explain that 'it was clear I wasn't going to be able to create value in the long term . . . I had to identify areas where new growth would come from.' 'Phood' offers this sort of opportunity in the €897 billion global packaged food industry, when brand extensions like purple Heinz Ketchup can do little to boost growth in the maturing convenience food market and where price competition from private-label substitutes is eroding growth rates for established brand leaders like those of Unilever and Kraft. Combining food and pharmaceuticals is appealing as an ageing consumer base becomes more health-conscious and premium-pricing structures for nutritionally enhanced products can be developed to earn double existing profit margins.

▶

Brabeck recognized the potential of nutrition from the outset and the ensuing competitive threats, 'if the pharmaceutical companies were starting to believe that they could add value to food, we had to be careful.' Hence, from day one, he has initiated a consolidation of Nestlé's nutritional assets, so that despite cost-cutting within the group, spending on nutrition has been protected. Nestlé now employs 3,500 R&D staff and it is estimated 20 per cent of their €470 million R&D budget is invested in nutritional research. This places them far ahead of Unilever and Kraft, for the moment. While product launch performance has been mixed so far, the failure of Nestlé's LC1 probiotic yoghurt range being the most significant flop to date, the company is trying to enhance internal functional integration especially between the science and marketing departments.

Source: adapted from *The Wall Street Journal Europe*, 18 March 2004, pp. A1–A4

Many large consumer products firms believe that trends are on their side; they believe that consumer markets worldwide are converging on standard products and services in demand by everybody, a feature of global markets noted in Chapter 1. The standardization of international marketing behaviour and practices for consumer products is predicated on a convergence in consumer tastes and values, especially among younger people. It is also due to increased and better information and communications.

There are a number of ways in which firms attempt to counteract or offset the effects of fragmented markets. Successful international firms frequently introduce standardized products covering most market needs, thereby replacing many specialized products. Volkswagen believes that providing a more standardized car and lowering costs are important factors in competing in international markets. The cost-cutting strategy involved reducing the number of car platforms along lines previously discussed – chassis, transmission and other components. Volkswagen is basing more and more of its four major brands – Audi, Seat, Skoda and VW – on the same platform. The danger is that while reducing platforms may cut costs at VW, it may cannibalize product versions. The result of this approach is a cost-cutting strategy that may save a lot of money but VW's four major brands compete with each other and with Opels, BMWs and other models. The marketing implications of the approach adopted may lead to unexpected and unwelcome outcomes in the longer term.

A Frankfurt based car dealer was not impressed with VW's strategy: 'Customers can come in and look at an Audi and turn around and see a Volkswagen with much the same technology at a lower price from a technical standpoint – it can be hard to convince people of the differences.' Soon after the strategy was announced a Skoda dealer in England advertised: 'VW engineering at Skoda prices.' Isn't a VW brand car simply a higher priced Skoda? is the question asked by prospective buyers. In response, VW argued that it had positioned the Skoda as the choice for Europeans seeking value. The company also claimed that it was attempting to position the image and price of VW and Audi closer to BMW and Mercedes. The company wishes to maximize the benefits from standardization through globalization of its four key brands. By following a cost strategy VW obtains the benefits of scale economies, reduced working capital requirements, lower marketing costs and reduced research and development costs. To avoid product line cannibalization as may arise from using common platforms, other companies attempt to make cars that are identical in ways that customers can't see but distinctive in ways that customers notice. A highly focused positioning strategy may protect VW's cost-driven strategy but ultimately customers will arbitrate.

There is, however, a double dilemma facing VW in reducing platforms. The first is that reducing the number of platforms may translate into weaker demand for up-market product versions of VW where profits were greatest. Second, EU regulators may eventually question the legality of price differences among VW's four brands especially if VW enforces recommended resale prices. The question may be: is this a price-fixing cartel? Renault, faced with similar product differentiation issues, has attempted to counteract the possible negative effects of common platforms by focusing on the brand (Exhibit 8.4).

Exhibit 8.4 Renault uses the brand to counteract possible negative effects of common platforms

After Renault took a 36.8 per cent position in Nissan Motor Company of Japan in 1999 the chairman, Louis Schweitzer, was asked in an interview: 'You had ambitious plans for sharing components like platforms and engines with Nissan. To what extent can you do that without hurting the brand images? You plan to go from 34 platforms to 10 by 2010.' Schweitzer replied: 'Brands are related to identity, culture and the nationality of the company. Almost by nature, a French company is different from a Japanese company. You have to make sure that design and styling do not collide. You can have common platforms and common components without confusing design. If you look at how car technology is developing, the technological ability to differentiate is increasing. Development costs are being reduced by computers, so it is easier to manage differences with commonality.'

Source: adapted from *The Wall Street Journal Europe*, Thursday 15 February 2001, p. 31

Market differences and the domino effect

A way of avoiding large-scale failures in foreign markets is to enter a smaller market first, one which is culturally and economically similar to the larger target market. French-, German- and Italian-speaking Switzerland could act as test markets for Germany, France and Italy, respectively, if care is taken in making the comparisons.

Competitive activity in the domestic market can force a firm to internationalize. Well-known brands such as Ford, Nissan and Sony were forced to internationalize because of competition at home. All three companies pursued very aggressive market-building strategies abroad in order to thwart and delay their principal domestic competitors, General Motors, Toyota and Matsushita, respectively. These firms built their competitive advantage abroad rather than at home and have managed to sustain their positions. Colgate-Palmolive also developed its competitive advantage abroad but varied the theme. It copied Procter & Gamble's products which were successful in the United States and pioneered them abroad. Colgate-Palmolive did not have a large R&D

facility and always relied on Procter & Gamble ideas, although it was first to internationalize them. Colgate, the first fluoride toothpaste outside the United States, still dominates many world markets. Colgate's innovation and competitive advantage was its ability to internationalize quicker and better than its rivals.

Developing competitive advantage may also mean appreciating cultural differences and the different uses for products in different markets. Guinness, considered a mild aphrodisiac in the Caribbean, an alternative drink with 'Green' associations in Germany, a typical Irish drink in Ireland, Scotland and Wales, is a British drink in England. Consumers in each market consume Guinness for different reasons and the perceived benefits and images are also considered to be different. These perceived differences are arguably due to the success of the Guinness company in positioning its brand differently in ways that matter in different markets while maintaining the overall global brand image for Guinness. Even with great promotional endeavours and attempts at unique positioning, most beers, however, continue to be commodities or near commodities. In blind tests most people cannot tell the differences among beer products. This is one of the reasons why the beer market is still largely local. Only a few beers have been sufficiently well branded to carry them to many foreign markets (Exhibit 8.5).

Exhibit 8.5   Beer the global commodity

The beer industry also remains fragmented. Budweiser, the biggest brand of all, has only 3.6 per cent of the 1.3 billion hectolitre world beer market, while Heineken's share is 1.6 per cent and the top 20 combined have barely more than a quarter. Most beers taste remarkably similar, so it is hard to charge a premium for it. 'Ninety-five per cent of beer is Pilsner,' says John Wakely, an analyst at Lehman Brothers. When Budweiser goes up against Tsingtao in China, what is the difference except price? The missing ingredient seems to have been marketing. 'There is a strong production and distribution tradition in the beer industry, less a marketing tradition,' says Heineken's CEO, Karel Vuursteen.

Source: adapted from *The Economist*, 20 January 2001, p. 65 and Heineken website.
The Economist © The Economist Newspaper Limited, London (20 January 2001)

New products and prime mover markets

The concept of product management in many international firms is often as a co-ordinating role with relatively little influence on product management in individual markets. Alternatively some international firms often appoint product managers with worldwide responsibility. These are managers who might have served in the regions before taking on a broader responsibility. The main functions of such product managers are to establish global and regional product market strategies, search for new product ideas and initiate their development to ensure maximum cross-fertilization of product information among regions and markets and to provide operating assistance in markets lacking particular marketing skills. Product managers develop worldwide or regional goals and strategies for their product lines. They develop branding, positioning, packaging, and frequently, advertising guidelines. These elements of the marketing mix would normally be adapted to local market conditions. When the positions of particular product in two adjacent countries are different and when their marketing communications spill over from one country to the other, as often happens in Europe, it may be necessary to coordinate efforts of the respective marketing organizations. When country organizations are unwilling to change, in the absence of a very centralized control, positions may be established independently which may clash. Citigroup, for example, is positioned as a mid-position bank in the US whereas in Asia it is positioned as a high-service specialized bank, two positions in conflict especially when customers are internationally mobile.

Large multinational companies often centralize the product innovation and new product development activities that, from a technical viewpoint, has advantages but from a commercial and marketing perspective has numerous pitfalls. Ideas for new products and innovations arrive at the centre from country markets to be tested in a research and development facility and developed there under the direction of head-quarters. These ideas are often tested in prime mover markets – markets that head-quarters believes show the best prospects for future growth. Headquarters promotion of new product ideas through prime mover markets such as France or Germany in Europe, Indonesia or Malaysia in Asia and Brazil in Latin America is motivated by market size; large and attractive enough to assume the financial risk of an unproven product. Success in one market would make it easier to persuade managers in other markets to adopt the new product. Because headquarters plays such a dominant role there is no guarantee that when subsidiary companies develop a new product concept that it will be chosen as the prime mover market. In such circumstances country managers become the customers for new product ideas imposed from headquarters, a situation usually disliked if not actually rejected.

In these circumstances new product ideas from subsidiaries and country markets quickly dry up when it is noticed that the benefits may accrue to the headquarters rather than to the originating company. There is a danger that innovation in country markets may take the form of product extensions under existing brand names rather than true new product development as the benefits, though likely small and short-term, accrue immediately to the local management team. One solution is to encourage the cross-fertilization of new product development ideas within the company and reduce the risks associated with developing and launching new products. Recognizing the possible damage that this lack of empowerment of managers can have, Unilever, through various means, has attempted to change the new product development culture in the organization and made it less risk averse (Exhibit 8.6).

Product category life cycles

An element completely ignored in the debate on product standardization and globalization is that markets develop at different rates and in some countries the development starts earlier than others. In such circumstances the consumer products company faces the predicament that its product category may be at different stages of the development cycle in different markets. An international product life cycle exists. This cycle and the firm's decisions regarding elements of the marketing mix are interrelated. A

Exhibit 8.6   Changing risk averse culture in product development at Unilever

'What we have been trying to do is change the culture, make it less risk averse; this involved empowering people to deliver against strategy and developing a greater sense of account-ability,' says Niall Fitzgerald, chief executive officer of Unilever. But it was his belief that Unilever should be taking more risks that lay behind Fitzgerald's biggest mistake during his 30-year career – the launch and recall of Persil Power in 1995. The new soap powder was so effective it could actually damage clothes, a fact seized upon by rival Procter & Gamble in an aggressive marketing campaign. Said Fitzgerald: 'It was not a mistake to launch it. The mis-take was not recognizing early enough that for a marketing company perception is reality.' The debacle was not without some benefits. 'It did convince people we were really serious when we said we wanted to be a risk-taking company. If I – or too many others – had been a casualty the company would have gone back into its shell,' says Fitzgerald.

Source: adapted from *The Irish Times*, Friday 2 April 2004, p. 6

product in the mature stage of the life cycle in one market can have undesired or unknown attributes in a market where the product is perceived as new and thus in the pioneering stage in the market. International marketing textbooks are replete with examples of mature products in one market being introduced in another and failing. An important dimension in evaluating the suitability of products for new foreign mar-kets is to determine, not the stage of the product's life cycle itself, but to understand the evolution of the entire product category. All marketing plans must include adapta-tions necessary to correspond to the stage reached by the product category in each new market.

Typically in the domestic market or in the first major foreign market entered, it is likely to reach maturity before even taking off in emerging markets. In this context it may be relevant to examine the evolution of the product category. If the managers of any of the myriad cream liqueur companies were to follow this advice they would examine how the development of the product category for cream liqueurs differs in different countries and how product development, market share and sales, differs in different countries. The differences from one country to the next may require a differ-ent marketing emphasis depending first on the evolution of the product category.

An application of these principles is shown in Figure 8.3. In regard to the develop-ment of the cream liqueur product category by country or area in south-east Asia, most of South America and in emerging markets in Eastern Europe, the category is not well-developed and the markets are very fragmented. In contrast Nordic countries, the Far East and Mexico are growing rapidly while markets in Australia, New Zealand and the Benelux countries are reaching maturity. Along with the United States, a number of EU countries are core cream liqueur markets. Product categories have their own life cycle and evolutionary process that should be monitored. By combining an analysis of the product category with the position of the firm's brand within the category, a subject discussed in Chapter 11, a number of strategic product and brand development alternatives may be identified.

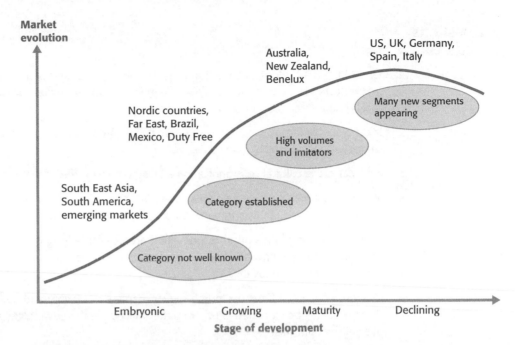

Figure 8.3 International development of the cream liqueur product category

Summary

Underlying this chapter is the view that consumer markets throughout the world are at different stages of development and require different approaches by the firm in regard to new product development and in managing products throughout the life cycles in different country markets. Particular consumer markets may be very advanced in one product area but less advanced in others that may cause a high degree of fragmentation in consumer markets. Product adaptation is usually necessary at three different levels: at the level of the core product, at the level of packaging and at the level of support services. The firm should recognize the cultural impact of its new product development processes both in regard to customers for the product but also within the firm itself. An open approach to communications and a high degree of flexibility are required at the early stages in the new product development process which has cultural consequences for firms that collaborate across countries in product development. At later stages in product development greater rigidity is required but which also requires cultural sensitivity.

New product development strategies based on the concept of platforms can cause conflict between true product innovation and the differentiation sought by consumers. Some firms attempt to overcome this difficulty by using modern information technologies to complement the dependence on product platforms as the foundation of their product strategy for international markets. Many multinational firms use prime mover markets to test and launch new products – a policy that can dampen new product development and innovation activities in smaller country markets. Because tastes and preferences are different in different markets the management of products across markets becomes a significant issue within the consumer products firm. Usually the firm must develop separate marketing mixes for its major international markets, although common elements may be found in a number of markets. In this context it is important to account for the evolution of the product category across international markets.

Questions

1. One of the major decisions the firm must take is whether and by how much to adapt its products and services for possible sale in international markets. Describe the three level changes that may have to be considered.

2. It is myopic of firms to consider the international product decision as an international market extension strategy. Do you agree?

3. How can cross-cultural communication affect the new product development process?

4. Many firms develop product policies based on the concept of product platforms. What are the advantages of this approach to new product development?

5. Novelty and continuous product innovation are key underlying concepts driving competition based on innovation and design. Describe the market conditions necessary for successful product innovation.

6. Many multinational firms use prime mover markets to identify and develop new products that may be launched in other markets. What are the advantages and disadvantages of this approach?

7. While the product life cycle model has some merit it is more important to examine the life cycle of the product category when judging which markets to enter and how to enter them. Discuss.

References

Grenadier, S. and Weiss, A. (1997) 'Investments in technological innovations: an options pricing approach', *Journal of Financial Economics*, **44**, pp. 397–416.

Im, S., Nakata, C., Park, H. and Ha, Y.-W. (2003) 'Determinants of Korean and Japanese new product performance: an interrelated and process view', *Journal of International Marketing*, **11** (4), 81–112.

Meyer, M. and Selinger, R. (1998) 'Product platforms and software development', *Sloan Management Review*, **40** (1), pp. 61–75.

Mohr, J. (2001) *Marketing of High Technology Products and Innovations*, Upper Saddle River, NJ: Prentice Hall.

9 The industrial products firm

Industrial marketing is considered to be complex because it involves an intricate network of influences. There are many people involved, each with a different background and perspective. Indeed, industrial buying in international markets may involve people drawn from different organizations in numerous countries. The technical nature of many of the products purchased adds to the complexity. Generally the size of the purchase in money terms is greater and the buying relationship can be long term. Relationships are often the focus of attention – individual transactions may be incidental. In industrial marketing myriad points of communication and contact exist.

Technology is a pervasive element, which frequently results in a production orientation rather than a marketing orientation. This production orientation is due to the greater amount of interaction and interdependence between marketing and other functional areas, especially manufacturing, R&D, inventory control and engineering. This interdependence may mean that the firm must internationalize a whole series of relationships in addition to its products and services.

After studying this chapter students should be able to:

- discuss the differences between marketing consumer products and industrial products;
- specify the key purchasing criteria in industrial product marketing in the international arena;
- outline the industrial buying process, with particular reference to the international market;
- specify the importance of international networking in industrial marketing;
- determine likely sources of competitive advantage for the industrial products firm;
- understand the new product development process for high-technology products as applicable to international markets;
- recognize the effect of international product standards on the sale of industrial products abroad.

Nature of industrial markets

Since an industrial product is purchased for business use and thus sought not for itself, but as part of a total process, buyers value service, dependability, quality, performance and cost, since the output of their own business is dependent to a large extent on the inputs used. Not all customers place the same importance on each dimension and therefore this marketing orientation which, typically, industrial firms have been accused of lacking is crucial in determining the product offering required by each customer.

The situation is further complicated when a firm operates in international markets where environmental factors differ. The level of economic development in a country is a major determinant of the demand for industrial products. The type of product needed and the level of demand are influenced by economic development (Day *et al.*, 1988). Culture has much less impact on industrial products than on consumer products. Culture, however, affects usage patterns, product features and product specifications.

Product quality includes both the physical product and the array of essential supporting services. The ultimate measure of high quality is customer satisfaction. Industrial marketing firms frequently misinterpret the concept of quality, which is not an absolute measure but one relative to use patterns and standards. Since use patterns frequently differ from one country to another, standards vary so that superior quality in one country may fall short of superior quality as determined by needs in another country. A number of factors reflect the nature of industrial markets:

- industrial products and services are classified according to their application, not the manner of their purchase as found in consumer markets;
- industrial buyers value service, dependability, quality, performance and value for money since the demand for industrial products and services is a derived demand;
- industrial buyers seek to acquire a system not just a single product or service;
- transactions between firms take place within a framework of established relationships – marketing activities in networks serve to establish, maintain, develop and strengthen relationships;
- the more technical the product the more homogeneous the marketing system; because of the large amounts of capital and technical expertise required to service the market, firms operate in close relationships;
- internationalizing the industrial firm means integrating supply relationships and networks across national boundaries.

The adequacy of a product must be considered in relation to the environment within which it is used rather than solely on the basis of technical efficiency. Equipment that requires a high degree of technical skill to operate, maintain or repair may be inadequate in a country that lacks a pool of technically skilled labour. This dilemma is particularly prominent in developing countries which demand the most up-to-date technology but lack the ability to absorb it.

Figure 9.1
Providing value
to industrial
customers in the
business system

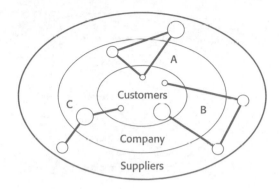

Network of international relationships

Most industrial products companies are highly 'customer-bound' when it comes to internationalization. Suppliers are usually very closely linked to their customers, even for industrial components. The internationalization strategy of an industrial products company is frequently co-determined with that of its customers. Since industrial marketing involves dedication to a small number of customers, the process of internationalization is likely to be a collaborative arrangement between customer and supplier. Internationalization of industrial products firms take place as part of the internationalization of a business system, so that one business system can more effectively compete with another in international markets.

Outsourcing is used by firms that seek other firms to provide elements of the value added chain more cheaply than can be done within the firm itself. In this way, the firm can be more competitive if it concentrates on producing those elements of the final product which give the highest value added. Many industrial firms discover that they are members of a networked supply chain in which the company deals with suppliers who may be located in one foreign country and customers located in another (Figure 9.1). The figure also shows how firms in different markets complement one another in terms of commercial and manufacturing relationships and the amount of effort contributed by each as represented by the location and size of the circles in the figure. In situation A most of the work is done by one of the firm's suppliers abroad while the company contributes less and the customer, in a different foreign country, very little. In situation B, the company provides no value, it is by-passed by the customer and the supplier. In situation C the company provides most of the value added while the supplier provides some and the customer even less. Cisco Inc., the well-known high-technology California based company, provides value to its customers by depending on a series of relationships in the business system (Figure 9.2). Firms in different markets complement one another in terms of commercial and manufacturing relationships and the amount of effort contributed by each firm.

The growing importance of knowledge-intensive suppliers based on highly specialized and technological capabilities has been a phenomenon in the growth of systems suppliers which enables the buying firm to reduce the number of suppliers. Fewer suppliers facilitate decentralization of decision-making and the reduction of coordination costs for large manufacturers in the car industry, for example.

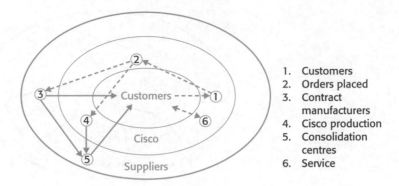

Figure 9.2
How Cisco networks provide value to international customers

1. Customers
2. Orders placed
3. Contract manufacturers
4. Cisco production
5. Consolidation centres
6. Service

Other factors bind independent industrial firms together in the business system. The development of specific technical interfaces, logistical arrangements and the special tasks related to the development of new product generations are important ways in which supplier and customer firms are linked. For many industrial products firms it is necessary to complement the product offering with product maintenance, repair service and allied support activities (Czinkota and Johnston, 1981). In business-to-business markets product quality is the most significant variable followed by delivery service (Chumpitaz, 1998).

Adapting to the specific product and service needs of customers increases the need for trust between the parties as switching costs rise. Adapting industrial products for international markets frequently runs foul of the customer's or importer's requirements (Morgan and Katsikeas, 1998). A number of reasons may be given for the higher cost of adapting to the preferences of industrial customers operating in different international markets: different business practices, different technical standards, logistical complexity of sending and receiving goods and different languages and culture. In summary, when dealing with industrial and technical products in international markets it is necessary to:

■ recognize that industrial products firms are highly 'customer'-bound – internationalization is usually a collaborative arrangement between customer and supplier;

■ treat industrial firms as part of a business system in discussing the internationalization process – value and supply chain relationships are created across markets;

■ acknowledge the growth of knowledge-intensive suppliers networked with other suppliers and customers across markets through technical interfaces, logistical arrangements and new product development programmes.

Markets as international networks

Industrial markets are highly interdependent and increasingly manifest a network of international relationships. Equipment, parts and component suppliers, for example, depend on the size and growth of the market for finished products. Demand in most industrial markets is, therefore, a derived demand, derived from further down the value-added chain or channel of distribution. Changes in demand or industry structure tend to have a knock-on effect back up the value-added chain and horizontally with other firms at the same level (Meyer, 1998). Firms in the car components supply business, for example, have discovered this network effect as the mergers between Daimler-Benz and Chrysler and between Renault and Nissan take hold.

With components accounting for up to two-thirds of the cost of a vehicle, even a few cents off a part could amount to millions of dollars over the life of a model. With Chrysler and Daimler-Benz spending an estimated $80 billion on parts, the scope for savings is immense; the first savings could come by redirecting existing purchases through fewer suppliers prepared to lower their prices for bigger volumes. In the Reanault-Nissan merger, new jointly developed vehicles are likely to be designed to share some components, increasing Reanault-Nissan's leverage over suppliers.

The context in which the firm operates also determines how firms interact competitively with others in the network. Business in any given relationship is often conditioned by relationships with third parties, such as the customer's customers, the supplier's suppliers, consultants, competitors, supplementary suppliers and middlemen, as well as public or semi-public agencies. The markets for most industrial products and services depend on the efficiency of networks of relationships. The concept of a relationship and the longevity of interfirm dealings is the key to understanding industrial products marketing in the international arena.

Organizing for industrial buying

Industrial buying process

The buying process for industrial products is often conceptualized as a sequential process involving a set of interrelated variables cascading down from the environment to the transaction (Figure 9.3). The sequence involves six steps:

- awareness of a problem;
- deciding on an appropriate solution;
- supplier search;
- accepting offers;
- placing an order; and
- evaluating the outcome.

Industrial marketing firms should be able to identify the type of decision and the decision stage and hence the key people to influence at a particular time. Before this can be done it is necessary to consider the make-up of the buying centre as well as the differences that exist between buying situations. One method of determining the make-up of a buying centre is to consider the levels of management, the functional areas, the roles that members fill and their interactions.

The buying centre includes all members of the buying firm who are actively and significantly involved in the purchase decision process. Membership is fluid depending

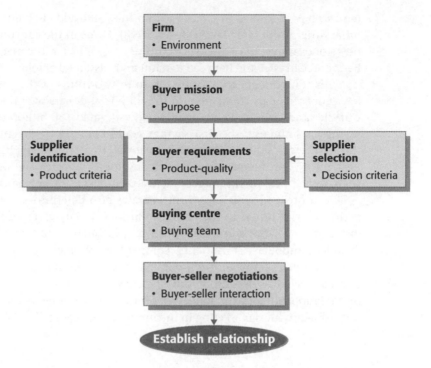

Figure 9.3
Influences on
industrial buying
behaviour

on product and buyphases. The management level is determined by the purchase-specific circumstances. The functional area composition of the buying centre varies with the product being purchased and the buyphase. Roles have been classified in various ways: users, influencers, deciders and gatekeepers (Webster and Wind, 1972). The importance of different organizational roles varies with the phase of the buying process. The make-up of a buying centre and the roles fulfilled changes depending on organizational factors, the organization size and the buying situation (Wind, 1978). In general it is necessary to understand five general aspects about the buying centre:

■ management level engaged in the process;

■ composition of functional area directly involved;

■ the roles accorded to individuals – user, influencer, buyer, decider or gate-keeper;

■ the identify of the people participating in the decision process; and

■ a professional profile of members of the purchasing department.

These functions and roles can be conceived fairly easily for the purchasing of products such as production materials. It is more difficult to specify roles for services, such as who within the firm is the user of transportation for inbound materials or outbound products, who is the gatekeeper, or who has the decider role.

Both domestic and international factors have a large impact both on the composition of the buying centre and on the manner in which the product is purchased. The business area in which the firm operates determines the importance of the purchasing function. Without an understanding of the customer's mission, other knowledge may be fruitless. Determining the mission is the first step in determining who in the buying firm will be interested in the decision-making process.

The issues that relate specifically to purchasing are how the product will be used, how the product benefits the buyer, the stage of the purchase decision, the buying process, the size of the purchase and the duration of any contractual commitments. Suppliers must know the range of potential uses of the product and priorities in the buying firm. At this stage product quality, complexity, delivery and service are important decision variables. Many industrial firms now seek suppliers from all over the world and use the Internet to establish contact and even to procure supplies of complex products.

Evidence is mounting that when companies shift their procurement online they make considerable savings. Lower prices for inputs come from different sources. They can be due to gains in efficiency among suppliers enabled by the Internet. Alternatively, they can be due to the removal of expensive intermediaries. Such intermediaries previously provided information to the buyer by connecting them to the supplier. The Internet presumably does this more cheaply than traditional intermediaries. The other source of lower prices is increased competition among suppliers as a result of the Internet. In addition, the Internet lowers the cost of processing the transaction with a supplier and allows companies to order supplies in a more timely manner and reduce the level and cost of inventories. The losers in this situation are suppliers of intermediary goods, such as car components, who face intense pressure to deliver productivity improvements or cut margins.

The level of management involvement in the buying situation should decrease as products progress from a new task purchase to a modified rebuy to a straight rebuy. Regardless of the industry or buyphase of the purchase, the decision-making process is shared for all but the smallest, most routine decisions. The firm in industrial markets must search for the individual who has the most influence at each stage, rather than for the sole decision-maker. It is important to understand the role and motivation of each member of the buying team.

The numerous stages involved in industrial buying mean that a cascading hierarchical dependency exists among the choice criteria. Numerous different sets of buying criteria are used. At the early stage because the intention is to restrict or screen suppliers, criteria based on supplier reputation, technical specifications and delivery capacity dominate. In evaluating bids the same set of criteria may be used, but now a rank order of preference among the suppliers is established. The relative importance of the criteria may change as the potential suppliers remaining meet the criteria imposed.

At the stage involving negotiations with one or two potential suppliers a third set of criteria may be used that contains only the most important attributes still having some variation across the bidders after the first two stages. At this stage in the negotiations the buyer's aim is often to get the best possible price without jeopardizing quality and delivery.

Numerous stages in the industrial buying process are more in evidence for high-value and complex buying situations where competitive offers are available. In simpler routinized buying situations the above stages will not normally be used. The stages phenomenon is complicated further by the presence of the buying centre influence on the criteria. The interaction of buying stages and buying centre members should also be assessed.

The industrial marketing firm must also determine the commitment level of buyers. This may be measured by examining the degree of complexity involved, the collaboration required, the life cycle effects and the money value of the business. Purchasing departments use money values as a management intensity criterion. In very small companies the purchasing manager has little influence in most purchases because the amount is relatively large, thus involving senior management. In medium-sized firms more authority is delegated to the purchasing manager as the relative size of each purchase gets smaller. Larger firms usually establish criteria and guidelines for individuals and departments, even for small purchases; therefore individuals have less flexibility.

Because demand in industrial markets is derived it is the life cycle of customer firms that should receive emphasis. The strategic changes by the buying firms during the life cycle of their products must be the focus of attention in an organizational buying model. Time has two effects on the organization for industrial purchasing decisions that need to be measured. First, as the time horizon increases, interactions can be made routine and delegated down the managerial hierarchy. Second, as they become routine, decisions may start to exceed the time allocated for such activities.

Assessing international competitive positions

Sources of international competitive advantage

Companies manufacturing capital goods and equipment have moved aggressively abroad in recent years in search of lower costs, more rapid growth or diversification or simply to follow their customers who have already moved abroad for similar reasons. Specifically, the motivations for going abroad include:

- profit advantage;
- product uniqueness;
- technological advantage;
- managerial orientation;
- competitive pressure.

As industrial products firms are very diverse, it is difficult to identify common competitive factors which more than a few share. Some industrial products firms succeed internationally by establishing strong local operations in key strategic markets while others continue to export.

There are three sources of competitive advantage among industrial products companies that are reasonably universal: strong management, low costs and financial strength. These competitive advantages may be elaborated into a longer list of elements which give many industrial products companies an internationally sustainable competitive advantage:

- low-cost manufacturing;
- global distribution strength;
- product quality and reliability;
- large installed customer base;
- technological leadership;
- dominance of narrow product niche;
- coherent corporate culture.

Applying the above criteria to selected industrial products companies active in international markets, it can be seen that the basis of sustainable competitive advantage ranges widely:

Company	Competitive advantage
ABB	Dominant in power generation, transmission and distribution equipment
Caterpillar	Strong distribution
Deere	Strong distribution, excellent products and strong brand loyalty
Emerson Electric	Global market and technology leadership
General Electric	Cost technology leadership
Sandvik	Dominant maker of cutting tools
United Technologies	Global presence and leadership

Segmenting industrial product markets

Segmenting industrial markets internationally can pay large dividends to the company. In a study of segmentation in the international car components industry, Dyer *et al.* (1998, p. 74) discovered that the Japanese car manufacturers Toyota and Nissan segment suppliers by dividing them into groups with whom they establish partnerships and others they keep at arm's length. This approach gives these companies a major differential advantage over competitors, whereas US and Korean firms do not segment suppliers and hence miss important marketing opportunities. Industrial markets are usually segmented on the basis of:

- industry;
- company size;
- operating characteristics;
- purchasing approaches;
- situational factors;
- personal characteristics of the people involved.

Industrial product markets are highly heterogeneous, complex and often hard to reach because of the multitude of products and uses as well as a great diversity among customers. They are usually relatively easy to identify, however. When the Swedish company, Alfa-Laval, developed its sophisticated ultra-filtration system with applications in the dairy, paint, pharmaceutical and water treatment businesses, it was a relatively easy matter to identify potential customers as they were few in number in each major market, e.g. France, Germany, New Zealand and the US. It was necessary, however, to segment these markets to ensure that Alfa-Laval reached customers for whom the new technology was appropriate and relevant. Formulating a coherent marketing strategy can be extremely difficult in such an environment; it usually requires a thorough approach to segmentation.

Failure to segment an industrial market properly can result in missed opportunities and even business failures. The benefits that accrue from standardizing elements of the marketing strategy are realized only when similarities among countries are identified. Universal needs and similarities in buying processes are far more evident in industrial markets than in consumer markets (Day *et al.*, 1988).

Before attempting to segment international markets, Day *et al.* (1988) recommend that the company should screen world markets in a preliminary manner in order to assess similarities among countries, thus making the task of segmentation more focused and less complex. Economic variables may be used to determine the level of economic development and hence the level of demand and the type of products needed. Countries can be grouped according to similarities exhibited in the analysis. Once this process has been completed a typical segmentation technique can be employed. There are certain limitations to this approach, however; there is a degree of subjectivity in selecting the type and number of variables needed to cluster countries and the difficulty in finding accurate data on international markets being the more important.

Macro variables such as type of industry, size of customer and product usage may be relevant. These segments may be subdivided on the basis of micro variables such as the characteristics of the decision-making unit. A number of points are relevant when attempting to segment industrial markets:

■ simple schemes can help discover different behavioural segments in industrial markets in different countries;

■ many large industrial buyers segment suppliers into groups depending on the degree of commitment to them;

■ universal needs and similarities are often present in industrial markets so there are elements of the marketing programme that can be standardized. Clustering methods may be used to place similar markets into suitable groups;

■ there is a need to monitor segments dynamically due to changing technologies and market boundaries.

Monitoring international market segments

Segmenting industrial markets is a continuous function as technology, customer needs, demand and other variables change unpredictably. Consequently it is necessary to monitor changes in markets and segments. According to Hlavacek and Reddy (1986) a four-step method which captures all the variables that help to monitor particular segments involves:

- identifiying segments;
- qualifying customers in these segments;
- assessing the attractiveness of the market segment; and
- monitoring each segment in regard to competitive activity and technological change.

The identification phase involves classifying the particular product and segmenting the market for it on the basis of location and typical end uses employing industry classification codes such as the SITC or BTN as discussed in (Figure 9.4). Once a segment is selected there is continuous monitoring of both competitive changes occurring in the domestic and international markets and technological changes arising among customers and other suppliers which could dramatically change the boundaries and attractiveness of segments. An example of the need for monitoring may be found in the X-ray film market. DuPont concentrated on and achieved a large market share in the X-ray film market, but developments in magnetic resonance imaging (MRI) technology has replaced part of the need for X-rays. Within each segment it is necessary, therefore, to qualify customers in regard to their needs, capabilities and readiness to accept the company's products and services. This is an important phase as establishing a fit between the supplier and buyer is an essential ingredient in the relationship. Lastly, the company determines the attractiveness of the market segment in terms of its size, growth rate, value and business distance.

Figure 9.4
Process of monitoring international market segments

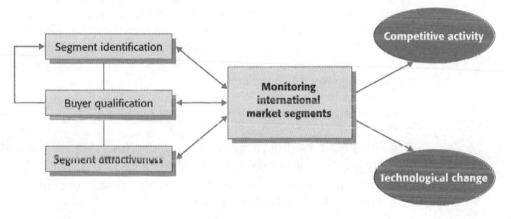

Source: Hlavacek, J. D. and Reddy, N. M. (1986) 'Identifying and qualifying industrial market segments', *European Journal of Marketing*, 20 (2), 8–21

Developing market positions

In developing a marketing strategy to enter foreign industrial markets the firm must pay attention to how it wishes to be positioned in the market. As a general rule, the company seeks parsimony in the ways it uses to position itself in the market. Building brands provides the company with such an approach in developing an international strategy. While branding in industrial marketing has moved beyond querying the

Figure 9.5
Competitive positions and buyer preferences for international technology suppliers

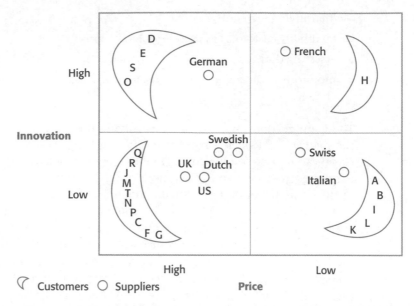

Source: Bradley, M. F. (1986) 'Developing communications strategies for foreign market entry', in P. W. Turnbull and S. J. Paliwoda, Eds, *Research in International Marketing*, London: Croom Helm, pp. 35–61

product trustworthiness to assessing whether the buyer can trust the company behind them, branding of industrial products is still in its infancy. In this regard it is recognized that while the potential power of industrial brands is great its value in terms of competitive positioning remains largely unexplained and untapped (McDowell Mudabi *et al.*, 1997, p. 445). Nevertheless, there are numerous examples of successful international industrial corporate brands, e.g. ABB, General Electric, Alfa-Laval, JCB. As a general rule, positioning strategy for firms such as these is usually conceived and implemented after considering the following factors:

■ the need for a distinct frame of reference – the firm's attributes, the competition and types of customers involved and branding;

■ buyer preferences, economic factors and other evaluative criteria are used to establish suppliers' competitive positions;

■ measures of competitive parity, the degree of product differentiation and the partnership potential which exists in the business system; and

■ size and identity of key market segments.

While there are many ways of measuring buyers' reactions to suppliers involving detailed lists of evaluative factors, managers frequently seek a parsimonious approach that would give useful managerial information in summary form. In a study of industrial buyers, Bradley (1986) identifies the preferences of 20 buyers of electric and electronic components used in numerous industrial markets (Figure 9.5). The analysis used here is based on a multidimensional scaling technique which elicits from respondents, in this case industrial buyers, their preferred positions on the two most important latent evaluative buying criteria: product innovation and price.

The 20 buyers, A–T, are positioned at their point of preference around the diagram. Ten buyers are located in cell 3, five in cell 2, four in cell 4 and only one, Buyer H, in cell 1. The positions of the companies are similarly evaluated and reflect buyer preferences. Thus the average position for French companies falls in cell 1, while Swiss and Italian companies fall in cell 2. The majority of companies fall in cell 3, while German companies fall in cell 4.

From this study of preferences it appears that the French firms are preferred by a segment dominated by Customer H, while Swiss and Italian firms are preferred by a segment containing five customers. The Italian firms, on average, are most preferred in this segment. German firms located in a very different market segment are preferred by a segment containing four customers. The largest segment, which contains ten customers, prefers to work with Dutch, Swedish, US and UK firms, with UK firms being the most preferred and Swedish firms the least preferred of this group.

A number of important lessons arise from this study. First, the relative competitive positions are established. Second, the size and identity of the key market segments become evident. Third, the match or fit of customer segments and supplier firms is specified. It becomes a managerial decision for the firm to choose to change position or otherwise to alter it in the light of the information supplied by the analysis.

Industrial product development

For industrial products firms serving global markets, the most important competitive weapon may prove to be the skilful management and deployment of technical resources rather than the resources themselves. A Booz-Allen Hamilton survey quoted in Perrino and Tipping (1989) demonstrates that:

- while markets are global technology developments occur in 'pockets of innovation' around the world;
- because of the need for expensive equipment and interdisciplinary teams there is a 'critical mass' necessary for technology development;
- external relationships through joint ventures and research consortia are used to spread costs and risks;
- higher levels of R&D do not guarantee success in global markets; greater benefits arise by linking research more closely to market and customer needs – large R&D budgets are not enough in themselves.

These product development considerations mean that many industrial markets, companies and countries are networked in tight relationships because of the large amounts of capital and technical expertise required to service the market. There are many joint ventures in this advanced composites industry, which allow companies such as Union Carbide, Celanese and Hercules in the United States access to a source of precursor materials, fibres and other fabricated materials in other parts of the world (Cammerota, 1984, p. 78). The network of relationships among manufacturers of sophisticated R&D

products demonstrates the complexity of industrial marketing for technical products, but also indicates the importance of maintaining good marketing relationships within the system. The network of relationships is indicative of the additional product development and market benefits these firms obtain from dealing with each other. The more technical the product the more homogeneous the marketing system facing the industrial products company and the greater the opportunities for collaboration.

Routes to international markets

The commitment of the firm to international markets may be measured by the way in which the firm organizes its resources to reach the market. For major customers in international markets, direct selling from the home base may be the most appropriate organizational form. Alternatively, access to the market with only minor investments may be obtained by the use of agents. To obtain a long-lasting presence in the market, however, a sales subsidiary, perhaps with local production facilities, may have to be used.

In a recent study of commitment by industrial firms to international markets, Morgan and Katsikeas (1998, p. 173) advocate that they:

■ ensure that exporting strategy is based on a well-founded approach to market planning;

■ visit export markets to obtain personal understanding of customers and their preferences;

■ cooperate with agents and distributors to develop a win–win position for all parties;

■ recruit specialized sales people with a proven track record in international marketing; and

■ select markets not adversely affected by exchange rate movements.

The path to internationalization of the industrial products firm may follow any one of four different routes (Andersen *et al.*, 1997, p. 240): follow its customers abroad; go abroad by being integrated into the supply chain of a large international company; be part of a domestic or foreign system supplier, or internationalize as an independent firm (Figure 9.6).

Following domestic customers abroad is a route used by suppliers whose products are of strategic importance to the customer. As the customer expands the foreign business, the market position may be strengthened, thereby requiring more product adaptation to local needs. As a consequence, the supplier firm finds itself increasingly in competition with local suppliers in the foreign market. If successful in the adaptation, the supplier becomes an indirect exporter and the firm adapts to the requirements of international markets. Eventually, the supplier may be encouraged first to locate service facilities and, subsequently, production facilities in the foreign market.

Figure 9.6
Routes to
international
markets for the
industrial
products firm

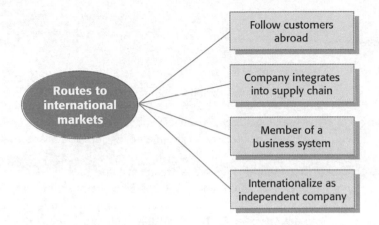

For firms whose products are not of strategic importance to customers, the situation may turn out to be quite different. These firms may reach the stage of being indirect exporters, at which point the customer may discover alternative suppliers in the foreign market who are better in some important way. These suppliers could easily fall out of the business system in the international and domestic markets. The second way an industrial products company can internationalize its activities is by integrating itself into the supply chain of a large international company. If successful with one division of the international customer, such business can rapidly lead to introductions to other divisions in other countries (Bradley *et al.*, 2000). In this case the firm internationalizes as part of a favoured supply chain to meet the requirements of customers in different international markets. As more and more customer companies outsource their requirements, additional opportunities arise for suppliers. International firms in the car industry, electrical businesses, computers and electronics generally are constantly searching for smaller supplier firms who can support areas of key competence – usually skills which complement the core competence in the customer firm.

Being part of a business system recognizes that, for the system to function properly, several fields of competence must be brought together and coordinated across borders. Frequently, firms internationalize through collaboration with other specialized firms located in different countries. Indeed, the design and management of the system assembly may be the responsibility of a key company located in one country with numerous suppliers located in other countries, all focused on providing a system for use by a customer in another country. Specialized small firms find this approach to internationalization attractive as it allows them to concentrate on their key skills while sharing resources and information on a need basis with others in the business system.

Motives to internationalize as an independent firm usually arise because of a stagnant or mature domestic market. Occasionally, specialized firms do not wish to share trade secrets and other technical information with companies which could subsequently become competitors. In such cases, they may prefer to develop new business abroad independently of others. This is the approach adopted most frequently by traditional companies. A major disadvantage of this approach to internationalization, especially for the small industrial products company, is the cost of establishing a sufficiently broad base of customers.

Summary

In the international marketing of industrial products technology is a more pervasive element, which frequently produces a technologically driven production orientation rather than a marketing orientation. This production orientation is due to the greater amount of interaction and interdependence between marketing and other functional areas, especially manufacturing, R&D, inventory control and engineering. This interdependence may mean that the marketing function is accorded a subservient role. The technical nature of many of the products purchased adds to the complexity of industrial marketing. The size of the purchase in money terms is greater and the buying relationship is more complex and long term. International industrial marketing takes place within a network of relationships between firms. Industrial products, because of their usage, are vulnerable to foreign government interference. Various laws and regulations often further restrict and determine how industrial products are marketed internationally.

Questions

1. Describe the main influences on industrial buying behaviour facing the international firm.

2. What are the key purchasing criteria in industrial products marketing? Are they different in domestic and international markets?

3. Describe the process of monitoring international industrial market segments.

4. What effects have international product standards on the sale of industrial products abroad?

5. Outline the industrial buying process and demonstrate how it is complicated in international marketing.

6. What role do cultural influences have on the marketing of industrial products in international markets?

7. How would the industrial products firm establish a position in international markets?

8. The pricing, selling and promotion of industrial products in international markets are complicated by the intervention of governments and multinational regulatory authorities. Discuss.

References

Andersen, P. H., Blenker, P. and Rind, P. (1997) *Generic Routes to Subcontractors' Internationalization*, Copenhagen: Handelshøjskolens Forlag, pp. 231–55.

Bradley, M. F. (1986) 'Developing communication strategies for foreign market entry', in P. W. Turnbull and S. J. Paliwoda, Eds, *Research in International Marketing*, London: Croom Helm, pp. 35–61.

Bradley, F., Kelly, A. and Meyer, R. (2000) 'Using first and second stage value chain relationships to compete in international markets', a paper presented at the *Third Annual Symposium on Multinational Business Management – The 21st Century Global Corporation*, School of International Business, Nanjing University, Nanjing, People's Republic of China, 10–13 December 1999.

Cammerota, D. A. (1984) 'Developing trade patterns for advanced materials', in *Proceedings of the International Research Seminar on Industrial Marketing*, Stockholm School of Economics, Sweden, 29–31 August, pp. 78–89.

Chumpitaz, R. (1998) 'Determinants of client satisfaction in business to business', in P. Andersson, Ed., *Track 1, Market Relationships, Proceedings, 27th EMAC Conference*, Stockholm, 20–23 May, pp. 167–86.

Czinkota, M. R. and Johnston, W. J. (1981) 'Segmenting US firms for export development', *Journal of Business Research*, 9, 353–65.

Day, E., Fox, R. J. and Huszagh, S. M. (1988) 'Segmenting the global market for industrial goods', *International Marketing Review*, 5 (3), 14–27.

Dyer, J. H., Cho, D. S. and Chu, W. (1998) 'Strategic supplier segmentation: the next "best practice" in supply chain management', *California Management Review*, 40 (2), 57–77.

Hlavacek, J. D. and Reddy, N. M. (1986) 'Identifying and qualifying industrial market segments', *European Journal of Marketing*, 20 (2), 8–21.

McDowell Mudabi, S., Doyle, P. and Wong, V. (1997) 'An exploration of branding in industrial markets', *Industrial Marketing Management*, 26, 433–46.

Meyer, R. (1998) The role of networking in the internationalization process of small and medium sized enterprises, PhD Dissertation, Graduate School of Business, University College Dublin, Dublin, 1 May.

Morgan, R. E. and Katsikeas, C. (1998) 'Exporting problems of industrial manufacturers', *Industrial Marketing Management*, 27, 161–76.

Perrino, A. C. and Tipping, J. W. (1989) 'Global management of technology', *Research Technology Management*, 32 (3), 12–19.

Webster, F. E. and Wind, Y. (1972) 'A general model for understanding buying behaviour', *Journal of Marketing*, 36, 12–19.

Wind, Y. (1978) 'Organizational buying center: a research agenda', in G. Zaltman and T. V. Bonoma, Eds, *Organizational Buying Behavior*, American Marketing Association, pp. 67–76.

10 The services firm

There are three reasons, stemming from the international marketing of products, why service firms have also internationalized. First, a manufacturing firm that pursues an international strategy requires detailed information on the size, composition and trends in foreign markets – information which is usually provided by specialized firms. Second, where it is essential to modify the product, the firm requires engineering and design services and, frequently, after-sales maintenance and servicing facilities. Third, as products move across borders they meet more obstacles than sales within the domestic market, e.g. distance, culture, language, customs, laws and regulations, and demand for services to remove these barriers grows. Many of the added costs of internationalizing in manufacturing are service costs. Services are independent of, but related to, developments in product markets. After studying this chapter students should be able to:

- evaluate the reasons for the international growth of services;
- describe the key characteristics of services in international marketing;
- evaluate the differences between international service marketing and international product marketing;
- analyze the problems that frequently arise in international service marketing;
- incorporate the two dimensions, tangibility and personal contact, into an international marketing strategy for services;
- determine the degree of service standardization and differentiation appropriate in particular circumstances;
- prepare and apply an analytical framework for the international marketing of services based on tangibility and contact.

Growth of services in world markets

The recent growth in services has occurred at the level of the household and at the level of the firm. At the level of the firm there has been a pronounced shift to arm's length sourcing of services as manufacturing industry reorganizes to take account of

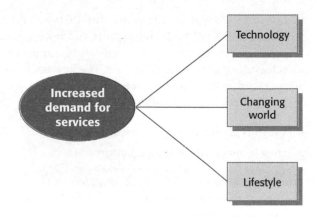

Figure 10.1
Reasons for
growth in service
businesses

the changes in the working environment mainly brought about through technological change. Technological change itself has introduced wide-ranging changes in the world and in life and in lifestyles generally. The growth in services internationally may be attributed to three principal factors: changing technology and the variety and complexity of products available on the market; the changing world affected by the increased complexity of life, increased life expectancy and ecological concerns; and a resulting change in lifestyles affected by affluence, leisure time and women in paid employment (Figure 10.1).

Defining a pure service business as one in which the service is the primary component on offer (similarly for a pure product), it becomes clear that few, if any, pure services exist. Only product benefits are subject to the market, not the products themselves, and these include both tangible and intangible elements. By deduction, the same applies to services. Following along these lines, Levitt's (1972) view that 'everyone is in service' is understandable. Levitt is saying that everyone is in services, not that everyone is in products, and hence the focus of attention should be on the service component of the 'thing' being marketed and this can only improve our understanding of service marketing.

Nature of services in international marketing

Many services are tradeable and more are becoming so. Through cross-border sales, joint ventures and foreign direct investment, companies providing financial, legal and business services, and consultancy, telecommunications and recreation services, experience many international marketing opportunities. Indeed, by combining or incorporating services in products, companies have discovered that it is easier to export services. The service exchange can be met through a wide set of modes of service delivery.

A service may be described as any activity or benefit that a supplier offers a customer that is usually intangible and does not result in the ownership of anything. The provision of a service may or may not be tied to a physical product. Services, according to the International Standard Industrial Classification (ISIC), include the following: wholesale and retail trade, restaurants and hotels; transport, storage and communications; financial, insurance, real estate and business services; personal, community and social services; government services. The key asset managed by the firm in each of the above businesses is a system for interfacing people and machines or equipment.

International services differ from domestic services in two respects;

■ they involve something crossing borders; and
■ they interact with a foreign culture.

They are similar to international products in this respect. Because services depend on people for their provision and delivery, cultural sensitivity is more critical. For these reasons, international services have been defined as 'deeds, performances, efforts, conducted across national boundaries in critical contact with foreign cultures' (Clark *et al.*, 1996, p. 15). In international marketing, services firms with large-scale facilities have no advantage as in many instances diseconomies of scale exist in service businesses. Small firms are often more efficient where personal service is the key to the business. Individualized, responsive service declines with size after reaching a threshold, e.g. personal and medical and management consulting.

Market needs with regard to services are diverse and buyer tastes for many services are fragmented. This fragmentation arises because of local and regional differences in market needs. In industrial markets there is considerable need for customized products and services, e.g. most fire engines sold are unique. The problem with fragmentation in the marketing of services is that an industry in which no firm has a significant market share means that no firm can strongly influence the industry outcome. There is also considerable indeterminacy in the industry since there are no market leaders with the power to shape industry events.

As with all aspects of marketing it is necessary for the service firm to research the market, to identify its target customers carefully and to aim its products and services at customer needs. The involvement of people is crucial in service marketing; the administration of human resources is a key way of competing. Most people in a service firm act in a selling capacity; all are engaged in the personal market communication effort of the firm. In such circumstances marketing training, especially in the areas of communications and selling, is essential for success. As all people in the service firm are engaged in marketing tasks, the firm must recognize the internal marketing task of service firms. The service must be successfully marketed to the people in the firm itself. This helps to avoid the possibility that the service might fail in its ultimate target markets. The staff are simultaneously the producers and sellers of the service.

Constraints on the international service firm

International service industries are fragmented. There are low entry barriers to service businesses as manifested by the many small firms sharing each market. There are few scale economies in many services owing to the relatively simple process involved,

Figure 10.2
Constraints on
international
marketing of
services

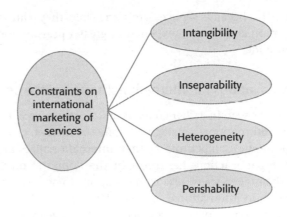

e.g. warehousing, or the inherently high labour content, e.g. personal care. The firm attempting to internationalize a service business faces four major constraints: service intangibility, service inseparability, heterogeneity of services and their perishability (Figure 10.2).

Because services are intangible, to trade them internationally they must be embodied in products, information flows or people which move from one country to another. Intangibility makes it difficult to differentiate services in different countries and cultures. Because they cannot be displayed easily, communication, especially across borders, is difficult.

Intangibility and personal contact are the critical elements of the product–service distinction in international marketing from which all other differences emerge. Intangibility creates several marketing implications (Patterson and Cicic, 1995, p. 60).

■ services cannot be easily displayed or communicated;
■ without inspection, buyers rely on cues, communications experience and word of mouth to make judgements;
■ the greater the intangibility, the more difficult it is to differentiate the services; and, hence
■ the higher the costs required to build a corporate image;
■ the more intangible the service, the higher the perceived costs and risks in internationalization.

Services differ from products also in that international marketing transactions frequently require consumers and providers to be at the same place at the same time; it is usually necessary for providers and consumers of services to cooperate if the service is to be provided. The simultaneous production and consumption of a service means that these two functions are inseparable. It is impossible to export a service on its own for this reason. Services are highly variable and require customization. Because services are heterogeneous, they cannot easily be standardized nor made in a uniform way; they are difficult to package and it may be difficult to ensure quality control across borders.

Lastly, because services are perishable they cannot be stored. Inventory is not an option and the firm experiences greater pressure for a 'just-in-time' system as a service provider.

Motivations for internationalization in the service firm

As was seen in earlier chapters, among the many reasons why product marketing firms go international are stagnant domestic market, growth in the market abroad, matching domestic competitors as they internationalize, opportunism, counteracting foreign company action, i.e. threat in the domestic market, and exploiting a competitive advantage. These reasons also apply to service firms as they attempt to enter and develop international markets. There is an additional motivation for services firms – the need to service customers who also have internationalized and expect their services to be provided at the new location.

The involvement of people in the process usually means that there is a degree of variability not experienced by the product marketing firm. Cultural diversities and social norms quickly come into focus in service marketing. The effect of these elements obviously varies with the degree of intangibility of the service offering and the extent of the contact involved. Unlike product firms, services firms usually cannot start the internationalization process with a service component but must provide the full service package.

Few services can be exported without also exporting the full 'service delivery system'. The service offering must be available in full from the day of entry to the market. In an international marketing environment, characterized by increased competition and slower growth in mature domestic markets, a system perspective allows the service firm to create a climate and culture of a relationship orientation in which customer retention is the key to profitability in the long term (Schneider *et al.*, 1997, pp. 19–20).

Retailers are especially proficient at customer acquisition and customer retention in their home markets but few have so far demonstrated great facility in this regard in international markets. Some large retailers enter international markets through acquisition while others do so through organic growth or, like the UK retailer, Tesco, by working with local partners. In the UK and elsewhere for many years it has been 'Every Little Helps', a slogan that has been the key to Tesco's slow and steady transformation from a vulnerable UK supermarket chain into one of the world's largest retailers (Table 10.1).

At home in the UK Tesco began to face a series of European discount stores which caused it to respond by changing its marketing to the adoption of the 'Every Little Helps' slogan. Next came the Value lines of own-brand products which started the current pricing architecture referred to as 'good, better, best', meaning that Tesco appeals to as wide a range of consumers as possible. Internationally, however, Tesco cannot depend on this marketing strategy nor is it large enough to compete successfully with giants such as Wal-Mart of the US or Carrefour of France as these large rivals appear to be preparing for more international expansion after a relatively dormant period. It is unlikely that Tesco's approach of focusing on emerging markets of Asia and Eastern Europe will be enough; more serious investment may be needed (Exhibit 10.1).

Table 10.1 Sales and international share in top global retailers

Company	Net sales (€ billion)	International sales (%)
Wal-Mart (US)	207.5	20.9
Carrefour (France)	65.6	47.5
Ahold (Netherlands)	52.3	83.5
Metro Group (Germany)	49.8	46.9
Kroger (US)	45.7	0.0
Tesco (UK)	41.5	18.6
Target (US)	39.8	0.0
Aldi (Germany)	37.4	37.0
Rewe (Germany)	37.4	28.6
Costco (US)	34.9	18.5

Exhibit 10.1   Tesco's tough challenge: internationalization

Five years ago Wal-Mart entered Britain with a €9.3 billion take-over of Asda, a move quickly followed by the merger of French hypermarket giants Carrefour and Promodés. Wal-Mart's purchase of Asda may have been a success but its earlier foray into Germany is still giving it problems while Carrefour is still suffering from post Promodés indigestion. Meanwhile, Tesco has been expanding internationally but in a different way. Tesco has focused on emerging markets in Asia and Eastern Europe and entered each by picking local partners. Each opera tion is run by local mangers with Tesco providing support systems and supply chain back-up. Excluding the Republic of Ireland Tesco operates in 11 countries outside its domestic base. It is profitable in all but two, Malaysia and Taiwan, and market leader in four. Recently, Carrefour has adopted Tesco's local partner model. 'Their old approach was more about leveraging their scale as a global purchasing power. Tesco is about getting local market dominance,' says Mike Dennis, retail analyst at CAI Chevreux Securities.

Tesco's achievements have worried some of its competitors. Wal-Mart's intense desire to buy Safeway in the UK last year stemmed in part from knowing that boosting Asda would threaten Tesco's stability at home, which is what allowed it to carve out its global footprint. Furthermore, now that Carrefour has resolved some of its difficulties it may become more aggressive overseas. Wal-Mart, meanwhile, has faced increasing criticism about its size in the US, making the rest of the world an alternative path to growth. If Tesco wants to be a true global player, judged alongside Wal-Mart, it will need more than emerging markets exposure; it will need a foot in mainstream continental Europe and the US. According to Charles Coates of Roland Berger, 'when Wal-Mart really decides to put its foot on the international acceler ator, the only real answer for Tesco will be a deal with a big competitor – Carrefour in Europe, say, or Kroger in the US, or even both – to create another global retail powerhouse. It may be another case of "Every Little Helps".'

Source: adapted from Voyle, S., 'Far from resting on his laurels, chief executive Sir Terry Leahy has already announced a further £1.7bn of investment to take . . . ', *Financial Times*, Tuesday 20 April 2004, p. 13

International marketing of services

Coping with service intangibility

Although the marketing concepts and many of the techniques are universal, marketing practices are often unique to particular situations. It should be remembered, however, that because both product marketing and services marketing are derived from the same general marketing theory, it follows that there are also many areas of commonality. Nevertheless, there are a number of differences.

Service systems with high customer contact are more difficult to control and to rationalize than those with lower customer contact (Chase, 1978). Customer contact is defined as the physical presence of the customer in the system. At the 'high-contact' end of the scale, it is likely that supply will seldom match demand for the service, given the customized nature of each delivery. At the opposite end of the continuum the potential for supply and demand to match exactly is much greater. In high-contact systems, the customer can affect the time of demand, the exact nature of the service and the quality of the service since, by definition, the consumer becomes involved in the process itself.

It is frequently better to view marketing in the firm as the marketing of a product–service system which consists of products which provide explicit benefits, where the emphasis is on product attributes; and services which produce tacit benefits, where the emphasis is on delivery to the customer (Figure 10.3). The explicit benefits associated with tangible products include the opportunity to standardize them and to support them with equipment where necessary. For products there is low personal contact and the focus is on production. The tacit benefits associated with intangible services, on the other hand, include the opportunity to customize them and to support them with trained personnel. For services there is high personal contact and a focus on process. The simplest approach in attempting to develop a continuum of services is to distinguish between pure service businesses on the one hand and product-oriented businesses on the other (Thomas, 1978). A market offering is classified as a service or a

Figure 10.3
Product–service system

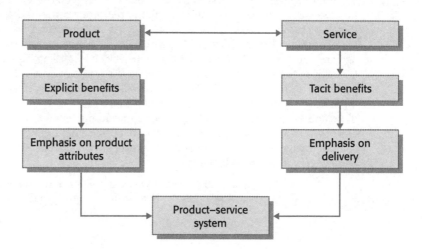

product on the basis of whether the essence of what is being bought is tangible or intangible. In this way, a continuum can be developed with varying degrees of dominance towards a product in one direction and a service in the other.

For example, toothpaste is almost totally dominated by a tangible object, i.e. a product, whereas intangibility dominates most medical services. A continuum exists between pure product and pure services; at the pure product extreme, emphasis is on individual manufactured or service products, e.g. a car; car hire; washing-up liquid; equipment leasing. At the other extreme emphasis is on pure services incorporated in integrated service system, e.g. educational services; medical services; financial services.

The more intangible the service, the greater the difficulty in exporting. Financial, engineering and medical services, for example, 'do not enjoy the same opportunities for learning from the gradual experience as the goods firm, e.g., via indirect or casual exporting. The international marketer of services has got no choice but to deal directly with the foreign customer' (Nicoulaud, 1989, p. 58).

Personal contact in services

For many services customer contact is a crucial issue: the provider must be in face-to-face contact with the customer. The closer the personal contact the richer the customer relationship. Many services fit this category – engineering projects, management consulting and tourism. These require a high degree of contact between the client and the provider. Other services, particularly financial services, medical diagnosis and telecommunications, may be delivered by technology and do not require high contact. Personal contact and the richness of the customer relationship are, therefore, lower. For high-contact services, there are marketing implications. A high degree of contact requires a local presence in the foreign market and customization. People delivering such services need high technical skills, but also they need culturally sensitive interpersonal skills, since they are involved directly in the provision and marketing of the service. For the services that require little contact, standardization is a possibility and a presence in the foreign market may not be required. Such services are not culturally sensitive and so marketing costs are lower. These low contact services may easily be provided to many customers, whereas high-contact services may have to be restricted to fewer customers. The extent of customer contact involved and the number of customers served in a given time period are factors which influence the international marketing of services (Figure 10.4).

Professional services involve very extensive customer contact and a small number of customers served. The nature of the personal contact between supplier and buyer is very rich, allowing strong bonds to be developed in the relationship. At the other extreme, standardized mass services such as equipment leasing, e.g. car hire; construction equipment, typically involve much less customer contact but a much larger numbers of customers served. Here the firm's ability to reach many customers is enhanced. Between these extremes are service shop operations such as fast food outlets; computer services firms and information providers. The degree of customer contact and the number of customers served have clearly defined consequences for attempts to internationalize a service business depending on where it is located on the richness of personal contact – reach of customers continuum. Personal selling of professional services

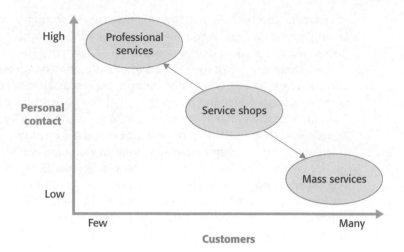

Figure 10.4
Contact and
customers
served

would seem appropriate whereas some form of franchising or joint venture partnership would seem to suit service shop operations and mass services.

Standardization and customization of services

Customer contact also dictates the extent to which services may be standardized or should be customized for international markets. Core services that are sold globally are more likely to be standardized than customized. The degree of standardization possible in a core service depends largely on the extent to which the service is 'people based' or 'equipment based'. A service such as an automatic car wash, eminently suitable for franchising, raises the level of standardization as it removes the human element. Because of the inseparability factor, the service sector is one which is highly labour-intensive. Investment in people and training is, therefore, one approach to standardized quality control. The difficulty of producing services of uniform quality which is necessary for successful branding, advertising and other mass-marketing activities makes the successful and sustained marketing of services more difficult than for products.

Standardization and customization of services, however, may be simultaneously possible by using local nationals as providers; the 'foreignness' of a standardized service may be overcome, e.g. the use of local cabin crews by international airlines (Lovelock and Yip, 1996, p. 72). The practice of augmenting a core service with many supplementary elements makes it relatively easy to provide a globally standardized core service augmented and differentiated by nationally customized supplementary service elements.

Scale and cultural effects

Certain scale and cultural effects in the international marketing of services must be considered when diversifying abroad, a point noted in Chapter 1. Some services businesses respond to scale operations, while others do not. It is important to recognize that services are also influenced by cultural factors. Some services are highly culture-bound and demand is strongly influenced by society. Some services, e.g. car hire, selected banking services (ATM services), recorded music, computer software and information services possess high scale effects and low cultural effects. Most firms should welcome this combination of effects. Other services such as the cinema, video, advertising, Internet and fast food, possess high scale effects but are also highly culture bound. Similarly, some medical services, particularly those dealing with human reproduction, the theatre, personal care and education manifest high cultural effects but possess few scale effects. Lastly, other medical services such as cardiology related treatments, management consulting and marketing research, possess few scale effects and manifest few cultural effects.

Integrated international marketing strategy for services

As a general rule service firms must choose from a reduced set of foreign market entry modes. As already noted only those services that are embedded in goods may be directly exported, e.g. software, videos, because their production and consumption can be decoupled by being produced in one country, embodied in the tangible product, e.g. a CD or DVD and training manual, and exported in the traditional manner.

Using the concepts of tangibility, contact and standardization discussed previously, it is possible to devise a framework which separates services in international marketing into four groups (Figure 10.5). Firms that sell pure services which require very little contact have been labelled 'location free' by Patterson and Cicic (1995, p. 67). Executives in these firms need only travel to the foreign country from the domestic base for relatively short periods to conduct an assignment. Then they return home. They do not require a permanent presence in the foreign market. The client is not expected to visit the company to obtain these services nor does the company spend much time with the client abroad. These are low-contact standardized pure services, such as market research, transportation and insurance.

Figure 10.5
Contact and tangibility in international marketing of services

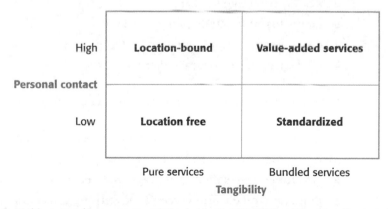

Source: adapted from Vandermerwe, S. and Chadwick, M. (1989) 'The internationalization of services', *The Services Industries Journal*, January, p. 85, and Patterson, P. G. and Cicic, M. (1995) 'A typology of service firms in international markets: an empirical investigation', *Journal of International Marketing*, **3** (4), 67

Where contact is high and the company is dealing with pure services, a customized service is required. These 'location-bound' services require relatively continuous contact with the client for successful delivery of the service. Such services are customized and the focus is on the home market. Staff providing them must exercise more executional discretion and adaptation during service delivery. Major engineering projects, long-term management consulting and project management services fall into this category.

Firms which sell standardized services tend to bundle the service with products. Because they are bundled and require little personal contact, these services tend to be exported in the traditional manner. There are few barriers and little customization.

Lastly, value-added customized services require a high degree of supplier–client interaction for successful service delivery. These services are highly customized in that the service component adds considerable value to the product component. High-contact bundled services include technical training and support, associated with major installations such as a telecommunications network or the building of a holiday resort.

Restrictions on international marketing of services

Restrictions by governments and public agencies are much more common for service firms than for product firms. After primary resources, host governments see services as a way by which foreign companies can 'take the most out of a country and leave little' (Carman and Langeard, 1979). The special nature of some services prompts governments into taking action – particularly when the service has some cultural, political or security sensitivity. Governments attempt to control services by measures such as licences, fees and special taxes. Administrative and investment-related barriers are quite common. Administrative barriers are often found in the form of:

■ delays in granting licences;
■ failure to certify certain professional services;
■ discriminatory implementation of statutory regulations;
■ inadequate access to local judicial bodies.

Investment-related barriers may also be experienced. These often take the form of:

■ employment requirements that control the personnel practices of the foreign firm;
■ restrictions on the extent of foreign ownership permitted;
■ government regulations biased against foreign service companies;
■ limitations on the firm's access to advertising and communications facilities;
■ discriminatory practices against specific service industries, i.e. higher reserve requirements for foreign bank subsidiaries or special capital requirements for foreign insurance firms.

Summary

In recent years there has been a very considerable growth in the international marketing of services. Many of the motives for international product marketing can be found in services marketing. Many of the added costs of internationalizing in manufacturing are service costs but services are independent of, though related to, developments in product markets. There are a number of characteristics of services that should be considered: their intangibility; the need for direct contact between supplier and customer; a recognition that customers participate in the production of the service; and that production and consumption occur simultaneously. There are three reasons, stemming from the international marketing of products, why service firms have grown and internationalized. First, a manufacturing firm which pursues an international strategy requires detailed information on the size, composition and trends in foreign markets – information which is usually provided by specialized firms. Second, where it is essential to modify the product the firm will require engineering and design services and, frequently, after-sales maintenance and servicing facilities. Third, as products moving across borders meet more obstacles than sales within the domestic market, e.g. distance, culture, language, customs, laws and regulations, there is a growing demand for services to remove these barriers.

Technology also plays a key role in the internationalization of the services firm. Technology allows the firm to be more cost-effective, it provides the ability to handle large volumes of some services while maintaining quality and it provides the ability to offer a wider range of services.

An integrated approach to the international marketing of services involves combining considerations of tangibility and personal contact that provide dimensions of an analytical framework which distinguish among location-free professional resources; location-bound customized services and standardized or value-added customized services. The international services firm sometimes experiences administrative and investment-related barriers to internationalization which should be considered by the firm.

Questions

1. The growth in services internationally has been attributed to changing lifestyles and a changing world. Do you agree?

2. A service has been described as any activity or benefit which a supplier offers a customer, which is usually intangible and does not result in the ownership of anything. Discuss.

3. Why are services more important to the economies of some countries than to others?

4. The problems and approaches to marketing of products and services are similar and there is no need to develop a separate treatment of services. Discuss.

5. For the firm in international markets is there any classification framework for its activities which is more appropriate than others? What is the appropriate role for a product service system?

6. What market entry options does the services firm have if it wishes to internationalize? Describe the need to consider contact, tangibility and the number of customers served.

7. There are fewer barriers to international services marketing than to international product marketing. Do you agree?

8. How useful can information technology be in removing constraints on the growth of the international services firm?

References

Carman, J. and Langeard, E. (1979) 'Growth strategies for the service firm', *Eighth Annual Meeting of the European Academy for Advanced Research in Marketing*, Groningen, The Netherlands, 10–12, April.

Chase, R. B. (1978) 'Where does the customer fit in a service operation?', *Harvard Business Review*, **56** (6), 137–42.

Clark, T., Rajaratnam, D. and Smith, T. (1996) 'Towards a theory of international services: marketing intangibles in a world of nations', *Journal of International Marketing*, **4** (2), 9–28.

Levitt, T. (1972) 'Production-line approach to services', *Harvard Business Review*, **50** (September–October), 41–52.

Lovelock, C. H. and Yip, G. S. (1996) 'Developing global strategies for service businesses', *California Management Review*, **38** (2), 64–86.

Nicoulaud, B. (1989) 'Problems and strategies in the international marketing of services', *European Journal of Marketing*, **23** (6), 55–66.

Patterson, P. G. and Cicic, M. (1995) 'A typology of services firms in international markets: an empirical investigation', *Journal of International Marketing*, **3** (4), 57–83.

Schneider, B., Schoenberger White, S. and Paul, M. C. (1997) 'Relationship marketing in an organizational perspective', in T. A. Swartz, D. E. Bowen and D. Iacobucci, Eds, *Advances in Services Marketing and Management*, London: JAI Press, **6**, 1–22.

Thomas, D. R. E. (1978) 'Strategy is different in service business', *Harvard Business Review*, **56** (July–August), 158–65.

Vandermerwe, S. and Chadwick, M. (1989) 'The internationalization of services', *The Services Industries Journal*, **9** (1), 79–93.

11 Building the global brand

The previous three chapters were devoted to how the firm internationalizes products or services. This chapter deals with how the firm builds the brand, product or corporate. Communicating brand values effectively in a relatively homogeneous domestic market is a difficult task; doing so across many markets is a serious challenge for most firms. It may be relatively easy to transfer some brand values to one or two adjacent markets but this requires significant strategic thinking and close attention to differences in the markets. Attempting to communicate and transfer brand values into multiple, culturally heterogeneous, international markets is a much greater challenge. Discovering the positioning and the subsequent image that help to build a global brand is a challenge only a few companies have faced down successfully.

This chapter examines three themes related to building the global brand. In the first section the major influences on the formation of international brand strategies are identified and evaluated. The second section is devoted to international brand positioning and the last section discusses ways that the global brand can be damaged and outlines remedies for such an occurrence. After studying this chapter students should be able to:

- evaluate ways in which firms develop and implement brand strategies appropriate for international markets;

- specify the characteristics of a global brand and understand why so few brands reach global status;

- determine the role of brand popularity and country of origin effects in building and communicating brand values internationally;

- determine how to harmonize brand strategies across multiple international markets;

- evaluate the relevance of the international brand life cycle and determine when brand extensions can profitably be used;

- avoid management traps that debase the brand in international markets;

- understand how the counterfeiting of brands is driven by unethical suppliers and misbehaving buyers and outline approaches to deal with this growing problem and thereby protect the firm's brand equity.

Branding phenomenon in international markets

Brands are a relatively new phenomenon in international marketing, but branding has existed in individual countries in a dominant form at least since the start of the twentieth century. Because they are targeted at the mass consumer market, consumer product brands are better known than industrial product or service brands. By the late nineteenth century most countries had passed trademark acts establishing the brand name as a protectable asset. Brands such as Coca-Cola (US), Mercedes-Benz (Germany), Persil (Germany) and Cadbury (UK) existed before the passing of the trademark acts.

Brands are usually developed within a country and then introduced to foreign markets as they become accepted through advertising, word-of-mouth promotion by visitors, adaptation and strategic development by the company. Another force for internationalization arose from the ease with which colonies could be guaranteed as markets for brands. A more natural expansion path was among countries of the same language and similar culture.

The main growth in international brands occurred, however, after World War II. Troop movements, especially the US military, have been associated with the successful introductions of many US brands to Europe and the Far East. With the resultant expansion of US culture across much of the world and through US business acquisitions and investments in Europe in the 1950s and 1960s, many US brands or US-owned brands became well known internationally: Ford; Opel; Pepsi; McDonald's. European brand names also began to spread during the 1950s and 1960s as a result of improved transportation and communications systems.

Japanese companies have also grown into highly developed brand-centred firms using corporate brand names rather than product brands as is more common in US firms, for example. Sony, Mitsubishi, Sanyo, Honda, Suzuki, Citizen, Seiko, Toyota, Suntory, Sharp, Casio and Pioneer are brands which are easily recognizable throughout the world. To date Japanese brands have been concentrated in the field of electronics, motor cars and heavy earth-moving equipment. This is changing, as a visit to Japan's neighbouring far eastern countries proves. Japanese branded foods, cosmetics (Shiseido) and clothing (Kenzo) are now widely distributed in the region and much sought after. They are also available in western markets though they have not yet dominated their segments.

These trends and variations raise some interesting questions for international brand managers. From an earlier discussion, especially in Chapter 5, it is expected that the values people fundamentally hold and the benefits that may be derived from products are reasonably universal. For example, everybody needs to feel safe and secure and be loved or appreciated in some way but do brands developed in one market provide those benefits in another market? To what extent do customers choose brands differently across cultures? Following from that, to what extent should a brand be global? Related to these topics is the issue of how people perceive communications through branding. While innovation is necessary to maintain market leadership, particularly in high-technology product-markets, it is also necessary to recognize that consumers in different markets may perceive the innovation differently and may require a focused form of communication, the role of the strong well-positioned brand, to ensure that the innovative product is understood and adopted (Exhibit 11.1). The structural representation of brands in the minds of consumers may change across cultural boundaries and require the company to engage in an unexpected brand adaptation process.

Exhibit 11.1 Siemens is inspired in communicating technical detail to global consumers

Referring to the advertising slogan, 'Be Inspired' for Siemens' SL-45 mobile telephone which focused less on technology and more on attitude, Jon Mathews, creative director of Weiden & Kennedy Advertising in Amsterdam, said: 'The product area can be a little too technical and feature focused. For a company to succeed in this market where the products are changing so fast, you need a brand that protects you from the competition, who at any point in time will have a longer list of features or a pricing advantage.'

Source: adapted from *The Wall Street Journal Europe*, 14 February 2001, p. 1

Characteristics of a global brand

Many features of the brand already successful in the domestic market may be used in international marketing – the logotype and symbols, the name, positioning product features, packaging, advertising copy and other elements of the marketing mix to a lesser extent. A brand is a product or service that provides balanced functional and discriminating benefits in a sophisticated form of added values that some consumers value sufficiently to buy. Brand values arise from the experience gained from using them – familiarity, reliability, risk reduction; and give the consumer a reference point during the purchasing process and afterwards. These are values that can be internationalized in many cases. The firm must make decisions about products, markets and brands. Much discussion has taken place on the decision to develop new products for new international markets. Here the discussion focus is on the branding question; local or global (Figure 11.1). Any move away from the origin of this three-way axis introduces complexity for the firm especially on the branding issue where culture and communication are main ingredients.

A large cash flow generated from sales in a large domestic market seems an important factor in the internationalization of the brand. Very few brands are well known in any one of the major regions of the world, in the US for example, and virtually unknown in Asia. A global brand has a minimum level of awareness and sales all over the world. Using this criterion, it is noteworthy that Nestlé has about 600 brands but 250 are present in only one country and only 20 are to be found in more than half of the countries where Nestlé operates. By this standard few companies can claim to be global.

Another dimension of the global brand is that the physical attributes of the products behind the brands tend to be very similar worldwide and meet the same, practically

Figure 11.1
Global markets,
products and
brands

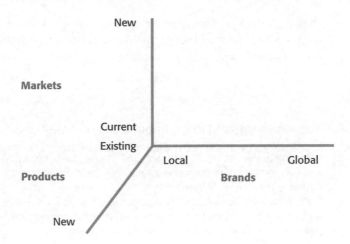

universal, needs of consumers. In some instances the physical product may vary for local reasons. For example, Guinness varies the sweetness levels of its dark beer depending on the market but the same basic need is satisfied in each. Global brands are positioned similarly in all markets. The way Baileys Original Irish Cream Liqueur is positioned throughout the world is very consistent – a spirit which provides sociable indulgent pleasure to be consumed with friends.

Furthermore, consumers of such brands value the country of origin. When Asian consumers buy a McDonald's hamburger or drive a Mercedes car they are participating in the lifestyle and material culture of two respected countries. The brand is embedded in a particular national culture – Baileys is embedded in the natural environment and tradition of Ireland while Chanel No 5 perfume reflects a strong association with France.

Most successful brands have a single product category focus. Being too diversified and spread across many categories makes it difficult for the brand to establish itself worldwide. Again, taking Baileys as an example, while the product is based on the successful blending of whiskey and cream, drawing from two separate product categories, it has built its reputation on the cream liqueur category which the company itself created. Lastly, in most successful international brands the corporate name is the same as the brand name. This may reflect the preoccupation of some large companies of concentrating their scarce resources on a few major brands.

By combining the main themes above, Quelch (1999, pp. 2–3) derives six measures by which a brand may be judged as global:

- dominating the domestic market; generating cash flow to enter new markets;
- meeting a universal consumer need;
- demonstrating balanced country–market coverage;
- reflecting a consistent positioning worldwide;
- benefiting from positive country of origin effect; and
- focusing on the product category.

International brand strategies

Impact of brand popularity

If a brand is to establish itself as a strong contender in the international market it should build or maintain its market position through its presence in the market. Being a popular brand in a geographical market, e.g. the United Kingdom, could create valuable intangible assets for the same brand in other geographical markets, e.g. Germany. Confirming this view Kim and Chung (1997, p. 379) note that in considering 'the transfer of brand image across different regions, brand popularity should be considered a key strategic variable for building long-term and global positions for a brand'.

Many well-known brands have established their popularity in all international markets of significance: Coca-Cola, McDonald's, Kodak, Heineken, Guinness, Honda, Ford, BMW, to name but a few. Popular brands are those that are widely sought after and are bought by a large cross-section of society. Brand popularity is considered as the accumulation of market acceptance and brand goodwill over time, promoted by word-of-mouth communication and advertising. Once a brand has become popular, the popularity component brings a positive contribution to the brand's loyalty, image or equity, or sales (Aaker, 1991; Kim and Chung, 1997).

Brand popularity positively influences brand performance not only directly in the short run but also indirectly in the long run by creating a favourable brand image. The successful consumer products company in international markets draws its strength from brand equity – real differentiation and genuine innovation that meet the needs of consumers while providing a good value proposition for the consumer; financial strength – company size measured by market capitalization and cash flow; and international distribution – international sales in the company to provide distribution scale effects to create high entry barriers (Figure 11.2).

Country of origin effects

Many successful consumer products companies expand abroad through acquisitions because it is the quickest and most efficient way to internationalize. In such circumstances, a strong financial position with healthy cash flows arising from previous

Figure 11.2
Sources of brand advantage

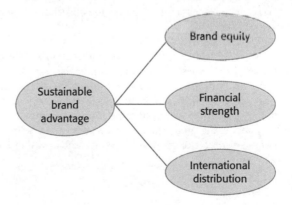

successes is essential. Dominant positions in a large domestic market like the United States, the United Kingdom, Germany or Japan are the source of a strong cash flow. Most of the world's best-known brands emanate from one of these markets.

There are a number of notable exceptions to this conclusion, e.g. Baileys, Heineken and Nestlé. Baileys' domestic market, Ireland, is very small and yet the brand dominates its category worldwide, selling in excess of 30 million cases. The same is true for Heineken. The Dutch market is very small relative to the US market and yet Heineken has become the most international of brewers – far larger internationally than Guinness or Anheuser Busch. Nestlé began in Switzerland, one of the smallest European markets, yet it dominates many sectors of the food industry. A narrow domestic base forced these companies to internationalize at an early stage. They obtained their critical mass internationally, giving them the requisite cash flow for brand-building. All of these brands made astute use of the country of origin in their advertising and positioning in the early stages of life cycle development. In later stages the country of origin effect is played down in favour of more broad based appeals. In evaluating a country's products, consumers consider product integrity, price and market presence in their own country and the perceived match with their own personal needs (Exhibit 11.2). Brand popularity in the domestic market and country image are, therefore, essential elements for the long-term success of brands in international markets (Kim and Chung, 1997, p. 361). The same elements apply to industrial and technical products where a combination of country of origin effects and advertising serves to build the industrial product brand (Bradley, 2001). The brand value mix depends on a superior product quality, acceptable prices and value for money.

Exhibit 11.2   Understanding product-country image

In today's global marketing battles, companies spend billions on campaigns designed to associate their products with a particular place. When Volkswagen, for example, advertises its 'German-engineered road sedans', it is trying to capitalize on images of German products, and even of Germany itself, that consumers are presumed to have. Yet how much do marketing people really understand about such product-country images? In evaluating a given country's products, consumers look most closely at factors having to do with product integrity, price and market presence in their own countries, and the perceived suitability of a country's products to their needs. In evaluating countries, they use standards connected with a country's level of advancement, their own feelings about its people, and their own desire for closer links with a country.

The general lesson from these findings is that the marketing value of a country's image may be so high that producers in other countries actually appropriate the image of their products, or so questionable that producers in a given country may wish to disassociate themselves from their own country's image. This would seem to validate the strategy behind a product name such as Australian Hair Recipe shampoo – which is actually made by a US company – or the tendency of some Japanese companies not to call attention to associations with Japan. Using product-country image as a marketing tool, then, requires an understanding of the disparate elements of an image and how they can be made to work together.

Source: *Insights*, Marketing Science Institute, spring/summer 2000, pp. 1–2

Figure 11.3
Building and
communicating
brand values

Building and communicating brand values

Branding influences customer decisions and ultimately creates value for customers. There is a need, therefore, to understand the differences in the buying decision process in different markets. As a general rule, based on quality and performance, customer goodwill transferred to a brand name in one market facilitates similar transfers across markets. As noted above many brands are readily identifiable globally. Featured attributes should give a competitive advantage in all markets; a combination of luxury, country of origin and prestige are the values that are usually sought. In the process international distribution and access to customers is essential.

A successful brand communications strategy in international markets depends on the performance of the firm in the domestic market, country of origin effects and specific endeavours on the part of the firm to address customer requirements in the international markets selected (Figure 11.3). Two other important factors contribute to the brand value mix – the ability of the company to recruit and retain customers in different countries and their level and frequency of consumption of the brand.

These factors, taken together, influence the brand value mix. Once the brand value mix has been established the company positions the brand in the market taking account of customer needs and competing brands. The brand is given a clear identity and the company attempts to develop an effective communications strategy to ensure that having built up the brand its values are properly communicated. These elements of advice may have been considered by Jean Claude Biver when he decided to relaunch the Blancpain brand by leveraging on a heritage that gave the watch a clear identity and communicated in a way to differentiate the brand from the quartz watches then beginning to have a strong foothold in the market (Exhibit 11.3).

Exhibit 11.3   Leveraging the heritage

Passion, history and visionary genius are key ingredients in reviving a brand. An old name, however distantly remembered, is a huge help when building a brand. This sense of connection with the past motivated Jean Claude Biver to relaunch Blancpain in 1982. Blancpain had been founded in 1735, but when he bought the name no Blancpain watches had been made since 1956. 'The benefit was that we were able to work on the traditional side of the brand. Because it was the oldest watch brand in the world and as no watches had been made for so long, the reputation was clean and we were able to build on that. The name was like a virgin.'

Biver's concept was to use the antiquity of the brand to establish it as a reference: thus, he made sure his watchmakers could massage the traditional complications or pillars of horology and that Blancpain would only use classic round cases. He was also able to use the memorable slogan, 'Since 1735 there has never been a Blancpain quartz watch and there never will be one.' As a soundbite and mission statement it was genius; it established Blancpain as a marque with pedigree stretching back over centuries and positioned it as a guardian of traditional craft skills unaffected by the stigma of quartz.

Source: adapted from 'Lessons on how to leverage the heritage', Financial Times Special Report –
Watches & Jewelry, *Financial Times*, Saturday 17 April 2004, p. 6

Brand positioning in international markets

Brands are perceived differently in different markets despite the product being the same. A Renault Clio may be exactly the same car except for the branding in order to maximize the goodwill from the consumer in each market in terms of brand recognition, country of origin stereotyping, social status of the brand and perceived performance. For these and related reasons brands originating in a particular country seem to create country-related intangible assets or liabilities that are shared by brands originating in the same country. Since brands from the same country tend to be perceived as similar, consumer perceptions may not be purely brand specific but rather country specific (Erickson *et al.*, 1992). There is a need, therefore, to recognize that the brand values built up in the domestic market should be considered in developing the communications strategy for international markets. By building on country-related intangible assets or country of origin images that are developed over long periods the company attempts to position its brand in such a way to make a positive contribution to sales and market share. The French publishing company Gallimard used a simple but unique approach in positioning its small innovative encyclopedias in different markets (Exhibit 11.4). The international brand positioning decision usually means developing:

■ consistent positioning in the minds of consumers across all markets;

■ a standardized marketing mix for products positioned as prestige high priced and scarce exclusive since the segments served are relatively homogeneous throughout the world, e.g. luxury items; and

■ different positions for mass market consumer products in different markets, e.g. detergents.

Exhibit 11.4   Gallimard Publishing Company

In the early 1980s Pierre Marchand, director of the French publishing company, Gallimard, thought of compiling a new kind of encyclopedia. He developed the idea of pocket-sized (18 × 12cm) paperback fact books which would treat a wide array of subjects such as history, literature, arts, music and technology. First targeted at children, the books rapidly were seen to appeal to the general public. The collection was very successful in France and was exported to other countries. The concept appeared to appeal to a wide range of people, and thus avoided a close segmentation of the market. The market positioning varied by country:

■ France – 'On n'a jamais vu autant de choses entre la première et la dernière page d'un livre' – stressed the amount of information provided by different sources in each book;

■ Italy – 'la prima biblioteca tascabile illustrata' – the emphasis was on the pocket-sized aspect and the power of the illustrations;

■ United Kingdom – emphasis was on the newness and the innovativeness of the concept, presenting it as a breakthrough.

Each book was translated and published with identical texts and illustrations as the French version. The cover and the testimonials were adapted depending on the culture, the history and traditions of each country.

Source: Catalog: 'New Horizons from Thames and Hudson',
'Découvertes Gallimard', 'Universale Electrea/Gallimard'

Harmonizing brand strategies

One of the difficulties of branding is that the brand name chosen for one market may not work in another. This is a special problem in a linguistic and culturally diverse region such as Europe. Some brand names lose their impact in different markets. The decision facing the manufacturer or brand owner is whether to change the brand name when entering a new market.

Many manufacturers decide not to change brand names that are well established in different countries, recognizing that the country loyalty factor might be lost in any such attempt. The Unilever brand names for its main detergent in various countries, Omo, Persil, Presto, Via, Skip and All, have been maintained because to change them the company fears it would lose customers. Recently Unilever has gone further. Recognizing that its family of brands differ so much from market to market the company has decided to focus on a small number of its more successful brands worldwide such as Dove, a soap sold in 75 countries. The costs of supporting its long list of weaker brands were eroding margins at an alarming rate. Packaging is, however, standardized so that travellers from one country to another would recognize the familiar shape and colour and hopefully remain loyal.

In some cases brand names translate so badly that they must be changed less they convey wrong meanings or cause offence. These pitfalls should be avoided but since they have been so well noted in the popular trade press and have become anecdotal and part of folklore they need not detain us further.

Figure 11.4
Baileys brand
development in
international
markets

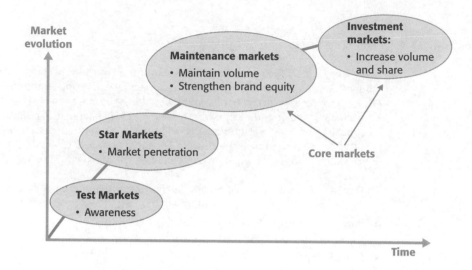

International brand life cycles

In Chapter 8 the issue of product category life cycle and its evolution was discussed. Turning now to the issue of brands and taking the Baileys brand as an illustration, we note that the position of the Baileys brand in each of the country clusters where it is sold shows how the brand evolves (Figure 11.4). Using the classification Test Markets, Star Markets and Core Markets it is possible to classify Hungary, Poland, Argentina, Venezuela, Columbia, the Philippines, Thailand and South Africa as test markets. In these countries the company's task is to create an awareness and test the brand proposition. In Norway, Sweden, Finland, Brazil, the Czech Republic and Korea, Baileys must attempt to penetrate the market, perhaps with an emphasis on heavy advertising and promotion. It continues to be necessary to recruit customers in these star markets.

Baileys has a number of core markets, some of which are maintenance markets while others are investment markets. In its key maintenance markets such as Australia, Belgium, Switzerland and Denmark, Baileys' marketing endeavours are focused on increasing consumption frequency and strengthening brand equities to maintain sales volumes. Lastly, in its investment markets such as the United States, the United Kingdom, Germany and Spain, the objective is to increase volume by increasing frequency and encouraging consumers to increase the occasions in which the brand is used. In these markets Baileys is engaged in changing the positioning of the brand from being a traditional special occasions spirit to being a mainstream spirit drink with an emphasis on pleasure for all sociable occasions. By moving from an occasional treat to a mainstream spirit beverage, sales volume increases and younger consumers are recruited thereby providing a cross-cultural loyal customer base.

By following this approach to the analysis of the Baileys brand it may be noted that there are country markets in different geographic areas that are similar in terms of the required marketing strategy. For illustrative purposes only, the likely category and brand position for each type of market are shown below (Figure 11.5). Using this brand-building framework, developed by Quelch (1999), it would be possible to notionally calculate country indices both for the development of the product category

Figure 11.5
Brand-building
objectives by
country

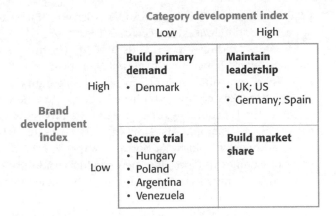

Source: adapted from Quelch, J. (1999) 'Global brands: taking stock', *Business Strategy Review*,
10 (1), p. 8

and the development of the brand itself. For illustrative purposes, countries are shown
in relation to the development of the cream liqueur category and the Baileys brand.
Different marketing strategies would be appropriate for each of these positions; the
appropriate approach to securing trial is very different from that required to build
primary demand, build share or maintain leadership.

Brand extensions in international markets

An effective way of internationalizing the company is to leverage product or corporate
brands through appropriate brand extensions. Brand extensions are new product introductions in which an existing corporate or brand name is applied to a new product
category. Brand extensions allow the company to reduce the marketing communication costs involved in building new equity or images for their products. Besides changing the product, R&A Bailey, owners of Baileys Original Irish Cream, developed very
sophisticated packaging for its 'Baileys Gold' – a brand extension containing 12-year-
old whiskey designed specifically for the Japanese market. Similarly, the same company developed 'Bailey's Light' – the 'Original' with half the amount of cream – for the
increasingly health-conscious US market.

Letting a product benefit from the competitive advantage of an established product
but using a variation of the marketing programme is a very popular approach for large
consumer products companies. The car and soft drinks industries are good examples.
Mercedes-Benz carries with it a very different connotation to Fiat or Toyota. Perhaps
better known are the soft drinks umbrella brands used to include diet soft drinks. Some
successful firms have used brand extensions to bring a range of new products to the
market and to transfer the success of the portfolio from one market to another.

In extending the brand to international markets a communication issue arises as to
whether the company should focus on product-category factors or corporate factors. In
the former the company focuses on the fit between the new product being launched
abroad and existing products that are part of the same brand whereas in the latter
consumers' attention is drawn to characteristics of the company providing the new

product. Both product and company-driven strategies can be successful but there appear to be differences between countries.

When extending their brands abroad, US firms seem to rely primarily on the product-related benefits or images of their products whereas Japanese firms and other East Asian companies seem to focus on corporate equities (Han and Schmitt, 1997, p. 78). When extending established equity into new product categories, Procter & Gamble, the US company, does not use the Procter & Gamble name but relies on the equity of, for example, its Tide and Crest brands, whereas Sony, a Japanese company, and Lucky Goldstar, a Korean company, offer a variety of products under their corporate names and introduce new products under the corporate name.

Clearly what works well with regard to brand extensions in the US may not succeed elsewhere and vice versa. The Japanese cosmetic manufacturer, Shiseido, provides a good illustration of the principle. Shiseido was successful with diapers in Japan but not in the US since Japanese consumers perceived the remote extension to be of high quality because it was done by a large well-known cosmetics firm while US consumers only considered the extension's low fit with cosmetics (Han and Schmitt, 1997, pp. 88–9).

Companies thinking of using brand extensions in international markets should pay attention to the relative importance of product-related and company-related brand equity communication strategies in the foreign markets under consideration. Brand extensions in international markets usually involve:

- transferring a product benefit from the competitive advantage of an established product using a variation of the marketing programme; and

- using an umbrella brand to bring a range of new products to the market and to transfer the success from one market to another.

The Armani brand, already considerably extended, will be extended further to a Middle East hotel chain raising the prospect of over-extension as has occurred in the past with brands such as Gucci, Yves St Laurent, Christian Dior and Pierre Cardin (Exhibit 11.5).

Exhibit 11.5   Brand extension, with Jacuzzi

The Armani brand is already highly diversified, to be seen on spectacles, watches and other such goods. What is more, fans may dine at an Armani restaurant in Paris, New York or London, purchase chocolates at Armani *dolce*, flowers at Armani *fiore*, or even enjoy Milanese nightlife at the recently opened Armani nightclub. The luxury goods brand is set to venture into a $1 billion hotel deal with Dubai's Emaar Properties. Mr Armani will be charged with developing four resorts and ten hotels over the next six to eight years. It is not untrodden ground; Donatella Versace designed a hotel on Australia's Gold Coast. Italian jeweller Bulgari, and Marriott, are each investing $70 million in a hotel located behind Milan's La Scala.

To sustain the brand's luxurious image, hotels must be as upmarket as possible and small, to maintain exclusivity in keeping with the brand. Luxury and travel follow similar economic cycles, both adversely affected in recent years by SARS, the war in Iraq and a rise in the euro's value. For this reason, hotels don't offer the business stability to hedge against the fickle nature of the fashion world. Another danger is brand dilution as happened to Yves St Laurent, Christian Dior and Pierre Cardin as they licensed out their brands losing control over core brand values. While Armani's hotel management will be performed by outside professionals, they will be located in Milan rather than Dubai. Ultimately while the venture may prove expensive and challenging, it will certainly garner publicity for the luxury brand, and if managed correctly, according to Rita Clifton of Interbrand, a strong product combined with the experience of staying at a branded hotel will combine to make a super-strong brand.

Source: adapted from *The Economist*, 28 February 2004, p. 67.
The Economist © The Economist Newspaper Limited, London (28 February 2004)

Protecting the brand

Avoiding management traps

There are many pitfalls in international markets for the unwary consumer products firm. Packaging and labelling in foreign markets are particularly important decision areas, not only with regard to compliance with local regulations but also with regard to product enhancement, information and promotion. Some markets place greater value on packaging than others. Far eastern markets value the decorative value of packaging a great deal and even industrial products are packaged to a much greater extent in Japan than in other western-style markets, for example. Packaging is very important for consumer products because it provides the first impression which, if negative, can be very difficult to overcome later. A related area which gives rise to many problems is that of language and instructions. Examples of poor instructions or no translation of instructions in packaged products abound.

Attempting to enhance the product by providing meaningless information is pointless, as was demonstrated by Volvo in Germany and the United States, where the firm found that the projection of 'Swedishness' and Swedish engineering did not help sales as the claims did not mean much to consumers in these markets. Similarly, the preparation of detailed copy to advertise a consumer product in Germany may be wasteful as Germans are believed not to be avid readers of advertising copy.

After-sales service is another minefield of traps for the unwary firm in international markets. The intensity of this requirement may vary from market to market and product to product. The after-sales service function for consumer durable products in particular is crucial to the success of the firm in international markets and may be a legal requirement.

Counterfeiting and forgeries

Competitive advantage can easily be eroded in some international markets owing to counterfeits and forgeries. Counterfeiting means that another company uses the firm's competitive advantage to supply products to consumers at lower prices. It is a term frequently used generically to include a range of forged or faked products. Forgeries occur principally in luxury products with a high brand image and require a relatively simple production technology such as branded shirts, travel luggage, ladies' handbags, and watches. Familiar consumer product counterfeits include Gucci and Cartier watches, Louis Vuitton bags, Nike sports shoes and Sony consumer electronics. There are many others. Less familiar counterfeits include aircraft parts, chemicals, computers, drugs, fertilizers, pesticides, medical devices, hardware and food.

Deceptive counterfeiting occurs when buyers do not know that they are buying counterfeit goods, often the case in product categories such as automotive parts, consumer electronics and pharmaceuticals. Given that buyers are unaware the only way of dealing with this form of counterfeiting is confronting the providers of the fakes. The quality assurance element is missing from these products when sold as counterfeits which frequently can have unfortunate repercussions for the unwary user. In contrast buyers are often aware of the fake and willfully buy it, being well informed about the specific qualities of the original and the counterfeit. The active role of the buyer as an accomplice in this non-deceptive form of counterfeiting requires ways of addressing unethical consumer behaviour. Buying a fake product means obtaining the prestige of branded products without paying for it (Cordell *et al.*, 1996).

According to the International AntiCounterfeiting Coalition, US manufacturers lose €250 billion a year through trademark counterfeiting (*Financial Times*, Wednesday 7 August 2002, p. 4) while the International Chamber of Commerce estimates sales of counterfeit products at 8 per cent of total world trade (*Forbes*, 5 April 1999, pp. 48–50). The European Commission regards counterfeiting as more profitable and less risky than drug-trafficking (European Commission, 2000). The low price of counterfeits compared to the original appears to be the key determinant for their purchase. In buying a fake the buyer obtains a different set of benefits than with the original. The image dimension is usually preserved, as the copy physically resembles the original. The price differential is, however, much to the advantage of the counterfeit product.

Counterfeits usually occur only where the trademark holder receives relatively high margins, where the brand is international and where the competitive advantage reflects a worldwide interest in acquiring the best in the market, irrespective of origin. In such circumstances brand logos are easily recognizable. The strength of the counterfeited brand logo rather than quality, which is usually inferior, carries the fake. The trademark owner attempts to ensure that the exclusivity of the brand is preserved because that element of the marketing programme is likely to have become the firm's principal competitive advantage, even superior to the product quality attribute. Counterfeiting is big business and a serious problem for many countries, especially in the developed world, and for many brand companies in those countries. While China may be one of the biggest offenders regarding the manufacture of forged consumer products, rising income there may encourage local consumers to seek 'the real thing' (Exhibit 11.6). Traditionally countries such as China and other Asian countries such as Pakistan and Indonesia were responsible for the largest proportion of counterfeits; producing such fakes has spread to Eastern European countries like the Czech Republic and Turkey (European Commission 1998, 2000).

Exhibit 11.6   Psst! Wanna real Rolex?

China may be one of the biggest and best producers of fakes in the world, but their consumption of foreign luxury brands is on the up. Swiss watch exports are growing fast, reaching almost $150 million in 2003. According to Kevin Rollenhagen, head of Swatch's Omega operations in China and Hong Kong, Chinese are not natural consumers of fake goods, 'if they can afford the real thing'. Omega opened its flagship store in Beijing in January where a man's Speedmaster Broad Arrow retails for more than 100,000 yuan or $12,000, while nearby $80 would pay for a fake. Sales are growing at 15 per cent a year which places China in the brand's top ten markets. The issue is that, while in general fakes are in demand, such customers are not in Omega's target market; some 50 per cent of Omega's Hong Kong outlet sales are attributed to wealthy Chinese mainlanders who perceive that the watches display the owner's status despite the abundance of replicas.

Source: adapted from *The Economist*, 24 January 2004, pp. 61–2.
The Economist © The Economist Newspaper Limited, London (24 January 2004)

Brands in the grey market

The most common activity in the grey market arises when an individual or firm buys products from a foreign distributor where wholesale prices are low and then diverts them to lucrative high-priced markets such as the US or the EU, where domestic distributors who have paid a higher price are undersold. Product diversion to grey markets occurs when manufacturers offer very different wholesale prices to different customers in different international markets. This issue of the grey market is intimately linked with attempts by firms to standardize some aspects of branding but to ignore or neglect others such as price and distribution policies, which creates opportunities for re-importers.

Currently, the grey market for cars in Europe causes concern for those in the trade but it benefits the customer. Where currency fluctuations exist, as for example among the US dollar, the euro and the pound sterling, significant price differentials may occur on individual models from one country to another. Competition from grey market products forces regular distributors to lower prices, which benefits customers. It also forces manufacturers to hold down prices to dealers in order to keep them competitive with the grey market. Because most of the re-importers are legitimate the product manufacturers' only hope of stopping them is to block the so-called renegade dealers from selling to the grey market. As the EU welcomes the activity of re-importers, because they serve to integrate the European market and benefit customers, the manufacturers' only recourse is to remove the franchise if a contractual agreement prohibiting sales to re-importers has been broken.

Summary

Underlying this chapter is the view that markets throughout the world are at different stages of development leading to the conclusion that only versatile brands that can respond to buyer needs at different stages of the life cycle are likely to succeed. There are, however, many benefits to companies of brand building as a means of entering and competing in many international markets simultaneously. Many well-known international brands successfully communicate desired values in many culturally heterogeneous markets but it is not an easy task. Because tastes and preferences are different in different markets the management of the brand across markets becomes a significant issue for the international firm. The issue of standardization of the marketing programme across markets also becomes an issue and, frequently, companies accept the trade-off between branding scale economies and niche strategies.

The firm must ensure that featured attributes present it with a competitive advantage in every market in which it operates which becomes a constant struggle as such competitive advantage can erode as a result of competitor activity and poor brand management. Usually the firm must develop separate marketing programmes for its major international markets, although common elements may be found in a number of markets. Harmonizing brand strategies is a fundamental concern for the firm.

Building and maintaining international brands represents a very heavy investment in marketing. Companies sometimes develop umbrella brands to be used in launching new products into markets. There are a number of pitfalls in international marketing related to branded consumer products – problems associated with packaging, labelling and after-sales service. Increasingly, the firm must protect its brands from counterfeits, forgeries and developments in the grey market. Counterfeits have become an invidious problem for many branded consumer and industrial products companies.

Questions

1. What is branding and what are the key attributes of a good brand? Are there any special attributes required for international markets?

2. How do firms use brands to enter international markets?

3. Is there such a thing as a global brand? How would you recognize one? How do firms maintain such a brand? Describe the sources of brand advantage in the global brand.

4. How would you build and communicate brand values in international markets?

5. Protecting the brand from counterfeits and forgeries is becoming increasingly difficult as many buyers throughout the world seek them. Why do the suppliers of fakes engage in deception and why do buyers display unethical behaviour in acquiring such goods?

6. Show how you can set international brand-building objectives for the firm by combining an analysis of the product category and the brand.

References

Aaker, D. (1991) *Managing Brand Equity: Capitalizing on the Value of the Brand Name*, New York, NY: Free Press.

Bradley, F. (2001): 'Country-company interaction effects and supplier preferences among industrial buyers', *Industrial Marketing Management*, 30, 511–24.

Cordell, V. V., Wongtada, N. and Kieschnick, R. L. J. (1996): 'Counterfeit purchase intentions: role of lawfulness attitudes and product traits as determinants', *Journal of Business Research*, 35, pp. 41–53.

Erickson, G., Jacobson, R. and Johansson, J. (1992) 'Competition for market share in the presence of straegic invisible assets', *International Journal of Research in Marketing*, 9 (1), 23–37.

European Commission (1998) *Combating Counterfeiting and Piracy in the Single Market* (Green Paper), Brussels: European Commission.

European Commission (2000) 'Customs: unions demand action against rising problem of counterfeit goods', *Combating Counterfeiting and Piracy in the Single Market* (Green Paper), Brussels: European Commission.

Han, J. K. and Schmitt, B. H. (1997) 'Product-category dynamics and corporate identity in brand extensions: a comparison of Hong Kong and US consumers', *Journal of International Marketing*, 5 (1), 77–92.

Kim, C. K. and Chung, J. Y. (1997) 'Brand popularity, country image and market share: an empirical study', *Journal of International Business Studies*, 28 (2), 361–86.

Quelch, J. (1999) 'Global brands: taking stock', *Business Strategy Review*, 10 (1), 1–14.

12 Selecting international markets

This chapter describes the various factors the firm must consider when selecting international markets to enter for the first time. Generic, strategic and operational approaches to segmenting international markets are identified and the mechanics of selecting international markets are specified. A market selection process based on two approaches is elaborated: the opportunistic approach and the systematic approach. Some firms start in the opportunistic mode and gradually shift to a more systematic approach. From time to time the international firm must review its product portfolio to ensure that it is not overinvesting or underinvesting in any of its international markets. A technique for evaluating the firm's international product-market portfolio is elaborated. After studying this chapter students should be able to:

- list and evaluate the factors that influence the international market selection process for different types of firm;
- evaluate generic and strategic approaches to segmenting international markets;
- describe the different ways companies become aware of international market opportunities;
- discuss the importance of information in analyzing markets and how this information is obtained;
- discuss the most common forms of international market-selection strategies;
- elaborate a framework for evaluating the firm's product-market portfolio.

International market selection process

The wrong choice of market is a frequent source of two types of cost: the actual cost of unsuccessfully attempting to enter the wrong market and the associated opportunity costs, i.e. the missed opportunities of entering markets where the product might have been successful. Choosing the right markets and the right sequence of entry is an integral part of international competitive strategy. Successful firms tend to operate in a balanced portfolio of markets, grouping markets according to their similarity, having a deliberate policy of concentrating or diversifying marketing efforts depending on circumstances and sequencing market entry to ensure optimum international competitive advantage. In designing the portfolio of markets a multicriteria approach to screening, identifying and selecting potential international markets may be necessary.

Segmenting international markets

International market segmentation involves seeking a balance in applying too many of the various segmentation criteria which are available as that can result in too great a number of segments for the company to manage. This is especially true if the company serves a number of international markets. In such circumstances the company attempts to aggregate customer dimensions into useful categories for the purpose of segmentation.

Market segmentation means dividing the market into customer groups who might merit separate marketing mixes reflecting different product benefits. Decisions regarding three factors assist in the segmentation process: those which relate to the technology embodied in the product, the customer segment served and the function performed (Figure 12.1). The level of sophistication in a country affects the propensity to accept new technologies and reject others while common segments across different country markets allow the firm to standardize its products and in situations where warranted customization may be appropriate. Frequently the function for which a product is used varies in different markets requiring the company to adapt accordingly. For example, in some countries of Latin America, Nestlé has adapted a porridge like food as a drink to serve a particular function in some countries but with a different set of enzymes is more similar to a traditional breakfast cereal in others.

Figure 12.1
Segmenting
international
markets

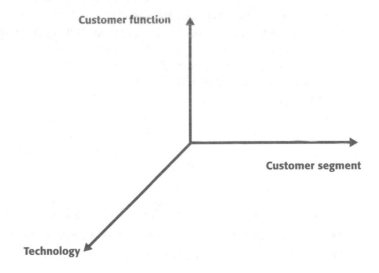

Generic market segmentation

Three generic market segmentation strategies have been identified which may be applied to international markets: an undifferentiated strategy, a differentiated strategy and a concentrated strategy. Companies sometimes make no effort to segment the market or the company does not recognize that the market is capable of being segmented. A firm following an undifferentiated strategy gives no recognition to market segments but rather focuses on what is common to all customers in the market, e.g. Coca-Cola. Products and services in such firms are designed and developed to suit the broadest possible customer appeals. The advantages of such a strategy are that it minimizes certain costs and helps to concentrate the attention of the competition in one or two areas of the market; assuming that competitors develop a wide-angle focus across a broad front but will select points where they are strong and the company is vulnerable.

According to Young *et al.* (1978) there are three sets of circumstances when it is inappropriate to attempt to segment the market as it is unlikely to provide any benefits:

1. the market is so small that marketing to a portion of it is not profitable;
2. heavy users constitute such a large proportion of sales volume that they are the only relevant target; and
3. the brand is the dominant brand in the market.

In relation to the market size, in some product categories the frequency of usage is so low that the market can only sustain one of the brands. Because such a brand must appeal to all segments, decisions on product positioning, advertising, distribution and pricing are based on an analysis of the entire market. When heavy users dominate the market for a product, conventional market segmentation is meaningless since most of the marketing effort will be directed at that group. If the heavy user group itself is large other segmentation criteria may, however, be applied. Lastly, when the brand is dominant it draws its customers from all segments. In such circumstances targeting a selection of segments may reduce instead of increase sales.

A differentiated strategy in contrast means operating in two or more segments using separate marketing strategies in each segment. A differentiated approach can have the effect of enlarging the size of the total market but costs are increased.

A concentrated strategy means identifying the various market segments that exist but operating in one segment only. Companies following such a strategy often attempt to seek dominance through specialization, e.g. Alfa-Laval in ultra-filtration. The key advantages of a concentrated strategy are that the company may be able to obtain specialization economies. The risks associated with such a strategy are usually greater.

Successful segmentation is related to company resources, the type of product, the stage in the life cycle, the degree of homogeneity among buyers and the strategies followed by competitors. The value of segmented markets increases if a number of conditions are present:

- the company possesses information on a relevant buyer characteristic;
- marketing efforts can be effectively focused on the chosen segments; and
- segments are large, profitable and stable.

Strategic country groups

Strategic approaches to grouping international markets raise a different set of problems. An appropriate system of classifying or grouping markets is an important aspect in clarifying a firm's understanding of its international operations. The grouping principle may also direct the selection of markets. Prior to a discussion of the possible relationship between market groups and market selection, it is necessary to consider the various techniques for classifying or grouping countries.

There are three reasons why it is important to identify appropriate macro variables to segment international markets:

■ international markets vary from each other with regard to their level of sophistication;

■ separating countries into different categories allows the firm to customize its marketing strategies; and

■ it may be possible to use a consistent umbrella strategy or positioning across a number of markets.

Geographic market segmentation

One of the simpler management approaches to market segmentation is to treat different geographic regions or countries as different market segments. This approach is very common in large market areas such as the United States or European Union. At a very general level some EU markets may be treated as similar based on language, geographic proximity and level of development.

The value of this approach depends on the existence of regional disparities in tastes or usage or some other important criterion. Usually there is a market variation in consumption patterns but this is not always the case. In some markets, especially markets like the US, mass media, transportation and multiple production locations have substantially eroded many of these differences based on geographic factors.

A segmentation approach based on geographical groups and the groupings of countries on the basis of trading patterns has a number of attractions. Trading pattern groups would include the former Eastern Bloc countries, the EU, the dollar markets of North and South America and the Pacific and the pound sterling areas. Such an approach leads to the concept of zones of influence and the marketing consequences which arise as a result of such groups. Basing market segmentation on country trading patterns is, however, much too crude an approach for most companies. In using macro variables to segment international markets it is essential for the firm to link market segmentation to market selection. In advocating an approach based on a geographical form of segmentation, Liander *et al.* (1967) provide a link between market grouping and market selection that is dependent on:

■ the levels of economic development;

■ political and cultural factors;

■ size of the firm's business in a country;

■ the firm's ownership or distribution pattern in a country;

- sales growth potential in the country; or
- the stage of development of the target market.

By following this approach the company can cluster country markets according to similarities in regard to their level of development or group them using a geographic criterion. Cluster analysis classifies countries into groups depending on their level of development. This technique emphasizes the degree of similarity between markets based on the number of attributes they share. In using this approach, a company proceeds to select markets as follows:

- assess the 'fit' between its products and each of the clusters and select the most promising cluster;
- select the most promising country from that cluster and, assuming favourable results from on-site research, introduce the product;
- in deciding to enter additional countries, select from the same cluster before moving on to another.

The second approach is similar to the first, except that countries are grouped by geographic location instead of by degree of development. The underlying assumption in this case is that countries of the same region display similar characteristics, e.g. culture, religion. As with the preceding approach, a company proceeds by:

- selecting a region; then
- a development level; and then
- a country within it.

In future market entries, the firm would first consider those within the same development level as the preceding country and then those at different levels of development within the same region.

Cultural market segmentation

The existence of local differences based on ethnic and cultural factors also presents the possibility of successful geographic segmentation. Culture may hinder or promote international marketing endeavours. In countries populated by heterogeneous cultures the firm's activities may be hindered. To measure this effect it may be possible to examine the size of the largest language group and the size of the largest religious group to provide an indication of the cultural impact. The market is likely to be more accessible the larger these groups.

Differences due to cultural and business distance reduce the level of commitment firms display to distant markets (Gatignon and Anderson, 1986). Countries or markets which are of close business distance are those which are politically stable, economically well-developed, culturally homogeneous and similar and provide many market opportunities but have few legal and trade barriers. Such markets are typically close geographically and the cultural disparities and problems of communication resulting from differences in social perspectives, attitudes and language do not constitute impediments to business. The more distant the market in terms of business distance the more likely is the firm to adopt an opportunistic exporting mode of market entry and the less likely it is to invest in these markets. Risk and lack of knowledge of such markets help to augment the business distance involved.

Country segmentation variables

The guiding principle in choosing from among country characteristics is their performance as measures of effective demand in various countries and the ease of market accessibility (Figure 12.2). The factors that appear to have the strongest effect on demand are cultural and social structure, level of economic development and degree of technical sophistication. Culture is acknowledged as a latent determinant of consumer behaviour in different countries but, because it is difficult to define and measure cultural characteristics, it is used in combination with other variables. Proxy variables are used – social structure of the society, education, living standards. Measures of economic progress or development are associated with rising incomes, industrialization, changing trade patterns and the accumulation of physical and human capital. Using GNP for industrial products and population for consumer products frequently proves ineffective, but trade data, energy consumption and production, and monetary variables have a strong explanatory power in measuring import demand for industrial goods. Different measures of income and stability of the currency are very important in explaining the import demand for consumer products.

Given the wide range of possible variables which are used to segment international markets, it is difficult for the manager to choose which are the more appropriate. As a result, a large set of variables are often used in an attempt to avoid making mistakes. Often there is no need to use a large set of variables – in most cases, a smaller set can be used, thus simplifying and reducing the costs of data collection.

In addition to estimating the effective demand for the firm's products in a country it is also necessary to examine a number of other variables that may determine the success of a particular segmentation strategy. In particular, the extent to which a country can be served as a whole and the level of demand concentrated in a small number of regions, rather than spread across a large number of small regions, must be considered.

Figure 12.2
International market development priorities

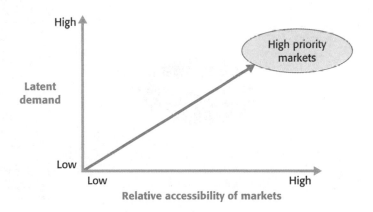

Measures of demand concentration include the number of large urban centres and the size of the largest city relative to the population of the country. In this regard companies often treat the United States as a series of regional markets with many separate urban clusters. China should be treated similarily because of the disperse population.

The level of economic development in the country is also a factor to be considered. Countries with high incomes tend to have better distribution and marketing infrastructure and communications which allows dispersed demand to be satisfied efficiently. In this regard the United States scores highly but other large countries such as China would not.

Many small emerging markets that have not developed sophisticated economic protection regimes may be open to foreign firms whereas some large countries such as Japan have well-developed protection rules and may be less open. A separate consideration arises in markets that are open but buyers prefer local products.

Mechanics of international market selection

An awareness of specific international market opportunities arises in two ways. In the first, certain stimuli bring a foreign market opportunity to the attention of the firm and it responds by entering the market; it may be said to choose its market opportunistically. The search and market identification are random or casual. In the second, awareness of specific market opportunities results from a systematic comparison of prospective markets and the firm expands by entering the market; this approach to market selection is termed 'systematic'. Frequently companies start with an opportunistic approach which on refinement and testing evolves into a systematic approach.

Opportunistic selection of international markets

Opportunistic selection of international markets is based on the receipt of an unsolicited order or enquiry for the company's product (Figure 12.3). Often the contact

Figure 12.3
Opportunistic
identification of
international
markets

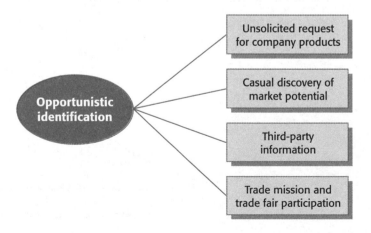

arises from idea diffusion whereby the idea of the product or service becomes known to a potential customer abroad who has no direct knowledge of the company's activities but is somehow motivated to make an unsolicited enquiry. Alternatively it may be the result of casual discovery of market potential by managers visiting foreign markets for some other reason, e.g. a holiday or attendance at a business meeting or conference. Sometimes market intelligence provided by third parties such as managers of non-competing firms or information supplied by government export promotion agencies may be the trigger to opportunistic identification of markets. Lastly, trade fairs and trade missions, while they may be part of a strategic plan, are often used in opportunistic ways, especially by the less experienced firm.

The firm's response to an international market opportunity is governed by a number of factors. The degree to which the company is affected by foreign country legislation, tariff and non-tariff barriers, health regulations or industrial standards is likely to influence its reaction. These barriers are beginning to fall, however, under pressure from the World Trade Organization. The extent to which a company is sensitive to competitive pressure may influence its reaction to foreign market opportunities that come to its attention.

The value to the company of adequate distribution in a foreign market may also influence its reaction to market opportunities. A company may be required to adapt its product to different tastes in each foreign market. In this regard it is quite possible that the company will react more favourably to market opportunities which need a minimal degree of product adaptation. While the selection of markets in an opportunistic way may occasionally produce positive outcomes, a dependence on the approach may be costly (Attiyeh and Wenner, 1981). Five hidden cost 'traps' associated with the opportunistic approach may be identified:

■ providing excessive production capacity for opportunistic business;

■ agreeing initial design and engineering costs to obtain the first order;

■ the additional costs stemming from low initial production efficiency, and repeat orders which do not materialize;

■ the cost of unsuccessful bidding for opportunistic business; and

■ the dissipation of the company's efforts that may result from constantly pursuing opportunistic business abroad.

For these reasons it is generally advisable to avoid such an opportunistic approach to the selection of international markets.

Systematic selection of international markets

Instead of merely responding to foreign market opportunities as they arise, the company may adopt a logical systematic procedure for market selection (Figure 12.4). In evaluating alternative international markets and customer segments within these markets the firm assesses its own strengths and weaknesses relative to those of its competitors, and it also considers market opportunities and threats. Following the broad framework provided above, this analysis leads the firm to the selection of target

Figure 12.4
Systematic
approach to
international
market selection

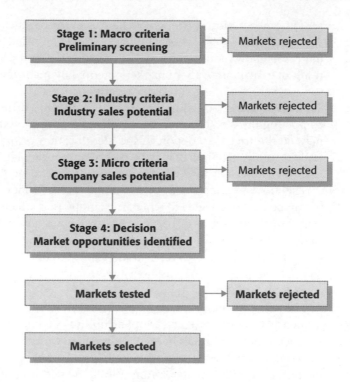

countries and to an evaluation of segments within those countries. A systematic way of proceeding further, emphasizing such evaluation and business strengths, segment by segment within each target country, is needed. By using the basic principles of segmentation analysis it is possible to proceed from country selection to customer selection. In the more systematic approach, therefore, the firm establishes criteria for:

■ market selection;
■ researching market potential;
■ classifying markets according to the agreed criteria; and
■ selecting markets which should be considered immediately and those suitable for later development.

The purpose of preliminary screening of markets in Stage 1 is to identify country markets whose potential size may warrant further investigation. In the preliminary screening stage the firm tries to minimize two errors: that of ignoring countries that offer good prospects for the firm's products and that of spending too much time investigating countries that are poor prospects. Preliminary screening thus requires a 'quick fix' on the market potential for the company's products in many countries. The criteria used in preliminary screening are, therefore, quite broad in their nature and include quantitative economic and social statistics, which should be readily available for most countries and be comparable across countries. These economic and social statistics cover areas such as GNP, GNP growth, income per capita, private consumption and population in each foreign market. These data are sometimes provided for regions and areas within countries, which is very useful.

The criteria that should be applied to preliminary screening may be found under three major headings:

1. Physical and geographical features of the market
   a. physical distance of each market from the home country
   b. climate in each market

   Measures: quantitative economic and social statistics, including GNP, income per capita, private consumption and similar measures.

2. Population statistics including total population figures
   a. geographical concentration and distribution by age group
   b. the number of males and females
   c. level of literacy

   Measures: indicators of the quality, concentration, current responsiveness of the market and its future growth potential.

3. Local economic conditions
   a. a large population may represent little potential if income per capita is extremely low

   Measures: wealth and purchasing power of potential foreign markets, e.g. the number of cars owned per family and the number of homes with Internet access.

Also related to local economic conditions is the financial well-being of a country and the consequent adverse movements in exchange rates. This may be an overriding factor when considering its possibilities as an export market since if the country cannot pay for its imports then business cannot be done under normal circumstances. Other modes of entry such as foreign direct investment, licensing or countertrade may have to be considered if entry is otherwise desirable.

Industry market potential

In Stage 2 of the systematic market selection process the firm examines the total potential for the product category in each promising market. This may be defined as the 'industry market potential' and involves an examination of the most probable total sales of a product by all sellers in a designated country over a strategic planning period. The markets with the most promising industry market potential should be examined to see whether the firm could gain a share of that potential in each case. This fine distinction is important, as it is clearly a waste of time and money for the firm to investigate how it will gain access to a market if there is no market for its product category in the first instance. For this reason the R&A Bailey and Company Ltd ignored all markets with any restriction on alcohol when first considering the market for Baileys Original Irish Cream.

There are several criteria by which the industry market potential may be examined:

■ imports of the product category;

■ consumption or sales of the product category;

■ product category sales forecasts;

■ consumer trends, social habits, local tastes and preferences.

In forecasting sales the firm must also take into account social habits, local tastes and preferences and consumer trends in the market. Because of a possible historical bias, it is important when using sales or apparent consumption data that managers estimate their likely values in the future or make the necessary adjustments for foreseeable changes in the quantities.

Social habits play an equally important part in determining the total sales potential of a product in each market. For example, in Italy the potential for DIY car maintenance products tends to be limited because the idea of asking a garage to care for the family car is firmly entrenched in the Italian mind. However, one should realize that such local tastes and preferences may be either short or long term because markets change continually.

Having identified countries with greatest total sales potential for the product category, the firm is then in a position to consider its own ability to gain a share of that potential in each case.

Company sales potential

During Stage 3 it is necessary to estimate the firm's sales potential. 'Company sales potential' is defined as the most probable sales that the firm's product in a designated country can attain over a strategic planning period. Company sales potential may also be viewed as its most probable share of a country's industry market potential. When investigating this, the company examines a number of factors:

■ local import legislation;

■ competition in prospective markets;

■ local market structure – competitive intensity;

■ distribution channel structure;

■ physical distance; and

■ language and cultural differences.

Local import legislation, which may take several forms such as prohibition on importing certain products, the imposition of high tariffs or legislation affecting the composition of a product, is among the more important which must be investigated. Competition in prospective markets is also a major concern. First, the firm must examine its own product in relation to those of its competitors in each market and decide whether it offers any real advantage. It is of little use trying to sell in a foreign market if the firm cannot offer the customer something which has some edge on the competition.

Distribution channel structure in each market also influences the company's sales potential. Here the company should concentrate on its ability to obtain adequate distribution in each foreign market and the degree to which it can match the distribution of the market leaders. The terms of distribution are also important, since it may be possible to improve them. If this is so, considerable success may be achieved.

Although it may have been considered initially in preliminary screening, the physical distance of each high industry market potential country from the home country may again be evaluated, albeit in greater detail. Here the firm may attempt to calculate transportation and other logistical costs to move the product from the home country to each of the foreign countries in question.

Language and cultural differences between the home country and each of the foreign markets may also be considered at this stage. For example, it may not be feasible for a telecommunications systems manufacturer to enter a small foreign market if all technical literature has to be translated specifically for that market.

At this stage of the process, the firm should be able to estimate its sales potential with some accuracy in a number of the most promising foreign markets. It should then be possible to place the most favoured markets in order of priority. The next set of questions is how many of these markets should be addressed, how to enter them and whether to do so simultaneously or in sequence.

Evolution from opportunistic to systematic market selection

In some situations market awareness initially involves an opportunistic approach to market selection. Rather than solely evaluating the specific market opportunity, however, the firm compares the opportunity to other markets not already entered. This comparison may resemble the systematic selection procedure already discussed. By following this approach the company which starts with an opportunistic approach may discover that it eventually evolves into a systematic evaluation procedure. Two factors influence the outcome of this analysis – the company's competitive resource position relative to the critical mass required to compete successfully in the market and the attractiveness of the markets under review. By combining the analysis of these two factors it is possible to develop a set of international market development priorities (Figure 12.5). This analysis suggests that firms whose competitive position is below the

Figure 12.5
Setting international market development priorities

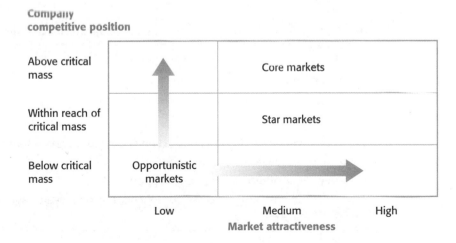

critical mass required to compete in selected international markets should treat such markets opportunistically no matter how attractive they are. Furthermore, an opportunistic approach is recommended for markets that are not attractive. Attractive markets in which the firm's competitive position is within reach of the critical mass required or above it should treat these markets in a systematic and strategic way, either to develop them or to maintain and expand them. Markets that are candidates for maintenance or expansion represent core strategic markets for the firm while markets that are candidates for development are star markets, hopefully, core markets of the future.

Role of information

Systematic market selection is essentially an evaluative process. It is now appropriate to consider the information sources which may be used in applying these criteria. The principal information sources available may be found under six headings (Table 12.1).

The use of management knowledge and experience accumulated within the firm is dependent on the product category and on the individuals involved in the market selection process; it can be important if the product category is specialized. Greater emphasis may be placed on management knowledge and experience in market evaluations where there is a lack of information from other sources. This emphasis, however, is influenced by a number of factors:

- amount of experience and knowledge possessed by managers;
- length of time they have worked in the product area;
- education and training; and
- degree of international exposure.

Some firms maintain extensive internal company databases relevant to key export markets while many others have access to commercially available computer-maintained databases which may be used as required.

Table 12.1 Information sources used in international market selection

Internal

- Knowledge and experience within the firm
- Company data

External

- Published reference materials, books, reports, business press, Internet
- Trade journals, magazines, newspapers
- Government or industry advisers and support services
- Trade associations, business clubs, consultants, market research agencies and market intelligence

Table 12.2 Research in international markets: approach to market surveys

- Measuring responses to exhibitions at local trade fairs, professional meetings and world trade centres
- Sampling of customer response by questioning (mailed, telephoned or face to face)
- Pre-testing the market via free samples
- Consulting local anthropologists and sociologists familiar with the area

---

Externally published reference publications on foreign markets are also available. The sources of information, such as country and industry status reports and trade intelligence, include central and commercial banks, chambers of commerce, embassies and consulates, trade associations and research institutes. Although externally published reference sources play a role in preliminary screening and in the estimation of industry market potential, they are less important in the firm's estimation of its own potential in each market.

Services provided by government- and industry-sponsored promotion agencies which are related to systematic market selection may be grouped under two headings: advice and facilities; support services. Under the first heading the agency may provide a firm with information and advice on many aspects of foreign markets, such as market size, patterns of demand, costs and prices, local standards, servicing requirements, purchasing and distribution methods, competition from domestic and other imported products and choice of representatives. Under the second heading the firm obtains market reports and surveys, profiles of foreign countries and other library facilities. Such support services would, therefore, have more in common with externally published reference sources than with direct contact with advisers.

Once management has satisfied itself that a relatively attractive demand exists for the company's products, that the firm can cope with the competitive conditions in the market and that the marketing costs are manageable, the next step is an on-the-spot survey. Various approaches for on-site market surveys have been used (Table 12.2).

Managing international product-market complexity

Segmenting markets also helps in managing the firm's product-market portfolio. Concentration on special segments may be a desirable strategy in particular circumstances. Whether because of resource constraints, company size or strategic focus, such concentration may result, for a number of reasons, in a reduction of product-market variety and management complexity. In developing international markets, successful companies frequently discover that initially they must provide a wide variety of products and product options to develop and maintain a customer base. Developing the product portfolio and customer base usually means that companies tend to expand into numerous markets over time or, at least, to accumulate a large number of customers. At some point it may be necessary to manage this variety, both on the product side and with regard to markets. One way of managing product-market variety is to

Figure 12.6
Complexity in
international
product-markets

Products / Markets	Core markets	Star markets	Marginal markets
Core products	Core product-markets		
Star products		Star product-markets	
Marginal products			Marginal product-markets

classify products and markets into three categories: core product-markets; star product-markets; and marginal product-markets (Figure 12.6). Core products are high turnover and high material value products, usually responsible for about 80 per cent of sales or profits but only about 20 per cent of the company's products. These products dominate the firm's portfolio. Star products are those that hold high future promise with the prospect of eventually reaching core status. Marginal products are low-cost, low-turnover products with a questionable future; these are unlikely to grow or be of much consequence for the firm.

In a similar way, it is possible to classify the firm's markets as core markets, markets which are indispensable to the company. The company and its customers experience a high degree of mutual dependence. Star markets are likely to contribute large profits in the future but now require investment. Marginal markets are never likely to be important to the company for whatever reason; returns are low and prospects for the future are low.

Most companies discover that they rarely recover the full costs of supplying marginal markets. It is a different matter, however, if marginal markets can be served with the same products as sold in core markets. In this way, it is possible for the firm to keep the extra costs of the added complexity due to excess product-market variety within manageable limits. By limiting market variety the company also benefits from the leaner product range which arises. This is achieved, not by reducing the number of products and introducing the risk of losing key markets, but by concentrating on core markets. The company supplies core markets with the products that are important in those markets, even if some of them are clearly marginal products for the supplier.

This type of analysis allows the company to judge the international product-market portfolio that maximizes its profits. In some cases, it may have to streamline its product-markets or even to discontinue some products or to withdraw from some markets.

Summary

The essence of international market selection involves the company becoming aware of international market opportunities and how best to structure them strategically. There are several influences on the international market selection process, some of which facilitate and others which hinder selection. Larger firms are more likely to be systematic in their selection of international markets. Companies dependent on international markets for a large proportion of their revenues are more likely to adopt a systematic approach. Company goals and the relative importance placed on them may influence selection by concentrating on a limited number of options. A systematic approach places emphasis on evaluating costs, competition, distribution and customer needs in prospective markets. Availability of information influences market selection.

The international firm must decide how to segment international markets. Three generic market segmentation strategies were identified which can be applied with good effect to international markets: an undifferentiated strategy; a differentiated strategy; and a concentration strategy. Two generic segmentation approaches are used: strategic country groups and cultural and geographic segmentation. Market choices may be linked or embedded in each other, which introduces the notion of sequencing the selection of international markets. Two principal forms of market sequence were identified: market diversification by which the firm carries out fast penetration into a number of markets and allocates limited resources to each; and market concentration by which the firm concentrates on a few markets and gradually expands; resources are allocated to a small number of markets initially. The mechanics of selecting international markets depends on the firm's choice among three approaches. In opportunistic market selection; market opportunities become known to the firm in a casual, unplanned way and should be pursued carefully. Systematic market selection means that the company becomes aware of opportunities as a result of exploring and evaluating many alternative markets; a more scientific approach to international market selection. Evolution from an opportunistic to a systematic approach, a possibility which often occurs in practice, allows the firm to obtain the best of both approaches.

In selecting international markets the firm must have access to various kinds of information: management knowledge and experience; internal company data; the Internet; trade journals and magazines and government agencies, industry-sponsored information agencies and marketing consultants.

Questions

1. Identify an appropriate set of criteria to be used in evaluating and comparing country markets in terms of opportunities.

2. In segmenting international markets traditional criteria include customer function, customer segment and the technology used but it is also important to segment on the basis of latent demand and market accessibility. Discuss.

3. Before the firm can take a decision to enter a specific foreign market there must be an awareness of opportunities in that market. How does the firm become aware of such opportunities?

4. What are the advantages and disadvantages of an opportunistic selection of international markets?

5. Outline and discuss the factors which influence the systematic selection of international markets. How is it possible to obtain the relevant information to carry out a systematic analysis of markets prior to selection?

6. How may the company set international market development priorities and manage complexity?

References

Attiyeh, R. J. and Wenner, D. L. (1981) 'Critical mass: key to export profits', *McKinsey Quarterly*, (Winter), 73–88.

Gatignon, H. and Anderson, E. (1986) 'Modes of entry: a transactions cost analysis and propositions', *Journal of International Business Studies*, **17** (Fall), 1–26.

Liander, B., Terpstra, V., Yoshino, M. Y. and Sherbini, A. A. (1967) *Comparative Analysis for International Marketing*, Boston, MA: Allyn and Bacon.

Young, S., Ott, L. and Feigin, B. (1978): 'Some practical considerations in market segmentation', *Journal of Marketing Research*, **15**, 405–12.

Part III Strategic challenge of international market entry

This part consists of four chapters each of which deals with a different aspect of entry into international markets. The simplest form of entry to foreign markets, exporting, is often seen as the preferred approach of the smaller firm. All firms active in international markets, at one time or other, become involved in exporting. These issues are considered in Chapter 13 Market entry – exporting. Many firms form partnership arrangements with other firms, usually in the host country, to enter foreign markets. Such partnerships may consist of marketing agreements, licensing, franchising or joint ventures. Entering international markets using these approaches is discussed in Chapter 14 Market entry – strategic alliances. Further commitment to foreign markets may be obtained by acquiring a firm in the host market or by investing in a new venture there. Entering foreign markets by investing is discussed in Chapter 15 Market entry – acquisition and direct investment. Because of the advantages and disadvantages of each approach and their suitability to different circumstances it is necessary to integrate the way firms select the mode of foreign market entry. By observing different sets of circumstances it is possible to develop a strategic approach to international market entry; this is presented in Chapter 16 Market entry – a strategic approach.

13 Market entry – exporting

Exporting is one of the quickest ways to enter a foreign market. For some firms it is also a very successful way of internationalizing. Often exporting is treated as a first step on the road to a deeper commitment to internationalization. Many firms, however, attempt to enter foreign markets through exporting but fail. Failure in international markets can be costly in terms of managerial and financial resources and the opportunities forgone. For these reasons, exporting as an entry strategy should be approached with care. Because of the impact on the balance of payments, governments frequently encourage and support exporting.

After studying this chapter students should be able to:

- list the set of factors that influence the firm's export decision;
- decide when exporting is the most attractive entry mode;
- acknowledge that exporting may be a step in the process of deeper commitment to internationalization;
- discuss the importance of managerial attitude to exporting;
- evaluate the costs associated with exporting;
- realise how pre exporting activities can influence the firm's initial exporting direction;
- recognize the relationship between export costing and export pricing.

Nature of exporting

Entering foreign markets through exporting

Besides being the quickest way, exporting is also the simplest way of entering a foreign market. The level of risk and commitment is minimized since investment of managerial and financial resources is relatively low compared with the other modes of foreign market entry. Exporting is often chosen as a means of entry when the following circumstances prevail:

225

- the firm is small and lacks the resources required for foreign joint ventures or international direct investment;
- substantial commitment is inadvisable owing to political risk, or uncertain or otherwise unattractive markets;
- there is no political or economic pressure to manufacture abroad.

From a macroeconomic viewpoint, exporting provides countries with foreign exchange, employment, opportunities for vertical integration of businesses and, with the resources obtained in international markets, a higher standard of living (Czinkota *et al.*, 1992). At the level of the firm itself, exporting may provide a competitive advantage, improve its financial position, increase the use of plant and equipment and improve the technology base in the firm (Terpstra and Sarathy, 1994). Generally, firms export for a number of reasons:

- geographic expansion;
- lower unit costs because of increased volumes; and
- the sale or disposal of surplus production abroad.

Unprocessed food products and commodities often fall into the last group. Apart from the disposal objective, exporting firms must consider the question of product adaptation and the adequacy of production facilities to meet increased demand and provide prompt delivery as already noted in Chapter 8. Occasionally it may be necessary to alter designs, which raises issues of technical and design features of the product, packaging, legal requirements, approval and certification and the cost of any modifications required. Lastly, the firm is concerned with sales and technical literature which may have to be made available in a number of languages, in metric and or Imperial measure, and aimed at the needs of local markets.

A matter of increasing concern to exporters is the availability of distribution and sales outlets for their products in export markets. The firm also considers standards and regulations, factors that can develop into non-tariff barriers, and the possibility of patent infringements. In summary, entering foreign markets through exporting is:

- the simplest way of entering foreign markets; risk and commitment minimized;
- ideal for firms with few resources or where resource commitment is inadvisable due to risk, uncertainty or unattractive markets; where
- objectives include geographic expansion, increased sales, lowering unit costs; and
- exporting is part of a continuum of market entry modes.

Exporting and commitment to internationalization

Exporting may be considered as part of a continuum of increasing commitment to internationalization. Being a very versatile mode of foreign market entry, firms frequently use it in conjunction with other entry modes (Figure 13.1). In direct selling the intensity of exporting activity is high but the level of risk and the degree of control is

Figure 13.1
Exporting is part
of a continuum

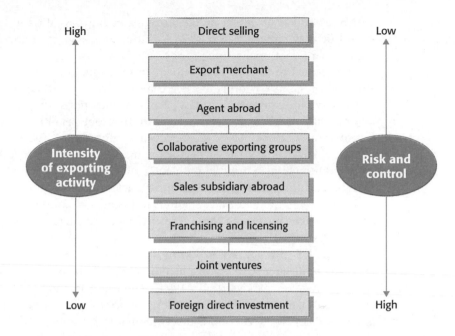

low. At the other end of the continuum, with foreign direct investment, for example, the level of exporting intensity is low while risk is high but so too is the ability to exert control. The greater the commitment the higher the risk but also the more control the firm has over its international operations.

Exporting may be found at the initial stages of internationalization and again at the more committed stages where the firm, having taken an equity position in a foreign market, decides to export from there to other third markets.

Determinants of export behaviour

The determinants of export behaviour are considered to emanate from three sets of influences on the firm: experience and uncertainty effects, behavioural and firm-specific influences and strategic influences.

Experience and uncertainty effects

Knowledge and learning with regard to exporting may be possessed by the firm and accumulated by it over time so that some firms become established exporters, while others with less knowledge of foreign markets have further to go in terms of learning. The necessary knowledge can be acquired mainly through operating abroad.

The key role of experience in export decision-making arises from observing that the firm's involvement in international markets is frequently a gradual process. This behaviour suggests a learning process as the firm adopts successively more complex export structures and as it enters markets of greater business distance over time. Indeed, exporting may be seen as a stage before strategic alliances and foreign production in the firm's internationalization process.

The gradual process of involvement in individual markets abroad may be understood as a response by firms to the greater uncertainty and ignorance which are associated with international business: 'Foreign operations are different from domestic and the difference is very much related to the problems of knowledge and the cost of information' (Carlson, 1975, p. 20). A firm beginning to export to a foreign market is not only likely to lack knowledge of the market itself but is also likely to encounter what has been termed 'frontier problems', which include potential problems involving both official procedures related to selling in a foreign market, e.g. customs regulations, and also foreign trade technical matters (Carlson, 1975, p. 7). The level of uncertainty and ignorance concerning these elements tends to increase the greater the business distance between the markets.

During the early stages of exporting, firms exhibit a more concentrated foreign market focus, while increased involvement in foreign markets encourages diversification to a wider range of markets (Dalli, 1994; Naidu and Prasad, 1994). Many factors may explain this behaviour. With expansion, the firm's resource base may increase (Naidu and Prasad, 1994). Furthermore, diversifying into a number of foreign markets reduces risks and exploits opportunities better than a concentrated strategy (Dalli, 1994). Also, the number of problems of managing a business in different foreign markets diminishes as the firm gains more export experience. With increased experience of foreign markets the firm is likely to commit more resources to the endeavour. Eventually this may mean establishing a special unit within the company to organize and manage exporting activities.

Acquiring knowledge of export markets

As a firm's knowledge of an export market increases, the uncertainty factor diminishes. The key type of knowledge required here, however, appears to be experiential knowledge, i.e. knowledge obtained through operating in the market or 'learning by doing' (Carlson, 1975, p. 8; Olson, 1975). It is this type of knowledge which, according to Johanson and Vahlne (1977, p. 28), gives a decision-maker a feel for the market and which allows the identification of concrete opportunities, as distinct from theoretical opportunities which may be apparent from objective or codifiable knowledge. The nature of objective knowledge is such that it can normally be acquired by, or transferred between, individuals relatively easily, e.g. operating manuals, but the acquisition of experiental knowledge is, by definition, a more gradual process.

This gradual acquisition of international experience suggests an explanation for the gradual involvement in foreign markets described above. Johanson and Vahlne (1977) have developed a link between these two processes:

■ as uncertainty is gradually reduced through experience the firm may be more willing to increase the level of its commitment; and

■ the nature of a firm's involvement will be gradual in the sense that it is likely to be an extension of the firm's existing activities in the market.

Export decision process

Behavioural and firm-specific influences

In general, traditional economic theories of trade have given way to more behaviourally oriented theories as explanations of export behaviour (Bilkey, 1978). Trade theories, while having a function at the national level of analysis, are inadequate at the individual firm level. More recent theories of exporting are strongly influenced by the behavioural theory of the firm, which stresses decision-maker characteristics, organizational dynamics and constraints, and ignorance and uncertainty as key variables in decision-making.

Exporting has been described as a developmental process based on a learning sequence involving stages (Bilkey and Tesar, 1977). Six learning stages are assumed by these authors (Table 13.1). The Bilkey and Tesar research is one of the few empirical attempts to take account of experience effects and other behavioural influences. The probability of the firm moving from one stage to the next depends on the firm's international orientation, on its perception of the attractiveness of exporting and on management's confidence of competing successfully abroad (Bilkey, 1978). In this framework unsolicited export orders and opportunistic business are critical to the firm becoming an experimental exporter. The movement between stages also depends on the quality and dynamism of management. Many small- and medium-sized enterprises wishing to become internationally traded companies seem to stall at the experimental exporter stage, Stage 4. Anything which lowers the perception of risk for the individual company and provides more favourable expectations of profit would encourage these firms. Usually elements of encouragement are treated as independent of one another and subsumed under the rubric of motivation, whereas there is good reason to believe that more complex interactions are involved, as discussed below. For the experienced exporter at Stage 5, the proportion of output sold abroad depends on the firm's expectations with respect to profits and growth of the firm.

The stages models of export development have been criticized on the grounds that they lack explanatory power and it is unclear how to predict movement from one stage to the next (Andersen, 1993, pp. 227–8). They provide, nevertheless, an intuitive

Table 13.1 Stages in internationalization

Stage 1:	No interest in exporting; the firm ignores unsolicited business
Stage 2:	Unsolicited business is fulfilled; the firm does not examine feasibility of active exporting
Stage 3:	Feasibility of exporting is actively examined
Stage 4:	Firm exports on experimental basis to country of close business distance
Stage 5:	Firm becomes an experienced exporter to that country
Stage 6:	Feasibility of exporting to additional countries of greater business distance is explored

Source: adapted from Bilkey, W. J. and Tesar, G. (1977) 'The export behaviour of smaller Wisconsin manufacturing firms', *Journal of International Business Studies*, **8** (2), 93–8

appreciation of the decision mechanism which cascades the firm forward toward internationalization. More important are the circumstances the firm must address at each stage in the process.

A number of export behaviour studies have suggested that direct stimuli, such as economic incentives and unsolicited orders, may be less important than internal behavioural influences in the firm. Four groups of variables internal to the firm (Cavusgil and Nevin, 1981) explain whether firms engage in exporting:

■ managerial expectations about the effects of exporting on the firm's growth;
■ the extent to which management systematically explores exporting possibilities and plans for exporting;
■ the presence of differential firm advantages, including firm size;
■ the strength of managerial aspirations towards growth and market security.

Model of the export decision process

A firm's pre-export activities influence the initial export step. Wiedersheim-Paul *et al.* (1978) suggest that a firm's domestic expansion pattern, i.e. whether the firm expanded interregionally or not, assuming a large domestic market such as Canada, Australia or the US, affects its likelihood of exporting. Firms which expand activities into regions outside their immediate area in the domestic market are more likely to export than firms which confine themselves to their home region.

Interregional expansion forces firms to develop skills in coping with uncertainty and in 'marketing a product at a distance' (Wiedersheim-Paul *et al.*, 1978, p. 51). The acquisition of these skills is more likely to predispose a firm toward exporting. A complex mix of factors and interactions among them produces a certain level of commitment to exporting.

According to Welch (1982), four groups of factors influence export commitment:

■ pre-export activities;
■ direct export stimuli;
■ latent influences on the firm; and
■ the role of the decision-maker.

A simplified version of Welch's model is shown in Figure 13.2. The pre-export activities of information search, questioning of customers and others with knowledge of the process and tentative experimentation such as attending trade fairs or visiting the market have a pronounced effect on subsequent exporting behaviour. Within this framework, there are a number of important feedback loops which integrate the framework. The decision-maker influences the nature of the pre-export activities carried out. The direct export stimuli also influence the decision-maker and there is an interaction between export stimuli and the latent influences on the firm.

Figure 13.2
Building
commitment
to exporting

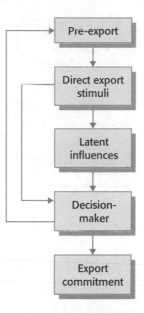

Source: adapted from Welch, L. (1982) 'Decision-making in the international context' in *Proceedings of the Seminar on Management Decision-Making*, European Institute for Advanced Studies in Management, Oslo, 1996, p. 96

Direct export stimull

Direct export stimuli may come from within the company itself as a result of evaluations carried out by management or they may derive externally from the market. Active exporters have higher profit perceptions concerning the effects of exporting and lower risk and cost perceptions than non-exporters (Simpson and Kujawa, 1974). The implication is that any direct stimulus, i.e. economic benefit, to exploit an export opportunity is likely to draw a different response from firms depending on their perceptions of exporting effects. Most companies attach limited importance to export stimuli relating to aspects of national export policy but the receipt of unsolicited orders from customers abroad is an important factor in stimulating export decisions (Katsikeas, 1996, p. 14).

Latent influences on export decisions

Latent influences on the process include the history of the firm and its background and experience. Firm characteristics such as its ability to innovate, its flexibility and its record for customer service are other important latent influences. The firm's actual and potential resource base can determine the company's commitment to entering new foreign markets. Similarly, the external environment must be considered. The importance of exchange rates, economic growth in the target market and accessibility should also be considered.

Figure 13.3
Influences
on the
internationalization
process

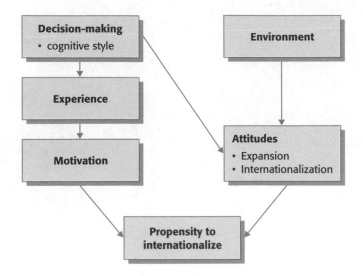

Export decision-maker

The role of the decision-maker is central to the export decision process. Decision-makers are people with different personalities who operate in different value systems, have formed different attitudes to international markets, have different cognitive styles and have different experiences on which to base their approach. Anything which lowers the perception of risk for the individual company and provides more favourable expectations of profit encourages firms to consider exporting. Usually elements of encouragement are treated as independent of one another and subsumed under the rubric of motivation. There is good reason to believe, however, that more complex interactions than motivation and attitude are involved. Decision-maker cognitive style and exporting experience are precursors of export motivation and cognitive style also influences attitudes. The propensity to export depends on a convergence of these influences (Figure 13.3).

A certain cognitive style or international orientation is a necessary prerequisite for the motivation to internationalize. Background influences identified in other studies include personality factors, which are believed to affect the firm's international orientation; 'A closed cognitive style reflected in the extent to which a manager is dogmatic about the international environment would seem to explain why potential exporters do not get started and are therefore not motivated to export' (Bradley, 1984, p. 253). The cognitive style of managers influences the experience the firm has when it does venture abroad. Open-minded managers are more likely to report a positive experience from tentative internationalization steps whereas, for closed-minded managers, the experience is more likely to be neutral or negative. The outcome of these experiences influences the firm's motivation to internationalize, which may be low or high. Many firms rely on third parties to take the initiative in developing export markets, which leads to low expectations and passive behaviour. The experience of international markets thus gained by the firm becomes an important determinant of international marketing behaviour. Presumably, successful experience has a positive effect on the internationalization process, whereas a poor performance has a negative effect (Bradley, 1987).

These factors are likely to affect the aspirations of management for goals such as growth, profits and market development. Aspiration levels are one of the determinants of risk-taking behaviour. The importance that the decision-maker places on the achievement of the firm's business objectives is believed to be a direct determinant. Empirical studies support this expectation by revealing a positive relationship between export marketing behaviour and the decision-maker's preference for certain business goals (Simmonds and Smith, 1968). Definite psychological motivational barriers to the internationalization process exist, which may be attributed to the absence of appropriate managerial aspirations.

A highly motivated firm with a positive attitude to growth is more likely to move from being a potential exporter to being a passive one to eventually being an active exporter, whereas a firm with low motivation and an indifferent attitude to company growth is likely to remain as a potential exporter or stall at the passive stage. The lack of advanced products in their portfolio was sufficient to stimulate the management of Tata Motors to acquire Daewoo Commercial Vehicle so that Tata could export to nearby markets and also sell a range of its existing products in South Korea (Exhibit 13.1).

Exhibit 13.1 Tata gains a foothold in heavy vehicle export market

When Tata Motors agreed to pay $100 million for Daewoo Commercial Vehicle, Ratan Tata, chairman of the Tata Group, one of India's largest conglomerates, said the acquisition provided a short cut to the advanced products Tata needed to compete with world-class manufacturers, especially in its export markets. 'We could have developed our own product range without Daewoo but it would have taken us longer and cost us more,' he said. 'We have 70 per cent market share in India but in other markets we don't have the products to compete with the likes of Volvo. Daewoo will give us a foothold in the export market.

Ratan Tata said the Middle East, South East Asia and China were among the markets the company planned to target following the acquisition. The deal also gives Tata a strong presence in South Korea, where Daewoo commands more than a quarter of the heavy truck market. 'We bought a profitable, debt-free company that is utilizing only 20–25 per cent of its capacity, so there is tremendous potential to grow,' said Mr Tata.

Source: adapted from Ward, A., 'Daewoo deal gives Tata SK foothold',
Financial Times, Thursday 8 April 2004, p. 28

Attitudes to firm growth and motivation to internationalize both determine the level of internationalization reached by the firm (Bradley, 1984). Attitude to company growth is influenced by the marketing environment, technology and the institutional environment. Attitudes are also influenced by the way managers think or by their cognitive styles, whether they are closed-minded or open-minded.

Size of firm and exporting activity

In many countries exporting is the preserve of the small firms. The key consideration is to what extent do smaller firms possess the critical mass, will and commitment required to enter and compete successfully in export markets. Research on small exporting companies in many countries shows this sector to be highly unstable. Only a fraction of small exporters become established. Many treat international markets opportunistically and some of these are soon forced out by competitive pressures. Small firms face the danger of too much, or not enough, success and they frequently overextend themselves. They also spread their managerial and financial resources too thinly across markets.

Advances in all forms of communication help the smaller firm. Improvements in telecommunications and international airfreight services permit them to internationalize much more easily than previously. Indeed, the role of the Internet has allowed many small firms access to customers in distant markets, once thought to be the preserve of large competitors; though great care must be paid to the actual approach adopted. Companies suddenly find that enquiries arrive from countries they wouldn't have ever considered as potential markets for their products and these opportunistic overseas enquiries often cause small firms to start exporting without proper preparation. Anecdotal evidence abounds of owner-managers rushing headlong into exporting without ever deciding how to deliver the goods or get paid for them and they often fail to agree terms and the currency of payment with customers. This approach is an obvious recipe for a disastrous financial outcome.

Small high-technology companies have been very successful in international markets. Specialized firms serving niche markets do not need to be big. Their strengths are built on knowledge, technology and customer service, not size. Indeed, many successful exporting firms tend to be high-technology firms, but this, of course, is by no means exclusively so.

Many factors appear to influence the decision to export and subsequent exporting activity. Size of the firm may be an influencing factor in some circumstances but is not the only factor, nor even the dominant influence in some situations. Size is not a significant influence on exporting for small- to medium-sized firms according to Czinkota and Johnston (1983) and Abdel-Malek (1978); other research results on the effect of size on a firm's propensity to export have been mixed (Bilkey, 1978, p. 36).

Export marketing groups

Frequently, firms form groups to counteract a common external threat such as increased import competition, entry by a new competitor or a new public policy that constrains their activities in some way. Size may also be a factor. Group marketing schemes are frequently found among small-scale firms attempting to enter export markets for the first time. Many such firms do not achieve sufficient scale economies in manufacturing or marketing because of the size of the local market, or the inadequacy of the management resources available. These characteristics are typical of traditional, mature, highly fragmented industries such as furniture, textiles, clothing and footwear but the principle also applies to high-technology firms.

Figure 13.4
Export
marketing
groups:
collaboration
and shared
interests

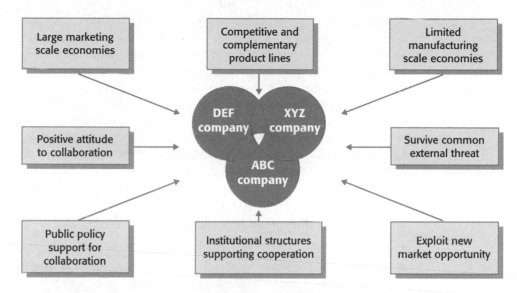

Source: adapted from Bradley, M. F. (1985) 'Market and internal organization in exporting for SMEs', *Developing Markets for New Products and Services Through Joint Exporting by Innovative SMEs Seminar*, Commission of the European Communities, Luxembourg, 6–7 March

There are many economic, institutional and behavioural reasons for collaboration among such firms (Figure 13.4). Small and medium enterprises working together learn a great deal about international markets, and the experience obtained serves to confirm these firms as established exporters. These groups are also formed to enter markets that are considered in some way to be 'difficult' and therefore require the critical mass of a number of firms operating jointly to ensure that successful entry is achieved. Collaborative endeavours may need institutional support especially from government export promotion agencies to ensure that the benefits accrue to small firms. Increasingly, small and medium enterprises become positively disposed towards export marketing groups when the benefits of such collaboration are apparent.

Other factors influencing the firm to join with others in such a group are the opportunities of effectively marketing a complementary product line, the presence of a positive attitude toward collaboration and the possibility of exploiting a new market opportunity. In forming groups firms try, as far as possible, to avoid competition arising within the group.

Lastly, and perhaps the central issue to be discussed in forming export marketing groups, is the matter of common or shared interest among the participating firms. Firms usually have different motivations for joining with others. Frequently, firms have conflicting views as to what the group should do and the area of common interest is thereby reduced. The size of the circles in Figure 13.4 attempts to indicate the extent of desire of three firms to participate in an export marketing group. In this situation the area of common interest, where the circles overlap, is smaller, indicating restricted scope for the formation of a group. Clearly, the fewer the shared interests the less likely is collaboration to occur.

In general, export marketing groups tend to be successful in situations where firms are already marketing oriented, financially strong and fully appreciate the benefits and limitations of the group structure (Bradley, 1985). Some of the problems associated with traditional export marketing groups may be avoided through the establishment of a jointly owned and managed sales company to serve the export markets of interest. Such a sales company, which would be owned in equal parts by a group of cooperating firms with complementary, but not competitive, products and services, would be established as an independent operation with profit-centre status. One of the major tasks of this company would be to balance the interests of the other stakeholders and adjudicate on contentious issues. A study of successful consortia suggests a number of guidelines for the creation and operation of a jointly owned sales company:

■ participant's products must be complementary;
■ products or services must be compatible in quality and technology;
■ for horizontally linked products, customer firms and, ideally, individual buyers should be the same for all members of the consortium; and
■ each participating consortium member should have one nominee on the board of the jointly owned sales company and have a single vote.

In regard to the first guideline the complementarity must be upstream and downstream if total packages are being offered and horizontally if a 'full-line' range is to be made available. The second guideline specifies that low-technology equipment, for instance, is unlikely to fit comfortably in a range of high-technology products. The essential ingredient is compatibility of corporate culture and, even more important, the compatibility of values among members of the board of the sales company.

Costs and competitiveness of exporting

Many firms new to exporting fail to realize that the cost of reaching the market can be formidable. A number of these costs are difficult to quantify but are nevertheless important. These include the cost of product modification and any packaging or labelling changes which have to be made and also the cost of researching the foreign market. The cost of obtaining customer and competitor information can be substantial.

At a more specific level the firm must estimate the cost of sending a consignment of a product to a foreign buyer. First there are the costs of extra people, e.g. an export executive or manager. It would be necessary to add the cost of travel based on a number of visits to the market in a year. Second, extra sales staff might be required to support the export manager. Third, it is necessary to allow for the cost of custom documentation, labels, samples and promotion. For some product groups these costs tend to be relatively high. Food marketing costs tend to be relatively high in foreign markets because of the cost of label changes, of complying with health regulations and of launching, including promotion through in-store tastings and price discounts.

By far the more important costs are those associated with the services provided by intermediaries such as distributors, wholesalers and retailers and agencies such as transport and insurance companies. Some of these costs are borne by the exporter while others are absorbed by the intermediaries and covered by their margins. In a study of the cost of exporting Australian wine to the United Kingdom, McDougall, (1989) estimates that the price received by the winery was less than one-third of the retail price. The single largest element in the cost was the retail margin, 33 per cent. This example illustrates the cost components that the exporting firm must consider. The information on the cost of the Australian wine was based on a cost plus approach to pricing, i.e. the final retail price was estimated based on identifying each cost element and accumulating them to find an estimated price at retail, a topic to which we return in Chapter 18.

In summary, when assessing export competitiveness the firm should consider the following cost factors:

■ cost of product modification, special packaging and labelling;

■ information costs – obtaining and interpreting relevant market based information;

■ payment – business practices, lapsed time between shipment and payment;

■ cash flow – significant for smaller firms particularly;

■ additional staff – export marketing and sales administration staff; and

■ services costs – distributor margins, agent commissions.

Summary

Exporting is the simplest and one of the quickest ways of entering a foreign market, requiring a low level of investment in terms of managerial and financial resources and consequently a low level of corporate commitment and risk. This makes it an ideal first step to internationalization for many firms and a useful strategy for firms in risky and uncertain markets. The export decision is influenced by three sets of influences on the firm: experience and uncertainty effects; behavioural and firm specific influences; and strategic influences on exporting. The firm's activities at the pre-export stage have an important influence on the firm's initial export direction. Several factors affect the firm's decision to internationalize: the degree of international orientation; the firm's previous experience; and managers' perceptions of risk and return. Government-sponsored export stimulation measures, product characteristics and unsolicited export orders also play an important role at the early stage of exporting.

Opinion among researchers and managers is divided on the issue of the relationship between firm size and export success. The importance of a positive managerial attitude to exporting and the necessity of committing managerial and financial resources to the internationalization process is crucial to the success of the firm, irrespective of size. The costs associated with exporting – market research, product adaptation, market visits, shipping and agency fees – have a strong influence on a firm's export activity; large firms may have an advantage over smaller firms. In assessing the cost of exporting and competitiveness, service, quality, design and product uniqueness must be considered.

Questions

1. Why is exporting frequently considered the simplest way of entering foreign markets and favoured by smaller firms?

2. Three sets of factors are believed to influence the firm's decision to export. Identify these factors and discuss their relative importance.

3. The behaviour and activity of the firm prior to exporting is thought to have a very great effect on the degree of success of the firm. How may the firm build commitment to exporting? Discuss.

4. Describe and explain the various influences on the internationalization process.

5. Size of firm is often cited as a barrier to successful exporting. It is argued that the firm must be large to succeed. Do you agree?

6. What is meant by export competitiveness? How might the firm determine its overall competitiveness in export markets?

7. What are the ideal conditions for collaboration in the formation of export marketing groups and why do they rarely occur?

References

Abdel-Malek, T. (1978) 'Export marketing orientation in small firms', *American Journal of Small Business*, 3, 24–35.

Andersen, O. (1993) 'On the internationalization process of firms: a critical analysis', *Journal of International Business Studies*, 24 (2), 209–31.

Bilkey, W. J. (1978) 'An attempted integration of the literature on the export behaviour of firms', *Journal of International Business Studies*, 9 (1), 33–46.

Bilkey, W. J. and Tesar, G. (1977) 'The export behaviour of smaller Wisconsin manufacturing firms', *Journal of International Business Studies*, 8 (2), 93–8.

Bradley, M. F. (1984) 'Effect of cognitive style, and attitude toward growth and motivation on the internationalization of the firm', in J. Sheth, Ed., *Research in Marketing*, Vol. 7, Greenwich, CT: JAI Press, pp. 237–59.

Bradley, M. F. (1985) 'Market and internal organization in exporting for SMEs', *Developing Markets for New Products and Services Through Joint Exporting by Innovative SMEs Seminar*, Commission of the European Communities, Luxembourg, 6–7 March.

Bradley, M. F. (1987) 'Nature and significance of international marketing: a review', *Journal of Business Research*, 15, 205–19.

Carlson, S. (1975) 'How foreign is foreign trade?', *Acta Universitatis Upsaliensis, Studia Oeconomiae Negotiorum II*, Uppsala, Sweden, Bulletin No. 15.

Cavusgil, S. T. and Nevin, J. R. (1981) 'Internal determinants of export marketing behaviour – an empirical investigation', *Journal of Marketing Research*, 18, 114–19.

Czinkota, M. and Johnston, W. J. (1983) 'Exporting: does sales volume make a difference?', *Journal of International Business Studies*, 14 (1), 147–53.

Czinkota, M. R., Rivoli, P. and Ronkainen, I. A. (1992) *International Business*, 2nd edn, Fort Worth, TX: Dryden.

Dalli, D. (1994) 'The exporting process: the evolution of small- and medium-sized firms toward internationalization' in C. N. Axinn, Ed., *Advances in International Marketing*, Vol. 6, Greenwich, CT: JAI Press, pp. 85–110.

Johanson, J. and Vahlne, J. E. (1977) 'The internationalization process of the firm – a model of knowledge development and increasing foreign market commitments', *Journal of International Business Studies*, **8** (1), 23–32.

Katsikeas, C. S. (1996) 'Ongoing export motivation: differences between regular and sporadic exporters', *International Marketing Review*, **13** (2), 4–19.

McDougall, G. (1989) 'Barossa Winery: penetrating the international market', *International Marketing*, **6** (2), 18–33.

Naidu, G. M. and Prasad, V. K. (1994) 'Predictors of export strategy and performance of small- and medium-sized firms', *Journal of Business Research*, **27**, 85–101.

Olson, H. C. (1975) 'Studies in export promotion. Attempts to evaluate export measures for the Swedish textile and clothing industries', *Research Paper*, University of Uppsala.

Simmonds, K. and Smith, H. (1968) 'The first export order: a marketing innovation', *British Journal of Marketing*, **2**, 93–100.

Simpson, C. and Kujawa, D. (1974) 'The export decision process: an empirical enquiry', *Journal of International Business Studies*, **5**, 107–17.

Terpstra, V. and Sarathy, R. (1994) *International Marketing*, 6th edn, Fort Worth, TX: Dryden.

Welch, L. (1982) 'Decision-making in the international context', in *Proceedings of the Seminar on Management Decision-Making*, Oslo: European Institute for Advanced Studies in Management, June.

Wiedersheim-Paul, F., Olson, H. C. and Welch, L. S. (1978) 'Pre-export activity: the first step in internationalization', *Journal of International Business Studies*, **9** (1), 47–58.

14 Market entry – strategic alliances

Various types of interfirm strategic alliances are used by firms to enter and compete in international markets. They form part of a continuum of foreign market entry methods. The first section in this chapter discusses the underlying philosophy of strategic alliances. Subsequent sections examine marketing partnership agreements, followed by sections on licensing, franchising and joint ventures. Most attention is given to the section which deals with joint ventures and ways of evaluating and controlling them in international markets.

After studying this chapter students should be able to:

- outline the main reasons for using strategic alliances;
- discuss the different alliance options available;
- understand the logic behind marketing cooperation agreements;
- evaluate the prerequisites for successful licensing;
- specify the risks, advantages and disadvantages involved in strategic alliances;
- develop a set of criteria for selecting a partner and determine how to choose a suitable partner.

Nature of strategic alliances

Strategic alliances allow firms to procure assets, and capabilities that are not readily available in competitive factor markets. A joint venture to gain access to complex technological or product development capabilities is an example as are intangible assets, such as reputation or brands (Oliver, 1997, p. 707). A global alliance formed with a local host to enhance the firm's reputation in the local market illustrates this point. As a mode of international market entry, strategic alliances allow:

- the firm access to assets not readily available in the market;
- access to technology, products and markets;

■ synergistic effects in the partner firms by combining technological and marketing advantages accruing to both.

Basis for a strategic alliance

Firms may form an alliance to compete in international markets based on the exchange of a range of assets. Product-market knowledge is such an asset. The basis for a strategic alliance usually involves a combination of the following assets:

■ product-market knowledge;

■ access to markets and distribution;

■ product and process know-how;

■ production capacity;

■ unique management resources.

These are assets possessed by some firms and sought by others, thereby giving rise to the possibility of a strategic alliance (Figure 14.1). In a marketing partnership, Company A in the home country possesses product and market knowledge and seeks to gain international market access and distribution for its product and process know-how by forming a strategic alliance with Company B, the international partner, located abroad, who possesses product and market know-how but needs a new product or technology to compete in the host country. Similarly, product and process know-how,

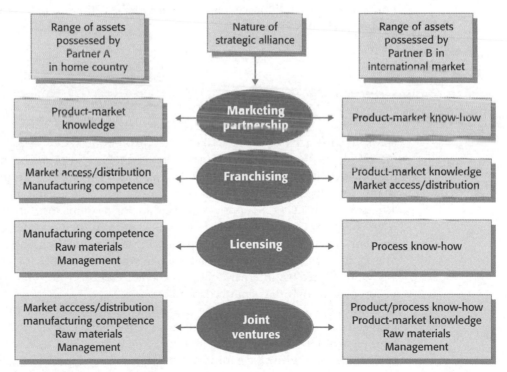

Figure 14.1
Complementarity in strategic alliances

spare manufacturing capacity, scarce raw materials and unique management resources may form the basis of a strategic alliance. In all cases Company B is located in the foreign market being entered by Company A – the internationalizing firm – through the form of strategic alliance specified.

The strategic alliance may take many forms. It may range from a simple contractual agreement to cross-distribute products to production agreements where the production stages of a product are shared. There are many types of marketing and production agreements, forming the basis of strategic alliances. A partnership which reflects greater commitment may be found under franchising, licensing and joint ventures. These various forms of strategic alliance represent a continuum of increasing commitment to the partnership. The commitment in marketing agreements may refer to one product market for a limited period, whereas joint venture agreements usually involve the commitment of financial, managerial and technological resources for a considerable time, usually years. Frequently, partners in a strategic alliance emphasize the scale economies and reduction in new product development and marketing costs that can result from a partnership.

As strategic alliances are nurtured and grow over time the partner firms may form closer alliances or bonds. With experience and a better understanding of each other's capabilities and objectives the form of the alliance may evolve toward a situation where the partners work together to gain access to new third markets and new technologies. Sometimes firms begin to develop and manufacture new products jointly. This dynamic convergence of resources, capabilities and business objectives may occur quite rapidly but is usually an evolutionary process taking a number of years to complete. The final point in the convergence arises when the firms decide to form a functional merger. Evolutionary complementarity reflects the strengths of each partner in the key assets to be exchanged.

Marketing partnership agreements

For firms with significant sales and physical distribution systems established in a large market such as the United Kingdom or Germany, there may be opportunities to market the products of, say, US firms suitably adapted for the market through the existing channels of distribution. For the smaller firm particularly, organic internal growth or acquisition may not be an option. A partnership on a complementary basis may be less risky and potentially more rewarding. Looked at from the opposite perspective there are many small- to medium-sized exporters in the United States who are not active in international markets but who provide a ready-made pool of well-equipped, technically sophisticated but internationally inexperienced firms who could serve as partners to European firms with guaranteed market access.

Airlines have discovered that partnership agreements, occasionally leading to full mergers, may be the only way to survive in global markets. Indeed, the larger airlines have recognized that none of them on their own is capable of serving the global needs of customers and many have formed marketing partnership agreements to provide, in theory if not in practice, a relatively seamless service to customers. Many such large alliances, e.g. Oneworld and Star, now exist which compete as business systems one with the other with the objective of gaining and holding market share of a growing global business.

Licensing to enter international markets

Licensing, the purchase or sale by contract of product or process technology, design and marketing expertise, avoids the risks of product and market development by exploiting the experience of firms that have already developed and marketed the product. It also provides a useful vehicle for the internationalization of small firms that might not have the capital or foreign experience to establish a joint venture or a wholly owned subsidiary abroad. The greater the possibility of internationally transferring technology in coded or blue-print form, as in licensing, the lower the cost of the transfer. Uncodified or tacit knowledge requires face-to-face communication for successful transmission and is, therefore, slow and expensive to transfer. Herein lies a major benefit of licensing; the costs of knowledge transfer are relatively low.

International licensing arises when a firm provides for a fee or royalty, technology needed by another firm to operate a business in a foreign market. Licensing of this form involves one or a combination of the following:

- a brand name;
- operations expertise;
- manufacturing process technology;
- access to patents; and
- trade secrets.

The licensor firm gains access to a foreign market with very low investment and frequently obtains the investment and market knowledge of a competent local firm. The licensee firm gains access to a foreign technology with very low investment.

International licensing may be a preferred strategy in some circumstances. It may be attractive in situations where: host countries restrict imports or foreign direct investments; the foreign market is small; and the prospects of technology feedback are high. Licence agreements generally fall into two categories: a current technology licence that gives the licensee access to the technology which the licensor possesses at the time of the agreement; and a current and future technology licence that gives access to existing technology and technology yet to be developed by the licensor in a specified product area during the life of the agreement.

Licence agreements vary depending on circumstances but normally contain aspects of a technical, commercial and organizational nature in addition to the patented technology being transferred. In summary there are several advantages and disadvantages in using licences to enter international markets (Table 14.1).

Table 14.1 Advantages and disadvantages of licensing in international markets

Advantages of licensing

- Access to difficult markets
- Low capital risk and low commitment of resources
- Information on product performance and competitor activities in different markets at little cost
- Improved delivery and service levels in local markets

Disadvantages of licensing

- Disclosure of accumulated competitive knowledge and experience
- Creates possible future competitors
- Lack of control over licensee operations
- Passive interaction with the market
- Possible exclusion of some export markets
- Organizing licensing operations: cost of adaptation, transfer and control

Benefits of licensing

There are several technological reasons why a firm would consider licensing to enter a foreign market. For bulky or heavy products of low value, transport costs may be so high as to make exporting prohibitively expensive. Sometimes a local manufacturer with product knowledge is required, especially when the product requires installation and service support. In such circumstances it is unlikely that an agent could provide the necessary back-up.

Frequently a complementary arrangement may be developed whereby the licensor exports a high-technology component and the licensee provides the less critical assemblies, harnesses, mountings and cabinets. This arrangement is more like a joint production agreement.

There are also territorial reasons why licensing could be an attractive means of entering foreign markets. Few firms have the sales force necessary to cover wide geographic markets in many different countries, nor do they have sufficient manufacturing capacity to service such large markets. Thus, where the potential market is large, licensing partners can be an attractive development option.

Impact of licensing on cash flow

Financial considerations may be an important determinant for the smaller firm in possession of advanced technology. Licensing in such circumstances may open foreign markets that might otherwise be beyond its reach. Small- and medium-sized firms attempting to expand and grow frequently experience cash flow and liquidity problems. Since licensing income is largely pure profit involving little extra investment, licensing for such firms may speed up the cash flow from new foreign markets.

Because technology licensing allows the firms to have products on the market sooner than otherwise, the licensee benefits from an earlier positive cash flow. In

Figure 14.2
Life cycle
benefits of
licensing

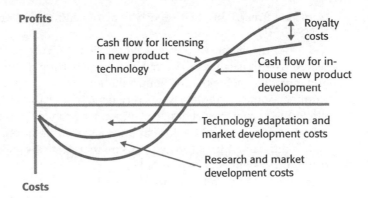

Source: adapted from Lowe, J. and Crawford, N. (1984) *Technology Licensing and the Small Firm*, England: Gower

addition, licensing of a technology means lower development costs for the licensor. As Lowe and Crawford (1984) show, however, licensing in rather than developing the technology in-house can mean fewer profits in the longer term. Quick access to new technology, lower development costs and a relatively early cash flow are, however, attractive immediate benefits of licensing (Figure 14.2). In ideal circumstances both licensee and licensor benefit.

Prerequisites of successful licensing

The licensor must have exclusive and internationally easy to transfer property rights to the product or process technology being licensed. It must also be possible to identify benefits associated with the licence, including the value of the licence to the partner firm. The licensor firm should be in a position to control the operation, including the geographic market area in which the licence is to apply. At the same time the licensee should have developed a level of technical competence sufficient to cope with the application of the technology in production and marketing.

Sometimes firms are opposed to licensing their technology. Opposition to licensing is usually centred on reluctance to divulge accumulated knowledge and experience that has been hard to develop; this fear stems from the situation where a company may find cheaper or improved versions of its own products competing against it at a later date. Other reasons for the decision not to pursue licensing include lack of real control over licensee operations, blocking off export areas, doubts about the suitability and transferability of technology and difficulties of organizing licensing operations in traditional manufacturing-oriented companies.

Assymetry in negotiating international licences

The market for licences is imperfect. The buyer located in the foreign market has a weak basis for bidding, especially for undisclosed technology, until it has been supplied. It is also very difficult to communicate subtle and complex technologies successfully from one firm to another, especially across cultures. There are heavy costs of knowledge transfer.

It is also difficult to police licences. The difficulty begins during the pre-signing period when a balance is required between whetting the prospective licensee's appetite and not divulging too much information, in the event of the negotiation falling through. Some technologies are very concise and the whole licence may depend on disclosure of some novel design or process: a problem of information disclosure which can sometimes support the formation of a new international firm.

It is difficult for the licensor to ensure that licensees maintain adequate quality control in production: a serious problem when the licensor's brand or trade name is used. It is difficult and expensive to police other clauses in the agreement, e.g. territorial limits. For these reasons technology leaders are often forced toward an equity involvement to protect their assets. Such pressure may ultimately force them to consider foreign direct investment.

Franchising to enter international markets

Nature of franchising

Franchising is a derivative of licensing whereby a business format is licensed rather than a product or process technology. Despite the recent escalation of publicity, franchising is not by any means a new phenomenon. It is frequently seen as a recent 'import' into Europe, particularly from the United States. The real pioneers of modern franchising, however, were almost certainly the British brewers of the eighteenth century who created a system of tied house agreements with their publicans which remains widespread to this day. Franchising, a derivative of *francorum rex* or 'freedom from servitude', is now a very significant organizational arrangement in the US economy accounting for approximately 40 per cent of all retail sales and 10 per cent of gross national product. In contrast, franchised retail sales in Europe are much lower so there is considerable interest in franchising as part of the firm's competitive strategy and internationalization process.

Franchising is a particular form of licensing of intellectual property rights (Adams and Mendelsohn, 1986). Trademarks, trade names, copyright, designs, patents, trade secrets and know-how may all be involved in different mixtures in the 'package' to be licensed. Franchising is a form of marketing and distribution in which the franchisor grants an individual or company, the franchisee, the right to do business in a prescribed manner over a certain period of time, in a specified place (Ayling, 1987). A more formal legal definition is provided by Adams and Mendelsohn (1986) who view franchising as a marketing method with four distinct characteristics, as follows:

1. the franchisor licenses the franchisee to carry out business under a name owned by or associated with the franchisor;

2. control by the franchisor over the way in which the franchisee carries on the business;

3. provision of assistance to the franchisee by the franchisor in running the business;
4. the franchisee provides and risks capital in the venture.

The relationship is a contractual one in accordance with a business format established by the franchisor. The franchisor provides assistance prior to commencement and throughout the period of the contract. The franchisee owns his/her business which is a separate entity from that of the franchisor.

There are various forms of franchises, job franchises, investment franchises and business format franchises being the most common (Brandenburg, 1986). The Swedish furniture manufacturer IKEA makes extensive use of franchising to expand internationally. One of the best known examples of international franchising, however, is Benetton. Benetton franchisees arrange their own finance, but they do not pay fees nor royalties. Their obligations are to:

■ carry only Benetton clothes;
■ achieve certain minimum sales levels;
■ follow guidelines for price mark-ups; and
■ adopt one of the standard shop layouts.

Factors contributing to the success of franchise arrangements include the quality of the business format system; the brand name associated with it; and the level of economic activity and business environment in the country where the proposed franchise is to operate.

Attraction of franchising as mode of entry

The major advantage of franchising is that it allows the company to rapidly enter a number of international markets thereby expanding the business over a wider area more quickly than is possible if done organically. This occurs because in franchising a business format is sold to someone who operates it in the manner which has proved to be successful, using the energies of a self-employed person with local knowledge. The franchising formula enables this expansion with minimum capital outlay. It creates additional income to the franchisor in the form of fees and royalty payments. A promising franchise attracts highly motivated operators. Furthermore, the franchisor's costs tend to be relatively low as the entire central organization usually consists of a few skilled experts and the franchisor is unburdened by day-to-day details which would arise in the case of many wholly owned outlets.

Franchisees are owner-managers who typically bear the residual risk of a local operation, because their wealth is largely determined by the difference between the revenue inflows to the operation and the agreed payments to the franchisor. From the point of view of the franchisor, the major risk is the possible bad effect the franchise could have on brand names. Legally, the franchisee is a firm dealing with another firm – the franchisor; the economics of the situation are such that the franchisee is far closer to being an employee of the franchisor than an independent entrepreneur so the bargaining power in the relationship clearly rests with the holder of the master licence.

Joint ventures to enter international markets

A joint venture is formed when two or more firms form a third to carry out a productive economic activity. A joint venture may be considered a mode of interfirm cooperation lying between the extremes of complete vertical integration of business activities within one firm and the opposite case where stages of production and distribution are owned by separate companies, which contract with each other through conventional market mechanisms. Joint ventures have increased in the variety and form they take and have become strategic rather than tactical in nature (Harrigan, 1985). While domestic joint ventures may seek collusive practices and access to the technological know-how of others (Valdés Llaneza and García-Canal, 1998, p. 62), international joint ventures are usually motivated by the desire of at least one of the partners for international expansion especially into difficult markets (Exhibit 14.1). Siemens expects competitors in different supply fields irrespective of geographic location to joint venture with each other to single supply the best and leading high-technology solutions so that Siemens can be at the leading edge of their product developments. In this way Siemens maintains its leadership position in the business system it creates to compete internationally.

Exhibit 14.1	International Herald Tribune and Asahi Shimbun strategic alliance

The International Herald Tribune and the Asahi Shimbun have formed a publishing partnership in Japan. Under the arrangement Asahi Shimbun ceases publication of the English-language Asahi Evening News and integrates a more precise version of that newspaper into the International Herald Tribune. By publishing together, the IHT and the Asahi Shimbun aim to reach both English-speaking readers, interested in Japanese news, and members of the international elite in the private and public sectors who require a concise and reliable daily source of international news.

The Asahi Shimbun Japanese edition has a circulation of 8.3 million with its morning edition and an additional 4.2 million with its evening edition. The IHT has a worldwide readership of 635,000. 'This is an important breakthrough,' Peter C. Goldmask Jr., the IHT's chairman and CEO, said. 'Businessmen, public officials and sophisticated citizens need to have a window in English on the life and government of Japan.' Mr Shinichi Hakoshima, president and chief executive of the Asahi Shimbun, said: 'As Japan's leading paper, we believe it is necessary to convey news about Japan's politics, economy, society and culture to the outside world. The combined efforts of the two newspapers will enhance our abilities to communicate with the world.'

Source: adapted from *The International Herald Tribune*, Friday 5 January 2001, p. 1

Various forms of joint venture are found in practice. Sometimes firms participate in a spider's web strategy consisting of many firms linked together in myriad ways. A spider's web strategy usually means establishing a joint venture with a large competitor.

Figure 14.3
Benefits of
international
joint ventures

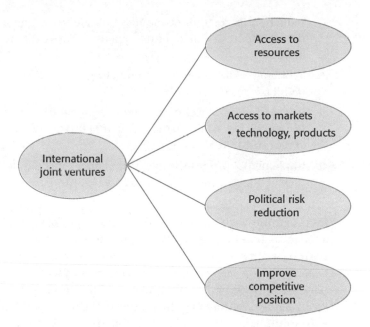

The smaller firm must avoid absorption through joint ventures with others in such a network. Two dangers are associated with this strategy:

■ indirectly forming a link with a competitor; and
■ the possibility of a take-over.

As an alternative, firms sometimes cooperate for a period of time and then separate; a go-together then split strategy, often used for time-limited projects such as large construction schemes. In contrast, other firms find their bonds with joint venture partners becoming tighter. In the third situation partners may finish up with a successive integration strategy having started with weak interfirm linkages that develop towards merger with a convergence of interests.

Benefits of international joint ventures

Joint ventures in international markets facilitate technology transfer, provide access to resources and markets, help to reduce political risk and can improve the firm's competitive position (Figure 14.3). In transferring technology, joint ventures deal with codified and uncodified knowledge and its conversion into goods and services. Through a joint venture it is also possible to discover the international market price of the technology. The formation of joint ventures is frequently cited as a way of reducing risk especially when the joint venture involves a large investment. It may also be beneficial in diversifying the portfolio of investments of one or all partners. In this context it has been noted that joint ventures make it possible to access the marketing knowledge of the partner firm immediately rather than waiting for the internal development of such skills. Four major advantages for joint ventures may be identified:

1. reduction in costs, or economies of scale from combining common administrative, transport and marketing expenses in two or more stages of production or distribution;

2. avoidance of interfirm contracting, transactions and negotiations costs (Williamson, 1975);

3. internalization of technological or administrative secrets within a firm which minimizes the risk of dissipation of competitive advantage arising from these secrets (Teece, 1981; Rugman, 1981);

4. implementation of technological changes more quickly and over more stages of production (Contractor and Lorange, 1988).

Joint ventures facilitate faster market entry and payback. This is of particular significance in such industries as pharmaceuticals where the certification process consumes a great deal of time. It is often possible in joint ventures to combine slack facilities and expertise in the partner firms. In such circumstances the cost of the joint venture to the partnership may be less than it would be to each partner operating independently. Lastly, a joint venture may enable a partial containment of the political risk associated with forming an alliance with a local partner. In such circumstances, the local partner would ensure that negative public policy interference was minimized while complying with host country industrial policy.

Access to resources and markets

Access to valued and scarce human resources with appropriate education and cultural background is a key factor in joint venture formation. One of the critical reasons why European and American companies enter joint ventures in Japan is the inability of companies on their own to attract local management as a result of their 'outsider' status. Indeed numerous joint ventures have been formed with the express intention of recruiting nationals with managerial ability. The local partner's participation in the development of the joint venture imposes less of a burden on its managerial capabilities than would a wholly owned subsidiary.

Access to capital is another resource frequently sought when firms enter a joint venture. Capital markets are characterized by significant transaction costs and credit markets are likely to be imperfect for young firms with little or no track record or experience. Transaction costs are also high for investments in risky projects that have no collateral, e.g. research and development (Hennart and Larimo, 1998). Small-scale technology based firms frequently encounter severe difficulty in securing funds for expansion, hence the attractiveness of joint ventures.

International joint ventures are also effective in gaining access to new foreign markets. Using joint ventures as a way of diversifying activities and obtaining growth, one of the partners frequently provides entrepreneurial enthusiasm, vigour, flexibility and advanced technology while the other partner provides capital, worldwide marketing support, channels of distribution and service. This combination allows for the rapid diffusion of technology based product innovation into large international markets. The synthesis implied can create a significant competitive advantage as experienced by Glanbia plc, the Irish food group and the US company Leprino Foods. In 2000 Glanbia plc entered into a joint venture with Leprino to expand further into the fast-growing European pizza cheese market. Leprino, which is the world's largest cheese producer, concentrating solely on mozzarella cheese, obtained a 49 per cent stake in Glanbia Cheese Ltd which was the leading producer and marketing company of pizza cheese in Europe.

The agreement provides Glanbia with access to leading-edge technologies, much needed cash and a strategic partner in a very important market. European demand for pizza cheese continues to grow at more than 8 per cent each year. It was the US company that approached Glanbia, group managing director, Ned Sullivan, explained: 'We had some discussion with them; the more we talked the more we saw the advantages of their technology, combined with our market share. It's a very important development in the cheese strategy because we're the leading player in Europe and this combines our position with the leading technical player in the world.' On the other side, James Leprino, chairman of Leprino Foods, said that Glanbia's leading position in Europe mirrored Leprino's position in the US. 'Taking a position in the European market has been a logical next step for Leprino for some time and this joint venture with the market leader will, I believe, offer significant mutual benefits,' he said.

Access to distribution channels is also an important motivating factor in the formation of an international joint venture. Strategic advantages under this heading include an existing marketing establishment, links with buyers, knowledge of the local market and culture, a recognizable brand name and market access. Joint ventures also enable the other partner to reduce its average distribution costs as there is a greater volume throughput. Equity positions in a partner company can be acquired strategically to strengthen marketing agreements.

General knowledge of the local economy is the key contribution a local partner can make to an international firm seeking entry to a new foreign market. Indeed some form of quasi-integration is likely to occur if the markets under consideration are outside Europe or the United States; in such circumstances a form of internal uncertainty is created by the business distance involved (Anderson and Gatignon, 1986). Cultural similarity between partners is, however, a critical antecedent for success in international joint ventures (Lin and Germain, 1998, p. 189). Cultural differences may be at least partly responsible for the failure of some strategic alliances. In studying the failure of the Volvo–Renault alliance Bruner and Spekman (1998, p. 149) report that 'one is struck by how much of it is explained at the interfaces of human behaviour: nation, cultures, allies, owners versus managers, and senior managers versus operating managers'.

Joint ventures and host country policies

Foreign firms sometimes express reservations over host government ownership restrictions. Imposing a joint venture on a reluctant international firm may curb its contribution to the new company, thereby reducing the venture's productivity. While joint ventures may have narrower product lines, smaller scale and less input of the investor's technology they are especially useful in obtaining access to difficult markets, such as the emerging markets in Central Asia, the Arab world and selected countries in Africa.

The People's Republic of China (PRC) and, more recently, countries in Central Asia, have formed economic and financial relationships through joint ventures with western firms. Companies such as Procter & Gamble, which has reported that this entry mode is inconsistent with its company strategy, have entered into joint ventures in China and other former socialist countries in Central Asia. The growth potential of these markets provides the incentive to overcome accepted company philosophies. The alacrity with which many western companies enter joint ventures in these new emerging markets may also be explained by noting that in these command or semi-command economies the governments control the ownership of the trading and industrial enterprises; they also control the country's resources and distribution channels and are important customers for imported goods and technologies (Child and Markoczy, 1993). Because of evolving government policies it may be prudent to delay entry into some of these newer markets particularly if joint ventures are being considered. Unambiguous first mover advantages do not appear to have existed in early entry to China through joint ventures (Exhibit 14.2).

Exhibit 14.2   In China it may pay to arrive late

First mover advantage as a competitive strategy may be turned on its tail when companies head east to exploit Chinese markets. Whereas restrictive property ownership laws and bureaucratic state-control initially bound foreign companies which entered China in the 1980s and 1990s, latecomers can enjoy a freer more liberal market environment complemented by China's recent membership of the WTO. Back in 1984, when Volkswagen AG came to China, 'there was no experience of dealing with foreign investors', says Walter Hanek, a managing director of VW Beijing. This learning curve wasn't the only challenge to surmount; 'your JV partner was not chosen by you, it was given to you', says Ernst Behrens, CEO of Siemens Ltd, China, alluding to the tangle of red-tape and state control which inhibited many business functions at Siemens. DaimlerChrysler AG and PepsiCo Inc are just two examples of early mover deals that went sour.

That said, Procter & Gamble's Austin Lally reasons the 'opportunity to build longer and deeper relationships with customers' outweighs the costs and frustrations of an early entry in 1988. While the Foreign Trade Law has facilitated sale and distribution of both domestically produced and imported products throughout China, a 50 per cent ownership cap still applies in the car maker's industry. Nevertheless, in general, it has never been easier for auto parts suppliers, food and drinks companies and even technology companies to do business in an ever more liberal Chinese market where JV liquidations and buyouts are an increasingly common occurrence. Whatever about the timing and mode of market entry, Ma Xiaoye, an ex-government official, advises 'any company that has the patience to stay here will profit eventually'.

Source: adapted from *The Wall Street Journal Europe*, Monday 5 February 2004, p. 1

In the non-EU countries of Eastern Europe the government, often represented by a privatization board, is the key stakeholder in joint ventures with western firms in that they control critical resources (Brouthers and Bamossy, 1997, p. 286). In strategically important industries such as oil and gas and telecommunications, governments as key stakeholders provide frequent and extensive influence in all stages of the negotiation of a joint venture including, most importantly, in the post-negotiation stage. In consumer non-essential products such as tea, coffee, milk and beer, key stakeholder influence appears to be very low, in both extent and frequency (Brouthers and Bamossy, 1997, p. 304).

Most of the investments in China in terms of number and value continue to be joint ventures, but as Vanhonaker and Pan (1997, p. 11) note, foreign managers are generally dissatisfied with the performance of joint ventures in China. The key problem areas for foreign managers are quality of local sourcing, the recruitment of skilled Chinese managers and the lack of clarity in laws and regulations. The least difficult areas are in exporting and financing (working capital) and foreign exchange.

Stability of international joint ventures

Joint ventures can be criticized because they are unstable; they often create a competitor, and the costs of control become too high. International joint ventures are believed to be inherently unstable and to be 'marriages of convenience'. International joint venture instability is, however, not necessarily an indication of failure as is often assumed. The fact that many are short lived may be attributed in part to their very nature and the strategic intent their parents bring to cross-border collaboration (Reuer, 1998, p. 167). Parents may select international joint ventures as a temporary gap-filling mechanism, as a means of taking an option on an emerging technology or market, as a structured choice suited to the features of exchange at the time of market entry or as a response to legal and political conditions in the host country.

Multinational firms are more likely to buy out their partners when they already control a majority of the shares of a company and are more likely to divest when they hold a minority shareholding. In this sense, joint ventures involving multinational companies may be viewed as 'instruments providing firms with flexibility in responding to trends that are difficult to predict' (Gomes-Casseres, 1989, p. 99). The change from joint ownership to wholly owned subsidiary for these firms is likely to occur in countries with which the international firm is already familiar.

Sometimes joint ventures create competitors unnecessarily; there exists the possibility for long-term opportunistic behaviour from the technology buyer when the technology supplier is no longer needed. This risk is reduced by a constantly changing environment when the pace of technical change is rapid and product life cycles are shorter. Moreover, in most cases the technology supplier constantly updates and improves existing products in order to maintain its competitive edge. Furthermore, joint ventures can raise difficulties for the technology buyer, particularly when the recipient uses the alliance to neglect investment in design and innovation.

This short-term orientation can result in a dependency spiral as the technology buyer contributes fewer and fewer distinctive skills. This may force the buyer to reveal more of its internal operations to keep the other partner interested.

Figure 14.4
Difficulties with
joint ventures

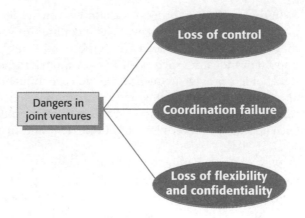

On a more general level the difficulties associated with joint ventures may be summarized under three major headings (Figure 14.4). Loss of control over foreign operations can arise when there is a large investment of financial, technical or managerial resources that would indicate the need for greater control than is possible in a joint venture. As the network of joint ventures becomes larger there is increased possibility of conflict of interest among the partners. The cost of controlling the joint venture becomes significant. The need for control strengthens the argument for unambiguous control within a single firm, as found in direct investment and acquisition modes of foreign market entry. Joint ventures are difficult to coordinate often due to a lack of adequate procedures for protecting proprietary information and shared decisions affect global marketing arrangements. There is also a loss of flexibility and confidentiality; a change in product-market mission by one partner may make the joint venture a liability. Sometimes partners are uneasy about sharing technology. Indeed, one partner may form an alliance with the other partner's competitor. Further dangers arise where there is managerial dependency between the joint venture and one of the partners.

Conditions for joint venture success

A number of conditions have been identified under which it is easier to operate international joint ventures. These conditions have been classified into dominant and shared partnership arrangements (Killing, 1980). The circumstances under which a dominant partnership works best are:

■ the international partner should be dominant when it is important to have long-term control of know-how; and

■ the local partner should be dominant when the international partner's skills are needed only temporarily and can easily be transferred.

In the first case the local partner should be passive and outside the industry. Shared partnership works best if the skills of both partners are required over time:

- choose a partner with complementary skills;
- give the joint venture autonomy; and
- allow partners to buy/sell out for a change in conditions.

In a study of international joint ventures involving Chinese firms, Ding (1997, p. 43) concludes that dominant managerial control exercised by foreign partners is significantly and positively related to performance, and conflicts between partners significantly hinder performance. International managers should recognize that the extent of managerial control they are able to exercise over a joint venture's activities increases the likelihood of meeting their expectations. It is advisable that partners formulate an effective conflict management strategy to resolve problems which generally arise in regard to quality control, export and import arrangements, wages and labour policy, and administration. These conflicts arise from divergent objectives, disparate expectations and priorities, incompatible business and management practices of the two partners and social and cultural differences between the home and host country. These fundamental deficiencies in know-how and process management allow the foreign partner to continue to dominate the development of innovative technologies in the belief that local counterparts will be slow to develop the skills and competencies to a level sufficient to compete with them. It was this philosophy that led General Electric to enter a joint venture with a Chinese firm to manufacture turbine engines (Exhibit 14.3).

Exhibit 14.3   China sets high price to gain market entry

In China it is called 'technology for market'. Effectively, to be considered in the bidding process for much needed electricity generation hardware, GE had to enter into a joint venture with a Chinese partner and agree to the Chinese receiving turbine designs that GE spent half a billion dollars to develop. The contract they won was valued at €720 million ($900 million). Ultimately the trade-off could translate as short-term sales gains in exchange for longer-term competition. Historically, Chinese firms have found it difficult, however, to leverage technology transfers because of a lack of engineering know-how. In GE's case, Chinese manufacturers have only recently mastered the technology to produce 40MW steam turbines, which GE introduced in the 1980s, while the American company is now poised to offer a cleaner 300MW turbine that is even cheaper to install.

The US domestic market demand is weak while China is expected to invest €8 billion a year building new power plants. The order for 13 of its advanced F9 turbines isn't straightforward. While GE maintains control over its most sensitive technology, some of the less sophisticated components will be manufactured by its Chinese partners. In addition, the metallurgic technology of the turbine blades will be made available to the Chinese. GE believe, however, that its rate of design innovation will sustain its advantage over its Chinese counterparts. What is more, China will be slow to build on this knowledge: 'the foreigners are now agreeing to tell us how and where to dig a hole, but we still do not know why to dig a hole there', commented one official.

Source: adapted from *The Wall Street Journal Europe*,
Friday, Saturday and Sunday 27–29 February 2004, pp. A1–A3

The performance of joint ventures is also influenced by the context in which they exist. In an examination of successful US–China joint ventures Lin and Germain (1998, pp. 189–90) discovered that cultural similarity between partners is a critical antecedent for joint venture success – the greater the cultural similarity the better the performance. These authors also discovered that only in limited circumstances is relative power an influence on performance. The greater the partner's relative power, however, the more likely it is to force its preferred solution when disagreement occurs. Lastly, Lin and Germain (1998) report that the longer a joint venture has lasted the better its performance. Obviously, selection is occurring in that only successful joint ventures are allowed to continue. Clearly, joint venture age breeds familiarity which translates into an open style of problem-solving to the mutual satisfaction of the partners.

Selecting a partner for a strategic alliance

The key to forging mutually satisfactory joint ventures is a realistic assessment of the firm's strengths and weaknesses in the proposed venture. In an attempt to take a share of the lucrative diamond jewellery market De Beers and LVMH formed a joint venture combining the prestige of De Beers with the retail knowledge of LVMH, their respective strengths. 'There is untapped opportunity for all of us in the diamond industry to . . . match the growth rates enjoyed by the leading companies in the rest of the luxury goods sector,' said Gary Ralfe, managing director of De Beers Group. 'In five years' time, we expect that the De Beers brand will be one of (the industry leaders)'. LVMH chief executive Myron Ullman said the venture will open five to seven De Beers flagship stores in major capitals. It is also necessary to assess the commitment of potential partners to the success of the venture and their willingness to contribute resources or to provide a market for the products in a manner that accommodates their partners' needs. In searching for an appropriate partner for the strategic alliance the company faces four dilemmas (Smith and Reney, 1997, p. 180):

- how to find local firms;
- how to assess compatibility;
- how to determine an operational fit with the prospective partner;
- how to specify and detail the nature of the project in the alliance.

Search costs are high as major companies do not as a rule wish to sell their technology and smaller companies are more difficult to locate since they do not generally advertise their position. It may be necessary to look beyond the obvious candidates engaged in the same business to companies with marketing and manufacturing capabilities in related or complementary products or services.

In some cases the process of partner selection is not performed thoroughly. The first candidate, generally discovered through contacts established through the Internet or arranged by a banker or a business colleague already established in the country, is often

Figure 14.5
Assessing
potential
partners in an
international
joint venture

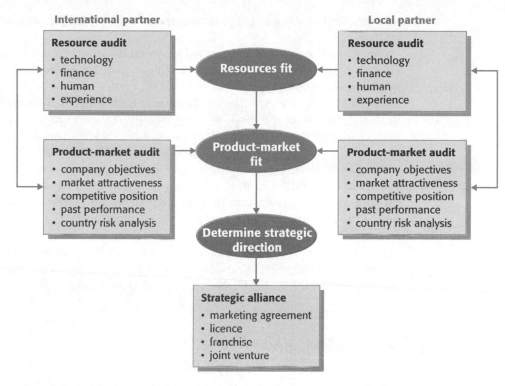

Source: adapted from Lasserre, P. (1984), 'Selecting a foreign partner for technology transfer', *Long Range Planning*, **17** (December), 43–9

the one with whom the company undertakes discussions. Little or no screening is done, nor is there an in-depth investigation of the motives and capabilities of the candidate. This situation is changing rapidly, however, as firms have become wiser in the ways of international markets and recognize the pitfalls that may be encountered if a strategic approach is not followed.

In more favourable cases, where the firm is already engaged in business in the country, the selected partner may be the agent who is already working for the company. For the foreign partner, there is the advantage of entering into an agreement with someone who is already familiar with the company's products and the parent company. However, the fact that a local company proves to be a good distributor does not guarantee that it will be as good in a joint venture involving manufacturing activities (Lasserre, 1984). To overcome this problem Lasserre proposes a method of assessing a partner based on analyses of the strategic and the resources fit of the firms involved (Figure 14.5).

In this framework potential partners examine their own resources through a detailed resources audit involving the firm's technology, financial and human resources and experience. Second, the potential partners then carry out a detailed product-market audit of their respective operations. A comparison of these two sets of audits presents the potential partners with a resources fit and a product-market fit. The next step is to determine the strategic direction for the alliance, if there is to be one. The alliance may take the form of a marketing partnership agreement, a licence, a franchise or a joint venture.

Lasserre maintains that this detailed approach to assessing a potential partner for an alliance is rarely implemented since it requires time, effort and investment in data gathering. A minimum period of one to two years of prior contacts and long-term missions by the foreign company to familiarize itself with the country, culture and the business practices of the local company would seem to be required in most circumstances, especially for strategic alliances requiring greater commitment, such as joint ventures.

Because both partners are likely to have similar expectations with regard to strategic value and the need for control, it is likely that franchising and joint ventures would produce a better resource and strategic fit than would marketing partnership agreements and licensing. The match in terms of resources and strategy for the latter two is frequently not as harmonious. Circumstances often arise where only one of the partners achieves the objectives established. For these reasons, marketing partnership agreements and licensing arrangements tend to degenerate over time and ultimately dissolve for partners who actively seek to attain their strategic objectives.

Evaluation of strategic alliances

The ability of the different forms of strategic alliance to cope with environmental and company policy changes are key considerations in assessing the performance of a strategic alliance. There are obstacles to performance measurement in strategic alliances that must be recognized. Since each partner has its own reporting processes and systems a common approach must first be agreed. Partners can have different objectives, gaining access to specific technologies or customers, so it can be difficult to agree what should be measured. Furthermore, the operations of an alliance can be intertwined with those of the parent company, a complexity which makes the determination of costs and benefits difficult to assess.

The issue of determining transfer prices for services rendered by the parents into the new alliance can be complicated. Measuring benefits is also a challenge. An alliance often generates extra sales of related products for the parent that must be considered. Then the issue of how to treat the intangible benefits arising from the opportunities for learning, access to new technologies and markets and improved competitive positioning.

How the parents meet these challenges determines the ultimate performance of the alliance and may strengthen or weaken the relationships with other firms in international markets. These relationships arise, as already seen, from contact with partner companies. Sometimes such contacts are very much at arm's length but frequently they involve the exchange of personnel for considerable periods of time. In joint ventures it is usual that training means the exchange of staff, and the development of joint ventures would need an extended two-way flow of key people between the partners. For these reasons it is important to examine how a particular form of strategic alliance responds to changes in the environment and how the partners in the alliance maintain contact (Figure 14.6).

Figure 14.6
Coping with
relationships
and
environmental
change in
international
strategic
alliances

Partner relationship

Environmental change		Weak	Strong
	Slow	Franchising	Marketing agreements
	Rapid	Licensing	Joint ventures

Source: adapted from Lorange, P. (1985) 'Co-operative ventures in multinational settings: a framework', Second Open International IMP Research Seminar on International Marketing, University of Uppsala, 4–6 September

Marketing partnership agreements are frequently established for a particular product-market and have a relatively short time scale. Usually an annual contract forms the basis of such a relationship with the option of extension where mutually agreed. In many situations, however, at least one party will not disclose full intentions regarding the longer-term development of the relationship and will reserve position to observe how the arrangement evolves. Sometimes firms see such relationships as a temporary measure until a more permanent arrangement can be found, e.g. a new product developed locally. In such circumstances the relationship may have only a temporary life. The continuation of the relationship depends very much on the two partners to ensure the performance of a specific task. Marketing partnership agreements are usually not equipped, therefore, with significant adaptive or environmental coping mechanisms and it is difficult to develop new business relationships within such partnerships.

Like licensing, franchising arrangements have the potential for being stable and mutually beneficial for both partners since they permit both to achieve their respective strategic values. Furthermore, both partners gain from the relationship. The extent of the links between the partners required to attain their respective objectives is low. One of the potential weaknesses of this form of relationship is the relatively low ability of franchising to cope with major environmental changes, e.g. varied attempts in different countries by McDonald's to cope with the demand for low fat and salt free fast foods.

In contrast, the level of day-to-day contact in licensing required between the licensor and licensee is low. The licence agreement forms the basis of the contact and may require an initial period of training but, once the operation is running smoothly, there is little need for extensive further contact between the partners. Because the licensee has obtained a unique know-how which gives a competitive advantage in the local market the licensing arrangement tends to be highly adaptable to changing environmental circumstances. The licensing contract is easily modified to accommodate changes in the environment (Lorange, 1985, p. 25).

A joint venture between two independent partners copes with environmental change as a matter of course. A well-designed joint venture can be well equipped to adapt to a changing environment, particularly if established initially with such flexibility as an objective. A joint venture can sometimes be much more flexible than its parents, while at the same time involving extensive continuous organizational links with the partners. These organizational links and mutually convergent objectives can sometimes lead to closer bonds between the parents even to the extent of effectively becoming a single entity as Renault and Nissan discovered after many years of successfully working together (Exhibit 14.4).

Exhibit 14.4   Renault and Nissan look to one future

Five years on, the Renault-Nissan alliance is getting tighter still. Carlos Ghosn who led the turnaround at Nissan will run both companies as one. Already, the French car manufacturer is planning to report sales and profit figures combined with those for its Japanese partner. This alliance commands a global reach, Renault is strong in Europe while Nissan flexes muscle at home in Japan and in the US, a market Renault pulled out of 20 years ago. Despite their partnership, the two compete in Europe where the Nissan Micra and Renault Clio retail in the same price range. Closer ties in terms of reporting geographical and product sales may clarify their cost structures and profitability, placing pressure on other car manufacturers. With combined earnings, they jump from tenth to fifth in the car-maker top ten, with 5.4 million cars sold globally, pipping Volkswagen's five million in 2003. While developing a stronger position to threaten the likes of Ford Motor Co. for the No 2 spot may be in sight, such close collaboration has also highlighted Renault's slim operating margins, 3.7 per cent contrasted with Nissan's 11.3 per cent, an imbalance unsustainable in a partnership where purchasing and platform development is shared. Projected profit growth may also depend on Renault's performance in the luxury car market, after their Vel Satis sedan disappointed; the company lacks the sales volume to compete with German luxury car makers – it is hoped Nissan can lend a hand.

Source: adapted from *The Wall Street Journal Europe*, Monday, 29 March 2004, p. 1

Summary

This chapter examines the various forms of strategic alliance found among firms in international markets. Four distinct forms of strategic alliance are discussed: marketing partnership agreements; licensing; franchising; joint ventures. Each involves the need to work closely with a firm located in a different market and culture. The greatest commitment to international markets is usually found among equity joint ventures established to transfer product or marketing technology. The form of alliance varies by product and marketing situation. Some product markets favour one form of alliance while others favour a different form.

   Marketing partnership agreements are usually established to serve special short-term needs in the market; often involving cross-distribution of the partners' products. Licensing is frequently found as a mode of entry in difficult and distant markets and is frequently used as a means of transferring product technology. Franchising, in contrast, usually involves a marketing technology transfer to a relatively similar or familiar market. Increasingly, franchising is a versatile means of market entry to secure more distant markets where initial demand is stimulated by international advertising and word of mouth from tourists and business travellers. Joint ventures are often the only means of entering some markets, especially those where public policy encourages the transfer of technology and know-how to local firms. Joint ventures tend to reduce the risk involved since capital is shared between the partners. The benefits of joint ventures include ease of technology transfer, access to resources, ability to comply with political pressure and access to markets.

The circumstances in which a strategic alliance partner might be selected and the form of alliance that might be favoured are identified in a simple framework which highlights ways in which the value of each form of strategic alliance may be determined.

Questions

1. Strategic alliances may be described as a set of methods of entering international markets which, in terms of commitment to internationalization, lie somewhere between exporting and foreign direct investment. Discuss.

2. What are the key characteristics of marketing partnership agreements?

3. When would you use licensing as a means of entering new international markets? What are the advantages and disadvantages of licensing?

4. Franchising is a common method of entering services markets abroad. What is the special attraction of international franchising to both partners?

5. Discuss the proposition that no firm should invest in a joint venture to enter an international market as it is always better to export the product or service or establish a plant abroad through foreign direct investment.

6. How can the firm ensure that it continues to obtain value from a strategic alliance?

7. What are the key considerations in selecting a partner for a strategic alliance?

8. Identify a firm located near you and assume it is considering entering a distant market. How would you decide the best form of strategic alliance for the firm? Would you suggest some other alternative?

References

Adams, J. and Mendelsohn, M. (1986) 'Recent developments in franchising', *Journal of Business Law*, 206–19.

Anderson, E. and Gatignon, H. (1986) 'Mode of foreign entry: a transaction cost analysis and propositions', *Journal of International Business Studies*, **17** (Fall), 1–26.

Ayling, D. (1987) 'Franchising has its dark side', *Accountancy*, **99** (112), 113–17.

Brandenburg, M. (1986) 'Free yourself from servitude', *Accountancy*, **98**, 11–18.

Brouthers, K. D. and Bamossy, G. J. (1997) 'The role of key stakeholders in international joint venture negotiations: case studies from Eastern Europe', *Journal of International Business Studies*, **28** (2), 285–308.

Bruner, R. and Spekman, R. (1998) 'The dark side of alliances: lessons from Volvo–Renault', *European Journal of Management*, **16** (2), 136–50.

Child, J. and Markoczy, L. (1993) 'Host country managerial behaviour and learning in Chinese and Hungarian joint ventures', *Journal of Management Studies*, **30** (4), 611–31.

Contractor, F. and Lorange, P. (1988) 'Why should firms co-operate? The strategy and economic basis for co-operative ventures' in F. Contractor and P. Lorange, Eds, *Co-operative Strategies in International Business*, Lexington, MA: Lexington Books.

Ding, D. Z. (1997) 'Control, conflict, and performance: a study of US–Chinese joint ventures', *Journal of International Marketing*, **5** (3), 31–45.

Gomes-Casseres, B. (1989) 'Joint venture in the face of global competition', *Sloan Management Review*, **31** (Spring), 17–26.

Harrigan, K. R. (1985) *Strategies for Joint Venture Success*, Lexington, MA: Lexington Books.

Hennart, J. F. and Larimo, J. (1998) 'The impact of culture on the strategy of multinational enterprises: does national origin affect ownership decisions?', *Journal of International Business Studies*, 3rd Quarter, 515–36.

Killing, P. (1980) 'Technology acquisition: license agreements or joint ventures', *Columbia Journal of World Business*, **15** (3), 38–46.

Lasserre, P. (1984) 'Selecting a foreign partner for technology transfer', *Long Range Planning*, **17**, 43–9.

Lin, X. and Germain, R. (1998) 'Sustaining satisfactory joint venture relationships: the role of conflict resolution strategy', *Journal of International Business Studies*, **29** (1), 179–96.

Lorange, P. (1985) 'Co-operative ventures in multinational settings: a framework', *Second Open International IMP Research Seminar on International Marketing*, University of Uppsala, 4–6 September.

Lowe, J. and Crawford, N. (1984) *Technology Licensing and the Small Firm*, Gower.

Oliver, C. (1997) 'Sustainable competitive advantage: combining institutional and resource based views', *Strategic Management Journal*, **18** (9), 697–713.

Reuer, J. (1998) 'The dynamics and effectiveness of international joint ventures', *European Management Journal*, **16** (2), 160–8.

Rugman, A. M. (1981) *Inside the Multinationals*, London: Croom Helm.

Smith, A. and Reney, M. C. (1997) 'The mating dance: a case study of local partnering processes in developing countries', *European Management Journal*, **15** (2), 174–82.

Teece, D. J. (1981) 'The market for know-how and the efficient international transfer of technology', *Annals of the American Academy of Political and Social Science*, **458** (November), 81–9.

Valdés Llaneza, A. and García-Canal, E. (1998) 'Distinctive features of domestic and international joint ventures', *Management International Review*, **38** (1), 49–66.

Vanhonaker, W. R. and Pan, Y. (1997) 'The impact of national culture, business scope, and geographic location on joint venture operations in China', *Journal of International Marketing*, **5** (3), 11–30.

Williamson, O. E. (1975) *Markets and Hierarchies: Analysis and Antitrust Implications*, New York, Free Press.

15 Market entry – acquisition and direct investment

Entry by the firm into international markets through acquisition and new venture investment represents the greatest degree of commitment and requires a greater investment of resources than the other modes of market entry. The firm is usually established with a geographical horizon limited to a locality, a region or a home country, but these horizons change. The change may be a result of internal forces such as decisions by senior management, the development of a new technology or product, observed need for a larger market and so on, or it may be the result of external forces such as customers, governments, the foreign expansion of a competitor or a dramatic event such as the formation or enlargement of a trade bloc such as the EU or the opening of new emerging markets such as those formerly dominated by the defunct USSR. Many companies believe that to avail of the opportunities represented by such forces it is necessary to invest in new foreign markets by establishing a new venture or acquiring an existing operation.

After studying this chapter students should be able to:

- determine how firms decide on an appropriate location to acquire a firm or to invest directly in foreign manufacturing operations;
- understand managerial motives for acquisition as a means of entering foreign markets;
- outline the steps involved in an acquisition strategy – determine why some fail and some succeed;
- understand managerial motives for foreign direct investment as a means of entering foreign markets;
- evaluate the conditions for success in using foreign direct investment as a mode of entry;
- compare the value of acquisitions and new investment ventures as a means of foreign market entry.

Obtaining locational advantage

Firms invest in manufacturing facilities in international markets primarily to obtain locational competitive advantage. In classical economic theory the firm is assumed to have perfect and costless knowledge of, and to be prepared to take advantage of, attractive opportunities wherever they exist. To operate successfully abroad, the firm must have certain compensating advantages that more than offset the innate advantages of local firms. Local firms, however, generally possess an intimate knowledge of the local economic, social, legal and public policy environment, and when the interest is in the local market only they do not face foreign exchange risks and misunderstandings which often arise in cross-cultural operations.

Firms engage in international horizontal and vertical investments. The objective of horizontal investments is to produce in foreign locations the same products manufactured in the home market. Vertical investments may be supply oriented, intended to produce abroad raw materials or other production inputs which are then supplied to the firm at home or to other subsidiaries. Customer demand also drives vertical investments in downstream activities. Increasingly, therefore, it is not a product embodied asset which drives firms abroad but the implicit contracts between suppliers and large customers located abroad, reflecting the international firm's ability to manage the logistics of continuous supply and adaptation to customer needs (Caves, 1998, p. 10).

Firms sometimes internationalize to create an internal market whenever transactions can be carried out at a lower cost within the firm. The creation of an internal market permits the firm to transform an intangible piece of research or understanding of the market into a valuable property specific to itself. The firm can exploit its advantage in all available markets and still keep the use of the information internal in order to recoup its initial expenditures on research and knowledge generation.

The propensity of a particular enterprise to engage in foreign production also depends on the locational attractions of its home country's endowments compared with those offered by other countries, including financial and other inducements to locate there. Differentials in the supply–demand relationship of resources among countries generate basic economic pressures for the international flow of resources and create opportunities for the multinational firm (Fayerweather, 1982).

Acquisition

Foreign acquisitions occur when one firm acquires a foreign based firm which possesses information, assets, brands, distribution networks or skilled management which can be used to improve the performance of the first firm.

There are many reasons for foreign market entry by acquisition. The most important production reasons are to be found in the areas of rationalization across different locations, restructuring of industry and achieving complementary of operations. A second set of motives are market driven – speed of market entry and strengthening of market position are also very important. The major attraction of entry by acquisition to a foreign market is that it is very much quicker than entry through fixed investment in new facilities and internal development of assets. Acquisition has two major advantages:

- the firm obtains assets that are already in use so the return is quicker than from fixed-asset investment; and
- acquisitions provide the firm with immediate market share without any increase in manufacturing capacity.

Speed may be an important consideration to allow the firm to enter new foreign product markets quickly and thereby to exploit first-mover advantage. Acquisition is a quick way of entering the market as it by-passes all the planning and negotiation stages which are necessary in building a complete new production facility.

Relying on the market might take a long time, be more expensive or be impossible. The lower transaction costs involved mean that acquisitions can be a better alternative to strategic alliances or organic growth through exporting. Deciding to enter foreign markets through an acquisition investment mode is akin to the big decision in the 'build or buy' alternatives facing firms as they expand. In summary, international market entry by acquisition:

- provides the firm with established means of market entry with institutional support and an established network of suppliers, intermediaries and customers;
- benefits from the innate knowledge of local economic, social, cultural, legal and public policy environment, possessed by the acquired firm;
- may be expensive but attractive if market potential exists – it is also quicker than investing in new facilities;
- focuses on acquiring well-known brands and access to a large customer base.

Nature of foreign acquisitions

Expansion by acquisition can take two general forms. At one extreme are acquisitions which are a complete legal integration of two or more firms. At the other extreme are acquisitions involving only changes in the ownerships of the firms involved. In the first case the assets and liabilities of two or more firms are transferred into a single firm, existing or new. This form of entry by acquisition involves major reorganization, from changes in the membership of the board to changes in products sold. Generally, legal acquisitions involve integration of the constituent parts of companies, a process which is not easily reversible. One of the major difficulties of this form of acquisition is that integration of management functions and determination of joint strategies may be a long and difficult process.

In the second situation, where a change of ownership allows an acquisition to occur, the take-over of one company by another is the most common form. Here both firms continue to exist as separate legal entities. This form of acquisition is performed by a purchase of shares or a public take-over bid. Acquisition in this way unifies the businesses while still maintaining a considerable degree of decentralization between the members of the new entity.

A complicated network of acquisitions of this form can result in a complicated structure, even involving subsidiaries large enough to make their own acquisitions. Although complex, they can be stable and profitable. Success in such firms is frequently due to flexibility and the decentralized management structure which continues.

A network of independent firms, although owned centrally through shareholding arrangements, is likely to be able to adjust better to changing social, political and business considerations in international product-markets than are firms which are single legal entities. Decentralized management allows the firm to withdraw from difficult situations.

Success factors in acquisitions

Somewhat curiously, given that cultural similarity is important for joint ventures, Morosini *et al.* (1998, pp. 153–4) argues that acquisitions are more likely to be successful the greater the cultural distance between the countries of the firms involved. The reason given is that cross-border acquisitions in more culturally distant countries are likely to provide a mechanism for international companies to access diverse repertoires of innovation, entrepreneurship and decision-making practices which have the potential to enhance the combined firms' performance over time. Successful acquisitions normally involve strategies to limit risk, to identify and assess elements of synergy, to achieve scale economies, to acquire sequentially and to maintain constant leadership from senior management (Figure 15.1).

A key influence in acquisition strategies is the possibility of reduced unit costs arising from better marketing and distribution arrangements and research and development work as applied to manufacturing. Centrally coordinated, such arrangements can produce scale economies. The successful acquisition of Rowntree-Mackintosh by Nestlé a number of years ago was motivated by similar reasons. Reflecting that success, Nestlé recently embarked on a programme of foreign acquisitions to re-invent itself.

Figure 15.1
Components of successful acquisition strategy

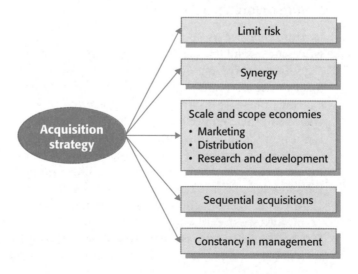

Early in 2000 the then new chief executive of Nestlé, Peter Brabeck, was considering the possibility of completely acquiring L'Oreal – 'we look to moving this company (Nestlé) from an agro-food business to something more of a nutrition, health, food, well-being company. 'Looking well and taking care of yourself will play a bigger role in the future. There will be more synergies and more overlap. Each would have to be run separately – L'Oreal would be run from Paris not Vevey (Switzerland) – but there would be a good fit' (adapted from the *Financial Times*, Monday 13 March 2000, p. 8).

Marketing effectiveness is increased if a standardized approach to positioning can be adopted. Similarly, distribution economies can be realized by integrating several minor distribution networks and increasing the number of product lines through an existing network. A higher degree of research and development specialization can be achieved through the consolidation of several similar research areas which may lead to shorter development time and quicker commercialization.

Disadvantages of foreign acquisitions

Acquiring an established firm in the foreign market provides the internationalizing firm with an established means of entry with institutional support and a working network of suppliers, intermediaries and customers. It may, of course, be much more expensive to enter the market in this way and other dangers of foreign acquisitions may be encountered.

- Foreign acquirers often pay more than would domestic buyers and hold inflated expectations of future synergies.
- Differences of language and culture may aggravate the integration of two management teams.
- Misperceptions about the new foreign market can lead to marketing mistakes.
- Employees tend to be even more frightened of new management if they are from another country.

The high cost of entry is frequently offset against the market potential which is presumed to exist. In recent years a number of large European firms have acquired US firms, since a strong presence in the growing US market is seen by these firms as an essential ingredient of their worldwide strategy. A similar pattern has also appeared in Europe, especially in food industries and branded goods businesses. Acquisitions frequently have as a central objective the ownership and international management of well-known brands.

Sequenced international acquisitions

A sequenced acquisition strategy can produce dominance in an industry sector or market. By targeting firms for acquisition in a clearly defined sequence a firm can become the dominant player in a region, or even in the world. In the early 1970s Electrolux was just one of several firms with a share in the appliance sector of the electrical products industry. By the end of the 1980s, with more than 250 acquisitions behind it,

Electrolux was the dominant player in this sector. The firm also maintains a low profile in the industry in that it retains most of the brand names of the companies it acquires. Electrolux follows a planned acquisition strategy in five steps (Eng and Forsman, 1989):

- a specific geographic market is targeted;
- a critical mass in the market is created by buying firms with established brand names;
- production is rationalized while taking account of the firm's capacity in other countries. Weak product lines are eliminated in favour of large-volume production lines;
- financial management is centralized and country marketing services are coordinated;
- all viable brands are supported to maintain customer loyalty in different markets and to hold shelf and floor space.

Acquiring firms sequentially to enter and dominate industry sectors across many international markets requires a stability of leadership policy in the firm. A mission to develop corporate and marketing strategies through internationalization by acquisition is a long-term strategy achievable only over many years. It is not a short-term strategy: dominance of market position is achieved only with patience, strategic thinking and a constancy of leadership in senior management. Sometimes the marketing logic is enough to overcome any organizational difficulties which would need to be faced. The marketing and manufacturing complementarity which existed between Electrolux and Zanussi was a large factor in facilitating that acquisition in the early 1980s. Electrolux had dominated the northern European markets for dry white goods, e.g. refrigerators, while Zanussi dominated southern European markets, particularly Italy, in wet goods, e.g. washing machines and dishwashers.

Public policy and cross-border acquisitions

Cross-border acquisitions are likely to continue growing and in general to be welcomed by policy-makers, as in most cases they do not adversely affect competition and the consumer should benefit. Unless the resulting market share held by the new corporate entity is substantial in the relevant market, such acquisitions and strategic alliances are more likely to benefit consumers. A case in point was the take-over battle in the UK confectionery industry for Rowntree-Mackintosh referred to above. Both Nestlé and Jacob–Suchard had small shares of the UK market and a merger between either and Rowntree-Mackintosh would not seriously reduce competition, whereas a merger with Cadbury and Rowntree-Mackintosh would. Frequently, however, the purpose of some foreign acquisitions is to deliberately reduce competition by removing aggressive competitors from the scene.

On purely commercial grounds a cross-border acquisition between either Nestlé or Jacob–Suchard and Rowntree-Mackintosh made marketing sense. Rowntree, with world brands such as Kit Kat, Rolo and After Eight, was a leader in the fastest-growing confectionery segment: chocolate-coated treats that frequently contain caramel,

Figure 15.2
Impact of
acquisitions on
competition and
efficiency

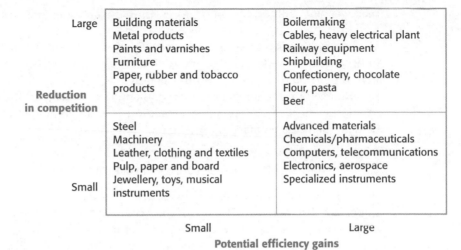

		Small	Large
	Large	Building materials Metal products Paints and varnishes Furniture Paper, rubber and tobacco products	Boilermaking Cables, heavy electrical plant Railway equipment Shipbuilding Confectionery, chocolate Flour, pasta Beer
Reduction in competition			
	Small	Steel Machinery Leather, clothing and textiles Pulp, paper and board Jewellery, toys, musical instruments	Advanced materials Chemicals/pharmaceuticals Computers, telecommunications Electronics, aerospace Specialized instruments

Potential efficiency gains

biscuits or nuts. In contrast Nestlé and Suchard were concentrated in the shrinking market for solid chocolate. This take-over activity in the United Kingdom reflected pressure to consolidate a fragmented European confectionery market.

The merger between Grand Metropolitan and Guinness in 1997 with a combined turnover of £13.7 billion allows the new entity, Diageo, to claim to be the world's largest spirit business. The two firms' portfolios of brands complement each other in Asia, where brandy and whiskey dominate, and in the US, where white spirits such as vodka are the tipple of preference. The merged company also experienced a decline in marketing and distribution costs.

Public policy interest in acquisition is frequently concerned with two issues: competition and efficiency (Figure 15.2). Governments view acquisitions as providing an opportunity for increased efficiency in industry. At the same time, however, they are concerned about any reduction in competition which might result from an acquisition. Situations where efficiency gains are large for a small reduction in competition are generally tolerated. In some cases small losses in competition would be traded for small gains in efficiency, depending on circumstances. In general, however, governments and public policy-makers resist acquisitions that produce only small efficiency gains for large reductions in competition.

Generally large efficiency gains for a small loss of competition arise when acquisitions occur in high-technology industries. Only small efficiency gains but severe loss in competition occur when acquisitions occur in low-technology areas.

Foreign direct investment

Foreign direct investment refers to the establishment of a new venture abroad and the management and effective control of the enterprise. Usually there is a heavy financial commitment involved. More important, perhaps, is the transfer of technology, management skills, production processes, manufacturing and marketing, and other resources.

The firm that invests abroad transmits equity capital, entrepreneurship, technology or other productive knowledge in the context of an industry-specific package. In most investments abroad where the firm replicates what it does well in one market, the importance of some unique asset or competitive advantage in the firm is recognized in another. It may be a potential invention or a differentiated product which is in demand in the target market.

Determinants of location of foreign direct investment

In manufacturing foreign direct investment, a number of factors are thought to be important determinants. The size of the market in the host country is likely to have a positive effect on the inflow of foreign direct investment. Since such investment is a commitment of resources in uncertain or unfamiliar markets, firms tend to invest in countries with larger markets to compensate for the risks involved.

Proximity of the host country measured on a business distance scale results in a general lowering of costs of managing foreign subsidiaries which would have a positive effect on the inflow of foreign direct investment. Production costs are a primary motivator of foreign direct investment. The size of the firm is correlated with foreign direct investment. Firm size is frequently taken as a proxy for a number of ownership-specific advantages possessed by the firm. Foreign direct investment requires significant funds to establish abroad. Larger firms seem to be more able to cope with the costs and risks involved. Previous experience gained through various forms of international operations has a positive effect on foreign direct investment. Existing investments or marketing experience gained in one country assist the firm when investing in another. The greater the international experience possessed by the firm the greater the learning.

Competitive factors also have a role to play. Firms in oligopolistic industries tend to mimic each other's foreign direct investment decisions in order to maintain a competitive equilibrium. Such oligopolistic reaction contributes positively to the level of foreign direct investment. In summary, the major determinants of foreign direct investment location are:

- size of host country market;
- proximity of host country;
- size of the firm;
- previous FDI experience;
- perceived need to mimic competitors' actions.

As the subsidiaries of multinational companies become more embedded in host countries it is likely to lead to a deepening of their value chains and a propensity for them to engage in higher-order or more innovative activities. This is most certainly the case in Ireland where government policy has promoted higher-order activities among the mobile multinational companies which have flocked there to capitalize on the spatial industrial clusters, existing nucleus of high-technology firms, a well-educated work-force, tax breaks and other locational advantages (*Wall Street Journal Europe*, World Business, September 2000, p. vi). These developments are well documented in various studies on the location of foreign direct investment (Papanastassiou and Pearce, 1997; Shan and Song, 1997). In general, high-tech multinationals operate three sets of criteria in making a location decision:

- Essential criteria:
  - access to a skilled and educated workforce;
  - proximity to world-class research institutions;
  - an attractive quality of life;
  - access to venture capital.
- Important criteria:
  - reasonable costs of doing business;
  - an established technology presence;
  - available bandwidth and adequate infrastructure;
  - favourable business climate and regulatory environment.
- Desirable criteria:
  - presence of suppliers and partners;
  - availability of community incentives.

Commenting on these and other findings, Dunning (1998, pp. 59–60) concludes that, with the gradual dispersion of created assets and as firms become more multinational by deepening or widening their cross-border value chains, from both the viewpoint of harnessing new competitive advantages and more efficiently using their home-based assets, the structure and content of the location portfolio of firms becomes more critical to their global competitive positions

Motives for foreign direct investment

Classical investment theory suggests that the reason for foreign direct investment is profit maximization, i.e. the factors of production move to where the highest rate of return can be earned; it is concerned with mobile factors of production. Behind classical investment theory is classical trade theory: the former is an extension of the latter; capital-rich countries tend to export capital-intensive products and to invest capital abroad. Labour-rich countries tend to export labour-intensive products and experience a migration of workers to better-off countries. Classical investment theory is a macro-economic theory which, however, does little to explain the investment decisions of individual firms.

Market based motives for foreign direct investment usually refer to the foreign market being attractive or conducive for the expansion of the firm's activities. These motives are based on access to raw materials, technology, intermediate goods and final products. Dunning (1998) has identified four reasons for foreign direct investment:

- Resource seeking – complementary resources.
- Market seeking – access to customers.
- Efficiency seeking:
  - deregulation of markets;
  - entrepreneurial environment;
  - enhanced competitiveness and cooperation among firms;
  - reduced costs – tax breaks.
- Strategic asset seeking:
  - exchange of localized tacit knowledge of markets;
  - access to different culture and market areas;
  - different consumer demands and preferences.

Resource seeking refers to opportunities to upgrading the quality of resources and the availability of local partners to jointly promote knowledge and/or capital-intensive ventures. Market seeking recognizes the increased need for a presence close to users in knowledge-intensive sectors and the growing importance of promotional activities by regional and local development agencies in foreign countries. Efficiency seeking acknowledges the increased role of governments in removing obstacles to restructuring economic activity and facilitating the upgrading of human resources, the provision of specialized industrial clusters (science parks), and the creation of an entrepreneurial environment and enhanced competitiveness and cooperation among firms. Strategic asset seeking refers to opportunities offered for the exchange of localized tacit knowledge, ideas and interactive learning, access to different cultures, institutions and systems, and different consumer demands and preferences.

This typology is useful for dealing with widely different markets and reflects the factor cost argument in international trade theory that markets at a lower level of development might be expected to attract a greater level of supply based foreign direct investment compared to more developed countries. Similarly, well-developed markets might be expected to attract a greater level of downstream or demand based foreign direct investment than less-developed countries.

Managerial motives for foreign direct investment

Many firms that internationalize through the direct investment mode do so to gain better access to scarce raw materials or intermediate products. More common is the situation where the firm's intention is to assemble final products for sale in local foreign markets. Investment in the foreign market may improve the firm's ability to serve that market and nearby markets. By designing products for local conditions the firm provides a better service to distributors and customers. The firm may be forced to establish in a local market to defend it from competitors. Local production may lower the final cost of the product through lower production and distribution costs. Local production

Figure 15.3
Motives for
foreign direct
investment

may be unavoidable where government policies and trade barriers are such as to make exporting unattractive.

Lastly, foreign direct investment occurs where strategic alliances make certain objectives unattainable. Sometimes firms are not in a position to control the use and exploitation of their technology by licences or joint ventures; those that depend for their competitive advantage on patents and similar forms of protection fall into this category. Foreign direct investment may provide the opportunity for a more efficient utilization of the technology and greater profits. The situation may be very different in services. Erramilli (1990) argues that customized services are likely to use integrated market entry modes that give the firm control over international marketing operations whereas entry for hard services such as software and engineering appear to be similar to that found in the manufacturing sector.

The specific reasons behind a firm's decision to invest abroad are operating efficiency, risk reduction, market development and host government policy (Figure 15.3). The basic motives for foreign direct investment are numerous. For some firms they include securing market positions in foreign markets, overcoming tariff and non-tariff barriers to trade, exploiting new markets, benefiting from government financial incentives, securing supplies and low-wage labour. In addition, firms engage in foreign direct investment because they have superior marketing skills. Firm-specific competitive advantages frequently reside in their marketing skills, their network of distributors and their well-established relationships with customers.

Operating efficiency and risk reduction

A firm increases the efficiency of the production process if it locates where the factors of production are cheapest. For example, in the early 1980s a number of German clothing manufacturers established production facilities in the Far East because German labour is relatively expensive. At the end of the 1990s other locations, especially in Eastern Europe, had begun to feature. Efficiency gains may also be possible if operations are closer to the source of raw materials, e.g. oil, ores and timber. Similarly, efficiency gains are possible when the firm produces closer to the market. It is essential for most service industries to locate in the market. Economies of scale in marketing and distribution may be a key factor in this location decision.

A second cost-related factor is economies of scale. Scale economies arise in several areas of the firm's operations, most often associated with production as occurs, for example, in car manufacturing in Europe where different components are produced in different countries. European and even global manufacturing networks are frequently more cost-effective than concentrating the production process in one location. Scale economies also occur in financing and marketing. Financial economies of scale may be obtained by a firm with international operations when the firm gains access to several capital markets. Marketing scale economies are evident in many products and services, especially franchised fast foods, soft drinks, clothing and cars. This explains the location of many US firms in Europe and Japanese firms in Europe and the United States. German motor manufacturers have located in the US and other countries both for cost and market reasons.

In regard to risk, firms sometimes internationalize through the investment mode to reduce it. Risk reduction is further enhanced through diversification since it is unlikely that all the firm's investment will perform at the same level of profitability. Because expansions and contractions in different countries are unlikely to occur at the same time, the firm should be able to stabilize its earnings by locating in several foreign countries.

Market development and government policy

Foreign direct investment may also be explained by the firm's desire to exploit the market. Some firms possess certain advantages in the design and development of products and services. The source of these advantages lies in the ability of the firm to differentiate its products and services. Product differentiation is a strong motive for foreign direct investment. Investment abroad allows such firms to internationalize product differentiation advantage to other countries where profitable. Because advantages stem from specialized knowledge, technology and patent protection, foreign based firms are usually not in a position to compete, hence the reason for foreign direct investment among such firms. Many of these are location incentives based on market imperfections which multinational companies are adept in exploiting. Multinationals are creatures of market imperfections. Two kinds of imperfections; structural imperfections, which may be natural, e.g. transport costs or man-made and imperfections inherent in transactions and markets themselves. The second is the more invidious to the well-being of the firm and has not disappeared, e.g. the uncertainty that a supplier will deliver on his promise; the volatility of exchange rates; the difficulty that customers face in evaluating unfamiliar products; the costs of negotiating deals; economies of scale in production, purchasing, research and development, distribution or marketing, which give advantages to existing firms and impose barriers against newcomers;

concerns about infringements of intellectual property rights; uncertainty about competitors' actions; the opportunity to spread risks through diversification. The modern international firm thus responds to these imperfection by organizing itself to adjust to market flaws and, indeed, to create such flaws.

Sometimes foreign markets grow faster than domestic markets, or better prices are available because of less competition. There are many markets throughout the world where only a few well-known brands share the market. Foreign markets may also open up to foreign competition due to income growth, population growth or the reduction of ownership barriers.

In regard to policy, governments frequently impose tariffs and quotas which force a firm to locate behind the barrier. In such circumstances foreign direct investment may be the only way for the firm to gain access to a market. One of the motives for Japanese car manufacturers in locating in Europe and the United States was to avoid import quota restrictions in these markets. Furthermore, as discussed earlier, governments frequently provide attractive incentive packages to firms considering foreign direct investment as a mode of entry to international markets. With the operation of the WTO it is increasingly difficult to use tariffs and quotas but non-tariff barriers such as blocked channels are still a problem. It is unlikely that exchange rate movements are the dominant factor in foreign direct investment decisions, at least in the short term but they may be a consideration. Such decisions are typically made in response to long-term market strategy considerations and cannot be implemented so rapidly as to accommodate short-term exchange rate fluctuations. A combination of factors usually motivates a move abroad as the move by BMW to the US confirms. Under attack from Japanese competitors and burdened with heavy manufacturing costs, Germany's BMW set up an assembly plant in Spartanburg, South Carolina in 1992. Eberhard von Kuenheim, BMW's chairman at the time, said an American factory was 'the next consistent step for BMW because it would help to minimize the effects of exchange-rate fluctuations [and] it also helps that production costs are 30 per cent lower in America than in Germany, and that the state of South Carolina was offering incentives, estimated by some to be worth up to $130 million' (*The Economist*, 27 June 1992, p. 74).

A decision to invest abroad requires several years to come to fruition and it is difficult, in the short term, to reverse such decisions. The possibility of exchange rate changes may, however, be a motivating factor to make or enlarge foreign investments. This is one of the reasons for the great interest by multinational companies in locating in the European Union as it allows them to serve customers in a very large market free of fluctuations in exchange rates now that the euro is so well established and accepted as the common currency across Europe. By locating production in several currency areas the firm can shift some of its production among locations and thus avoid potential exchange rate losses; hence, the interest by the same multinationals in the United States, Europe and the Far East.

One of the greatest motivations for foreign direct investment is the benefit accruing to consumers; the ability to raise local living standards. Many companies enter foreign markets stimulated by market potential not by the attraction of low costs or the possibility of producing cheap goods for export. Local consumers benefit most from market seeking investment. After foreign companies arrive in a market consumers enjoy lower prices or a better selection of goods and services. Prices tend to fall because foreign

Figure 15.4
Foreign direct
investment –
motives and
impact

Motives		Low	Medium	High
New markets			Food retailing Retail banking	Consumer electronics
Avoid barriers				Cars
Cost			Information technology	Business processes
		Low	Medium	High

Impact on recipient

companies improve efficiency and productivity by introducing new capital, tech-nology and management skills and by forcing less efficient local companies either to improve their operations or to close. Although some local companies may close or lose market share consumers benefit from lower prices which in many cases leads to a increase in demand and to the creation of new wealth. In most cases foreign direct investment leads to unambiguous benefits to the company entering the market and also to the recipient economy (Figure 15.4).

Evaluation of new foreign ventures and acquisitions

Comparison of acquisitions and new ventures

New venture foreign direct investments are frequently less costly than acquisitions since the scale of the firm's involvement can be precisely controlled and the produc-tion facility can be expanded exactly in line with achieved market penetration. In gen-eral, smaller firms prefer the new venture approach because they lack the financial resources for a take-over; another reason is because the choice of location is open to the entrant and a least-cost site can be selected, which frequently comes with an attractive incentive package provided by the host government because of the technology transfer and employment potential of the new facility.

New venture foreign direct investments also avoid inheriting problems which may exist in established firms, while at the same time it is possible to introduce the most modern technology and equipment. For larger firms new venture foreign direct invest-ment can be the best alternative market entry mode when suitable candidates for acquisition are not available.

By acquiring a foreign-based firm, other advantages accrue to the firm. Generally the acquisition route means a quicker payback and cultural and difficult management problems may be avoided. The major advantage of the acquisition mode of entry is the purchase of critical assets, products, brand names, skills, technology and, above all, distribution networks. Access to channels of distribution has been central to many of the recent large acquisitions and attempted acquisitions in Europe. Lastly, acquisitions do not usually disturb the competitive framework in the host country and for that reason are often not hindered greatly by public policy, provided they meet the criteria outlined above.

There are a number of thorny problems, however, in pursuing the acquisition route. Firms frequently find it very difficult to value the assets being acquired, e.g. the value of brands. Furthermore, it is often very difficult to determine the degree of synergy that will exist between the firm's existing assets and the acquired assets. As noted above, there may be considerable costs associated with integrating a previously independent company into a larger group. Lastly, the search costs to find a suitable firm to acquire can be substantial.

In summary, a number of factors are relevant in evaluating market entry through new ventures and acquisitions:

- new ventures are often less costly than acquisitions since customization of production to market needs is possible;
- small firms prefer new ventures because they lack finance for acquisitions;
- new ventures allow free choice of location and avoid inheritance problems;
- suitable take-over candidates are not always available;
- acquisitions allow purchase of critical assets – especially distribution networks;
- acquisitions may remove aggressive competitors from the market; and
- it is difficult to value some assets, e.g. brands, and it is difficult to assess the extent of synergy between firms in an acquisition.

Management view of foreign direct investment

From the point of view of the firm there are market entry advantages and disadvantages associated with the two forms of foreign direct investment. Each can be judged in terms of its effect on the firm's costs and on its product markets (Figure 15.5). The cost

Figure 15.5
Evaluation of acquisitions and new venture modes of foreign market entry

	Advantages	**Disadvantages**
Cost factors	Reduced transport costs Scale economies Host government incentives Reduced packaging costs Tariff and duties elimination Access to resources	High initial capital investment High information and search costs Nationalization or expropriation
Product-market factors	Management control Market access Effective marketing	Management constraints Loss of flexibility Increased marketing complexity

advantages of foreign direct investment lie in the areas of reduced transport costs, unit production and marketing costs and access to materials and cheaper labour. The cost disadvantages arise from the high initial capital investment, high information and search costs and the threat of nationalization and expropriation. The product-market advantages of foreign direct investment as a mode of entry are threefold:

- greater management control;
- better access to markets; and
- more effective marketing.

Disadvantages arise because of increased marketing complexity from the need to co-ordinate subsidiary and headquarters marketing programmes.

Summary

Participating in international markets through foreign direct investment is often considered to be the most intense form of commitment to international markets. Foreign direct investment may take the form of acquisitions or new ventures. Acquisitions are by far the more popular of the two forms, since market entry is quick and can be very effective. It is an expensive option, however, especially if the acquired firm is already well established in the market through the possession of a well-known branded product. Foreign direct investment, even cross-investment, is a prevalent feature of international business. Foreign direct investment through new ventures is favoured by smaller firms generally and by firms motivated as much by manufacturing reasons as by market reasons. Scale effects can be an important determinant of the new venture mode of entry to international markets. Foreign direct investment through whichever form may cause concern at the political level in either the source or host country. The benefits of foreign direct investment, particularly if motivated for marketing reasons, have been judged to outweigh the costs. The advantages for the firm in entering international markets through foreign direct investment are: reduced costs; more effective marketing; and greater control of manufacturing and marketing.

Questions

1. Foreign direct investment is the most expensive option when considering ways of entering international markets. Discuss.

2. Describe the components of a successful foreign strategy and outline the common motives for this form of foreign market entry.

3. Foreign direct investment is more suited to industrial products firms than to consumer products firms. Discuss.

4. Explain the recent interest by large companies in acquiring branded consumer products firms abroad.

5. Some commentators argue that more open markets encourage foreign direct investment while others argue that it is protection which determines such investment. How can you reconcile these contrasting positions?

6. What are the advantages and disadvantages of acquisitions and new ventures as options within foreign direct investment?

7. By what criteria would you judge a particular foreign acquisition or direct investment activity to have succeeded or failed? Illustrate your answer.

References

Caves, R. E. (1998): 'Research on international business: problems and prospects', *Journal of International Business Studies*, **29** (1), 5–19.

Dunning, J. H. (1998) 'Location and the multinational enterprise: a neglected factor?' *Journal of International Business Studies*, **29** (1), 45–66.

Eng, E. and Forsman, A. (1989) 'Mergers and acquisitions – Swedish efforts to gain access to the Common Market', *International Marketing Seminar*, Department of Marketing, University College Dublin.

Erramilli, M. K. (1990) 'Entry mode choice in service industries', *International Marketing Review*, **7** (5), 50–62.

Fayerweather, J. (1982) *International Business Strategy and Administration*, 2nd edn, Cambridge, MA: Ballinger.

Morosini, P., Shane, S. and Singh, H. (1998) 'National cultural distance and cross-border acquisition performance', *Journal of International Business Studies*, **29** (1), 137–58.

Papanastassiou, M. and Pearce, R. (1997) 'Technology sourcing and the strategic role of manufacturing subsidiaries in the UK: local competences and global competitiveness', *Management International Review*, **37** (1), 5–25.

Shan, W. and Song, J. (1997) 'Foreign direct investment and the sourcing of technological advantage: evidence from the biotechnology industry', *Journal of International Business Studies*, **28** (2), 267–84.

16 Market entry – a strategic approach

Various means of foreign market entry are related to the firm's choice of international market strategy. The relationship between market strategy, complexity of international markets and mode of market entry must be integrated to allow the firm to make an optimum choice of entry strategy. The two principal reasons why firms enter international markets are to source components more competitively than at home and to enter new growing product markets that hold more promise than the domestic market.

After studying this chapter students should be able to:

- define the meaning of international market entry from a managerial point of view;
- identify the factors which influence international market entry decisions in the firm;
- discuss the different market entry strategies available and the circumstances in which each may be used;
- develop an analytical framework in which to specify appropriate courses of action for the firm;
- compare market penetration and market skimming as generic international market entry strategies;
- use the product-market familiarity matrix to decide the optimum foreign market entry strategy;
- discuss the concept of sequencing and why it is important in the long term for international firms.

Dynamics of international market entry

The international firm has a number of choices available as it attempts to enter international markets – the modes of entry discussed in the previous three chapters. The firm must consider the dynamic aspects of its market entry decisions – the sequence of decisions taken by the firm determines the path of internationalization. In broad terms the firm may first decide to export a single product to its first international market.

A combination of entry modes may be used later: exporting and joint ventures, for example. At a later stage again it may be appropriate to commit greater investment to some markets by establishing or acquiring a production plant to serve important markets. There is no clear path through this decision maze. Circumstances, markets and customers, competition and the company's position influence the most appropriate foreign market entry mode over time.

By slowly deepening its involvement in international markets the firm learns from mistakes and successes so that it can control its continued growth through internationalization. Learning by exporting means that the firm becomes familiar with the demand conditions in the eventual host country: the selling methods, distribution system or mode of transfer of products and services. By agency representation, the firm learns how to do business with a host country organization. Agencies also allow the firm to cope with legal and cultural constraints. In a sales subsidiary the firm learns how to control a foreign firm in the host country. It begins to coordinate its policies with the home firm and thereby obtains the experience of management at a distance. Only then does the internationalizing firm have to cope with the problem of organizing foreign production through foreign direct investment.

Many international firms shift slowly to foreign direct investment after first establishing a sales branch abroad, which in turn commonly precedes the establishment of a contractual relationship with a foreign sales agent. Agency contracts are frequently unsatisfactory, containing vague and difficult to enforce performance criteria. Attempts to support these criteria by attempting to specify quantitative budgets for travel, advertising, engineering and support, as well as certain inventory levels in the agent's premises, often prove unsatisfactory.

The transition from agency to branch sales office is facilitated by the manufacturer's gradual accumulation of information about the foreign market. This information is acquired through monitoring its foreign agents and by expanding sales volumes to levels which would support a facility of minimum economic size. The establishment of a sales branch also demonstrates to customers a more solid commitment on the part of the manufacturer to support the market in question.

Often triggered by the failure or termination of an agency, the establishment of a foreign sales subsidiary subsequently becomes the platform upon which a manufacturing investment may be made. Looking at the cost side of the equation the transition to manufacturing, however, depends on the relationship of production costs abroad to production costs at home in addition to tariffs and transportation, as well as control considerations. This is the outsourcing decision facing many companies today.

The foreign direct investment process is stimulated by more than just economic incentives. An initiating force that galvanizes the firm into action is often required. The presence of a sales office also assists in collecting information and providing a better understanding of market opportunities, thereby significantly lowering perceptions of uncertainty and raising the probability that the firm will engage in foreign direct investment if the underlying cost conditions permit.

Foreign direct investment stems from the possession by the firm of a competitive advantage or certain unique assets. The ability to develop and protect the profits associated with these assets often requires the extension of some kind of control structure over productive assets that are distributed internationally. The implications of such control for the location of manufacturing facilities and the marketing of its output vary from time to time and may be unique to the firm in question.

Entering new foreign markets may be achieved, therefore, in a variety of ways, e.g. exporting and its various derivatives, strategic alliances in their various forms including marketing cooperation agreements, licences, franchising and joint ventures, and foreign direct investment and acquisition. Each of these ways of entering the foreign market places its own unique demands on the firm in terms of organizational and financial resources. It is necessary, therefore, to determine the most appropriate market entry mode for a given set of circumstances.

International market entry – concept and modes

Appropriate market entry mode

The appropriateness of a specific entry mode relates to the ease or difficulty with which a firm can enter new international markets (Gannon, 1995). Successful foreign market entry requires a superior performance on all aspects of marketing: 'Entry is one of the supreme tests of competitive ability. No longer is the company proving itself on familiar ground, instead it has to expose its competencies in a new area' (Yip, 1982, p. 85). In deciding the appropriate mode of entry to foreign markets, firms must answer two questions:

■ What level of resource commitment are they willing to make?
■ What level of control over the operation do they desire?

These two questions can only be evaluated in the context of the risk that the company believes it may encounter in the country being considered for entry (Brouthers, 1995, p. 10). In high-risk countries, firms may not be willing to commit resources. In countries they perceive as low risk, they may desire control over the operation assuming that they are as capable of managing the foreign operation as the domestic. Risk perception, therefore, shapes the evolution of the two questions which in turn leads to entry mode choice. The challenge of entering new international markets is formidable and successful companies use varying modes of market entry. Indeed, some companies use a variety of entry modes at the same time but normally in sequence depending on the nature of the market and strategy employed at different times or stages of the life cycle. Because of demand uncertainty in international markets, firms whose principal product is in the introductory or decline stage of the life cycle tend to avoid high-control foreign market entry modes, whereas firms in the growth and mature stages may prefer high-control modes (Bradley and Gannon, 2000).

The principal modes of entry include exporting, strategic alliances and foreign direct investment. For example, Heineken typically first enters a new international market through exporting; then it licenses a local brewer to produce its beer and eventually it acquires the same brewer or another as a way of establishing a full investment commitment in the market.

Figure 16.1
Choosing a
foreign market
entry mode

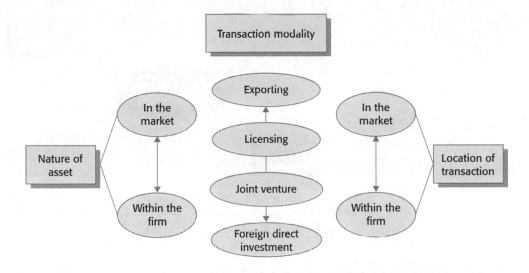

Choosing the entry mode

The international market entry mode may be determined by specifying the extent to which the knowledge or know-how embedded in the asset being transferred is explicated. The greater the codification or explication of the knowledge and know-how associated with the product or asset being transferred the more likely will the transfer be through exporting. When knowledge and know-how in the asset is tacit and difficult to codify, organizational and marketing factors raise the transaction costs associated with exporting and thereby promote the use of other forms of exchange. These pressures are shown as a movement in transfer modality from exporting through licensing and joint ventures to the establishment of a full international firm (Figure 16.1). The market entry mode is a continuum. By their very nature commodities, mature products and innovative products are high-touch, easy to define and separate from the firm.

In contrast, technical inventions, product coordination competences, technical skills and strategic marketing skills are to be found more towards the high technology end of the continuum. Firms whose competitive advantage or uniqueness derives from technical skills, product coordination skills or marketing skills seldom resort to exporting activities, joint ventures or licences since product bundles and constantly changing marketing strategies are difficult to contract out and hence are likely to be performed within the firm. The mode selected for foreign market entry depends on:

- the explication of knowledge in asset being transferred abroad; the decision reflects a fear of knowledge dissipation;

- the greater the codification or explication of knowledge the more likely exporting or some other form of non-investment entry mode will be used;

- when knowledge is tacit and difficult or expensive to codify, investment entry modes are used – joint ventures or foreign direct investment.

Figure 16.2
Foreign market
entry decision
framework

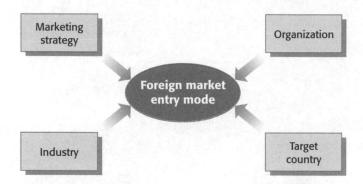

Source: adapted from Gannon, M. (1993) 'Towards a composite theory of foreign market entry mode choice: the role of marketing strategy variables', *Journal of Strategic Marketing*, **1**, 48

Framework for international market entry

Four sets of factors are thought to be critical to the entry mode choice decisions (Gannon, 1993, p. 47): marketing strategy variables, organization-specific variables, target country variables and industry-specific variables (Figure 16.2). Gannon subsumed into his framework the myriad entry mode variables identified by researchers over a period of half a century. A comprehensive examination of the entry mode choice is necessary given an environment characterized by shortened life cycles, rising R&D costs and the commercialization of innovative products and processes, the reduced lead time between the launch of innovative products and the arrival of imitative ones and radical political change (Bradley and Gannon, 2000). The choice of foreign market entry mode is influenced by the company's overall marketing strategy, its organizational structure, the industry and, of course, the target country market. These issues are discussed below.

Market concentration and market diversification

The firm in international markets faces two generic market entry strategies (Ayal and Zif, 1979): a market concentration strategy; or a market diversification strategy. In the first the firm concentrates effort on a few attractive markets while in market diversification the firm spreads its effort over a large number of markets (Figure 16.3).

Market concentration has been described as the purposeful selection of relatively few markets for more intensive development. Such a strategy is characterized by a slow and gradual rate of growth in the number of markets served. Its advantages, by no means universal to all industries, include specialization, scale economies and growth by penetration.

The firm following a market concentration strategy selects the more easily available international market targets while minimizing risk and investment. A market concentration strategy is based on a longer-term view of opportunities in international markets. In this case the firm supports its entry to the market with a heavy commitment of

Figure 16.3
Market, segment
and competitive
positioning

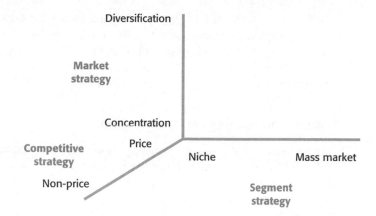

Source: adapted from Ayal, I. and Zif, J. (1979) 'Market expansion strategies in multinational marketing', *Journal of Marketing*, **43**, 84–94, and Piercy, N. (1982) *Export Strategy: Markets and Competition*, London: George Allen and Unwin

resources in pursuit of longer-term profitability through market penetration. A market concentration strategy favours high control, and firms with technically sophisticated products are more likely to choose a high-control entry mode (Bradley and Gannon, 2000). For some firms this may mean direct investment in local manufacturing facilities or local acquisition of an operating firm. Longer-term marketing relationships are established to ensure that the firm's products and reputation are well known and accepted. Close contact with customers, suppliers, distribution outlets and the government is cultivated. Prices are determined with an objective of sales growth. Short-term profits may be sacrificed. The firm adapts its products and services to the precise needs of each international market. A market concentration strategy recognizes that there may be direct competition with local firms and other international firms.

Market diversification involves a relatively equal spread of resources across many markets. The objective of a market diversification strategy is to obtain a high rate of return while maintaining a low level of resource commitment. The relative advantages of such an approach include flexibility, a reduced concentration and a way to capitalize rapidly on some significant competitive advantage. The method of market entry most frequently used in market diversification is some form of exporting or licensing. The success of exporting depends very much on the choice of agents and distributors. The responsibility for marketing and distribution falls to the partner abroad. Product modification is unlikely to be more than that required to meet standards and general market preferences. This is essentially a market skimming strategy.

Of course, the firm may pursue a mixed strategy in which it follows neither a pure concentration nor a pure diversification strategy but, instead, sells to a large number of markets while concentrating its resources on a selection of these. It is easy to see how such a situation could arise as firms often receive opportunistic business, outside the geographic markets in which they are concentrating.

Neither market concentration nor market diversification is a universal remedy for the international expansion problems facing the firm. Each strategy has its own strengths and weaknesses, which requires the decision-maker to find a match between the firm's situation and a possible strategy. In the longer term a strategy of diversification frequently leads to a reduction in the number of markets. This is a result of consolidation and abandonment of less profitable markets. With limited budgets and managerial resources, the level of resources allocated to each market under a strategy of diversification is lower than with concentration.

Market entry strategy and competition

The two strategies of market concentration and market diversification should lead to the selection of different levels of marketing effort and different marketing approaches in each market. The level of resources allocated to each market in a strategy of market diversification is likely to be lower than under a strategy of concentrating in fewer markets. Specifically, a lower level of marketing effort implies less promotional expenditure, more dependence on agents and a stronger tendency for price skimming. On the other hand concentration involves substantial investment in market share and using an aggressive competitive strategy based on heavy penetration pricing.

The strategic choices facing the firm suggest, therefore, taking account of segment strategies within countries (Figure 16.3). A country and segment concentration strategy means concentrating on specific market segments or niches in a few countries and on a gradual increase in the number of markets served. In this case competition on the basis of non-price factors tends to be very prevalent owing to the need to specialize to serve the needs of the segments.

A country concentration and segment diversification strategy means concentrating on markets but spreading the firm's product appeal across a number of different segments within those markets. One would still expect competition on non-price factors but the firm seeks a price advantage by capitalizing on economies of scale in promotion.

A country diversification and segment concentration strategy means concentrating on segments or niches while spreading across many country markets. Firms following such a strategy would be expected to seek a price or cost advantage by economies in promotion or production. Non-price factors, however, still play a significant role owing to the segment specialization. Lastly, a country and segment diversification strategy is based on a dual spreading in both segments and markets. This aggressive strategy is sometimes followed by firms with a product line appealing to many segments. Only the large well-resourced multinational companies are in a position to follow such a strategy. Price factors play an important role in the competitive strategy as the firm seeks a fast entry into the market. This strategy is sometimes attempted by smaller firms using commission agents which may allow a superficial coverage of the markets. The resource implications generally prevent smaller firms from following such a market entry strategy.

Linking market strategy, complexity and entry

Because of the complexity of international markets it may be necessary for the firm to shape its entry strategy to accommodate the specific needs of the market. Complexity

Figure 16.4
Market strategy,
complexity and
foreign market
entry

Market strategy	Market diversification	Export	Strategic alliances
	Market concentration	Strategic alliances	FDI
		Low	High

Market complexity

arises in dealing with customers, competition, intermediaries and governments in different country markets. The added dimension of different cultural and competitive situations adds to the difficulty of interpreting signals from such an environment.

Processing of market signals from diverse situations can be quite difficult, especially for firms new to international marketing. Market complexity forces the firm to carefully choose its entry mode from the wide range of available options (Figure 16.4).

Strategic international market entry must consider market complexity. Two possibilities are identified:

- low market complexity – the firm intent on market diversification might choose to export or a strategic alliance if the decision is to concentrate on a few markets;
- high market complexity – it may be advisable to form a strategic alliance if the firm wishes to diversify or acquire a local firm or invest directly in the market if concentration is the objective.

The degree of complexity existing in the market is likely to affect the choice of entry mode. A highly complex market might favour a direct investment or acquisition mode, whereas a situation of low marketing complexity might favour exporting as a means of entering international markets. Pernod-Ricard acquires strong local brands and then piggy-backs its own international brands on these to enter new unknown and, for Pernod-Ricard, more complex markets (Exhibit 16.1). Strategic alliances fall somewhere between the two extremes. The firm facing a relatively complex marketing environment may form a joint venture or other alliance with a partner firm abroad to reduce the complexity factor. In this regard many western firms considering entry to the Chinese or Japanese markets seek local partners, since the local culture is so strange to them that they need somebody with similar interests to mediate between themselves and local customers, employees and government agencies.

A strategic alliance can, however, increase marketing complexity for the firm in certain circumstances. A major cause of failure in joint ventures is the inability on the part of one of the partners to understand the external environmental factors: cultural differences; government rules and regulations; the market; sources of supply; competition; currency movements. Complexity may also be increased by a failure to understand the decision-making process. In many oriental countries firms place a heavy emphasis on a consensus decision-making process, whereas in the West the emphasis is on the outcome or decision itself.

Exhibit 16.1   Pernod-Ricard piggy-backs on local brands to enter foreign markets

While many of the large brand companies are reducing their portfolios to concentrate on a handful of international mega-brands, Pernod-Ricard has been buying up strong local brands to develop beyond their domestic borders while using their weight in the home market to build distribution networks to sell the group's core brands. As the market leader in Russia and Armenia, Yerevan's brandy is boosting Pernod-Ricard's commercial presence there. Another recent acquisition, Wyborowa, a Czech bitter aperitif, is serving the same purpose in Central Europe. 'Wyborowa allowed us to finance the creation of a strong distribution network to allow us to import our other brands. From three sales representatives, it's grown to 60', says the managing director, Thierry Jacquillat.

Unlike groups like Diageo, Pernod-Ricard believes tastes remain largely local, and that respecting them makes economic sense. 'The demand for strong local brands will remain,' Mr Jacquillat says. 'We need strong local brands to be able to impose our international brands. We think this is the right policy for us, and for the moment, our big strategic brands are growing faster than the rivals.' Some base strategic brands started out as 'local' brands. Kentucky-born Wild Turkey bourbon, for instance, one of the jewels of Pernod-Ricard's crown, was mostly a national brand in 1980 when the French company bought it. Now it sells more outside the US than inside. Pernod-Ricard is pursuing a similar strategy with its recently acquired Spanish gin, Larios, which is gradually pushing beyond Spain into other Mediterranean markets and next into Latin American ones. 'Who knows – maybe some day Larios will have as much snob appeal as Gordon's,' Mr Jacquillat muses.

Source: adapted from *The Wall Street Journal Europe*,
Thursday 25 November 1999, p. 6 and Pernod-Ricard

Selecting mode of international market entry

Entering new international product-markets

Competitive market factors associated with internationalization may be characterized in terms of business distance: domestic, similar or distant. The distance or newness of a market refers to the degree to which the products of the firm have not been sold in a particular foreign market. It is a matter of market familiarity. Familiarity with the market refers to the extent that the characteristics and mores of the market are understood within the company, but not necessarily as a result of participating in the market. For example, the managers of the R&A Bailey Company had some knowledge, gleaned from secondary sources and discussions with others, of the workings of the US market before the Bailey brand was launched there.

A similar three-way classification can be applied to products and underlying technologies: existing products, similar products and new products. Newness of a technology, process or service embodied in the product to be sold abroad refers to the degree to which that technology, process or service has already been used in the company. Some products require considerable adaptation and modification before they

Figure 16.5
International
product-market
decisions

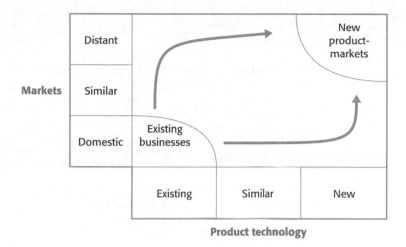

can be sold in most foreign markets and, therefore, may require a technology which is new to the firm.

Using these categories of newness and familiarity it is possible to classify new opportunities in an international product-market development matrix (Figure 16.5). Positions in this matrix may be further classified into those which are more or less demanding on the resources of the firm. In the bottom left-hand corner there is no extra pressure on the firm as this cell represents existing businesses, i.e. serving existing markets with existing products. As the firm moves away from this point in any direction the strategies become more demanding. The most demanding is to develop totally new products to serve distant markets. The further the firm moves from the origin the less familiar it is with the market and product requirements and the demands on the firm's resources.

Familiarity of the firm with its products and familiarity with the market being considered are the critical variables that explain much of the success or failure in approaches to internationalization. Related expansion strategies, i.e. strategies similar to those already being used by the company, tend to give better results than other unrelated strategies. Unrelated diversifications abroad usually provide lower returns while the highest profitability is associated with the use of related strategies. Successful international companies typically do not attempt to exploit potentially attractive new opportunities which require skills that they do not already possess. Market entry decisions in these firms acknowledge the core capabilities of the companies concerned.

Determining optimum international market entry strategies

Entry strategies which require high corporate involvement are usually reserved for new businesses with similar market characteristics and product requirements. Entry mechanisms requiring low corporate input seem best suited to unfamiliar situations (Roberts and Berry, 1985, p. 10). Large-scale entry decisions outside the sphere of the firm's familiarity are liable to miss important characteristics of the product market, thereby reducing the probability of success.

Figure 16.6
Product-market
strategy and
foreign market
entry

Markets		Product technology		
	Distant	Alliance	Invest	Invest
	Similar	Export	Alliance	Invest
	Existing	Present situation	New products	Alliance
		Existing	Similar	New

Product technology

Source: adapted from Roberts, E. B. and Berry, C. A. (1985) 'Entering new businesses: selecting strategies for success', *Sloan Management Review*, Spring, 5 – 6

This suggests a two-stage approach when a firm desires to enter unfamiliar new foreign product-markets. The first stage should be devoted to building corporate familiarity with the new area. Once that is done the firm can then decide whether to allocate more substantial resources to the opportunity and, if appropriate, select a mechanism for developing the business. Active nurturing of a minority investment in a foreign company allows the firm to monitor new technologies and markets. Over time, active involvement with the new investment may help the firm to move into the not-so-demanding similar product-market positions from which it may be easier to exercise judgement on the commitment of more substantial resources.

Acquisitions of small, high-technology, rapidly growing entrepreneurial firms may provide a more transparent window on a new product or market which can assist the transition towards higher familiarity. Before the firm reaches this stage of maturity in international marketing it will normally consider strategies involving less commitment.

Based on an adaptation of the Roberts and Berry (1985) framework the firm has a number of choices available to it (Figure 16.6). First it may decide to develop existing product markets, which is the least demanding option. Usually this is done by encouraging a greater penetration of existing markets such as the US. So far the firm is concentrated in its domestic market; it has not internationalized in any respect.

The firm could choose to develop a range of similar products for sale in existing markets, an option slightly more demanding. This product development strategy is quite common, especially among firms in large competitive markets. Alternatively the firm may decide to develop new markets nearby which are similar in terms of business distance to those already served, an option still slightly more demanding in terms of market development. The firm would normally enter such markets by exporting. In these circumstances a Spanish firm, for example, might export its food processing equipment to Tunisia.

A more demanding strategy is to develop a range of similar products for entry into similar international markets. In such circumstances a strategic alliance may be worth considering: licensing may be a useful alternative since it offers rapid access to proven products. A joint venture may also work since it gives access to a new market for a range of jointly manufactured products which may be similar to the firm's existing range.

A strategic alliance in the form of a joint venture may be an attractive proposition for the firm seeking to enter distant markets with an existing set of products. In this case the firm understands the product technology very well but seeks assistance in a distant market which would normally require a very different approach, which could be supplied more readily by a local firm. A strategic alliance in the form of a licence may be attractive for the firm seeking to develop new products for an existing market which has changed or become more competitive, for example. In such circumstances, joint ventures between large firms providing access to large lucrative markets like the United States and small European firms providing technological products may also be particularly appropriate. Alternatively the Spanish food equipment manufacturer might consider a joint venture to enter the China market.

Lastly, for the firm attempting to develop a range of similar products for distant markets, the entry method favours acquisition or foreign direct investment. The same is true for the firm attempting to develop entirely new products for markets which are similar. Acquisition or direct investment seems appropriate for new products in distant markets.

There is, therefore, no unique combination of product-market situation and entry strategy. Indeed, managers recognize that in choosing modes of entry it is necessary to recognize considerable interaction among them (Agarwal and Ramaswami, 1992). No one strategy is ideal for all new businesses. Within familiar markets virtually any strategy may be adopted and exporting or acquisition is probably most appropriate. In unfamiliar areas, however, these two high-involvement approaches are risky and greater familiarity should be established before they are attempted. Small-scale investments and small selective acquisitions constitute ideal vehicles for building familiarity and are often the preferred entry strategies in unfamiliar situations. In making a foreign market entry decision the firm must, therefore, consider the risk that can be tolerated and the control desired and the resources required to manage the balance between the two (Figure 16.7). In situations of low risk and low control, exporting, which

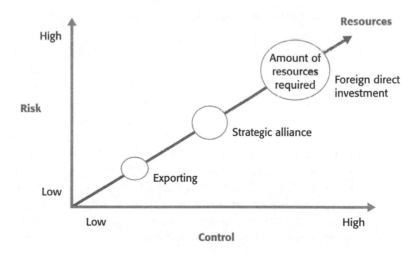

Figure 16.7
Foreign market entry, risk, resources and control

requires a commitment of fewer resources, would seem appropriate. Strategic alliances are used where the risk is greater and require considerably more resources. With strategic alliances, however, there is the possibility of greater control. For high risk markets greater control through heavy investment in new ventures or acquisitions may be required.

Choosing an entry mode for services

With respect to market entry strategies, the options open to the service firm are similar to those available for the product marketing firm: exporting; strategic alliances; acquisitions–direct investment. Exporting has already been shown to be difficult for the services firm since the delivery system must accompany the service. By embodying services in a product, it may be easier to access foreign markets. This is a particularly attractive option when barriers to trade in services are greater than barriers on merchandise trade. By embodying services in products, the company moves towards the tangible dominant part of the product–service continuum. Service contracts sold as part of an equipment purchase package are an example: Levi Strauss embodies a design service in the famous denim jeans which are branded and sold in many markets. Benetton similarly embodies design and style in clothing sold through leading retailers throughout the world. Forms of strategic alliance such as joint ventures abound and are used more often than in product marketing due to the cultural element of services and the different people involved. Locals can overcome many barriers confronting the service marketing firm.

The licensing of a service operation has never been as widespread as it is for products but, as was seen in the previous chapter, franchising of services operations is growing. The service firm must offer a substantial payment in return for the licence fee. To avoid the foreign counterpart 'taking the idea and going it alone', Winter (1970) suggests that an acceptable arrangement should include the following:

■ a strong name;
■ a well-designed marketing strategy;
■ a complete manualized operation system;
■ substantial opportunity for profit.

The name of the firm and the goodwill attached to the trademark are crucial elements in the service offering process; this is an essential aspect of franchising. When a product is taken to international markets, these markets are generally familiar with the product. For a service marketing firm such will not be the case; the firm's name and reputation are critical to selling the service successfully and these must be given before purchase of the service can begin. The confidence of the prospective client or customer must be won initially. The firm's name and existing experience may not be sufficient, however. The conditions in the marketing environment must be conducive.

Franchising appears to be a good market entry choice for service companies, affording a greater degree of control over the elements of the service component. Franchising is frequently used in the fast food industry.

Joint ventures, acquisitions and foreign direct investment decisions for service firms, in the form of a branch or subsidiary, may also be appropriate but the firm must consider the costs of the investment compared with other market entry modes. Consideration must be given to the obvious scope for greater control, particularly quality control with such modes of foreign market entry.

For services companies there may be no clear path through the maze. Indeed service companies face unique difficulties in obtaining international competitive advantage, particularly locational advantage. This is the belief among the large law firms now actively seeking ways of entering and expanding in international markets on both sides of the Atlantic. Accounting firms, banks and advertising agencies generally follow their customers abroad by establishing local offices and outlets. Law firms until recently have been reluctant to join the international race whether because of prudence or patience or simply that they were unable to determine the best approach. Exporting law services does not work well where local knowledge is important. Joint ventures hold more promise while acquisitions may be preferred by some; organic growth through investment, though slow, may be preferred by others (Exhibit 16.2).

Exhibit 16.2   The battle for global supremacy among law firms

Business went global, accounting firms chased it round the world, but law firms have yet to finish the race. Nevertheless, the global elite is split into three groups heading towards the inevitable shake-out in the field, the potent, the prudent and the patient. At the moment, 81 of the top 100 law firms ranked by revenue are US based; however, their 15 UK counterparts, 'the magic circle', typify the potent group. While the potent strive to be one of the surviving firms in an envisaged global shake-out, the prudent follow a strategy, less focused on such risky investments like acquisitions, but banking on success through performance rather than scale. In between lie the patient, mostly American firms with the exception of Slaughter and May, the UK's most profitable firm, who are not chasing mergers, opting to maintain integrity in the partnership.

The key to any global strategy will be establishing top-tier practices on both sides of the Atlantic, not easy for either group. UK firms enjoy strong presences in Europe and Asia while finding it tough to break New York, the bastion of US practice and the most lucrative market in the world. While organic growth via hiring new staff may be expensive, mergers pose issues of culture clash, as Clifford Chance found when it took over New York's Rogers and Wells and Germany's Punder, Volhard Weber and Axster both in 2000. Difficulties in integration in their case were offset by the platform the merger created from which the business could pursue its global ambitions.

Structurally, UK firms and US firms differ greatly in their remuneration systems, where the Americans' 'eat what you kill' attitude may lose out to the hierarchical lockstep approach of the magic circle. Ultimately, copying the growth strategies of banks and accounting firms may facilitate global ambitions; however, this shouldn't be at the expense of profits and a tried and tested successful business ethos.

Source: based upon an article by Sherwood, B., 'The battle for supremacy', *Financial Times*, Monday 22 March 2004, p. 11

Sequencing international market entry

Strategic sequencing of international market entry raises a different set of problems which the firm must consider. As a result of long-term objectives, market choices may be linked and embedded in each other. Here concern rests with deciding on the second and subsequent foreign markets to enter having successfully entered the first one. The implication is that the first entry influences subsequent entries and, therefore, it is important for the firm to examine not just the first foreign market entry but also to consider the sequence of possible entries as a process to be managed. Many international companies have developed global networks of subsidiaries and a global scanning capability. Furthermore, initial production does not necessarily occur in the market which inspired the innovation. The location of production is usually suggested by costs and factor availability. Very often, for cost reasons, it is necessary to locate initial production in low-cost countries in order to compete. Many new products are launched simultaneously in numerous markets; global roll-outs are a common feature in many product-markets.

The strategic sequencing of entry to international markets is, therefore, a key decision area for the international firm. In sequencing foreign market entry Ayal and Zif (1979) suggest a hierarchical approach that produces a slow sequence of entries to different markets depending on their receptivity. This approach has been dubbed the waterfall model (Ohmae, 1989) to depict the situation where innovations trickle down in a slow-moving cascade from the most to the least receptive country. According to this approach, after a successful domestic launch of a new product, the company introduces it into other receptive markets and then into less receptive markets. Baileys Original Irish Cream liqueur was first launched in the Netherlands – a very receptive market for international products, later into Belgium, Denmark, France and Germany – markets that at the time were less receptive.

Global competition does not always force a firm to introduce a new product simultaneously in all its markets (Kalish *et al.*, 1995). The determining factors appear to be the nature of the product, the market cost conditions and competition. Firms are attracted to the waterfall strategy, according to Kalish *et al.* (1995, p. 115), when:

- the product has a long life cycle;
- the foreign market is small relative to the domestic market;
- the foreign market is not innovative and growth is slow;
- there are weak competitors in the foreign market and they collude;
- the entering firm enjoys a monopoly position in the foreign market.

The rapidly changing marketing environment, however, the integration of regional markets, the rapid diffusion of technology and the worldwide access to communications and information technologies would indicate that most of the above conditions do not always hold for the majority of companies active in international markets. The market receptivity approach may need to be modified or calibrated somewhat.

As already mentioned a market sequencing strategy based on concentration or diversification is widely discussed in the literature (Hirsch and Lev, 1973; Ayal and Zif, 1979; Sizer, 1983). As was seen above two generic strategies may be used to modify the market receptivity approach:

■ enter a small number of the most promising markets initially; only after a 'presence' is established in these markets and the potential of the product proved are new and less lucrative markets entered;

■ enter simultaneously as many potential markets as possible; initial wide diversification is followed by a period of consolidation where less profitable markets are abandoned.

These two approaches to market sequencing have implications for different elements of the marketing programme, especially pricing.

After a number of years, both strategies may result in the firm operating in the same number of markets (Ayal and Zif, 1979). The alternative expansion routes may generate totally different consequences in terms of sales, market shares and profits over time. A rapid rate of market expansion is usually accomplished by devoting limited resources and time to a careful study of each foreign market prior to entry. With this approach the firm may make more mistakes and may be more likely to enter unprofitable markets. The strategy chosen usually depends on the nature and extent of the resources that the firm is able and willing to invest in the markets examined. It also depends on the relative attractiveness of its domestic market, in particular its size and growth rate.

An alternative approach is to develop a strategy based on sequencing and market groups. As illustrated earlier, the sequence of market entry may be dependent on the firm's policy of grouping foreign markets. Hence, the sequence of entry might be as follows:

■ clusters of countries selected on the basis of common criteria, e.g. size, culture, language;

■ select the most promising cluster of countries and then select the most promising country from that cluster;

■ in deciding to enter additional countries, select from the same cluster before moving on to others.

Market groups may also influence the entry sequence in other ways. Many firms find that they need more than one foreign market to provide sufficient volume of sales to justify the modifications to products and production methods involved and to allow these to be made economically. The firm may, therefore, group markets with similar characteristics, and a product for a group of markets having been adapted, all markets in that group may be entered simultaneously or at least rapidly in sequence depending on other characteristics. There are many examples of this approach, as may be observed in firms that manufacture products customized for linguistically homogeneous markets.

Summary

The strategic aspects of the market entry decision and the various means of market entry are related to the firm's choice of market strategy. The relationship between market strategy, complexity of international markets and market entry must be considered. A series of approaches was discussed and an attempt was made to integrate them into a form which enables the firm to make an optimum choice of entry strategy. The chapter is divided into sections that examine the concept of international market entry; generic market entry strategies; the various ways of entering international markets in practice and the issue of sequencing subsequent entry into additional foreign markets. The concept of entry to international markets was discussed in the context of how the firm uses information about opportunities in foreign markets; how it acquires resources, accesses the markets and overcomes entry barriers.

Two generic market entry strategies may be used by the firm in international markets: a market penetration strategy by which the firm concentrates in a select number of markets; and a market skimming strategy by which it enters a large number of markets simultaneously or in rapid succession. These strategic alternatives apply to country markets and to segments within each country market. The greater the range of choice the more complex the decision.

A framework based on product-market familiarity is used to help the firm to decide its optimum entry choice. Entering foreign markets may be achieved in a variety of ways: exporting and its various derivatives; strategic alliances, especially joint ventures, licensing, and foreign acquisition and direct investment.

The choice of one market may be linked to the choice of another. For this reason it may be important to examine a combination of entry methods involving a sequence of decisions over time for related markets. A framework based on product-market familiarity may be used to decide the optimum choice. Sequencing may be seen, therefore, as a generic long-run strategy for the firm in international markets. Two alternatives are discussed: the possibility of entering a small number of promising markets initially; or simultaneously entering as many markets as possible. The advantages and disadvantages of both approaches were examined.

Questions

1. Discuss the commonly held belief that there is no single market entry strategy which is appropriate in all circumstances.

2. Why does the international firm often have to combine different levels of market entry to reach world markets effectively?

3. Discuss the proposition that the nature of the asset being transferred between markets and the location of the transaction should determine the type of foreign entry mode to be used.

4. What are the strengths and weaknesses of each mode of market entry for a medium-size firm selling a patented sophisticated electronic component? The firm at present is

working close to full capacity and demand for the component is doubling every two years. An immediate decision is required.

5. Describe the market entry decision framework based on market and product familiarity developed in the chapter.

References

Agarwal, S. and Ramaswani, S. N. (1992) 'Choice of foreign market entry mode: impact of owership, location and internationalization factors', *Journal of International Business Studies*, **23**, 1–27.

Ayal, I. and Zif, J. (1979) 'Market expansion strategies in multinational marketing', *Journal of Marketing*, **43**, 84–94.

Bradley, F. and Gannon, M. (2000) 'Does the firm's technology and marketing profile affect foreign market entry?', *Journal of International Marketing*, **8** (4), 12–36.

Brouthers, K. D. (1995) 'The influence of international risk on entry mode strategy in the computer software industry', *Management International Review*, **35** (1), 7–28.

Gannon, M. (1993) 'Towards a composite theory of foreign market entry mode choice: the role of marketing strategy variables', *Journal of Strategic Marketing*, **1**, 41–54.

Gannon, M. (1995) *Towards a Composite Theory of Entry Mode Choice*, PhD Dissertation, Graduate School of Business, University College Dublin, Dublin, March.

Hirsch, S. and Lev, B. (1973) 'Foreign marketing strategies – a note', *Management International Review*, **6** (73), 81–8.

Kalish, S., Mahajan, V. and Muller, E. (1995) 'Waterfall and sprinkler new-product strategies in competitive global markets', *International Journal of Research in Marketing*, **12**, 105–19.

Ohmae, K. (1989) 'Managing in a borderless world', *Harvard Business Review*, **67** (May–June), 152–61.

Piercy, N. (1982) *Export Strategy: Markets and Competition*, London: George Allen and Unwin.

Roberts, E. B. and Berry, C. A. (1985) 'Entering new businesses: selecting strategies for success', *Sloan Management Review*, **26** (Spring), 3–17.

Sizer, J. (1983) 'Export market analysis and price strategies', *Management Accounting* (January), 30–3.

Winter, E. L. (1970) 'How to license a service', *Columbia Journal of World Business*, **5** (September–October), 83–5.

Yip, G. S. (1982) 'Gateways to entry', *Harvard Business Review*, **60** (September–October), 85–92.

Part IV International marketing operations

Developing an international marketing strategy and an international marketing entry strategy without a detailed implementation or application plan are fruitless exercises in themselves. They must be accompanied by a detailed consideration of how the firm distributes its products and services internationally, how it prices them and how it sells and negotiates with foreign based customers. This part consists of four chapters dealing with these three important topics while the last chapter in the book is devoted to assessing international marketing operations and performance. This chapter pays special attention to the international planning context in which performance measurement should occur. Attention is given to performance measures that address traditional short-term financial requirements and the broader strategic objectives of the firm.

17 Channels of international distribution

Although recognized as a subject of study in its own right many firms fall into the trap of functional myopia by failing to integrate decisions on distribution and channels with other key management decisions. Channel access to international markets and customers is a key decision area facing companies. Accelerating product life cycles and increasing capital requirements for research and development in many product areas require rapid international market entry to numerous markets. The ability to maximize the number of markets successfully entered requires access to a highly developed distribution system characterized usually by coordination of the activities of interdependent firms that may have multiple and conflicting objectives.

From a strategic perspective, most firms establish channel policies which are uniformly applied to all intermediaries, but this may be suboptimal. Because customers in different geographic segments are different, they require different distribution services, so different quality service levels should be provided. Competitive advantage may be gained by differentiating the service provided by market segment. Astute use of the perceived quality of distribution service significantly affects the closeness of exporter–importer relationship. After studying this chapter students should be able to:

- evaluate the relevance of various channels for the international distribution of different types of products;
- specify how and why distribution channels vary from country to country;
- specify the role of the Internet in the possible disintermediation of international distribution channels;
- understand the factors to be considered in motivating channel members;
- understand why channel conflicts occur and how they can be resolved.

Nature of international channels of distribution

While distribution channel decisions face all international firms at some time or other they are very much the concern of firms that decide to enter foreign markets through

Figure 17.1
Channels of
distribution in
international
markets

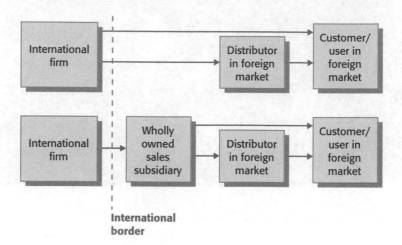

exporting. At the same time, firms that enter using other modes such as alliances or acquisition or investment usually discover that exporting and, hence, distribution feature in the decision at some stage in the internationalization process. There are myriad distribution relationships which arise in the transfer of products and services from a provider located in one country to a customer located in another. One of the more important differences between establishing a domestic or international distribution system is the complexity of the variables involved. The firm frequently finds that it must serve each foreign market with a different kind of distribution system. Thus, the key success factors in one market may not be transferable to another.

Distribution networks in different countries may also have much in common, so observing similarities rather than differences may be worthwhile. There is also a greater emphasis on direct distribution from point of manufacture to point of use or consumption. Direct distribution in international markets is quite common for industrial products and systems but it is also found in other areas including computers, cosmetics and some packaged goods (Figure 17.1). Distributors may be found in consumer products markets and for small industrial goods such as compressors, small motors and other equipment. In many situations the international firm establishes a wholly owned subsidiary in the foreign market and serves customers in that market directly or indirectly through distributors.

Complicated channel systems which are long and involve margins at each stage are sometimes considered as barriers to international market entry. In other situations, multitiered distribution systems which have evolved over many generations make it very difficult for the international firm to penetrate. Sometimes foreign governments claim that such distribution structures prevent trade and are, therefore, a barrier to international competition.

There are a number of key differences between domestic and international channels of distribution:

- higher complexity of variables involved in the international distribution channel;
- different markets have different distribution requirements;

- a successful domestic approach not always transferable abroad;
- common elements may exist which are transferable;
- the interaction of cultures in both the domestic and foreign markets must be considered.

Role of channel intermediaries

By clearly specifying channel roles, cooperating firms reduce the potential for conflict and improve the performance of the entire channel system. Roles define appropriate behaviour for firms occupying each position in the system. Role consensus enables channel members to anticipate the behaviour of others and to operate collectively in a unified manner. Establishing that consensus is especially difficult among firms operating under different business practices and in different cultures and language.

There are five important roles for international marketing intermediaries:

- coordinate and assemble international buyer demand and product availability; reduce bargaining asymmetry between buyers and sellers in different countries and cultures;
- protect buyers and sellers from opportunistic behaviour; to serve as agents of trust in cross-cultural context;
- reduce market transaction costs;
- match buyers and sellers in different countries – establish contacts and customer relations in selected markets;
- provide the physical distribution/logistical support necessary for the company's product category.

With regard to the first point, the intermediary aggregates the demand of many customers and the products of many suppliers located in many different international markets and so avoids the need for each customer to negotiate individually with a corresponding supplier. The potential benefits include a reduction of transactions costs, achieving the advantages of scale and scope economies and reducing asymmetries in the bargaining power of customers and suppliers located in different countries and cultures. On the second point, intermediaries may be able to prevent parties to a market exchange or relationship from behaving opportunistically. Because of their experience in the market and being subject to a different legal system, intermediaries have significant incentives to ensure that market exchanges are completed and that both the supplier and the customer comply with their agreement. They become an agent of trust in a cross-cultural context.

With regard to providing information, exchange between companies is expensive especially if it involves implicit contextual knowledge that cannot easily be explicated. In these instances, the intermediary can facilitate the exchange of information by coordinating the process and translating the information that moves between suppliers and customers in different markets. This is a particularly important function in international marketing where culture, language and different business practices intervene.

Because of the differences in a number of companies and customers, intermediaries can also reduce the overall processing and coordination costs.

Lastly, the need of customers to locate an appropriate supplier and for suppliers to locate appropriate customers can be accommodated by an intermediary that becomes the focal point of this match. In these circumstances intermediaries can provide a better price discovery mechanism and acquire better knowledge of the characteristics of market demand and supply preferred by individual customers and suppliers.

Integrated channels for international distribution

The issue of deciding which activities should be performed by the firm itself and which should be performed by others outside the firm was discussed earlier in the context of the business system within which the firm operates. Here the same issue is discussed from the point of view of effective control and cost regarding the international channel. Internalizing international distribution within the firm gives rise to a trade-off between cost and control. Some firms, especially strong brand companies, insist on owning their international distributors where possible. This policy of ownership or shared ownership is followed to ensure complete control of brand positioning in each international market and to ensure that the company has access to its customers. The choice of approach can be interpreted as a transactions costs problem. The balance of control and cost evaluated in terms of transactions costs, broadly defined, determines whether international distribution should take place through subsidiaries of the firm or through independent distributors.

Transactions costs are closely linked to psychic distance of markets and experience already obtained in international markets (Klein and Roth, 1990, pp. 30–2). Integration offers the benefit of having a captive outlet in each international market entered. Such extensive control implies the commitment of many resources, which means that failure is thereby much more expensive. In contrast, the use of an independent distributor implies specialization and associated benefits. Ready-made access to markets means that learning costs are low and entry is quickly and effectively expedited.

As already mentioned, the value of independent distributors with regard to channel loyalty and control of the marketing programme is questionable. Benetton, an Italian knitwear manufacturer, believes in distributing its products through its own agents wherever possible. This has allowed Benetton to standardize its promotions and distribution: inventories; type of outlet; shipment; types and sizes.

Firms are sometimes advised to use independent distributors if the market is competitive. Other influencing factors include the cost of monitoring the performance of the intermediary, the stage of the life cycle for the product and the degree of standardization applied to the marketing programme.

Constraints on channel design

In designing an international distribution network, territorial exclusivity is a matter of concern to manufacturer-exporters and intermediary partners in the distribution system. Attention is focused on exclusive territories because manufacturers wish to maintain a brand's image by selling only through a certain type of retailer or because the product requires a high level of customer service. To accomplish these objectives, the manufacturer-exporter may require retailers to invest in special training and equipment. Since this often involves large commitments by both parties, the manufacturer may insist that its retailers may not sell a rival's products. When such practices provide an adequate combination of service and prices, consumers benefit. Under this arrangement, there is an incentive for the manufacturer to raise prices and/or to contract with another retailer nearby. In this way, the manufacturer obtains a larger share of the profits or encourages greater sales through competition at retail level. With an increased number of retailers, the manufacturer is free to raise prices to all. To protect itself from the possibility of such behaviour, the retailer seeks an exclusive territory before making any commitments. In these circumstances, territorial monopolies can be beneficial to all parties. Retailers understand that manufacturers cannot exert power over them and manufacturers realize that their products will be treated loyally and that both parties can serve customers well and make profits in the process.

In some circumstances, however, retailer monopolies can raise prices to consumers. This occurs in many parts of Europe where regulations inhibit potential competitors from entering the market. These retailers demand exclusivity from the manufacturer as a price for carrying the products but leave consumers with a restrictive choice.

The situation is particularly aggravated in the European Union, when potential sales outlets are tied up by competitors, e.g the beer market. A major purpose of the EU is to promote a single competitive market throughout its territory. In doing so, the Commission of the EU deals with restrictive agreements among manufacturers, wholesalers and retailers or so-called 'vertical restraints'. Some vertical restraints may reduce competition, but others may benefit consumers. A manufacturer may attempt to force all retailers to sell its products at the same price or it might require distributors who sell its products to refrain from selling those of rivals. The Commission blocks any arrangement that grants a retailer exclusive rights to serve customers in its area (European Commission, 1997).

The task facing the European Commission is to determine the negative impact of territorial protection on a case by case basis, depending on industry structure and the particular country market. If there is not much competition among rival brands, exclusive territories strengthen the monopolist's position and reduce benefits to consumers. If there are many rival brands, however, a territorial monopoly in a single brand may do little harm to consumers. With many specialized retailers, one for each brand of car, for example, customers would be able to shop around easily both nearby and even across European borders.

Structure and function of channels of distribution

There are a number of things which are common in all channels, domestic and international. Participants in the channel usually include manufacturers, distributors and wholesalers, retailers, end-users and consumers. There are many alternative channels

Figure 17.2
Multiple
channels serve
international
markets

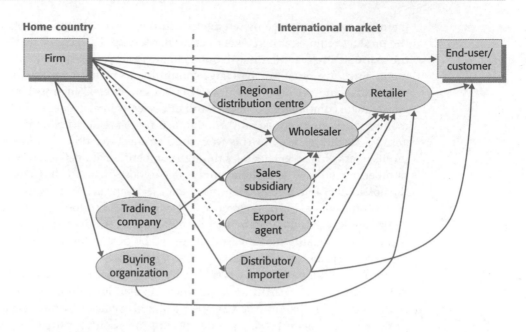

for the firm in international markets to choose from and many decision areas which need to be managed (Figure 17.2). The nature of the distribution activities performed in the various distribution channels, in some cases, can be quite similar but in other circumstances additional services and support are provided, including storage, transport, customs clearance and packaging. In selecting an international distribution channel the firm must make two decisions:

■ decide the way in which its products and services will be made available to users in designated foreign markets;
■ decide the combination of intermediaries and services to be used.

As already noted, the most direct distribution is from the firm to the end-user or customer. One of the most indirect ways is through a buying organization located in the domestic market usually owned by large international retailers or department stores such as Bloomingdales in New York. Trading companies are commonly used for commodities exported from new emerging markets and countries where central government interference in trade is high. International firms often sell directly to regional wholesalers in large country markets such as the United States. Sales subsidiaries are outlets in international markets owned by the firm which give the firm a presence in the market to keep close to the customer.

Agents and distributors are the most popular type of intermediary although, strictly, agents represent the international firm as principal and do not take title to the goods. There are important differences between agents and distributors which the firm should consider. The agent abroad is a contractor who knows the market, acquires orders and carries out other tasks, making the agent in effect the company's salesperson in the foreign market. The agent introduces the company into direct contact with customers to whom the company supplies the product. Once the goods are sold the agent is entitled to a commission, the amount depending on the nature of the product and services provided.

An agent typically does not need more than a good communications system to operate successfully. The agent, however, must be extremely knowledgeable about trends in the market. Apart from getting paid, the agent has no other financial interest in the sale. It is the company's responsibility to deliver the goods on time according to the agreed specifications and to collect payment from the customer. A proven skill derived from market knowledge, business contacts and market experience are essential characteristics when appointing an agent. As the agent is a foreign based sales representative and a key member of the company's team though not an employee, it is also crucial that the agent's culture and style blend with that of the company. A distributor on the other hand is the company's customer who buys and imports the goods, stores them and makes a profit by selling them to a third party. Exporting may not be the appropriate choice if the firm is unable to provide user support in distant markets; in such circumstances the firm may have to choose a recognized distributor (Burgel and Murray, 2000). A distributor typically has warehousing facilities, a sales and distribution network and an after-sales service capable of providing technical assistance if necessary. In many respects appointing a distributor is a much stronger arrangement for representation abroad and often easier to make. The problem of finding customers and getting paid fall to the distributor. Appointing a distributor is most effective where there is large number of relatively small customers for the company's products. Using distributors is less suitable in more concentrated industrial markets where technical sales and servicing can only be provided by the company's qualified staff.

Usually distributors handle large volumes of fast-moving goods such as those sold in supermarkets or department stores. They also handle standard industrial items such as building materials, components, low-cost machinery and smaller items of equipment where the customer is relying on a ready supply in the market. Clothing, footwear and textiles and the more expensive customized items of capital equipment are more usually the business of agents.

Distributors provide a stronger presence in the market, a capability to keep product supplies available to customers and, because they take title to the goods, relieve the exporting company of the task of collecting payments from the ultimate customers, which can be a major task. Because distributors absorb the cost of holding inventory and providing a sales force, sole and exclusive distribution rights in a defined territory are usually expected. This, however, may not be legally possible under local or EU competition laws.

An increasingly important feature of international distribution is the emergence of the regional distribution centres, primarily a feature of food marketing, established to serve the large supermarket chains. In the United Kingdom such distribution centres are usually owned and integrated by the supermarket chains. In continental Europe they are usually independently owned so integration is not a feature. These distribution centres assemble products from a wide range of suppliers from all over the world, maintain inventories for a number of supermarkets in a region and provide a just-in-time delivery service to the individual stores. There are considerable cost savings in distributing through regional distribution centres rather than to individual stores but

Figure 17.3
Nature and
direction of
international
channel
activities

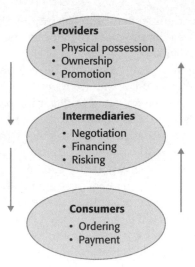

there is a loss of control over the way branded food products are merchandized. Regional distribution centres complement the rise of private label especially in the UK where private label is such a large part of the business of supermarkets chains, the owners of the regional distribution centres.

Functions of the international channel

Companies may appoint different types of intermediary in the foreign market to serve as their local representative. Managing channels of distribution is about improving the performance of eight different 'flows' which move up and down the channel (Figure 17.3). Physical possession, ownership and promotion move from the provider to the consumer whereas ordering and payment move in the opposite fashion. Other important flows – negotiation, financing and absorbing risk – move in either direction, depending on custom and practice in the industry and the power of individual channel members. While they are activities found in all channels of distribution, in international marketing, however, these activities require considerable attention as new economic, cultural and legal factors intervene. In particular the firm must consider the skills required to effectively negotiate finance across borders and to be able to communicate among channel participants. Hence, the choice of channel is constrained by numerous factors which may influence the efficacy of a particular route to customers located abroad.

Selecting an international intermediary

Appointing an agent or a distributor depends on the nature of the product and the expected sales volume and the risks involved. In addition to the normal financial and risk factors there are a number of things the company should consider when appointing an agent or a distributor:

- geographical area and market segments covered – the need to avoid domain conflict among agents or distributors;

- range of products and companies already represented – complementary or competitive;

- customers served and trade contacts used – nature and number;

- product knowledge and application experience;

- servicing and after-sales service capability;

- level and form of commission or margins required.

Many of the above points are obvious but one, after-sales service, requires particular attention by both parties. Ultimately, after-sales service is delivered mostly through intermediaries so a firm's attempt to provide after-sales service can be foiled by un-cooperative intermediaries (Asugman *et al.*, 1997, p. 25). The firm should select inter-mediaries so that it can effectively compel them to support its after-sales service. It should be possible at the recruitment stage to select intermediaries who understand the importance of after-sales service and are committed to serving customers. The international firm may also be in a position to reinforce and reward the intermediary's role in the successful delivery of after-sales service in the market.

Frequently situations arise where it is not clear whether the company's represent-ative is acting as an agent or a distributor. In some cases a representative may be an agent in respect of some of the company's products and a distributor in respect of others. In such cases it is as well for the company to note that the legal relationship between it and its agents and distributors is a matter of contract. It arises from the actual nature of the relationship, agreements with them and the provisions of the appropriate law. It does not simply depend on the title conferred on them or used in practice. That title, however, may greatly affect the legal relationship with third parties who take it at face value without understanding the private arrangements between the company and the foreign market representative.

Most firms also attempt to ensure that agents or distributors do not acquire the legal status of employees which can arise by implication of law unless the contract appoint-ing them is clearly expressed. Contracts of whatever kind usually confer legal rights and responsibilities on each party and can come into being by an exchange of letters or a phone call or, as one manger once noted, 'by an enthusiastic discussion over a busi-ness lunch'. It is usually advisable, therefore, in establishing representation in foreign markets to seek legal advice.

Trade-offs and conflict in the distribution channel

Manufacturers and intermediaries in international channels have very different perspectives. It is necessary to achieve a subtle blending of the needs and objectives of all parties in the system: manufacturer, intermediary and user/consumer. These per-spectives are manifested in the criteria that each uses to select the other and thereby reach a channel equilibrium (Figure 17.4). Expectations of the distribution channel by customers and other users include the traditional issues of product, price, delivery and service satisfaction.

Figure 17.4
Balancing
channel
member
requirements

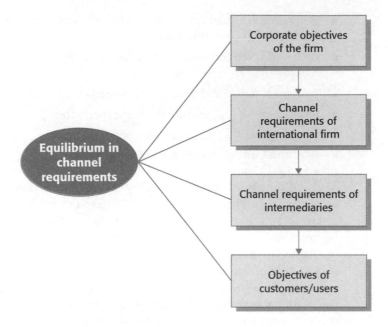

The factors important to the manufacturer in selecting intermediaries usually involve final consumer considerations, company strategic issues and financial returns. These corporate objectives revolve around matters of market share and profits, intermediary and consumer loyalty and reseller control. The manufacturer-exporter usually evaluates potential channel partners on the basis of their contacts and relationships with customers in target markets and their capabilities, reputation and past performance in respect of sales and service. The manufacturer normally checks that the functions provided by the intermediary complement those provided by the manufacturer. In this regard the manufacturer also evaluates the potential contribution of the product or service to the intermediary's needs; profit; contribution; and gaps in product line. Here the manufacturer is attempting to determine the probability of effective long-term working relations. Lastly, it is necessary to examine the potential intermediary's financial status and management ability.

Manufacturers evaluate potential foreign intermediaries using four broad criteria:

■ resources of firm and product characteristics;
■ buyer procurement strategy and commitment;
■ markets and market segments served; outlet penetration, channel inventories; and
■ firm's marketing programme, promotion and selling support, market intelligence, value added downstream.

Factors important to intermediaries in establishing relationships with manufacturers usually involve the manufacturer's product and/or brand image, the support and assistance provided and the compatibility of the product with the intermediary's existing line. The intermediary is also concerned with the trade reputation of the manufacturer and the potential profit contribution of the product to the intermediary. Sometimes it is difficult for a manufacturer to break into a distribution system for reasons known only to the intermediary. The manufacturer is concerned with the expected reaction of channel members to the attempted entry by the manufacturer to the channel system. Lastly, intermediaries examine the estimated investment costs of adding the new product to the existing business. Intermediaries evaluate potential exporter manufacturers using a range of criteria:

■ product or brand image, reputation of the manufacturer and commitment;

■ assistance provided – marketing and sales support and start-up costs for new product launch, credit terms;

■ complementarity with existing product range and area exclusivity;

■ financial stability of manufacturer;

■ supply capacity of manufacturer; and

■ potential profit contribution; acceptable margins and high sales turnover.

Value added in the downstream channel is essential to suppliers and the ability to replace suppliers is essential to intermediaries (Kim and Frazier, 1996, p. 21). For suppliers, the extent of value added is the most crucial for the existence of a channel system and the achievement of channel goals. Downstream value-added activities include basic economic values such as the reduction of transaction costs, but they also include social values, such as mutual support and trust. Members of Japanese channels of distribution consider social as well as economic factors in developing and managing channel relationships. When the value added in downstream activities is high, suppliers take a greater interest in enhancing cooperation and coordination with channel partners. When value added is low, suppliers are less likely to be worried about relationships with intermediaries.

Replaceability of suppliers refers to the ease with which suppliers can be changed. Supplier replaceability reflects the general value of supplier relationships to intermediaries. When suppliers are easy to replace, intermediaries are unlikely to commit strongly to them. When suppliers are difficult to replace, for whatever reason, intermediaries are likely to be more concerned about their relationship with them (Heide and John, 1988). Suppliers may be difficult to replace because of social concerns, loyalty and reputation factors experienced by intermediaries (Czinkota and Woronoff, 1986).

Cost effectiveness and control in international distribution channels

Cost effectiveness in international channels of distribution

In deciding a distribution strategy for international markets or in assessing existing channels the firm must consider the cost of the alternative chosen, the barriers to entry in the market, the orientation of intermediaries, the ability of the channel to distribute the range of the firm's products and the characteristics of the product or service and the customer. Distribution costs, in particular delivery costs, were one of the reasons IKEA, the Swedish self-assembly furniture group, went abroad to source supplies. It was founder Ingvar Kamprad's fear of paying delivery costs that gave him the idea of producing build-it-yourself items in the early 1950s. When Swedish competitors imposed a boycott on the fledging IKEA in the late 1950s, threatening to stop doing business with suppliers who sold to IKEA, Kamprad made contact with Polish producers and secured deliveries of inexpensive components that could be packaged flat for home assembly. Cost effectiveness, whether it refers to exports or to imports, is an important decision area for the firm. At the same time it is essential that factors other than cost are considered simultaneously. An effective way of evaluating these factors is to use a framework based on Cateora's (1993) five Cs:

- coverage – ability of channel to reach customers to achieve market share and growth objectives;
- character – compatibility of channel with the firm's desired product positioning;
- continuity – loyalty of channel to the firm;
- control – ability of the firm to control total marketing programme for the product or service;
- cost – investment required to establish and maintain the channel – variable associated with sales level. Fixed costs required to manage the channel: inventories, facilities, training of sales force.

Considerations of market coverage usually refer to the firm's objectives regarding market penetration and market share or merely sales. The firm attempts to find that channel which is optimal in terms of sales and the ability of the channel to service the product or product line.

In most cases the firm is intimately interested in the character or suitability of the channel for its particular product or product line. Occasionally this becomes an issue of whether the intermediary fits the overall positioning strategy for the product. Here concern lies in determining the suitability of the channel in the overall market positioning of the product. The character of the channel addresses the broader aspects of managing the channel.

Distributors frequently change their loyalties depending on the returns they receive. The contribution the intermediary receives is the principal determinant of the continuity of the channel. Small-scale exporters frequently complain of the lack of continuity in international channels.

Generally, control diminishes with the length of the channel. Control may be increased by investing in control systems which send information back to the firm; it is usually proportional to the capital intensity in the channel. Control in longer distribution channels, frequently found in developing countries, is difficult to attain. Generally, the more different and distant is the foreign market entered the less likely that the firm will invest in company-owned sales operations and other assets likely to give greater control of the operations (Gronhaug and Kvitastein, 1991).

The firm tries to reduce or optimize the effect of cost. Here the firm is concerned with the capital cost, which refers to the expenditure by the firm on sales force training, the investment in safety stocks and the initial marketing and distribution costs. These costs are generally fixed or at least periodic. The firm is also concerned with the cost or investment required to develop and maintain the distribution channels. Firms aim to minimize these costs, which are usually variable and associated with the level of sales. The variable costs associated with using web based hotel reservations systems can be so high as to discourage customers and even withdraw their patronage from some of them (Exhibit 17.1).

Exhibit 17.1 Costly online distribution of hotel rooms

Who should control online distribution in the hotel reservations sector? It seems that Hilton Hotel and Starwood, whose brands include Sheraton, are not happy with online travel intermediaries like Expedia, whose strategy is eroding their profits. Steve Bollenbach, Hilton's chief, feels online mark-ups of 30 per cent make rooms too expensive. Sites like Expedia have gained significant market share and control over the distribution of hotel rooms. They operate as merchants, charging the customer up-front, depositing the cash at interest and paying the hotel upon check-out.

While HHC, owners of the Hilton brand, will invest $175 million to 'outspend everyone' in delivering online distribution, Expedia defend their business on the basis of increased customer value. The proliferation of such sites has transformed the industry model; 'over the next five years the Internet will dominate travel', according to Mr Cotter of Starwood.

However, it remains to be seen whether hotel companies can improve direct sales and reassert control; websites should be designed for the requirements of the consumer rather than those of head office.

Source: based upon an article by Garrahan, M., 'Web agencies too costly say hotel', *Financial Times*, Friday 19 March 2004, p. 32

Cross-border cooperation, conflict and trust

Cooperation is an essential ingredient of distribution channel effectiveness because of the multiplicity of firms, many of which are independent decision-makers and not under common ownership. The situation is complicated by culture, distance, legal factors and different business practices in international markets. Functional interdependence in the marketing channel requires cooperation to accomplish the channel task. Because of the complexity and number of levels in international distribution the issue of cooperation is crucial. Obtaining cooperation in complex channels may be difficult due to the number of participants at different levels. In some businesses many different levels of distribution are required to reach the customer effectively. These circumstances are illustrated by the importation and distribution structure for rattan furniture in the US market (Figure 17.5). Here international suppliers have a choice of dealing with specialized importers, manufacturers in the US or distributors in the US. These in turn deal with many different types of intermediary all of whom serve the customer, whether final consumer or institutional customer such as hotels. In a wide distribution system there is plenty of scope for conflict and cooperation.

Figure 17.5
Channels of
distribution
in the United
States for rattan
furniture

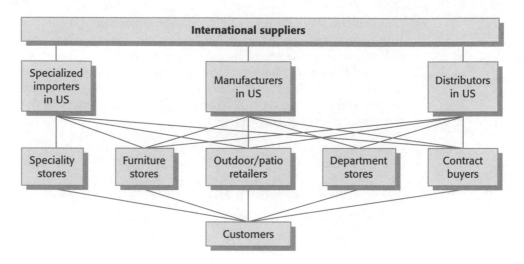

Channel conflict arises when one channel member perceives another to be imped-ing the achievement of its goals. Frustration arises from a restriction of role perform-ance. There are three sources of such conflict, already alluded to:

■ incompatible goals between large manufacturer exporters and small retailers located abroad;

■ domain conflict where manufacturers compete with wholesalers for market territory; and

■ incongruent perceptions of the distribution task and how it should be performed.

This last difficulty is often due to technical communication issues which produce a dif-ferent basis for action in response to the same situation. Some conflict in the channel is manageable but coping with too much is difficult. If conflict becomes destructive, i.e. pathological moves are made which impede the performance of the conflicting parties and the system itself, then the channel system is likely to disintegrate, even though channel objectives are attained in the short run. Channel conflict is highly positive so long as it does not pass the malignant threshold and impair the output of the system.

Trust is also an essential ingredient in effective channel relationships and one that gives rise to special problems in international marketing. Trust has been defined as 'existing when one party has confidence in an exchange partner's reliability and integrity' (Morgan and Hunt, 1994, p. 23). Trust, like commitment, is believed to be positively affected by dependence (Kumar *et al.*, 1995), which suggests that the more dependent a partner is on a relationship, the more trust is developed; it may be built on shared values regarding the business system in which the partners operate. Trust is developed through interpersonal relationships and is directly related to cooperation indicating the need for effective communications across cultures and many visits of key personnel. National cultures have a systematic impact on such behavioural rela-tionships (Kale and McIntyre, 1991, pp. 43–4). Channel participants use various forms of influencing strategy and sometimes conflict arises. A benign mix of such behaviour contributes to the success of international marketing channels.

Communication and information exchange between partners promote good inter-firm relationships in international distribution and reduce conflict. Information exchange between partners manifests itself in three sets of behaviours (Leuthesser and Kohli, 1995) all of which are highly culture-bound:

■ initiating behaviour;
■ signalling behaviour; and
■ disclosing.

Initiating behaviour involves effort to understand better the partner's needs and to help the partner to add more value so that the cooperating firms improve their respective positions in the business system. Signalling behaviour refers to the provision of advance information to the partner about changes in marketing plans for the country, product design or packaging, for example. Disclosing behaviour refers to the extent to which a partner is perceived to reveal sensitive information which may affect the other's position. Communication and information exchange have a positive influence on cooperation in the channel and communication also affects commitment to the relationship where commitment is defined as a 'desire to develop a stable relationship, a willingness to make short-term sacrifices to maintain the relationship, and a confidence in the stability of the relationship' (Anderson and Weitz, 1992, p. 19).

Improving channel performance

Distribution performance is improved with the attainment of four desired objectives for all the parties in the distribution system (Figure 17.6). Appointing and managing foreign market representation is a process, not an event. The agent or distributor, although independent, is part of the company's team. Within the business system they are partners. It is essential to monitor performance, to relate to the representatives and to seek ways of improving the economic circumstances of all parties concerned. It is essential that the company continually seeks ways of motivating the agent or distributor, otherwise the relationship withers. The ability of the firm to monitor and control its intermediaries internationally is a key part of any distribution strategy.

When the company has appointed an agent or a distributor, however, it is important that the company supports them in carrying out the tasks expected. There are

Figure 17.6
Performance measures in distribution

many ways of doing this, among which the more important measures the company can take are:

- to provide sales and promotional materials written in the local language;
- to visit the agent or distributor regularly and to visit customers together;
- invite agents–distributors to company premises regularly;
- to ensure that the price structure provides a genuine financial incentive;
- to provide updates on products, markets and company developments.

The provision of various kinds of information to intermediaries can strengthen the manufacturer's position. Successful firms regularly provide information on their products, margins, credit terms and advertising support available. By monitoring the distributor's sales volume, customer base and market penetration, the firm can improve the performance of the international marketing channel. By making distributors accountable for operational and economic results, while providing them with the freedom to select the most efficient and effective local marketing actions, export productivity may be enhanced (Bello and Gilliland, 1997, p. 34). Close monitoring is particularly important for firms that export highly technical products, since they are exposed to the risk of opportunistic behaviour on the part of the intermediary. In such cases, exporters attempt to influence the process by which intermediaries sell their products to end-users. They do so in various ways to ensure that the correct technical benefits are emphasized and that only appropriate applications are allowed.

There is a need to monitor the performance of the distribution channel and seek ways to improve it. Performance may be improved by seeking ways to:

- increase profits and require less capital investment;
- reduce customer complaints;
- increase repeat business;
- provide information and support;
- devote immediate attention to intermediary grievances; and
- reduce training costs.

Power in international channels of distribution

It is important that the firm knows where power lies in the channel and is able to note changes in its location over time. It is generally accepted, for example, that retailers possess the power in the apparel and furniture industries and, above all, in food. In alcoholic beverages, cars and some household appliances manufacturers have established brand names and greater relative power. International firms note that it is strategically wise to avoid channels with undesirable power balances if alternatives exist. Changes in power structure can have strategic implications, e.g. legislation for generic drugs has shifted power to retail pharmacies; Internet-available information has shifted power to users and consumers. International firms and intermediaries, aware of these power shifts, adopt countervailing power strategies to influence and control the channel and distribution of their products. The power of knowledge derived from information available through the Internet and other sources is not the sole preserve of any one group – it is universally available.

Channel leadership and sources of power

Channel leadership is based on the power relationships implied above. One of the primary functions of the channel leader is to provide leadership in one or more markets. Channel leaders use power to coordinate and to specify and implement channel synergy. Power is correlated with asymmetrical dependence arising from three sources:

- ability to reward compliant channel partners;
- ability to coerce recalcitrant channel partners;
- product-market knowledge.

The ability to reward refers to the belief by one firm that the second has the ability to mediate rewards for it, e.g. provide wider margins or better promotional allowances in fast-moving consumer products. Channel service quality may be used as a reward element of power to influence and control the decisions and behaviour of channel partners (Keith et al., 1990). This may be even more applicable to international channels owing to distance, diversity of channel levels, time zones and risk (de Ruyter et al., 1996, p. 22). In international channels, producers have less control over service levels, so a quality service may convey a manufacturer's intention to cultivate and maintain strong partnerships in addition to traditional power dependence themes. In effect this is brand building; power derives from the firm's ability to brand the 'reward structure' in the channel and the provision of quality service. Successful franchisors make very obvious use of this power in controlling international channels.

The ability to coerce refers to the belief that privileges will be threatened if the partner fails to conform, e.g. margin reduction, slowing shipments, reduced territory rights. Frequently, manufacturers squeeze the margins of intermediaries who are not performing well. New agents may be appointed to overlapping territories to cover markets poorly served by established distributors. A supplier–exporter doing business with a smaller foreign intermediary may be tempted to influence that intermediary coercively, which may lead to an unstable relationship and an inability on the part of the exporter to influence a much larger intermediary. Where the choice of intermediary is limited, the exporter may face a decision between forming a relationship with one intermediary who is totally compatible with the exporter or consider a different form of market entry, since, if the goals of the parties are not aligned, the relationship may be unstable and prove to be unsatisfactory in the longer term (Karunaratna and Johnson, 1997, p. 28).

Threats and coercion are negative incentives used when relationships in the channel have broken down. Channel participants usually rely on non-coercive approaches, however, because they are generally more supportive of continuing a cooperative relationship whereas coercive relationships in a channel usually imply the likely disintegration of the relationship. Large multinational companies frequently coerce intermediaries into using standardized marketing strategies whether or not such strategies are appropriate. Large brand companies use their power to threaten partners in the channel who are perceived to be uncooperative. Indeed, many brand companies change channels of distribution or acquire existing ones outright to ensure their wishes are heeded. Similarly, large brand distributors and retailers exert their coercive power to ensure that foreign suppliers comply with their procurement needs. Again, coercive power may arise from the power of branding.

Product-market knowledge refers to the firm's perception that another possesses special knowledge: manufacturers providing managerial training for marketing intermediaries or detailed technical manuals for the sales force of sophisticated industrial or medical product are examples of this form of power. Understanding customers in defined product-markets and the ability to transfer that knowledge internationally can be converted into power in the distribution channel. Product-market knowledge combined with direct customer contact and a sophisticated logistics system allows Zara to sustain its competitive advantage in the fast-moving fashion business. When Amancio Ortega started Zara in La Coruña, Spain in 1975 based on his vision of affordable fashion for all, he decided to avoid the usual route of distributing through retailers to reach his customers. Instead he decided to sell directly (*The Times*, Thursday, 18 September 2003, p. 31). Ortega understood the fashion business, especially the shopping behaviour of women who regularly seek new styles and colours in their local shops and department stores. Success came rapidly. Zara ships to many stores in Spain and worldwide. After a few years, direct selling was no longer feasible, given the nature of the business. Establishing a supply-chain system based on a sophisticated logistics system became a central feature of Zara's marketing programme that allowed it to supply its wholly-owned or highly-controlled retail outlets very frequently, some as often as twice weekly! This regular up-dating of the product range has generated a high degree of loyalty among an extensive customer base. The product-market knowledge thus obtained has allowed Zara to diversify into related product-markets such as home furnishings. Zara Home stores are now highly visible in many locations. Zara responds to customer preferences quickly; it focuses on market segments that have expressed preferences for fashion, quick response, good quality and acceptable prices. While competitors provide some of these product dimensions they do not match Zara in terms of speed and flexibility. Zara's success may be attributed to its control of every step in the supply chain from design to clothes rack.

Product-market knowledge also includes the ability to adapt the marketing strategy to different circumstances. For example, product-market knowledge is more valuable in the early stages of the life cycle for high technology products especially. At these stages education is an important marketing tool – the potential adopter must be educated in how best to use the product. A thorough understanding of customer needs and how likely they are to accept an innovation is the key to success. The US multinational animal feed ingredients company Alltech Inc recognized the need to educate animal feed compounders when it launched its natural animal feed additives, including yeasts and enzymes based on natural fermentation technology, by developing its highly successful *Marketing Through Education* programme. Through its educational endeavours Alltech Inc demonstrates its superior innovation and research capabilities, factors desired by the target market. The power derived from product-market knowledge is usually captured in the brand. As brands are a unique way of providing information, the brand owner possesses power which can be exerted in the channel.

Market interactivity and shifts in channel power

Traditionally, having the right product, the firm controlled the channel and the entire business system; continuous product innovation was the key competitive weapon in this system. In such a regime power rested with the manufacturer. With the rapidly decreasing cost of communication and the use by consumers and users of information freely available on the Internet, international markets have become interactive. Information and knowledge has shifted channel power partially towards the customer or user. The availability of near perfect knowledge provides the possibility of reviewing and evaluating products and services from all parts of the world. In this regime customers dominate the channel in some cases.

The customer can exert power in the channel and choose to obtain product requirements from any of a number of different channels that in turn obtain supplies from myriad foreign companies located in countries around the world (Figure 17.7). In these circumstances the power of product-market knowledge is dominant; reward and coercive power are less important. Power has shifted towards the customer. This potential for the use of power in the channel is, however, symmetrical. In such a regime customers may not dominate the channel entirely. Successful intermediaries, observing the power relationships and the role of the Internet, can offer value-added information services and reduced transaction costs in the channel. The balance of power depends on who successfully appropriates and brands the values added.

With such interactivity the firm's primary sustainable competitive advantage is its customer information base, its skills in building channel relationships with intermediaries and customers and its brands. By branding its products and myriad services the firm attempts to shift competitive power in its favour, giving it intangible values as a basis for competition. As Figure 17.7 indicates, numerous manufacturing companies can obtain product parity with the best technically available products and as such may not be distinguishable in the eyes of distributors or end-users. Manufacturers have traditionally used the power of branding to reward, coerce and understand product-markets and thereby shift power back to the company. With increased similarity and a convergence in manufacturing technologies, product parity among myriad manufacturers has become a feature of the market that continues to support the shift in power towards the customer.

Figure 17.7
Impact of
information on
locus of power
in international
channels of
distribution

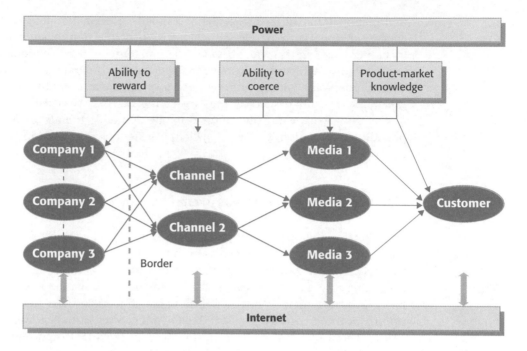

One of the outcomes of power shifts in the channels of distribution due to trade-offs in brand power possessed by the international firm and knowledge power possessed by customers has been the rise of international direct distribution.

International direct distribution

Successful direct distribution presumes that the firm has sufficient resources available to support a direct marketing approach; the establishment of a sales force as in Dell Computers, for example. It is also necessary that the firm already possesses experience in the marketing of similar products to comparable markets abroad, i.e. that direct international marketing channels exist.

Direct distribution may also be possible where the manufacturer's personnel are required to sell and service the product or service because of its complexity, e.g. computer sales and service. Microsoft's European distribution centre in Dublin provides warehousing and distribution services for its European customers and removes the need to carry inventory in each country. According to Bernard Vergnes, president of Microsoft Europe: 'Microsoft is a software company, not a distributor and if we are to continue to be successful we must focus on this . . . [as] . . . more companies want to do business at a pan-European level.' When product technology is changing rapidly, direct distribution may be favoured.

The direct distribution decision is also influenced by the nature of the market segments served, e.g. industrial equipment. Market segments with relatively few customers, where the unit purchase is large in terms of quantity or price and where customers are concentrated geographically, tend to favour direct distribution. There must also be a sufficient margin to support frequent personal visits and direct contact with myriad people in the customer firm. Furthermore, when the purchase decision is a major long-term commitment by the buyer, direct distribution may be an attractive proposition.

There are four sets of factors (very similar to the criteria used by manufacturers to evaluate intermediaries) which influence the firm's decision to distribute direct:

■ resources and technology in the firm;

■ characteristics of the product or service;

■ market segments served; and

■ the marketing programme – how the firm provides, communicates and delivers value to its customers.

Intermediaries and the Internet

Information is the key competitive advantage possessed by intermediaries. To be useful, information must be rich – accurate, current, relevant, customized and interactive. Cost factors, determined by the number of people who share the information, must also be considered. Traditionally there has been a trade-off between richness of the information and the number of potential customers reached (Figure 17.8). If this trade-off disappears distributors have no reason to be in the business system. A major threat, beside the compromise between richness and reach, is the rapidly falling cost of information due to new communications technologies. As seen already, the power base in the business system is knowledge; something now largely controlled by the customer which leads to the disintermediation of the channel.

When information technologies allow the information richness-customer reach curve to be displaced upwards to the right it allows the company, or more likely new competitors, to offer greater reach and richness simultaneously. This may result in a direct threat to existing distributors. Usually the innovator or new entrant moves

Figure 17.8
Disintermediation in the channel of distribution

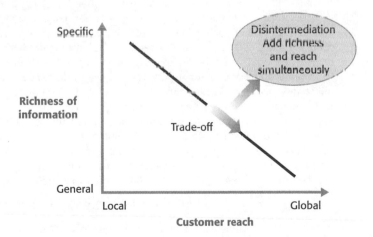

Source: adapted from Evans, P. and Wurster, T. S. (2000) *Blown to Bits*, Harvard Business School Press, Boston, Massachusetts, p. 70

down the curve providing greater reach in what amounts to a re-segmentation of the market, e.g. Dell computers, amazon.com. Having established this position the new technologies allow the firm to move off the curve to provide a richer relationship with the customer. This is the threat to existing intermediaries – the extent to which low-cost information, arising from the use of new information technologies combined with an innovative approach, in providing richness and reach simultaneously can challenge existing intermediaries. Sony and UMI, recognizing the power of mobile telephony among young people, the target market for music, joined with a mobile telephone company, T-Mobile of Germany, to deliver some of their products to an important market segment (Exhibit 17.3).

Selling through the Internet allows a company to move off the richness-reach trade-off. Dell offers online technical support and encourages its customers to access detailed product line descriptions that allows them to make a product selection having designed the exact configuration that they want and see instantaneously the price implications of the choices they make. In this case Dell interacts with the customer towards the end of the decision process. With further application of existing technology Dell interacts with customers at the needs identification stage and then guides the customer to configure the kind of equipment appropriate to those needs.

Exhibit 17.2 T-Mobile phones to download songs

The recorded music industry has suffered greatly since the 1990s from mass piracy through the introduction of new entertainment media and a slew of new acts. Companies like Universal Music International, part of Vivendi Universal SA and Sony Music, part of Sony Corp., are facing shrinking markets and must devise innovative ways to exploit their resources in the transformed marketplace. That is why both companies have signed a deal with T-Mobile, a unit of Deutsche Telekom AG with 61 million customers worldwide.

Specially remixed top artists' works designed for sale through mobile phones in short format, offers a new connection with the consumer. T-Mobile have already compiled a library of 200 songs; the venture will begin in April in Germany, Austria and the UK, with a similar launch in the US at a later date if successful in Europe. Estimates that music sales through mobile phones could reach 20–30 per cent of all music sales by 2006 make this an attractive niche. The global market for ringtones is already worth €3–€4 billion a year.

While product and channel providers believe customers will pay a premium to hear an abbreviated version of a new song, it remains to be seen whether consumers will take them up on an early yet different version of the song, with a starting price of €2.50 per song. Mobile phones 'are a key channel for tomorrow, but it is very important to rethink the way content is produced and delivered', states Cedric Ponsot, chief of UMI's mobile division. Indeed, mobile operators are also looking for new products and services as voice traffic growth slows and investment in more advanced networks capable of transmitting, voice, video and Internet access ensues. It seems music and mobile phones may make noisy but natural bedfellows.

Source: adapted from *The Wall Street Journal Europe*, 18 March 2004, p. A10

For the manufacturer exporter the Internet supports this disintermediation and presents an alternative to vertically integrating foreign channels through acquisition or by using independent distributors. Manufacturers can use the Internet to reach customers taking on functions previously performed by distributors. Intermediaries also use electronic markets and assume important roles that include aggregating information, providing trust relationships and ensuring the integrity of the market, matching customers and suppliers and providing marketing information to suppliers (Bailey and Bakos, 1997, p. 18).

In consumer markets, characterized by a large number of products and infrequent purchases, the matching role of intermediaries is usually more important. The movement to electronic markets does not seem to reduce the number of intermediaries in use, as electronic markets require intermediation services, albeit in ways that differ from traditional physical markets. Markets with fewer suppliers and customers and frequent purchases, such as the machine tools or car components markets, have less need for matching intermediaries. Manufacturer designed and maintained web based supply systems are more effective in these situations.

The growing use of the Internet has significant implications for international marketing companies. The Internet has demonstrated its power for building relationships in the physical world of goods and services. The emphasis on creating value in the business system receives a further endorsement from use of the Internet; the ability of the firm to provide value is emerging as a core marketing capability. In terms of channel functions the Internet is well accepted by customers as an information source and reservation system but as a physical delivery channel it has not been accepted, irrespective of product group (Van den Poel and Leunis, 1999, p. 254).

The challenge for the international marketing company is to adapt to the new information and communication technologies and to cope with customers in different countries and cultures.

The low barriers to entry to the Internet are both an attraction and a limitation for the international firm. Any small firm can create a site on the Internet, so every firm is difficult to find. The challenge is how to be noticed by browsers. This gives an advantage to the big brands as people tend to go first to the brand names familiar from the real world. Indeed, these brands are quite adept at promoting their websites in the more traditional media.

Once the international company receives an order, however, and agrees the terms of the sale, it must fulfil the order. In international marketing this is simple in theory – the company delivers the product when, where and how the customer wants it. Implementing this delivery strategy, however, is not so easy in practice as the product crosses national boundaries. The use of the Internet, therefore, places even greater demands on the fulfilment aspect of international distribution. Fulfilment of orders is still an issue except for some firms like amazon.com who provide books to be sold online and have so successfully reduced return rates that 'category killers' like Borders and Barnes and Noble have been forced to enter the online arena (Bucklin et al., 1997). In summary, the competitive interaction of intermediaries and the Internet depends on the ability of intermediaries to:

- aggregate information effectively;
- provide trust relationships;
- ensure the integration of the market;
- match customers and suppliers;
- provide added value marketing information to foreign based suppliers.

Direct cross-border shipments

With the removal of trade barriers in the EU, NAFTA and other areas the costs of transport and distribution have fallen. The abolition of border checks, expensive administration form-filling procedures and circulation restrictions have significantly improved the distribution of goods in the EU. The cross-border physical distribution of goods is the fulfilment aspect of delivering the value to customers irrespective of the nature of the channel, traditional or Internet based.

Under the old physical distribution regime manufacturers exported goods from one European country to another. Under the new regime it is possible to dispatch the goods. Under such a regime, direct cross-border shipping becomes increasingly attractive for many firms that have historically consolidated shipments to replenish inventories in local national warehouses (Figure 17.9a). The alignment of warehousing operations with natural service areas irrespective of national border is an expected result of this improved situation (Figure 17.9b). Companies in large markets like the EU are better positioned to secure benefits from a reconfiguration of market logistics. To obtain the benefits the company must ensure that regional or country sales and marketing activities are coordinated effectively with logistics when the change from a geographic based structure to a market based structure is implemented. Direct

Figure 17.9
Alternative cross-border shipping methods:
(a) Traditional cross-border shipment in Europe;
(b) Future direct cross-border shipment in Europe

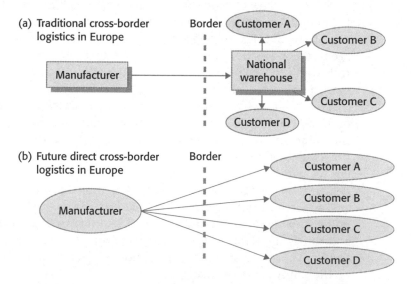

Source: O'Laughlin, K. A., Cooper, J. and Cabocel, E. (1993) *Reconfiguring European Logistics Systems*, Oak Brook, IL: Council of Logistics Management

distribution is to traditional logistics what the Internet is to channels of distribution – a disintermediation.

The task facing the company is to select from among the available alternatives the combined transportation mix that best fits its market logistics needs. The selection of the transportation mix must be fully integrated into the overall market logistics configuration in order to design a cost-effective service-balanced system.

Summary

Access to international markets and customers through effective use of distribution channels is one of the key decision areas in international marketing. Gaining and holding access to markets relies heavily on good distribution channel management, which must be seen as an interactive process between manufacturer and the foreign based intermediary who may dominate the path to the final user or consumer. The relationship is further complicated where different historical developments give rise to different distribution structures. Agreements between manufacturer and distributor involve a range of factors including physical performance criteria related to the sale of the product or service and financial criteria related to profits and return on investment. Because objectives may be different at different stages in the distribution channel, conflict between the members can arise. The resolution of conflict requires one or a subset of channel members to use power to bring about interorganizational harmony for the good of the entire channel. Specifying channel roles in advance can minimize channel conflict. Large consumer brand companies pay close attention to control in distribution channels, the primary objective of which is to maintain the desired position of their brand in the market. Frequently international companies go to the extreme of acquiring their distribution partners to ensure this control based on the view that access to customers is paramount and that relying on an independent distribution system may be too fickle. The ability to maximize the number of markets successfully entered requires the international firm to have access to a highly developed distribution system, characterized by coordination between marketing and production, and using the most modern technologies such as the Internet where appropriate.

Questions

1. Describe the major differences that exist between domestic and international channels of distribution. What criteria should the firm apply when selecting channels of distribution to simultaneously serve a number of international markets?

2. Explain why different countries have different channel structures. A number of examples of distribution channels were outlined in the text. What are their common elements? How are they different?

3. How can the firm motivate channel members in foreign markets?

4. Discuss the need for control and market coverage in selecting and managing an international distribution channel.

5. Why does channel conflict occur? Is conflict more likely to occur in international marketing? Explain and present some suggestions for such conflict resolution.

6. Describe how power in the distribution channel can shift with unwelcome outcomes for the international firm.

7. What role has innovation in international channel management? How can a firm maintain or gain market share by innovating in the channel of distribution? Does the Internet have a role to play?

References

Anderson, E. and Weitz, B. A. (1992) 'The use of pledges to build and sustain commitment in distribution channels', *Journal of Marketing Research*, **29** (February), 18–34.

Asugman, G., Johnson, J. J. and McCullough, J. (1997) 'The role of after-sales service in international marketing', *Journal of International Marketing*, **5** (4), 11–28.

Bailey, J. P. and Bakos, Y. (1997) 'An exploratory study of the emerging role of electronic intermediaries', *International Journal of Electronic Commerce*, **1** (3), 7–20.

Bello, D. C. and Gilliland, D. I. (1997) 'The effect of output controls, process controls, and flexibility on export channel performance', *Journal of Marketing*, **61** (January), 22–38.

Bucklin, C. B., Thomas-Graham, P. A. and Webster, E. A. (1997) 'Channel conflict: when is it dangerous?', *McKinsey Quarterly*, **3**, 37–43.

Burgel, O. and Murray, G. C. (2000) 'The international market entry choices of start-up companies in high technology industries', *Journal of International Marketing*, **8** (2), 33–62.

Cateora, P. R. (1993) *International Marketing*, 8th edn, Homewood, IL: lrwin.

Czinkota, M. R. and Woronoff, J. (1986) *Japan's Market: The Distribution System*, New York, NY: Praeger.

de Ruytner, K., Wetzels, M. and Lemmink, J. (1996) 'The power of perceived service quality in international marketing channels', *European Journal of Marketing*, **30** (12), 22–38.

European Commission (1997) 'Green Paper on vertical restraints', January.

Evans, P. and Wurster, T. S. (2000) *Blown to Bits*, Harvard Business School Press, Boston, Massachusetts.

Gronhaug, K. and Kvitastein, O. (1991) 'Distributional involvement in international strategic business units' in *17th Annual Conference*, European International Business Association, Copenhagen, 15–17 December.

Heide, J. B. and John, G. (1988) 'The role of dependence balancing in safeguarding transaction-specific assets in conventional channels', *Journal of Marketing*, **52** (January), 20–35.

Kale, S. and McIntyre, R. P. (1991) 'Distribution channel relationships in diverse cultures', *International Marketing Review*, **8** (3), 31–45.

Karunaratna, A. R. and Johnson, L. W. (1997) 'Initiating and maintaining export channel intermediary relationships', *Journal of International Marketing*, **5** (2), 11–32.

Keith, J. E., Jackson, D. W. Jr. and Crosby, L. A. (1990) 'Effects of alternative types of influence strategies under different channel dependence structures', *Journal of Marketing*, **54** (July), 30–41.

Kim, K. and Frazier, G. I. (1996) 'A typology of distribution channel systems: a contextual approach', *International Marketing Review*, **13** (1), 19–32.

Klein, S. and Roth, V. J. (1990) 'Determinants of export channel design: the effects of experience and psychic distance reconsidered', *International Marketing Review*, **7** (5), 27–38.

Kumar, N., Scheer, L. K. and Steenkamp, J-B. E. M. (1995) 'The effects of perceived interdependence on dealer attitudes', *Journal of Marketing Research*, **32** (August), 348–56.

Leuthesser, L. and Kohli, A. K. (1995) 'Relational behaviour in business markets: implications for relationship management', *Journal of Business Research*, **34** (3), 221–33.

Morgan, R. M. and Hunt, S. D. (1994) 'The commitment–trust theory of relationship marketing', *Journal of Marketing*, **58** (July), 20–38.

O'Laughlin, K. A., Cooper, J. and Cabocel, E. (1993) *Reconfiguring European Logistics Systems*, Oak Brook, IL: Council of Logistics Management.

Van den Poel, D. and Leunis, J. (1999) 'Consumer acceptance of the Internet as a channel of distribution', *Journal of Business Research*, **45**, 249–56.

18 Pricing in international markets

International price decisions are influenced by both managerial and marketing factors and by behavioural and attitudinal factors within the firm. The firm must take many variables into consideration in setting prices for different international markets. It is rare to have the same price prevail in all world markets because of currency fluctuations, different factor costs, different product requirements and government regulations, standards and official limits on pricing and discounting. At best this differential may be contained within a few percentage points across different markets. Otherwise, there is the ever-present danger of parallel importing taking place.

Having studied this chapter you should be able to:

- specify the general influences on international pricing including technology, competition and government policies;
- determine the impact of exchange rates and their volatility on prices;
- identify approaches of coping with currency differentials and exchange rate movements;
- understand the advantages of using absorption and marginal cost pricing;
- demonstrate the value of break-even pricing for different stages of the life cycle;
- specify how the international distribution system affects price levels;
- develop a market based approach to international pricing and select a feasible price level from a range of possible prices.

General influences on international pricing

The company considers a multitude of factors in deciding prices in international markets: the nature of the product and the industry, the location of the production facility, the distribution system, the foreign market environment and foreign currency differentials (Cavusgil, 1996). It is also necessary to consider the company's international marketing objectives for pricing; the pricing objective may be to price penetrate

Figure 18.1
Influences on
international
pricing

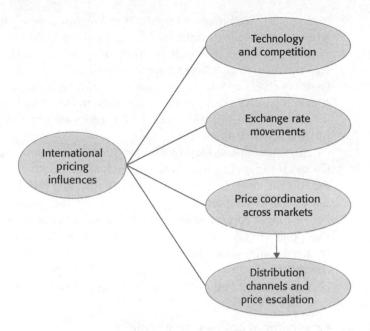

selected markets or it may be to use a price-skimming strategy to enter a particular segment in many markets simultaneously, a topic discussed in Chapter 12. The characteristics of the international market and the position of product in the life cycle in the new market may also influence the pricing decision. The company also must account for competitor activity in the market. Some markets are more competitive than others, warranting a different approach to pricing. Lastly, the company's financial and marketing strengths may influence the discretion the firm has in setting international prices. These myriad influences may conveniently be analyzed under four general headings (Figure 18.1).

Technology and competition

The nature of the product and the degree of competition in the industry influences the degree of price discretion available to the firm. A firm with a knowledge based competitive advantage in high technology, for example, has a greater room for manoeuvre in setting prices than a firm in agricultural commodities. Very often high-technology products do not have direct indigenous competition in new international markets; this is particularly true at the early stages in the life cycle. Furthermore, high-technology products rarely face trade barriers since government policy in most countries favours the importation of new technology and the upgrading of skills in their countries. In such circumstances the firm may decide to use a price-skimming strategy. The opposite is often the case for commodities and mature manufactured products. With the diffusion of technology and increased competition the firm may need to change its pricing strategy. In the mature stage of the life cycle the firm may face aggressive pricing from low-cost competitors from different parts of the world seeking a share of lucrative markets. Sometimes new firms enter the market with a unique competitive mix of high-quality, well-designed products at low prices which provide an irresistible challenge to potential customers and an awkward situation for incumbents. For IKEA, the Swedish self-assembly furniture group, it is the products themselves, their low price, and their design that keeps buyers satisfied and loyal. 'Most nicely designed products were very, very expensive, and we were blocked from main suppliers and producers,' Ingvar Kamprad, IKEA's founder, remembers. He relishes the memory of being thrown out of a Swedish furniture fair for asking 'would it be possible to make well-designed products at a reasonable price level?'

The value of most high-technology products is determined by the cost of alternative solutions to the customer. Where there is no alternative, pricing is a matter of attempting to value the solution for a particular customer problem; there is no necessary connection between that value and the cost of the product. As products mature they become quasi-commodities so the value of the solution is increasingly determined by the price of comparable but not identical products. In such circumstances prices of quasi-commodities are related to the cost structure of lower-cost competitors and their willingness to accept lower margins. These competitors may operate in the firm's domestic market but more likely they operate in a low labour cost foreign country.

Government policies on pricing

Government intervention and political interference also influence pricing in international markets. National government regulations concerning maintenance of good trade balances, development of national resource bases, promotion of national security and provision of employment can all have a considerable impact on prices. Industrial goods, e.g. capital equipment, are particularly susceptible since they are often used in economic wars waged to win the political allegiance of developing countries. As a result, international marketing firms are sometimes confronted with impossible price competition because prices are shaded by a foreign government for political rather than economic reasons.

Though becoming less frequent due to government vigilance and the activities of international institutions, dumping affects prices and revenues in international markets. One school of thought argues that dumping of goods is an unfair trade practice in all circumstances since it is based on international price discrimination, which occurs when a product is sold abroad for a lower price than the seller charges for the same product in the home market. This normally occurs when the home country's demand is less elastic than is the foreign market. A second school of thought argues that dumping is a phenomenon based on costs – using a different cost basis on which to calculate prices for domestic and foreign markets. In the domestic market full absorption costs are used and when the domestic market is much larger than the foreign market it may be possible to use a particularly virulent form of marginal cost pricing to obtain foreign sales. In either case 'dumping', however defined, attracts much political attention.

Transfer pricing in international markets

Transfer pricing, which refers to the prices at which products and services are transferred within the corporate family across national frontiers as they move globally, division to division or to a foreign subsidiary or joint venture, can pose a number of management issues to be resolved. Transfer pricing sometimes becomes a problem within the company. Where a profitable international division is an intermediary there will be an inevitable conflict over price when products move from the manufacturing division to the international division and from there to the foreign subsidiary. For the manufacturing division the price should be high enough to encourage a flow of products for export and build up an export trade. Low prices result in poor returns for the manufacturing division, and losses can disillusion workers. From the viewpoint of the international division, however, the transfer price should be low enough to enable it to be both competitive and profitable in the foreign market.

Market price is by far the most usual method of transfer pricing, followed by standard unit full cost with a fixed mark-up added. Several reasons may be identified which are likely to induce high transfer price above arm's length prices for flows from parents to foreign subsidiaries:

- corporate income tax higher than in parent's country;

- pressure from workers to obtain greater share of profits;

- political pressure to nationalize or expropriate high-profit foreign firms;

- political instability;

- high inflation rate;

- price of final product controlled by government but based on production cost;

- desire to mask profitability of subsidiary operations to keep competitors out of the market.

Impact of exchange rates

Fluctuating exchange rates and price volatility

Exchange rate fluctuations tend to be cyclical among currencies that do not have a fixed exchange rate. The introduction of the euro has fixed the exchange rates among the countries that have signed the single currency agreement – EU members with the exception of the UK, Denmark and Sweden. Among the 15 new members that joined the EU in 2004 none has so far accepted the euro as their currency as a number of years adjustment will be necessary before taking such a crucial decision. Exchange rates among the major world currencies still fluctuate considerably depending on economic conditions in different regions and countries. Exchange rates among the US dollar, the yen, the euro and pound sterling can fluctuate so much that an otherwise well-planned marketing strategy can be jeopardized. Circumstances can arise whereby the company moves from price advantage when its domestic currency is undervalued to disadvantage when the currency is overvalued. Because of fluctuations in currencies many companies resort to using forward exchange markets. These circumstances require appropriate pricing strategies for different markets during different time periods to correspond to movement in exchange rates. It is not a straightforward matter to evaluate exchange rates on their relative movements alone. It is necessary to examine how much of the company's trade in its final products take place between the currencies of interest while also accounting for the possible counterbalancing of trade in factor inputs. There are numerous perspectives which should be considered (Exhibit 18.1).

Foreign based customers, distributors and importers seek low prices but they also seek stable prices. High price volatility due to fluctuating exchange rates, however, may be a more important consideration, hence the importance of stable exchange rates. A strategy based on a relatively high price but low volatility may be more acceptable than a low-price strategy where prices are volatile due to fluctuating exchange rates. Exporting companies also seek the comfort of stable exchange rates and stable prices. The move towards a more benign exchange rate environment addresses this issue.

Exhibit 18.1   Europe's exporters get the greenback blues

The EU's 15 members send 38 per cent of their merchandise exports outside the union – a figure that has stayed consistent in the past five years. The dollar's weakness has a big impact on those exports. And that's not to mention dollar-pegged currencies like the Chinese renminbi or the Hong Kong dollar. Sweden's Atlas Copco could tell you all about it; taking all dollar linked currencies into account their dollar sales jump 10 per cent to 50 per cent while only 20 per cent of production costs are in dollars and approximately 50 per cent remain in euros. This is worrying Savino Rizzio, president of VIR, a leading valve-maker located in Valduggia, northern Italy. VIR export 95 per cent of their product, and three-quarters of this goes beyond the eurozone, so a considerable chunk of exports are affected by the 30 per cent slide in the dollar's value since 2002. He is not the only one worrying.

On the other hand, the euro has eliminated currency fluctuations in trade among eurozone countries. Thus German toolmaker Trumpf are relatively unperturbed by the dollar's slide despite a considerable export market, because roughly two-thirds of their annual €1 billion in sales occur within the eurozone; 'having the euro is a big relief to us'. Spreading bets like this globally has helped other manufacturers neutralize currency fluctuations. Heineken's hedging strategy has so far protected them from any major impact of currency fluctuations. One-third of operating profits come from the Americas region which may, however, expose the firm's bottom line in the longer run. Philips spreads risks by localizing production in the country where sales take place. Thus high eurozone exporting costs may be balanced by the cushioning effect of dollar sales in other parts of the company thereby reducing overall losses. Of concern, however, for such greenback dependent companies are sluggish eurozone recovery figures which could just give them more of the blues.

Source: adapted from 'Europe's exporters get the greenback blues',
Financial Times, Thursday 11 March 2004, p. 12

Coping with exchange rate movements

Exchange rate movements against the company's national currency can be favourable or unfavourable. These currency movements are important for exporters because they directly affect profits. Depending on the length of time and the volume of trade

Figure 18.2
Relative prices
and exchange
rate movements

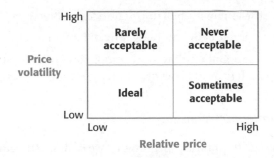

involved the consequences may be critical for the exporter. Indeed a mix of high relative prices and high price volatility is a difficult combination to defend. Very high price volatility due to constantly changing exchange rates and high relative prices of the goods themselves is never acceptable (Figure 18.2). High price volatility and low relative prices are rarely considered by buyers and make it difficult for the exporting firm operating under such a regime, as many UK manufacturers experienced in exporting to the US in the 1980s and 1990s due to the highly fluctuating exchange rates between the US dollar and the pound sterling. In this period UK firms had difficulty holding market share; indeed many firms lost share.

Low price volatility and high relative prices are occasionally accepted due to the certainty provided by the stable exchange rates, but the acceptance is reluctant. In the same period Japanese firms in the US gained market share though their prices were relatively high but, crucially, price volatility was low due to the fixed nature of the exchange rates. The ideal situation for the exporter is to have a low relative price and a low price volatility, circumstances faced by many low-cost producers with currencies fixed to the US dollar.

The situation is less serious where a large proportion of raw materials is also sourced from the same export market. Many EU countries now have the protection of the euro which removes the adverse effects of exchange rate movements for the growing intra-EU trade. Once prices of competing products have been converted to the euro it becomes relatively easy to judge where a product is cheaper. Within the euro system, however, it may also be necessary to harmonize for different tax regimes in different countries to obtain full price transparency (Caller 1999, p. 34). Much of the international trade not denominated in the euro is carried out in US dollars and, hence, provides a similar protection against unexpected exchange movements.

For trade outside either of these currency systems companies may attempt to minimize the currency risk associated with export marketing by diversifying the range of export markets. Another way is to negotiate with the foreign buyer for payments to be made in the company's own currency. A further option, increasingly used by exporters, is to hedge against future exchange rate losses or gains by entering into forward foreign exchange contracts to protect against fluctuations. Many banks offer forward foreign exchange contracts for all major traded currencies. The objective of such hedging, though it may be considered expensive, is to protect the exporter's receipts from exchange rate movements over a period of time, usually ranging from three weeks to two years. Funds do not change hands until the contract completion date. The principal advantages for exporters of contracting forward are:

334 ■ International marketing operations

- the elimination of uncertainty regarding the value of foreign payments;

- accurate cash flow budgeting of foreign receipts;

- a recognition that most companies do not wish to enter into currency speculation, preferring to concentrate on their core business activities.

Strategic responses

When the firm is operating in weak domestic currency it is advisable to stress price benefits, expand the product line, move manufacturing to the domestic market, minimize foreign currency expenditures and invoice in the stronger currency (Cavusgil 1996, p. 69). Customers in a strong currency country may welcome the additional product attributes at competitive prices and most certainly the lower prices permitted by the weaker currency would be welcomed. For larger companies with plants located in many different countries it may be possible to move some manufacturing to the domestic market. While it may not be feasible to move entire plants, at least in the short term, it may be possible to provide some of the value there, e.g. final assembly and packaging. Clearly in such circumstances the firm attempts to minimize expenditures in the strong currency of the host country but instead make all necessary purchases of services such as advertising, insurance and transportation in the domestic market. Lastly, the firm in the weak currency country should attempt to invoice foreign customers in their currency and should the currency relationship persist it may also be possible to speed up the repatriation of foreign-earned income and collections.

Pricing in a strong domestic currency usually means following the opposite of the above advice. Firms operating from a country with a strong domestic currency often follow a non-price strategy by improving quality, delivery and after-sales service. These are circumstances that faced Japanese firms in the United States during the past 20 years. For most of the time the yen was stronger that the US dollar. This was the period of greatest investment by Japanese firms in the US market. Japanese companies invested in manufacturing and distribution facilities in the US on the basis that protecting access to customers in the US was something that fluctuating exchange rates should not be allowed to jeopardize.

Firms sometimes attempt other approaches to protecting their foreign markets. It may be possible to reduce profit margins and use marginal-cost pricing but as noted elsewhere in this chapter this provides only temporary respite. The ability of the firm to insist on any of these approaches in dealing with currency strengths and weaknesses depends on the relationship and power it possesses relative to customers abroad. Some firms may be able to take advantage of the possibilities offered while others may not. In most situations companies would prefer not to have to deal with fluctuating exchange rates and the relative strengths of currencies in which they trade. Indeed, many large multinationals, recognizing their ubiquity, set their own internal exchange rates and abide by these rates irrespective of currency movements in the financial markets. Siemens and other large enterprises, for example, fix their own internal rate of exchange for the US dollar and the euro at parity. As these companies trade so much using the dollar and the euro presumably the benefits and losses even out over time. This approach is not an option for the smaller single-plant companies.

Standardized international prices

Firms that attempt to pursue a global marketing strategy require uniformity of prices across markets. Since such companies encounter the same competitors in many markets they usually attempt to coordinate strategies including pricing. Furthermore, greater price transparency across markets may force international firms to standardize their pricing. For example, in Europe there are literally thousands of different ways to be charged just by receiving or placing a telephone call but several European operators, however, have started to offer one international rate that eliminates roaming charges for large parts of Western Europe, making it easier to compare prices. Firms with brands designed and available for homogeneous market segments in many countries and positioned similarly across markets may require central control of pricing. The pricing policy of a large multinational brand company may be cited as an example: 'the brand must always be premium priced relative to local products where the premium is at least 15 per cent but not more than 20 per cent above the price of the most expensive locally produced item'. Another advantage of uniform prices is that parallel imports may be avoided.

There are a number of circumstances where it is more appropriate to allow price decisions to be made locally. Competitive conditions may be such as to suggest that full pricing autonomy should be given to subsidiaries. For example, the timing of a price decision may be crucial; a quick response to price changes by competitors may be needed. If the firm's product is one of many in the market, the company may have to follow the market leader in changing prices to remain competitive and to hold relative market share. Customer characteristics may dictate a local approach to pricing. For example, low income markets may require significant deviation from central pricing guidelines, especially when the company is attempting to establish a foothold in the market. In setting prices in international markets there are a number of obstacles to standardization:

- currency fluctuations;
- different factor costs;
- different product requirements and government regulations;
- standards and official limits on pricing and discounting;
- extent of dumping;
- requirements of transfer pricing policies.

Framework for pricing in international markets

A low cost-low price strategy is difficult to defend in international markets. Low prices give the firm a distinct competitive advantage but low prices that depend on low costs is a difficult strategy to defend over time. The danger is that new entrants may be able to deliver a competitive product at lower prices; a new start-up firm may be able to reduce the overhead structure or leverage scale economies of its business system partners, particularly its suppliers, to compete with the incumbent in the market.

For many businesses cost is the only basis for establishing export pricing policies. Many United Kingdom industrial products exporters, for example, use a form of mark-up pricing in determining their export pricing (Tzokas *et al.*, 2000, p. 201). This is understandable as individual cost elements for materials, labour and overheads can be measured and sometimes compared with those of competitors. The two most common cost-oriented approaches to pricing are full absorption costing and marginal costing. Manufacturing costs are the basis for most pricing decisions because the elements which make up these costs can be sourced from within the company itself and are readily understood by everybody in the company. The costs of materials, direct labour overheads and a margin to allow for fixed costs and profit, are added together to establish an appropriate price.

Cost approaches to international pricing

Absorption costing aims to recover or absorb the fixed costs of the exporting business. Costs are estimated and each unit sold is expected to carry or recover its share of variable and fixed costs. A difficulty arises with regard to the allocation of fixed costs and in particular the use of an unchanged recovery rate for all subsequent pricing decisions made in the planning period. The firm usually decides the recovery rate for fixed costs at the beginning of the planning period based on a forecast of the number of units expected to be sold. Forecasts are difficult enough in uncertain domestic markets but are far more difficult in uncertain and highly fluctuating international markets. Accountants usually advise a price based on full cost at normal capacity but where the actual number of units sold deviates from plan the overhead recovery rate used to calculate cost and fix price will be incorrect. If actual sales volumes fall below expectations the price charged will be insufficient to recover fixed overheads and losses may ensue. If sales exceed expectations fixed overheads will be recovered and leave a surplus. In such circumstances it may be possible to reduce price without adversely affecting profit targets.

While in the long term all fixed costs must be recovered, otherwise the company goes out of business, the use of absorption costing is not especially helpful in making short-term price decisions. This is where marginal pricing may be used. Despite these difficulties absorption costing rather than marginal costing is the most common system found in industry. Absorption costing is most frequently used to establish the prices of new products where:

■ specified sales levels are expected and a separate production facility to serve the international market is planned;

■ the company aims to recover its investment quickly allowing a price reduction later;

■ the company adopts a price-skimming strategy with a progressive reduction in price over the longer term.

Figure 18.3
Marginal cost-pricing in international markets

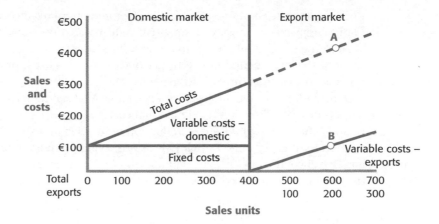

The first element above is the conventional assumption when the company plans to recover all costs from the outset while the presence of the second may encourage competitors to offer product parity but at a lower price. The reverse of the third, a low price to penetrate the market quickly and then to increase price progressively, is generally not feasible.

Marginal cost-pricing in contrast may be used in a very different set of circumstances. Marginal costs are those which, at a given level of output, are incurred when one additional unit is produced. Whereas absorption costing is used in primary pricing decisions for standard products, marginal costing is often used in what might be described as secondary pricing decisions, e.g. export orders, unusual quantities, once-off deals or subcontracting. An example will illustrate the use of this approach to pricing. Assume the fixed costs faced by a firm producing a simple industrial component are €100 and that the unit variable cost is €0.50 (Figure 18.3). The total cost of producing 100 units amounts to €150 (€100 fixed cost and €50 variable cost – €0.50 × 100 units). Assume further that the domestic market is saturated at 400 units of the component and that the company decides to export, point A in the figure. The issue of pricing arises. Assuming export sales and using the conventional full-cost approach, the price charged would be €0.67 for each unit (€400/600 total units sold). If instead the company's total fixed costs have already been absorbed in the domestic market operation the company may decide to use marginal cost pricing – using only the variable costs associated with the exporting activity. Assuming for the present that these are the same as occur on the domestic market (this assumption is easily relaxed) the price would be €0.50 (€100 variable cost/200 units sold), point B in the figure. Using marginal cost-pricing the firm obtains a distinct price competitive advantage in the export market.

Marginal analysis helps to answer the question: what happens to total profits if the selling price is changed? In this way marginal costing is future oriented; all past costs are sunk costs. With marginal cost-pricing the company attempts to establish prices in order to maximize the total contribution to fixed costs and profit. Marginal cost-pricing is useful when surplus manufacturing capacity is available in the domestic market to produce additional foreign sales without any increase in fixed costs. This is usually a short-term phenomenon as in the longer term fixed costs must be recovered. Many companies in highly competitive industries work below full capacity and are able, in the short term at least, to increase output by more intensive utilization of the plant or the introduction of overtime working. Marginal cost-pricing may be effective for low introductory pricing to generate high acceptance for a new product in an export market. It also exploits experience curve effects and may be used for the sale of surplus capacity. Firms resort to marginal cost-pricing when life cycles are expected to be short due to the imminent introduction of new technologies. Marginal cost-pricing is often used in secondary pricing decisions, special export orders, unusual qualities, and in subcontracting. A major limitation of all cost-oriented pricing systems is that they do not take into account what the customer is prepared to pay for the product.

Pricing and distribution channels

In the previous chapter it was noted that many firms attempt to control all aspects of the distribution system to ensure guaranteed access to their customers on the terms decided by the firm. Distribution through subsidiaries or foreign based manufacturing facilities provides greater control over final prices than do other forms of distribution arrangement. Firms that sell through distributors, for example, can only control the landed price as distributors mark up prices, sometimes substantially. As was seen in the previous chapter reducing the number of intermediaries between the manufacturer and the customer can reduce the adverse effects of successive mark-ups. For this reason it may be advisable to sell direct to end users in many industries to ensure control over final prices. This is especially the case in pricing large industrial systems or technical equipment. It is also true in other product and service markets. Ryanair, one of the low-priced airlines in Europe, uses the Internet to reach most of its customers directly and thereby by-passes travel agents and the general media. Customers using the Internet to make reservations with Ryanair are rewarded with lower prices (Exhibit 18.2). Longer channels tend to escalate prices in the international distribution system.

Exhibit 18.2   Ryanair wins Internet booking race

Ryanair, the largest of the low-cost carriers in Europe, now sells 64 per cent of its seats over the Internet. The company claims that its website is now Europe's largest Internet travel service, dealing with 250,000 transactions a week. Crucial to the airline's online success has been its determination to break up the travel industry's existing distribution channels. Air fares have traditionally been sold by travel agents using computer reservation systems. 'The computer reservation systems are very useful for multi-sector trips, or trips where you have to change airline or book kosher meals, but we don't do any of that. And they are charging us $4 per sector booking,' says Tim Jeens, Ryanair's sales and marketing director.

Ryanair has also attempted to stimulate Internet interest by placing its cheapest fares on the web, making the next cheapest available through its call centres, and its most expensive on computer reservation systems. Jeens says booking patterns follow the rhythm of a normal office day, rather than surging at night. 'We have a big lunchtime peak in our booking rates – both the UK lunch hour and the continental lunch hour. People are not booking these seats from home.'

Source: adapted from *Sunday Business Post*, 25 February 2001, p. 14

Price escalation in international channels

Managers of international firms who visit foreign trade fairs or participate in trade missions abroad frequently encounter products similar to their own, selling at what appear to be much higher prices. The immediate and understandable reaction of some managers is to conclude that distributors, wholesalers and retailers are making excess profits, due to large price mark-ups. In these circumstances the international firm might then attempt to sell to these markets in the belief that its product and price levels would be attractive to the foreign customer and that existing competitor products would be replaced. This line of reasoning may be accurate in some situations but is often incorrect since in most cases added costs are the cause of the seemingly disproportionate difference in price; a phenomenon referred to as price escalation in the marketing channel, particularly troublesome in international markets. Price escalation reflects the situation where the ultimate consumer or user prices are different as a result of shipping costs, tariffs, longer channels of distribution, larger wholesaler and retailer margins, special taxes, currency values and fluctuations in exchange rates (Figure 18.4).

Figure 18.4
Factors influencing price escalation in international markets

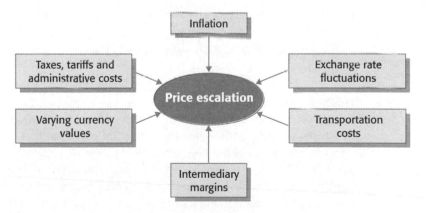

Source: Cateora, P. R. and Ghauri, P. N. (1999) *International Marketing*, European Edition, McGraw Hill Publishing Company, London

Table 18.1 Price escalation in the international channel

Source of price escalation	Domestic market	Wholesaler*	Distributor	Longer channels
Net price to *manufacturer*	200.00	200.00	200.00	200.00
Transport, CIF	–	8.00	8.00	8.00
Tariff at 20%		41.60	41.60	41.60
Distributor pays			249.60	249.60
Distributor margin (25% on cost)			62.40	62.40
Regional wholesaler pays	200.00	241.60	312.00	312.00
Regional wholesaler margin (33$\frac{1}{3}$%)	66.67	80.45	103.90	103.90
Local wholesaler pays				415.90
Local wholesaler margin (33$\frac{1}{3}$%)				138.49
Retailer pays	266.67	322.05	415.90	554.39
Retailer margin (50%)	133.34	161.03	207.95	277.20
Consumer/user price	400.00	483.08	623.85	831.59

* Assume a regional wholesaler who imports directly

The possible effects of these factors are illustrated in Table 18.1. Assume that a firm produces a range of hand-held heavy-duty electric drills and has observed retail prices in foreign markets which it considers to be exorbitant. Because costs and tariffs vary so widely from market to market, a hypothetical situation is examined. In the following illustration it is assumed that:

■ a constant net price is received by the international firm irrespective of market destination for the drills;

■ domestic transportation costs are absorbed by the various intermediaries and reflected in their margins; and

■ intermediaries in foreign markets work with the same margins as domestic intermediaries.

This last assumption is later relaxed to demonstrate the effect of larger margins on the foreign retail price of the drills. In this illustration retail prices vary over a wide range which demonstrates the difficulty facing international firms that attempt to control prices in foreign retail markets. No matter how much the international firm may wish to sell its drills in a foreign market at a price equivalent to €200 it may discover that it has little opportunity for doing so. Assuming the most optimistic conditions, those assumed for the domestic market, the international manufacturer of drills would need to cut net prices by almost 30 per cent to absorb the freight and tariff costs so that the products could be priced at the same level abroad as in the domestic market. To achieve the same objective under the remaining conditions assumed, the price cuts would be much greater. As a consequence, the firm should approach the international pricing issue with considerable care. Price escalation in international marketing channels requires an understanding of the role of intermediaries and the effects of marketing costs such as transport and insurance, in addition to the tariffs and local taxes which prevail in each particular market.

In particular, the situation depicted for the longer channel as might arise, for example, in a developing country market or in a large country like the United States, where there are many distribution levels, price escalation may be considerable. In the circumstances assumed, prices escalate from €200 in the domestic market to €831.59 abroad. Even in the case of using a distributor the final price is more than three times the domestic price.

In practice the levels of margins may differ in different countries and at different levels in the distribution channel. The example nevertheless illustrates the impact of price escalation in international distribution channels and lends truth to the view that transactions costs represent the largest cost element overall. The price escalation phenomenon, particularly if manufacturers and customers decide that insufficient value is being added in the channel, is a powerful incentive to disintermediate the channel as Ryanair and other low-cost operators have done through the use of the Internet.

Market based pricing in international markets

While a cost approach to pricing in international markets is very common it should be complemented by also taking account of retail prices in the market and working backwards. It is necessary, therefore, to examine the market, the customer's needs and the effect these are likely to have on price. The successful firm attempts to maintain flexibility and discretion in price decisions; i.e. too much concentration on the cost side of the equation gives rise to an extremely jaundiced view of the scope available. The market and its potential should be the starting point and costs should be used only to determine whether what is desired by the market can be produced at a profit. Successful international firms base their international pricing on a mixture of criteria involving a combination of the following steps:

■ estimate the price of the product 'landed' in the foreign market by considering international customer costs, e.g. documentation, freight, insurance, etc;

■ determine the price the distributor or importer is likely to charge by accounting for tariffs and the margins of intermediaries;

■ specify the target price range for end users, lowest price, most likely price and highest price;

■ assess company sales potential at different price levels.

In following these steps the firm attempts to determine the effect of a market opportunity on profits or contribution by working backwards from the established or accepted range of market prices and simultaneously working forwards from the cost side (Figure 18.5). The special allocation for export overheads includes agents' commissions,

Figure 18.5
Market and
cost factors in
international
pricing

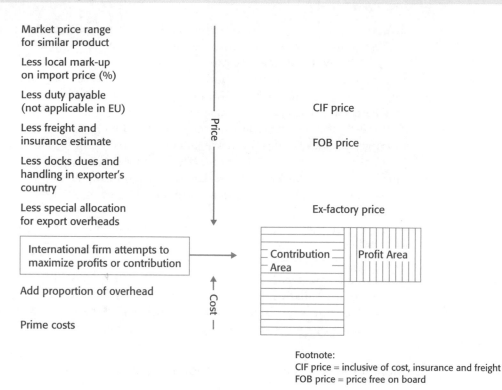

Market price range
for similar product

Less local mark-up
on import price (%)

Less duty payable
(not applicable in EU)   CIF price

Less freight and
insurance estimate   FOB price

Less docks dues and
handling in exporter's
country

Less special allocation   Ex-factory price
for export overheads

International firm attempts to   →   Contribution   Profit Area
maximize profits or contribution   Area

Add proportion of overhead

Prime costs

Footnote:
CIF price = inclusive of cost, insurance and freight
FOB price = price free on board

promotion costs, travel, extra staff attributable to the exporting activity, any interest on special loans and factoring discounts. The addition for overheads on the cost side include a contribution for salaried staff, indirect wages, rent, and any special services. The prime costs include materials consumed, direct labour, power and packaging.

The difference that remains, if there is one, presents the firm with an estimate of profits, the smaller box in Figure 18.5, or contribution to overheads, the larger box. Where there is no difference the firm should examine its costs more carefully or examine the potential of other market segments or different markets. This is a generic framework: the precise circumstances faced by the firm in its pricing decision, e.g. tariffs, duties and taxes, would need to specified.

An illustration of this procedure for a hypothetical situation demonstrates its value. Assume that a United States manufacturer of ultra-filtration systems has been asked by one of its existing customers, a dairy cooperative in France, to quote in euro for a number of small motors used to drive the ultra-filtration units which have been adapted for the cooperative's small cheese plants. The firm knows that similar motors are available from original equipment manufacturers as initial market research in France has indicated that competitors were supplying similar motors for around €10,000. Given the previous discussion on absorption and marginal cost-pricing there are two things the firm needs to know: will there be a profit or, at least, will there be a contribution to overheads? Applying the principles outlined in Figure 18.5 and given the hypothetical situation assumed it is possible to price from the demand side and the cost side, to see what profits or contribution can be made (Figure 18.6).

Figure 18.6
Costing and
pricing in export
markets

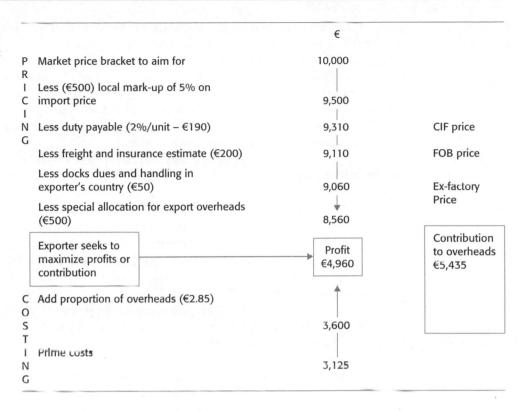

It is worth noting that there are many charges or costs which at first sight may not be obvious. Local wholesaler and retailer mark-ups, here assumed to be 5 per cent (€500), and duties, here assumed to be 2 per cent (€190/unit), are perhaps the two most important. Allowing for these costs we arrive at the cost, insurance and freight price (CIF). From the CIF price thus derived it is necessary to allow for freight and insurance to arrive at the free on board (FOB) price, here assumed to be €200. Other deductions include assumed dock handling charges in France and the allowances to cover the direct export costs. Two sets of costs are assumed, direct manufacturing costs and an allocation for overheads. All figures are in euro to facilitate the discussion of the two approaches. By following this procedure two sets of residuals are computed: profits or contribution to overheads depending on circumstances. Many firms find that when this kind of analysis is performed the profit area is much lower than anticipated or disappears altogether and the area of contribution may not be substantial. The example illustrates the importance of performing a detailed cost and price analysis before deciding whether to export to a particular market.

Life cycle effects on international pricing

Prices charged by the firm vary by stage of the life cycle. Earlier it was shown that products evolve through a life cycle both across different country markets and over time. At the introductory or embryonic stage of the life cycle the manager, planning to export to a number of foreign markets, might consider a price-skimming strategy or a penetration strategy depending on the company's overall pricing objectives and the situation it faces in various markets. Limited capacity may rule out a penetration pricing strategy and restrict the firm to charging a particular price. In these circumstances the strategy should be to select an introductory high price with a view to lowering it as demand elasticity increases, additional capacity becomes available, and competitors respond or are attracted to the market.

Alternatively, if there were no capacity constraint a penetration price might be selected which would yield high sales volumes initially accompanied by slow competitive imitation. Penetration pricing, however, is associated with low unit profits and may, therefore, not suit the company's intentions. The firm must examine the circumstances and make a decision based on the trade-offs involved. In some instances the international firm relies on a penetration price to maintain the firm's share in an existing market which is growing and thus avoid having to resort to successive price reductions. In such circumstances the firm normally operates with lower variable costs as it moves down the learning curve.

In setting the price, the firm must also consider the profits dimension. A very low penetration price does not normally make sense at the embryonic stage of the life cycle if the objective is to maximize short-run profits.

At the maturity stage the firm has far less discretion over selling prices. Prices tend to fall in real terms during the growth stage as a result of scale economies and pressure from competitors, and to decline even further in the maturity stage but eventually to stabilize. Consequently, the firm must be prepared for a number of real price changes during the life of the product. At this stage of the life cycle the firm would probably be well advised to maximize short-run profits, ignoring the doubtful potential of higher prices.

In the decline stage, the firm typically seeks to obtain as much profit as possible while seeking to divest itself from this market. One strategy is to cease promotion which should increase profits while killing off the product. Raising price can have the same effect.

Most firms modify prices over time as the product moves through the life cycle. To fully achieve the benefits of life-cycle pricing it is necessary to estimate the product demand elasticities in each market the firm wishes to enter and to consider how these elasticities may be altered so as to improve the product's competitive position. This means that the firm must be prepared to vary the emphasis given to price and the other marketing variables such as advertising, product improvement and packaging for each stage of the life cycle. It is necessary to examine the entire mix of marketing effort rather than to treat prices in isolation. An increase in advertising should be evaluated to ensure that the increase in total contribution at least exceeds the advertising outlay. The increased advertising expenditure, however, is reflected in increased fixed costs and a higher breakeven level of product units at a given price.

Pricing for exporting competitiveness

Successful international firms consider a combination of objective managerial factors and behavioural related variables such as attitudes, values and norms in setting international prices (Holzmüller and Stöttinger, 1996, p. 48). A mixture of factors influence price competition in international markets – influences which relate to managerial, marketing, behavioural and attitudinal factors. The reality of pricing in international marketing is, therefore, that many factors must be considered:

■ the company's international marketing objectives – is the firm attempting to penetrate or skim the market?;

■ the exchange rate regime;

■ the position of the product in the market and in the life cycle;

■ the activities of competitors;

■ other elements of the marketing mix.

Even acknowledging the relevance of all of the above factors the firm is still faced with making a decision on what price to charge. Unfortunately there is no way of determining what the best price should be. Prices can range from the low level suggested by marginal cost pricing to a price higher than the competition on the assumption that the product can carry a premium for quality or some other benefit. For new products which are innovative a price skimming-strategy may be used. Marginal cost-pricing can be used to set the minimum prices to be charged. Successful companies use absorption costs to set long-term prices. It is also essential to consider competitor products and prices when setting prices. Such a balanced approach to pricing, incorporating concern for customers and competitors as well as product factors, is recommended (Tzokas et al., 2000, p. 202). Lastly, for the international firm the financial stability of the respective currencies of buyers and seller must be considered. Taking all these factors together suggests that a range of possible prices from the low of marginal cost price to the high upper price limit that represents a premium for product quality over competitor prices should be considered (Figure 18.7).

Figure 18.7
A range of
feasible prices

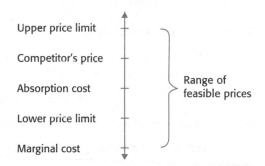

Summary

The nature of the product and the extent of competition in relevant international markets limits the amount of price discretion available to the firm; a knowledge based competitive advantage in high technology gives greater room for manoeuvre. It is also necessary to consider government macroeconomic policies in a number of areas as they may influence price levels in international markets. A number of additional issues must also be considered by the international firm. Transfer pricing among units of the same international firm can cause many managerial and administrative difficulties. Market prices are the most common method of transferring prices followed by standard full unit cost with a fixed mark-up added. Fluctuating exchange rates pose many problems for the international firm. They cope with them in numerous ways: diversifying sales among a mix of currency areas, hedging, and developing strategic responses by preparing a marketing programme suitable for weak or strong currencies depending on the situation faced. Price volatility appears to cause customer firms as much concern as high absolute prices so trading in euro, US dollar or pound sterling alleviates some of the difficulty. Many large firms set their own internal fixed rates of exchange among volatile currencies to ensure that prices to their customers abroad do not fluctuate widely.

Standardized prices across many markets are difficult to maintain because of currency fluctuations, different cost structures, government policies and transfer pricing requirements. It is necessary, however, to maintain some order on prices to avoid the possibility of parallel importing. Prices between domestic markets and foreign markets escalate for many reasons to do with added costs and margins incurred in international distribution channels. Price escalation is greater in longer channels. Market rather than cost based approaches to international pricing are recommended. Costs should be considered as the base below which the firm should not go whereas market based prices are the highest in the range of feasible prices. In setting prices for the first time it is recommended that the firm start with current prices in the market and work backwards to determine the level of profit or contribution remaining after costs have been considered.

Questions

1. Describe the major external influences on international pricing in the firm.

2. Price volatility due to exchange rate movements makes it difficult for some firms to compete in key international markets. Discuss.

3. When might you use marginal cost-pricing in international markets?

4. What is meant by price escalation and why should the firm be concerned about it?

5. Demonstrate why it is necessary to examine market demand factors and cost factors in arriving at an appropriate price.

References

Caller, L. (1999) 'The consumer meets the euro: likely effects and implications', *The Journal of Brand Management*, **7** (1), 27–37.

Cateora, P. R. and Ghauri, P. N. (1999) *International Marketing*, European Edition, McGraw Hill Publishing Company, London.

Cavusgil, S. T. (1996) 'Pricing for global markets', *The Columbia Journal of World Business*, Winter, 66–78.

Holzmüller, H. and Stöttinger, B. (1996) 'Structural modeling of success factors in exporting: cross-validation and further development of an export performance model', *Journal of International Marketing*, **4** (2), 29–55.

Tzokas, N., Hart, S., Argouslidis, P. and Saren, M. (2000) 'Industrial export pricing practices in the United Kingdom', *Industrial Marketing Management*, **29**, 191–204.

19 Selling and negotiating in international markets

International marketing strategy is implemented through the marketing team and the sales force operating abroad. It is the sales and marketing team that directly interact with customers in the market and become the eyes and ears of the company. In international markets, the sales force faces an additional challenge – communication across different cultures, languages and business backgrounds. The role of the sales force is emphasized since personal selling is a key function in most international firms. Furthermore, the supplying firm in one market usually deals directly with a purchasing firm in another, but only indirectly with the consumer market. The strategy is one of promoting products and services through the channel from producer to agent or intermediary or user. Rarely does the international firm sell directly to the consumer mass market internationally although with the growth in direct marketing and the Internet this occurs in some areas but yet accounts for only a small proportion of total international sales. Frequently, the firm sells directly to industrial users. Hence, much of the emphasis in this chapter on personal selling applies to international business-to-business marketing.

After studying this chapter students should be able to:

- understand the buying and selling process in a cross-cultural setting;
- specify the role of the sales force in international markets;
- define communication and its importance in the international marketing exchange process;
- recognize the importance of negotiation in the international selling process; and
- outline the key factors to be considered when selecting an international sales team.

Selling and negotiating in international marketing

International marketing negotiation is concerned with cross-border exchange activities and building subsequent marketing relationships and the manner in which such exchanges and relationships are established and nourished. We distinguish between discrete exchanges where only weak relationships are established between the parties and negotiated exchanges where buyers and sellers are actively involved in a process which may result in the formation of longer-lasting and deeper marketing relationships such as marketing agreements, joint ventures and investment. To avoid strategic errors in international marketing exchange and negotiations, companies must have access to complete information, including information on how to cope with cultural differences, how to assess management processes and styles, and how to understand the political economy of the target country (Marshall *et al.*, 1998, p. 19). Negotiated exchanges in international markets have a number of distinguishing features. At least two parties, usually from different cultures, are involved; there may be a conflict of interests but the parties come together in a voluntary relationship concerned with the exchange of tangible and intangible assets. Negotiation is defined as:

> any sequence of written and or verbal communication processes whereby parties to both common and conflicting commercial interests and of differing cultural backgrounds consider the form of any joint action they might take in pursuit of their individual objectives which will define or redefine the terms of their interdependence.
>
> (McCall and Warrington, 1989, p. 15)

Negotiation means talking about a relationship before doing something about it. Negotiations are mixed-motive situations, however: each party has a motive to enter into negotiation to reach a mutually acceptable solution while, simultaneously, each may have a motive for competition. The negotiations process is a four-stage sequence of activities involving: a) the presentation of demands by one or both parties; b) their evaluation; c) possible concessions and counter proposals; and d) closing with an agreement which, in an ideal situation, benefits both parties. While a 'win–lose' situation may arise it is assumed that it is possible for both parties to achieve their objectives – a win-win outcome: 'where both parties perceive the process of negotiation as a process to find a solution to a common problem [where] one party's gain is not dependent upon the other party's concession' (Ghauri, 1996, p. 4). Four features distinguish win-win negotiations in international marketing:

■ disclosure of objectives by both parties;

■ a search for a solution that satisfies both parties;

■ a recognition that both parties have common and conflicting objectives; and

■ the negotiation task is to find common and complementary objectives acceptable to both sides in a cross-cultural context.

Nature of international marketing exchanges

In an international marketing exchange we are concerned with the transfer of assets which may consist of products, services, ideas, information or rewards associated with the transfer of industrial and consumer products, licensing and joint venture agreements, distribution and agency agreements and information. Such exchanges are central to marketing, as they represent the point of convergence of the selling process and the buying process. Concern also involves understanding the process of exchange including personal selling, marketing negotiations and managing the resulting relationships. The selling firm in the home country and buying firms abroad are linked through these products and processes.

International marketing negotiations

Buyer–seller communications

Communication is defined as a 'process of convergence in which two or more participants share information in order to reach a better mutual understanding of each other and the world in which they live' (Barnett and Kincaid, 1983). Open sharing of expectations and information is even more critical when it crosses national boundaries because of the increased difficulty of understanding the needs of remote customers (LaBahn and Harich, 1997, p. 34).

Communication is a two-way process of interaction (Schramm, 1971, p. 4) involving a sender, a message and a receiver. Both the sender and the receiver play an active role in the transmission and reception of the message. The Schramm model conceives of participants in the communication process as having separate frames of reference (Figure 19.1). First there is the frame of reference or field of experience of the internationalizing firm and a counterpart field of experience of the customer located abroad. The seller, influenced by culture, chooses words and symbols to encode a message, written, verbal or pictorial which is transferred abroad through some medium such as advertising, personal selling, mail or the Internet. The customer abroad who receives the message uses a set of words and symbols, likely to be different, to decode the message. In international marketing effective communication can only take place in the area of overlap between the frames of reference of the two countries and cultures involved. The greater the degree of overlap, the broader the range of issues about

Figure 19.1 Factors affecting shared meaning in international marketing

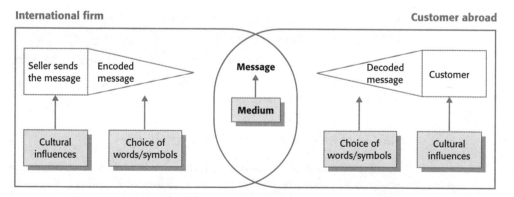

Source: adapted from Schramm, W. (1971) 'How communication works', in W. Schramm and D. F. Roberts, Eds, *The Process and Effects of Mass Communications*, Urbana, IL: University of Illinois Press

which companies located in these two countries can communicate. The area of common frame of reference also determines the possible depth of communication.

The message may be conveyed verbally or otherwise by means of a code which, in personal selling particularly, includes oral and written language accompanied by a set of paralinguistic features, such as stress and loudness. Personal selling may also contain non-verbal phenomena such as gestures and facial expressions. Coding and decoding are the ways in which participants in the buying and selling process negotiate and define new knowledge, new understanding, new joint priorities and new values as a key to understanding the intercultural communication process. Throughout the international marketing communications process, many opportunities exist for distortion and loss of messages.

Cultural filters and 'noise'

Language is both a facilitator and an impediment of shared meaning in cross-cultural communications. Impediments may take two forms, filtration, where messages are only partially transmitted, and distortion, where the intended meaning is altered during the transmission of the message (Marschan *et al.*, 1997, p. 595). These authors also argue that 'An important first step might be to include language aspects at the highest level of strategic planning and implementation [as international firms] cannot allow language to become peripheral, given that it permeates virtually every aspect of their operations' (pp. 596/7). The two faces of language, as facilitator or as impediment, may emerge in a range of situations between the company and its customers, all of which affect the company's ability to communicate. There are two factors that cause a distortion in a verbal communication, which may affect the buyer's or seller's ability to understand what the other is saying (Gourlay, 1987):

- filters refer to forms of internal psychological distorting mechanisms which alter the counterpart's message;
- 'noise' in the system that relates to background distraction which has nothing to do with the substance of the message but can complicate the communication process.

In regard to filters it is easy for a buyer or seller to assume that they know instinctively what the counterpart seeks but such expectations can lead to difficulties. If the seller expects the buyer to be difficult, the seller may distort the buyer's communications to fit the expectation.

The context of the communication is also important (Francis, 1991). This is particularly difficult in cross-cultural communications especially where one party incorrectly uses the paralanguage of the other. The double messages which result are a great source of mistaken understanding and confusion. This is one of the reasons why television advertising attempts to rely on messages with universal meanings and avoids themes which may be interpreted differently in different countries. A key decision facing the selling company is the extent to which communications should be standardized across markets or customized to address better communication needs within individual markets. In some countries such as the US, the UK, Germany and the Nordic countries the emphasis is placed on the universal – legal systems, contracts, higher obligations, objectivity and on only one correct way of doing things. The communications approach required for markets like these is very different than that required for countries such as France, Japan, Spain, Latin America and China where the emphasis is more on the particular – relationships, personal systems, trust, duty to friends and family and the acceptance of myriad approaches to doing things.

The firm's ability to standardize communications messages depends on the kind of message involved. An advertising campaign, using an emotional appeal, for example, may be difficult to standardize across countries since the success of an emotional appeal depends on viewers bringing similar cultural values to the situation (Ueltschy and Ryans, 1997, p. 491). Douglas Daft, former chief executive of Coca-Cola, believes that advertising has to reflect local markets. 'I think global advertising is really an oxymoron, because global advertising tends to look at the similarities between people. But it's the differences you need to focus on. English advertising I can appreciate as an Australian. It tends to be a bit risqué and have double entendres and by some standards be almost politically incorrect. But it is very funny. If you transfer that to Germany they don't know what you are talking about.'

All markets experience 'noise' which includes physical noise and idiosyncrasies of the communicators in a personal selling situation. Cross-cultural noise which derives from gestures, behaviour seeming overly or insufficiently courteous, clothing, office surroundings and the speaking distance between the parties to the exchange represents a more serious challenge to effective communications. Such noise may lead to conflict with expectations and may result in a misinterpretation of the situation, a change of intent on the part of the counterpart or even a change in the meaning of the message itself.

Fields of cultural experience

The overlap between the fields of experience of the sender in the home country and the receiver in the foreign country establishes how effective the communication is likely to be. If there is little common experience or culture, successful communication is difficult. Overlap in the sender's and receiver's culture is necessary for successful cross-cultural communications (Samli *et al.*, 1993). Striving to understand the field of experience of the counterpart is a necessary step in facilitating a successful communication process. The more divergent the experiences of individuals, the more difficult it is for effective communication to take place. It is important, therefore, to be sensitive to the national business culture of potential business partners. Sensitivity to national business culture refers to the firm's understanding of and adaptation to its exchange partner's domestic business practices as perceived by the partner (LaBahn and Harich, 1997, p. 31). Furthermore, sensitivity to national business culture is an important prerequisite for the cross-cultural adaptation necessary to lessen misunderstanding and disagreement (Reardon and Spekman, 1994).

With some common ground in experience and culture, buyers and sellers share similar expectations of a situation, the decisions to be made and the implications of those decisions. They also understand the style and pattern of communication to be used, plan to discuss similar topics and choose to use similar forms of communication

(Schuster and Copeland, 1996, p. 152). The more each partner understands the other's situation, perspective and culture, the easier it is to create verbal and non-verbal symbols that can be encoded and decoded similarly by both.

Culture and effective communication

Cultural barriers militate against effective communications and increase the likelihood of total breakdown in communication. Cross-cultural communication problems arise because of language and language behaviour, non-verbal behaviour, different value systems and different cognitive styles or thought patterns. Misunderstandings at the level of language are usually very obvious and easy to correct but at the higher levels of values and cognitive styles they are not so obvious and therefore often go uncorrected.

A major difficulty arises when we assume that implicit assumptions and habitual ways of thinking about our own circumstances have universal applicability. As already noted this self-reference criterion trap gives rise to many problems in international marketing (Hall, 1960; Lee, 1966). As a consequence, confusion turns full circle in cross-cultural communications, when the mind not only places its own stamp of meaning on an incoming message but begins to project that same meaning to the counterpart in the negotiations (Fisher, 1980, p. 15). One form of unconscious projection that wreaks havoc in negotiations, according to Fisher, is attribution of motive. Motives attributed reflect the buyer's or seller's experience in dealing with others. An example of an assumed motive that does not need to be thought through to complete an exchange when operating in a single culture would be: 'he is hesitating because he thinks that the price is too high or that my offer could improve'. In such circumstances the probability of being correct in assuming motives is relatively high in western cultures. The probability falls rapidly, however, when dealing with an oriental culture where silences and slow responses do not necessarily indicate a reluctance by the counterpart to consider the proposition. The complexity of the subject matter exacerbates the communication difficulties which arise (Figure 19.2).

Culture has a benign effect on communications when the parties attribute very similar affective meaning to the communicative stimuli used, when the experience of the parties converges sufficiently for effective communications to take place, and when the firm is sensitive to national business culture which helps to establish a network of shared meanings.

Figure 19.2
Culture and international communication

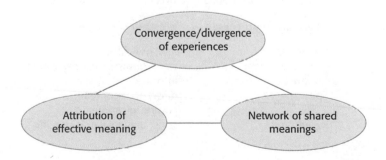

Impact of context on communication

A crucial aspect of the influence of culture on communication is the context in which it takes place (Hall, 1976). By context Hall refers to situation-specific factors such as the roles of participants, their power and status, the physical environment and the subject of interest. As discussed in Chapter 5, the content of communication can be understood only in the context of these factors. The relevance of context also applies to negotiations. In high-context countries the content of the communication in negotiation is not as important as the role of participants. In such situations communications depend greatly on the context or non-verbal aspects of the communications. In low-context countries the focus of attention is on the content or words used. For example, in France the role of the negotiator influences results, whereas in Germany role or context has no importance (Campbell *et al.*, 1988, p. 57), leading these authors to claim support for Hall's (1976) characterization of Germany as a low-context culture.

For marketing and sales people the analysis of social structure in high-context countries is essential to obtain useful insights to a selling or buying situation. As an example of high-context negotiations process it is instructive to examine Chinese cognitive structure and its effect on international negotiations. In business negotiations the Chinese tend to elicit as much information as possible before disclosing their hand to avoid losing face or displaying ignorance. It is generally accepted that the Chinese and other oriental people assimilate data in intuitive lumps or bundles and understand in terms of systems. In such circumstances appreciation of technologies may be limited until they have grasped how the diverse elements fit into an entire system. Culture influences the entire negotiations process in different ways depending on the region and countries involved including the number of delegates attending a meeting, the manner in which decisions are taken, general conduct and speech and the way agreements are implemented (Table 19.1). In western countries fewer people tend to be involved in the negotiation process, compromise is often an outcome, communications are informal and direct and agreements tend to be specific and have a legal basis while in eastern countries the opposites prevail.

Establishing the negotiation range may, therefore, be unimportant where the assimilation of information is a major element in the interaction. The problem-solving element assumes a greater importance for the development of the relationships between the negotiators. It is not a gradual move, but one of attaining an agreed position in one well-considered step. In such a buying–selling regime foreign negotiators must make

Table 19.1 Impact of culture on negotiation processes

Negotiation processes	Western countries	Eastern countries
Delegates	few, individuals	many, collectivism
Decisions	compromise, majority voting	group, consensus
Conduct	informal	formal
Speech	direct, low-context communications	indirect, high-context communications
Agreements	legal, universal and specific	trust and mutual respect, particular and diffuse

their points as cogently as possible within the relationships that they can establish and trust that their package is accepted.

Following these guidelines suggests that the international firm should present a summary close to the negotiations involving a simple package so that the buyer understands the complete offer before being asked for a response. A summary close is more appropriate than a concession close, provided that the timing is right. A concession close may be more appropriate in western countries where the seller attempts to lead the buyer through a series of stages in a linear way towards an acceptance of the offer. In such circumstances, in order to obtain an acceptance sellers often offer a concession to close the deal.

Selling and negotiating strategies

Personal selling is the dominant demand-stimulating element in the international marketing communications mix; this is especially true for industrial products. In such situations sales people work primarily to stimulate demand while also providing a range of other customer services.

From once being an adversarial function selling has become much more cooperatively and collaboratively driven. Noting this trend for industrial products has led Hutt and Speh (1989, pp. 521–2) to refer to consultative and negotiative selling. In consultative selling the sales person assumes the role of a consultant helping to improve the client's profitability. Here face-to-face contact is important, and questioning and listening are crucial skills. The sales person provides analysis and problem-solving assistance in an attempt to offer more value than competitors. A negotiations style is adopted to optimize the benefits of a marketing transaction for both the buyer and seller. The objective is to establish a partnership across cultures between buyer and seller with common objectives, mutually beneficial strategies and a common defence against third parties.

Convergence of buying and selling

Buying and selling processes in international markets tend to converge and are greatly influenced by the ability of the parties to communicate and share information. Throughout the process of sharing information about preferences and priorities the parties endeavour to understand what the other side wants to achieve. Because of cultural differences and different business practices this usually means probing below the surface of the counterpart's position to discover latent needs.

Experienced negotiators create a free and open flow of information and they use their desire to satisfy both parties as the perspective from which to structure their discussions. This is the essential ingredient of a 'win–win' situation in international marketing negotiations. Buyers attempt to learn what is available that can solve their perceived problems, and the buying process involves many people at many stages. Similarly, sellers must communicate with potential buyers to obtain their attention to convey offers and to prescribe possible solutions to identified problems. Hence, there are many opportunities for communications breakdown in the various stages of the buying and selling processes which are exacerbated when communicating across cultures.

The buying process

The anatomy of the buying process consists of five discrete phases (Figure 19.3). Buyers first recognize their need to buy; the buyer identifies and defines a need. Need recognition may arise within the firm, e.g. the need for supplies of components or it may be stimulated by sales people or advertising. Three buying situations may be identified, a new purchase, a modified repurchase or a routine purchase of some low-cost uncomplicated product. A new need is the most complex of these three buying situations. The amount of interaction between the buyer and seller is also usually quite significant and takes place at several points in the respective organizations. In such circumstances there are many opportunities for a break-down in cross-cultural communications. In a modified buying situation, e.g. a change in a production process, the buyer may have to search for a new solution but, because of previous experience, the decision process is much simpler than the first time such a purchase was made. Nevertheless, communication problems can easily arise. A routinized buying situation results in the purchase of a product that has been bought many times before; the buying process is simple and often automatic as both buyer and seller know the solution to the buyer's problem. Cross-cultural communications problems are less likely to arise in these circumstances.

The roles of the various parties engaged in buying depend on the buying situation. A new need may require a number of people both within and outside the firm to be involved in the buying decision. For example, the purchase of a new aircraft by an airline would require considerable involvement from purchasing, engineering, finance, senior management, outside consultants, banks, leasing firms and even government departments. At the other extreme, for a routinized need, it is probably only necessary for the buyer to become aware that a purchase needs to be made. Depending on the situation, therefore, the buying decision involves one or several people, influencers, users, gatekeepers and the people who make the actual purchase. In such circumstances

Figure 19.3
Convergence
of buying and
selling processes

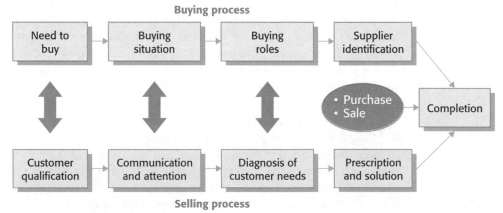

it is important that the seller understands that there are important differences in the way in which different people search for information and make buying decisions.

Before buyers begin to search for information they develop criteria by which the information collected can be evaluated. These criteria serve as a guide in the search process. For the seller it is important to know and understand the buying criteria used. The search process is directed at identifying and qualifying potential suppliers. At this stage buyers shortlist potential suppliers. Specifications are prepared that establish criteria in terms of product performance, characteristics, quality, acceptable price ranges, repair, maintenance, installation and advice.

The last stage involves a comparison of competing offers to choose the best possible package of price, quantity, delivery, quality and service in making the purchase. At all stages there are valuable opportunities for interaction by the selling firm which assist in the problem-solving process outlined. Availing of these opportunities requires considerable understanding of cross-cultural communications and negotiations.

Stages in the selling process

The selling process may similarly be divided into five definable but interdependent stages, each of which corresponds with its equivalent stage in the buying process (Figure 19.3). The first step is to qualify the customer to prepare for the ultimate sale. Here the seller is interested in identifying possible problems in the customer firm. The selling firm begins to identify the nature and range of issues to be resolved in a possible encounter with the buyer. It is important to plan the negotiation strategy, to incorporate trade-off possibilities and to allow for contingencies. The seller or sales force also establishes authority limits for dealing with the potential customer. All activity at this stage is carried out before meeting the customer.

The communication and attention phase is critical in international selling. Obtaining the buyer's attention may be a very long process involving research, much travel and an analysis of the needs of potential customers to short-list the more promising. It also usually involves the preparation of suitable promotion materials and the use of other media to reach the potential customer. All subsequent stages in the selling process depend on successful completion of this one. Cross-cultural communications and differences in cognitive styles add to the possible distractions or interference in the communication between buyer and seller which reduces attention. In launching its new S60 model in the United States only through the Internet, Volvo believed that attention and awareness levels could be raised in its target market – younger and technically knowledgeable people – even though the Internet is not known for its strength in awareness-building for a new product. Customers use the Internet to learn more about a product or to decide among a few, so a blend of online and offline advertising might have been more appropriate.

During this stage, too, factors which affect the relative power of the parties are identified. The seller and the buyer begin to determine how best to approach the negotiation. Indeed, if the work of the first stage is not carried out accurately it may be decided not to proceed. Both sides also attempt to establish the needs and preferences of the other party. Face-to-face communication is normal at various points in this stage of the process.

Figure 19.4
Context and
empathy in
cross-cultural
communications

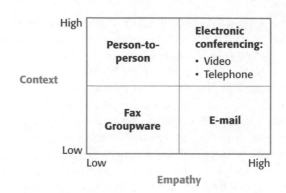

Indeed many different forms of communication are used, some of which are appropriate in high-context situations while others are acceptable when a low-context situation is faced. Furthermore, the degree of empathy established between the parties also influences the choice of appropriate or advisable communications methods (Figure 19.4).

Diagnosing customer needs and the buying situation consists primarily of collecting facts and qualitative information about the potential customer. The seller attempts to identify the buyer's dominant reason for buying the product or service. Diagnosis and evaluation clearly indicate the problem-solving aspect of selling. This is a highly interactive stage and very demanding on interpersonal skills, especially those concerned with communicating and influencing across cultures. It is important to maintain flexibility; experienced buyers and sellers keep issues linked as proposals and counter proposals are made, a difficult thing to do in markets characterized by different cultures. It may be necessary at this stage to reformulate objectives and strategies in the light of new information on tangible and intangible issues.

The next step in the selling process is to begin to prescribe a range of possible solutions. A well-prepared and executed selling programme usually convinces the potential buyer of the seller's purpose. The seller at this point demonstrates a clear understanding of the buyer's problem and shows that the seller's range of products and services can help solve that problem. The seller attempts to influence the buyer–seller negotiations by assuming a knowledgeable role and concern for and proper understanding of the buyer's problem.

The seller moves towards an agreement, conditional on acceptance of a package of products, services and conditions for their exchange. Having obtained acceptance for the prescription offered, the seller must convince the buyer as to the appropriateness of the proposed solution. This means explaining the purpose, use, features and benefits of the product or service so clearly that the buyer completely understands and accepts what is said.

Lastly it is necessary to close the sale which means employing an effective approach to direct the buyer to the point of decision. It also involves recognizing when the buyer has made such a decision. The objective of closing is to influence the buyer to make a decision to purchase the product or service and to ensure that all formalities are completed. At this stage the seller resorts to an appropriate closing technique. As discussed in a previous section, in some situations it is more appropriate to close a sale by summarizing the agreement, while in other circumstances making a concession to the buyer is more appropriate. The choice depends on the situation, the product-market and the circumstances. Lastly, good marketing relationships usually call for revision when circumstances change.

Selling and promoting industrial products

Selling industrial products

Personal selling is the most important method of promoting and selling industrial products internationally. The reason that personal selling is so important in the industrial markets is inherent in the types of purchases that are made. The need for sales people who are well trained and experienced within their individual technical discipline when marketing high-technology industrial products is well documented in the literature and in trade journals. Most such purchases are large and arriving at the sale often takes considerable time. Often the purchaser is not exactly sure of what is available in a company's product line or requires a special item for which specifications need to be worked out and a price and delivery date negotiated. This is a particularly complex matter when a company is launching a new innovative high-technology product for the first time. Obtaining a launch customer for expensive technical products is key to success as other orders from other customers quickly follow. The decision by Singapore Airlines in 2000 to buy up to 16 A380 super-jumbos, referred to in Exhibit 4.2, p. 71, meant that a leading airline had agreed with Airbus that an all-new super-jumbo was the appropriate way to serve the increasing demand for air travel. With the Singapore launch, Airbus could look forward to receiving further orders for its new 680-seater civil aircraft; other airlines such as Qantas and British Airways, which are heavy users of Singapore Airlines' domestic hub, would sooner or later feel obliged to offer the last word in big-jet travel. Airbus could not have hoped for a better, more high-profile launch customer. The deal was won only after a vicious pricing battle with Boeing. Those operating in another culture need to be familiar with various negotiation strategies employed there and how the negotiation process is similar to and different from that which exists in their own culture.

By dealing with a sales team, many of the final details concerning the product can be resolved. For new, maintenance, repair and operating service products end-users often determine which products are purchased and are most influenced by advertising, but closing a sale may still require many calls from the sales person to the organization's gatekeepers. Because of culture and distance these aspects to selling abroad require considerable commitment on the part of the industrial products firm. Commitment to international marketing among industrial firms is determined by the way the firm organizes its resources to reach the market:

■ for major international customers, direct selling from the home base is an appropriate organizational form;

■ market access with only minor investment can be obtained through agents;

■ sales subsidiaries and foreign direct investment may be necessary to obtain a long-lasting presence in the market.

Promoting industrial products

Trade journals, trade fairs and exhibitions are the principal communications media used by industrial buyers. In a recent study of a large sample of US industrial firms, the Internet was discovered to have only a very modest initial impact on sales and profits but a very significantly improved public relations and communications effect among suppliers, customers and employees (Honeycutt *et al.*, 1998, p. 71). A website allows industrial products firms to enter the world of electronic commerce and allows them to communicate internationally in a direct and effective way with selected customer groups.

Trade fairs continue to be a most valuable means for reaching the hidden buying influences not reached by regular sales people or by trade publications. A sales person can talk to more prospects in a three- or four-day trade show than could be reached by personal calls in a much longer period. Many members of the buying centre of targeted companies frequently attend trade shows. In the marketing of high-technology industrial products, exhibitions and trade shows play a very important role at the interest–awareness stage as well as the evaluation and selection stage. The benefits of international trade shows according to Rice (1992, p. 33) include:

- lower customer contact cost than sales calls;
- it is possible to examine opportunities before investing in foreign markets;
- ability to monitor regional–global competition efficiently;
- managers can identify new product opportunities in discussion with visitors;
- evaluation of reactions to a new product;
- building relationships with existing and potential customers.

Product sampling is a very effective way to introduce and stimulate interest among end-users and influencers for industrial supply items which are relatively inexpensive. More expensive products, however, may be promoted in this way by offering a free trial period. Various restrictions are imposed on the industrial marketing firm's chosen communication mix in international markets. The EU directive on product liability influences the content of a particular communication mix.

Cultural integration of negotiation and selling

In this section we attempt to understand the role of culture, more precisely, cultural familiarity, in buyer–seller negotiations in international marketing and how it affects the style of negotiation adopted by the parties in the exchange or relationship. Successful international firms recognize that foreign customers judge their performance on their ability to be culturally accommodating (Harich and LaBahn, 1998, p. 97). Three types of culturally responsive negotiation strategies, reflecting Weiss's (1994a, 1994b) framework based on the familiarity that the negotiator has with the counterpart's culture, may be identified. By combining negotiation styles and cultural familiarity

Figure 19.5
Cultural
familiarity and
negotiation style

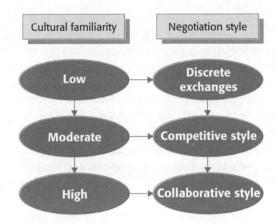

three distinct approaches to integrating culture and negotiation may be envisaged (Figure 19.5).

Negotiation and discrete exchanges

In situations where the company is not familiar with the counterpart's culture it may be advisable to hire an agent or advisor who is familiar with the culture of both parties. Agents and advisors may be effective for companies that have little awareness of the other's culture and little time to become aware. Alternatively, it may be possible to introduce a mediator. Mediators who make introductions and then withdraw from the negotiation process are quite common. Frequently, however, mediators are present throughout the negotiation and take responsibility for orchestrating the entire negotiation process. Throughout Europe, interpreters and language schools have played the role of mediator, providing both parties with a deeper understanding of the cross-cultural negotiation process. Neither of these approaches involves a full-blown commitment to cross-cultural negotiation but they represent a starting point and may evolve into something more substantial. In this situation the parties to the exchange may still be avoiding substantial engagement with the other or they may be following a very competitive style of negotiation.

In these circumstances a low level of concern for the other's situation by both parties may exist which leads them to avoid each other in terms of establishing a marketing relationship but there may be opportunities for discrete exchanges. In this case the product or service is expected to sell itself or the purchase is a very routine affair in the customer firm. Neither buyer nor seller emphasizes any aspect of the exchange. This type of avoiding behaviour in international negotiations can result in a break-down of weak relationships and no exchange may result.

Competitive negotiation style

The competitive style revolves around a hard sell, pressure on the buyer or seller for better terms, disregard for the other side and emphasis on the product or value of the deal. The competitive buyer or seller, manifesting moderate familiarity with the counterpart's culture, enters the negotiation to take advantage of the other party and is usually suspicious and untrustworthy. The outcome of an exchange based on a competitive style turns upon the location of power in the relationship. A competitive style by one party to the exchange must be matched by complete accommodation by the other side, otherwise agreement is unlikely. A competitive style implies exploiting the exchange situation, especially when the other party is cooperative. A competitive style is often associated with an adversarial approach in buying and selling, often leading to a win-lose situation. To succeed as a negotiating style one of the parties must accept the aggressive position adopted by the other. Such acceptance is unlikely where there are alternative ways of obtaining the product or service in question. Such circumstances can arise, at least initially, when a company in a low-context country attempts to negotiate with a company in a high-context country.

In this aggressive approach an attempt is made by the aggressive party to induce the counterpart to follow a particular negotiation approach. There are many ways of doing this, ranging from a firm request to insisting strongly that the suggested way is the best. It can also be done more subtly by continuing to respond in the 'home' language to the requests of counterparts because 'you cannot express yourself well enough in their language' (Lewicki *et al.*, 1994, p. 431). Two can play this game, however, as the counterpart may have a strategic advantage and may attempt more extreme tactics and, if they do not work, excuse them on the basis of 'cultural ignorance'.

When the company is more familiar with the counterpart's culture and approach it may be possible to be more accommodating within a competitive negotiations style and to make conscious changes to the negotiation approach so that it is more appealing to the counterpart. In this approach this may mean maintaining a firm grasp on the preferred approach but making modifications to help relations with the counterpart. The challenge in adapting to the other party is to know which behaviours to modify, which to eliminate and which to adopt. Furthermore, it is not clear that the counterpart will interpret any modifications made in the way intended.

Collaborative negotiation style

As the company becomes more experienced in doing business abroad and becomes very familiar with negotiating in different foreign cultures it may begin to adopt a win–win or collaborative style in its negotiations over time. One way of doing this is to embrace the counterpart's approach, which requires the negotiator to be completely bilingual and bicultural. This is an expensive strategy and places the negotiator under considerable stress. There is much to be gained by this approach, however, since counterparts can be approached and understood completely on their own terms.

As an alternative to embracing fully the counterpart's approach both parties may customize or improvise an approach to suit a specific situation. In improvising an approach both parties must be very familiar with the counterpart's culture and have a strong understanding of the individual characteristics of the other party. This is a very flexible approach.

A very collaborative negotiation style may be observed when both parties attempt to 'transcend exclusive use of either home culture by exploiting their high familiarity capabilities' (Weiss, 1994a, p. 58). This approach has been referred to as a symphony as it involves both parties working together to create a new approach that may include aspects of either home culture or adopting practices from a third culture. Use of this strategy is complex and involves a great deal of time and effort. It works best when both parties are very familiar with each other, familiar with both home cultures and have a common structure for the negotiation (Lewicki *et al.*, 1994, pp. 432–3; Weiss, 1994a, pp. 58–9).

The collaborative style to buying and selling is based on consultation with a focus on customer benefits and the need to find a good result for both parties. Concern is high for both sides. The collaborative style seeks both a good purchase and a good selling decision. Emphasis is on solving problems; a joint problem-solving operation provides the best mutually attractive result. In collaborating, both parties recognize the possibility of increasing the shared benefits. Collaboration relies on believing that business negotiations lead to longer-term relationships when the benefits are shared on a win–win basis.

Bridging cultural differences in negotiations

Bridging cultural differences in international negotiations is not easy to accomplish without effort on the part of all parties. Successful international marketing negotiations require that both parties form a strong desire to make things work for their mutual benefit. In international marketing negotiations the parties have different and often conflicting expectations regarding outcomes. Overcoming these differences, manifested in the stereotypes outlined in Exhibit 19.1, requires the ability to see the differences for what they are – the product of diverse cultures rather than definite signs of incompatibility or threats to successful negotiations.

Exhibit 19.1   Negotiation style – impact of culture

The French pride themselves on reasoned discussion. They dislike being rushed into decisions, preferring instead to examine various options in decisions. Negotiations are likely to be in French unless they occur outside France. Punctuality is expected. They tend to be formal in their negotiations and do not move quickly to expressions of goodwill until the relationship has existed for some time.

In Japan, business often goes to the party respected the most. Recognizing who is deserving of such respect takes more time than most. The Japanese consult with all parties involved before they make decisions. And they also tend to spend time becoming acquainted with the potential partner before developing the framework for a partnership.

American negotiators usually operate as if today is the last day of their lives. They negotiate with conviction and interpret delays and hesitation as signs of stalling or ineptitude. Most do not speak languages other than English. American negotiators exhibit words and behaviours that are often perceived as tough or insensitive. Winning is part of their psyche. Once they are assured that they will not lose, it is possible to redirect their attention to mutual gains.

Creating the right environment in Sweden, however, is not the same as doing so in Italy. For example, the Swedes tend to be formal in their relationships, dislike haggling over price,

▶

expect thorough, professional proposals without flaws, and are attracted to quality. Italians tend to be extremely hospitable, but are often volatile in temperament. When they make a point, they do so with considerable gesticulation and emotional expression. Moreover, they enjoy haggling over prices.

Of course, these are stereotypes that individuals [from most countries] may violate. They demonstrate, however, that business people of different cultures come to the negotiation setting with different expectations and different styles of conducting business. Blind to these differences, the foreign negotiator can expect to create a negative impression. Once that impression is formed, it is difficult to establish positive rapport.

Source: adapted from Reardon, K. K. and Spekman, R. E. (1994) 'Starting out right: negotiation lessons for domestic and cross-cultural business alliances', *Business Horizons*, **37** (1), 72–3

Relationship domains in international marketing

Where there is a convergence between the needs and wants of both parties and the expected benefits are high, both parties become intimately involved in managing the relationship (Figure 19.6). Where the needs and wants of the seller dominate or the expected net benefits are higher than the buyer's, the seller is likely to manage the relationship. The same is true for the buying firm when its needs and wants are met or the expected net benefits are higher.

In establishing a marketing relationship involving buying and selling it is necessary to recognize that a range of outcomes is possible. By examining the mutual expected net benefits of a marketing relationship, we can observe that in some situations the seller attempts to dominate and manage the relationship, while in other situations the

Figure 19.6
Domain of
buyer–seller
relationships in
international
marketing

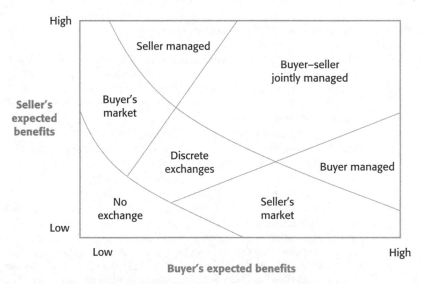

Source: adapted from Dwyer, R. F., Schurr, P. M. and Oh, S. (1987) 'Developing buyer–seller relationships', *Journal of Marketing*, **51** (April), 15

buyer attempts to dominate and manage the relationship depending on the benefits each expects to obtain (Dwyer, Schurr and Oh, 1987).

In other situations the relationship is jointly managed (Figure 19.6). Where the expected net benefit from the relationship is equally high for both parties a joint arrangement is likely to operate. The seller manages where the pay-off is high for the seller but neither high nor low for the buyer. The buyer manages where the pay-off is high for the buyer and neither high nor low for the seller. A relatively large area remains which is designated as a buyer's or seller's market depending on the relative benefits, which are likely to be dominated by discrete exchanges. In circumstances where the benefits or pay-offs are low to both parties it is unlikely that any exchange will occur.

Sometimes, however, conflict occurs between the parties that is not always easy to resolve. When participants in a conflict are from the same culture, they are more likely to perceive the situation in basically the same way and organize their perceptions in similar ways. The people involved in cross-cultural conflicts must be careful, however, not to assume that the perception and values of the counterparts or adversaries in the conflict are the same. Conflict in international markets can be difficult to resolve. The methods used by society for dealing with conflicts reflect the basic values and philosophy in that society. Considerable assistance in avoiding or reducing conflict may derive from an understanding of buyer–seller negotiation styles and the impact of culture on the various positions adopted by the parties concerned.

The international sales team

For the international sales person to succeed it is necessary to have a comprehensive knowledge of the business culture as well as an ability to adapt to a foreign culture if necessary. A number of skills have been identified as important in adapting to a new culture (Hutton, 1988). Most important among these are the following:

- tolerance of ambiguity and a willingness to change objectives;
- a low task orientation to allow flexibility to different circumstances;
- open-minded non-judgemental view of life;
- empathy;
- ability to communicate across cultures;
- self-reliance.

Flexibility does not mean that the sales force relinquishes its own ways of doing business and goes 'native' in the face of difficult circumstances but here the role of language becomes important. A facility in the counterpart's language is a basic ingredient for successful interpersonal relations and affects results.

Most sales people and negotiators require a mix of technical and social competencies. Both sets of capabilities are required in most situations involving the international

Figure 19.7
Multiple
linkages in
communication
and negotiation

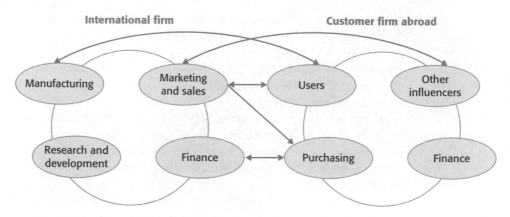

Source: adapted from Turnbull, P. W. (1987) 'Interaction and international marketing: an investment process', *International Marketing Review*, **4** (4), Winter, 7–19.

marketing of technical products. The international firm discovers that it requires a team of people in the selling and negotiation process since so many separate points of contact exist within the customer firm (Figure 19.7). For example, marketing and sales people must communicate and negotiate with users, the purchasing department and other influencers while the users abroad are also in contact with the manufacturing section of the selling firm. The mix of technical and social capabilities tends to vary in emphasis, however, from country to country. Counterparts from traditional societies may operate much more on the basis of their social competence, i.e. who they are, their connections and social class. Most North Americans tend to believe in technical competence when credentials are being checked. Thus North Americans frequently find they are dealing with counterparts who place more stock on their social competence than seems reasonable to them. An underlying difference in this role definition helps explain some of the feeling of social distance in achieving agreement both within and outside the negotiation process.

Selecting the team

The firm has three choices when selecting a sales team; it can hire expatriates, host country nationals or third country nationals. Expatriates are home country sales people and are favoured by industrial products firms because of their technical competence and ability to provide after-sales service (Boyacigiller, 1990). While there are benefits in using expatriates, there are also costs. Frequently expatriates:

■ do not cope easily in a foreign culture and so can be ineffective;

■ they are also more expensive than locals;

■ comprehensive training in and sensitivity to the foreign culture are required before sending expatriates abroad.

This means providing detailed knowledge of the area's language and culture as cultural alienation renders a sales person ineffectual.

The second option, hiring a host country national, has the benefit of retaining somebody with extensive market and cultural knowledge, language skills and familiarity with business customs. Locals tend to be less expensive, except for some advanced economies, such as Japan, the US and Germany. The adjustment period is shorter as a local sales person can be effective in a relatively short period. There are, however, two disadvantages in using locals:

■ they may not have the detailed product knowledge required; and usually

■ they do not understand the company or its culture.

Where response to the market and its culture is deemed to be more important than communication between the person in the field and headquarters, a national of the country is usually employed.

The third option open to the firm is to hire third country nationals who, if selected from the region, may be culturally sensitive and have the language required. This is certainly true in European countries and in Asia. Third country nationals are a welcome compromise for regionally focused companies. There are, however, some disadvantages in hiring third country nationals:

■ they may feel that they do not belong to the company or the host country;

■ they may feel that their career path within the firm is ill-defined and uncertain; and

■ they may also cost more than the others.

The advantages and disadvantages of each type of sales person have been identified by Honeycutt et al. (1998) and are summarized in Figure 19.8.

Figure 19.8
Selecting the international sales team

Composition of sales team	Advantages	Disadvantages
Expatriates	• Product knowledge • High service levels • More control	• Highest cost • High training costs • Ineffective
Host country people	• Market knowledge • Language skills • Cultural sensitivity • Quick response time • May be economical	• Lack product knowledge • May not be loyal
Third country sales people	• Language skills • Cultural sensitivity • Regional sales coverage • May be economical	• Identity problems • Career moves in jeopardy • Lack product knowledge • May not be loyal

Summary

The interaction between buyer and seller in international marketing is very complex. The marketing exchange may refer to a simple discrete transaction or, alternatively, it may refer to a long-standing, well-developed relationship between two firms operating in two very different cultures to attain mutually beneficial objectives. Understanding the selling and negotiations process is important whichever situation is present. Communication, negotiation and personal selling in international markets is more difficult due to differing cultures and languages and the interaction between the familiar and unfamiliar and the context of the relationship. In international marketing most exchanges are between firms. The supplying firm in one market deals directly with a purchasing firm in another, but only indirectly with the consumer market, hence, the emphasis on international selling and negotiation applies mostly to international business-to-business marketing. In deciding appropriate roles for the sales force it is necessary for the firm to acknowledge the existence of both a buying process and a selling process which converge to produce a satisfactory result to both parties to the exchange. The successful outcome of these processes of convergence is dependent, to a large extent, on there being a high degree of cultural understanding and affinity between the partners. This affinity arises through culturally sensitive communications between the parties involved. International marketing adds a new and complex dimension to the communications process. Successful buying and selling strategies are based on establishing mutually beneficial marketing relationships.

Questions

1. What is meant by the convergence of buying and selling processes?

2. Discuss the importance of communications in buying and selling in international marketing. What is the effect of culture on communications?

3. How do different cultures affect 'shared meaning' in international marketing? What is meant by the attribution of effective meaning in negotiating across cultures?

4. Explain how context and empathy can affect cross-cultural communications.

5. The negotiation style adopted by the international firm is dictated by cultural familiarity. Discuss.

6. A distinction was drawn in the chapter between discrete exchanges and exchanges which occur as a result of a longer-term relationship. What is your opinion regarding this distinction?

7. In developing a selling or negotiating strategy the firm may use a particular buyer–seller style. Outline the more important of these and discuss their relevance to the firm in international markets.

8. What are the key factors to consider in picking the international sales team?

References

Barnett, G. A. and Kincaid, L. D. (1983) 'Cultural convergence: a mathematical theory' in W. B. Gudykunst and B. Hill, Eds, *Intercultural Communication Theory*, London: Sage Publications, Chapter 10.

Boyacigiller, N. (1990) 'The role of expatriates in the management of interdependence, complexity and risk in multinational corporations', *Journal of International Business Studies*, **21** (3), 357–81.

Campbell, N. C. G., Graham, J. L., Jolibert, A. and Meissner, H. G. (1988) 'Marketing negotiations in France, Germany, the United Kingdom, and the United States', *Journal of Marketing*, **52**, 49–62.

Dwyer, R. F., Schurr, P. M. and Oh, S. (1987) 'Developing buyer–seller relationships', *Journal of Marketing*, **51** (April), 11–27.

Fisher, G. (1980) *International Negotiation*, Chicago, IL: Intercultural Press.

Francis, J. N. P. (1991) 'When in Rome? The effects of cultural adaptation on intercultural business negotiations', *Journal of International Business Studies*, **22** (Third Quarter), 402–28.

Ghauri, P. (1996) 'Introduction' in P. N. Ghauri and J.-C. Usunier, Eds, *International Business Negotiations*, Oxford: Pergamon, pp. 3–20.

Gourlay, R. (1987) 'Negotiations and bargaining', *Management Decision (UK)*, **25** (3), 16–27.

Hall, E. T. (1960) 'The silent language of overseas business', *Harvard Business Review*, **38** (May–June), 81–98.

Hall, E. T. (1976) *Beyond Culture*, New York, NY: Anchor Press/Doubleday.

Harich, K. R. and LaBahn, D. W. (1998) 'Enhancing international business relationships: a focus on customer perceptions of salesperson role performance including cultural sensitivity', *Journal of Business Research*, **42** (1), 87–101.

Honeycutt, E. D. Jr., Flaherty, T. B. and Benassi, K. (1998) 'Marketing industrial products on the Internet', *Industrial Marketing Management*, **26**, 433–46.

Hutt, M. D. and Speh, T. W. (1989) *Business Marketing Management*, 3rd edn, Chicago, IL: Dryden Press.

Hutton, J. (1988) *The World of the International Manager*, Oxford: Philip Allan.

LaBahn, D. W. and Harich, K. R. (1997): 'Sensitivity to national business culture: effects on U.S.–Mexican channel relationship performance', *Journal of International Marketing*, **5** (4), 29–51.

Lee, J. A. (1966) 'Cultural analysis in overseas operations', *Harvard Business Review*, **44** (March–April), 106–11.

Lewicki, R. J., Litterer, J. A., Minton, J. W. and Saunders, D. M. (1994) *Negotiation*, 2nd edn, Chicago, IL: Irwin.

Marschan, R., Welch, D. and Welch, L. (1997) 'Language: the forgotten factor in multinational management', *European Management Journal*, **15** (5), 591–8.

Marshall, G. W., Brouthers, L. E. and Lamb, C. W. Jr. (1998) 'A typology of political economies and strategies in international selling', *Industrial Marketing Management*, **27**, 11–19.

McCall, J. B. and Warrington, M. B. (1989) *Marketing by Agreement*, Chichester, Wiley.

Reardon, K. K. and Spekman, R. E. (1994) 'Starting out right: negotiation lessons for domestic and cross-cultural business alliances', *Business Horizons*, **37** (1), 71–80.

Rice, G. (1992) 'Using the interaction approach to understand industrial trade shows', *International Marketing Review*, **9** (4), 32–45.

Samli, A. C., Still, R. and Hill, J. S. (1993) *International Marketing*, New York, NY: Macmillan.

Schramm, W. (1971) 'How communication works' in W. Schramm and D. F. Roberts, Eds, *The Process and Effects of Mass Communications*, Urbana, IL: University of Illinois Press.

Schuster, C. and Copeland, M. (1996) 'Cross-cultural communication: issues and implications' in P. N. Ghauri and J.-C. Usunier, Eds, *International Business Negotiations*, Oxford: Pergamon, pp. 131–52.

Thurnbull, P. W. (1987) 'Interaction and international marketing: an investment process', *International Marketing Review*, **4** (4), Winter, 7–19.

Ueltschy, L. C. and Ryans, J. K. Jr. (1997) 'Employing standardised promotion strategies in Mexico: the impact of language and cultural differences', *International Executive*, **39** (4), 479–95.

Weiss, S. E. (1994a) 'Negotiating with "Romans" – Part 1', *Sloan Management Review*, **38** (Winter), 51–61.

Weiss, S. E. (1994b) 'Negotiating with "Romans" – Part 2', *Sloan Management Review* (Spring), 55–99.

20 International marketing operations and performance

Managing international marketing operations means ensuring that the international marketing strategy developed for each market entered is implemented and controlled. This means that in planning the programme the firm pays attention to difficulties that may arise subsequently. Successful firms institute control systems to complement the alignment of their strategy to expected performance. The key issues arising in implementing international marketing plans involve a hierarchy of control systems. First, we examine how firms develop international marketing plans and use operational control systems. This is followed by a section dealing specifically with financial performance. Finally, the appropriate role for strategic control in the firm is discussed. After studying this chapter students should be able to:

- explain the importance to the firm of planning and measuring international marketing performance;
- outline the criteria to be used when evaluating the effectiveness of a firm in international markets;
- develop a set of 'hard' and 'soft' performance measures applicable to the international arena;
- establish a system for measuring and controlling the rate of return on investments in international markets.

Strategic planning framework

In forming a vision and strategy for the company it is necessary to discuss goals, objectives and targets in the context of a strategic planning framework. The strategic planning framework should consider the company's mission, its purpose, its values and its distinctive capabilities and how these are blended together. A strategic planning framework should also set out how the company intends to measures success of the strategies it considers appropriate. The manager needs a framework to assist in forming a relevant vision and selecting appropriate international marketing strategies.

Figure 20.1
Strategic
planning
framework for
the international
firm

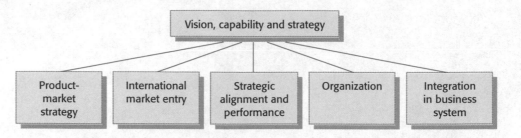

The international competitive environment has become increasingly complex and dynamic. Successful international firms first examine the competitive environment before identifying appropriate marketing strategies. In developing an international marketing strategy the firm requires a clear indication of how to combine the various product-market options available.

A strategic planning framework designed to integrate and prioritize existing and future investments in the company is required. Given the rapidly changing international marketing environment, the company requires distinctive capabilities under a number of headings in order to respond to changes in the environment and to fulfil its declared mission. Every successful company possesses an overall vision and a set of distinctive capabilities (Figure 20.1). Vision refers to the firm's shared purpose and values while the distinctive capabilities distinguish the firm in its competitive performance. The firm must be able, however, to measure the firm's ability to deliver the performance desired. Based on the firm's distinctive capabilities it develops strategies and decides on the appropriate way of entering international markets. These are issues that have been discussed in the previous 19 chapters of this book. The firm must also decide how it should align its strategy and performance and how it should integrate itself into the business system of which it is a member. For the strategy to work the firm must state how performance is to be measured and how the firm implements strategy through operational guidelines.

The company must deal with each of the above in an integrated way with particular reference to the way they affect its performance. Together with the company's mission these capabilities constitute the five elements through which the company interacts positively within the business system. Under each heading the company should identify its distinctive capabilities, i.e. the core capabilities or competencies required to fulfil its mission. Furthermore, the company must determine how to measure performance, i.e. the indicators of success in operationalizing its distinctive capabilities. Lastly, the company must specify its various strategies and approaches to implementation, i.e. the critical things the company must do to reach the distinctive capabilities, required for that success. This framework emphasizes a process rather than something fixed and unchangeable.

Continuous improvement and change are essential ingredients of success in the company and in the personal success of each individual employee. Keeping abreast of new product developments, ways of entering foreign markets and managing the brand image are the key factors that sustain the international success of Royal Selagor (Exhibit 20.1). Company strategies should reflect the firm's environment and the resource allocation should reflect the strategies selected (Christensen, 1997, p. 142).

Strategy at a corporate level represents the cumulative direction of the organization given the nature of the industry, the competitive environment and internal factors related to production, finance, marketing and personnel. Strategies regarding the core capabilities should be implemented in a three- to five-year period.

Underlying the mission of the company is a value system which drives it and motivates its customers and conditions its competitors, actual and potential. It is necessary to explicitly consider company values and how they impinge on what the company does and how it is done. A five-step process may be sufficient to reflect what should be done:

- identify the appropriate values for the company;

- select the values of interest and match them with the needs of customer groups;

- provide the value in terms of products and services which has implications for scope and differentiation of the company's activities;

- communicate the value which means dealing with many issues such as advertising, communications, but centrally involves positioning of the company and its products and services; and

- delivering the value which has strong implications for modes of foreign market entry, distribution channels, pricing, logistics, selling and negotiations.

Exhibit 20.1 Royal Selagor – the pewter king

The only way to keep the business thriving is to keep abreast of current developments says Yong Poh Kon, managing director of Royal Selagor: 'Even though you have lots of history, if what you are designing or producing is not relevant, it'll be difficult.' It is not an easy task to remain relevant in an age when consumers throughout the world are inundated by a wide array of choices. That's why Royal Selagor has come up with 60 to 80 new designs and items each year. It draws inspiration from a range of sources, ranging from nature and Malaysia's traditional woodcarving to the modern preference for sleek and simple designs, and even books.

The acquisition of rival companies over the years has also contributed significantly to Royal Selagor's standing as the largest pewter maker in the world. In 1987 Selagor Pewter, as the company was then known, bought 300-year-old Englefields, the last remaining London pewterer that made Crown & Rose pewter. Pewter items appealed to the upper classes and the older generation at that time. Failing to ride on the name Crown & Rose to penetrate the UK market, Englefields was renamed Royal Selagor UK several years later and the products were promoted as Crown & Rose by Royal Selagor. With new marketing strategies in place and collaboration with Arthur Price, the English cutler and silversmith, in 1998, sales picked up again and the company turned in its first profit that year.

Commenting on these developments, Yong Poh Kon says the change of name from Selagor Pewter to Royal Selagor gave the company a good opportunity to redirect its branding focus; with the new name, consumers could associate the brand with a certain lifestyle rather than with pewter alone. 'We were able to move beyond pewter and further reinforce our direction that when consumers buy our products, it is not necessarily for the material,

▶

pewter, but for what it represents, either a lifestyle product that they would like themselves, to use or as a gift to give to their friends or loved ones for a special occasion', says Yong.

The most recent large acquisition, in 2002, aimed at expanding the company's market share in North America, was Seagull Pewter, Canada's largest pewter maker. The Royal Selagor group also includes the jewellery business Selberan, which it set up in 1972, and the London silver company Comyns, which it acquired in 1993. All the company's products are crafted in Setapak in Malaysia's Selagor state. The factory produces about 1.5 million pewter items a year, including tableware, tankards, wine accessories, photo frames, and other gift items. Two-thirds of the company's production is exported to more than 20 countries; its pewter pieces are sold in retail outlets as renowned as Harrods and John Lewis in the UK and Wako in Japan. In the 1970s less than 2 per cent of the company's production was exported. History alone may not be enough for success in international markets but it helps.

Source: adapted from Cindy Tham: 'Pewter King', *Asia Inc.*, April 2004, pp. 18–21

Elements of strategic planning framework

Company mission

The purpose, values and vision implied in the company's mission must be reviewed periodically to ensure that they reflect the real complexity of the tasks facing the company in the future. Managers must constantly ensure that the values that the company upholds are long term, otherwise the company's ability to cope with complexity and, hence, its purpose, would be severely compromised. Most challenging for the company, however, is how it can best couple the above longer-term vision with the short-term day-to-day activities. For that the company needs a well-conceived strategy; a strategy which may change over time as most firms discover. Creating and implementing the strategic direction that oversees and guides all aspects of what the company does, that creates good systems and information on customers and markets, and encourages best practice and innovation at all levels in the company is fundamental to success.

Shared purpose and values

Successful companies usually have as an objective the provision of products and services with attributes that set the company apart in serving customer needs in many international markets. Core values of such companies might consist of a selection of the following and other values:

■ willingness to change and accept diversity of approach in dealing with myriad customers in many international markets;

■ partnerships, innovation and flexibility while being responsible in striving for excellence in dealing with customers and competitors;

- commitment to continuous improvement and increasing aspirations in regard to knowledge-creation within the firm;

- the discovery of new ideas and creatively applying existing knowledge to new products and new markets.

A value system such as the above drives the company while reflecting its core values or what the firm stands for in society. To serve this mission, the company must continue to:

- create and develop innovative products and services;

- nurture a high-quality approach to international marketing strategy;

- promote extensive linkages within the business system; and

- focus on continuous improvement of management.

Distinctive capabilities and measures of success

The likely diversity of the company's products and customer groups will normally oblige it to apply strategic thinking to how company endeavour should be focused in the future. As a way of measuring success the company must decide whether it possesses the appropriate degree of customer orientation; how it avoids complacency in dealing with customer complaints and observations; how it delivers added-value services in an effective and efficient way.

Successful companies attempt to differentiate themselves from competitors in order to attract the best customers and ensure that the company controls a dominant share of the relevant market. For this reason it may be necessary to deliver higher quality products and services in more flexible ways using appropriate new technologies. In responding to these challenges, there are a number of dangers and challenges:

- the danger that the company might be attracted by short-term responses which would give a relatively immediate, but short-lived, impact;

- developing instant new products aimed at trendy specialized niches, in competition with the company's existing products – such product-market cannibalization is a failure in strategic thinking;

- the proliferation of undifferentiated products and services lacking in distinction – this is a mere waste of resources.

The real challenge is to position the company for the longer term; the appropriate response is to focus; for without focus, there will never be enough resources to succeed in any market, national or international. Successful firms align their international marketing strategies in the context of the chosen focus. Alignment of strategies means considering changes at the level of the customer, competition and the environment generally, and the resultant likely impact on profits (Figure 20.2).

Figure 20.2
Aligning
international
marketing
strategy with the
company vision

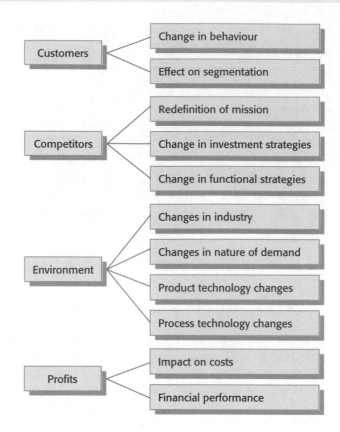

Aligning international marketing strategies

It is generally accepted that the objective of the company is to maximize stakeholder value; shareholder value in particular. In practice such a broad goal rarely dominates the strategic thinking of managers. Managers display additional objectives usually involving a combination of sales, profits, and return on investment. Sales are important because they are a source of profit growth in the company and reflect management rewards such as bonuses and promotion. Profits are important because they are used to satisfy stakeholders and are required in raising new capital.

These two objectives are in potential conflict since sales can be increased by lowering prices which would have the adverse effect of lowering profits. Increasing marketing expenditures like advertising or encouraging myriad frivolous sales trips abroad should result in increased sales but this would raise costs and could easily reduce profits. A particular problem facing the company is that the conflict between sales and profits 'becomes much more acute when the time dimension is added. Specifically, while positive marketing actions (lowering prices, boosting advertising) have these positive effects on market performance and negative effects on profitability, the positive effects come slowly and the bad effects come quickly' (Doyle and Hooley,

Figure 20.3
International
marketing
performance
and control

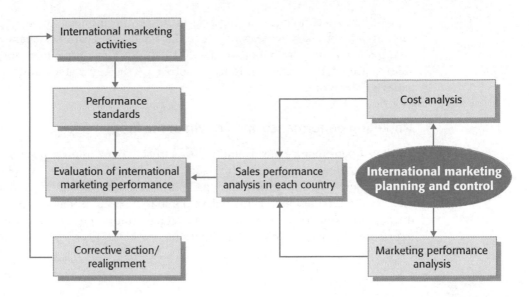

1992, p. 60). The management objective becomes one of balancing short-term profits with long-term market performance.

Successful firms first develop a plan for each international market entered and an overall plan for the firm's entire operations. The plan has associated with it two key elements – a cost analysis of the strategy and a performance analysis of each foreign market (Figure 20.3). These two sets of analyses provide the firm with a sales performance analysis which in turn allows the firm to evaluate international marketing performance. This evaluation depends on having an agreed set of performance standards for each international marketing activity so that, if necessary, corrective action or realignment of strategy and objectives may be made.

Marketing performance analysis

The firm is linked to its environment through customer–supplier relationships, competitive relationships and relationships with firms that complement the company. This linkage arises within the cultural, economic and political environment which defines and controls the nature and boundaries of the relationships formed within the business system. Only effective firms survive in this environment. Effectiveness derives from responding adequately to the various interest groups in the business system upon which the firm depends for resources and markets. Successful firms constantly test their effectiveness in this system by monitoring performance.

International marketing managers sometimes assess performance based on their degree of satisfaction with overall performance or the perceived success and degree to which objectives have been fulfilled (Zou *et al.*, 1998, p. 52). While these are crude measures they are often used to obtain a general assessment of performance. In assessing performance in a more methodical way, however, firms are concerned with measuring the efficiency of the use of marketing inputs such as marketing and investment expenditures, technology and physical facilities, the influence of mediating factors such as market characteristics, product characteristics, customer characteristics and task characteristics (Bonoma and Clarke, 1988). Very few firms measure all the variables outlined but many firms use a subset of these variables and monitor their behaviour over time.

Marketing performance and growth of the firm

Improved performance means finding ways of achieving improved sales, or improved profits or a combination of both (Figure 20.4). Four distinct ways of obtaining sales growth may be identified: penetrating the international market; new product development; new international market development; forward integration in the market through investment and acquisition. Market penetration means selling more products to existing customers in current international markets. This may be difficult where the

Figure 20.4
Improving
international
marketing
performance

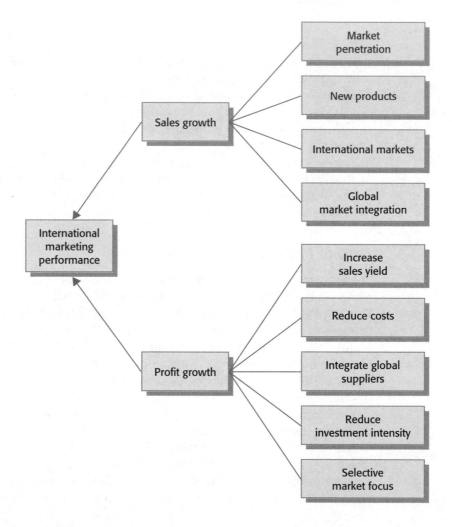

firm is already strong, the market is saturated, or where there are entrenched competitors with very large market shares. An aggressive strategy would be to take market share from competitors by attracting their more profitable customers. The nature of the industry may make it difficult for the firm to discourage competitors by raising the stakes. Big-brand companies frequently raise advertising stakes or use preemptive pricing and announcements of capacity additions to discourage competitors. With regard to new product development a firm might use its own people or consultants. Alternatively, it could license or joint venture from overseas where appropriate. Many firms start out as single product firms and soon realize that it is necessary to possess a portfolio of products in order to serve chosen markets. It is likely, therefore, that a new product development strategy would be part of the firm's internationalization strategy.

Developing new international markets means identifying markets abroad not yet properly served. It could also mean using new distribution channels or information sources such as the Internet. Market integration would probably mean establishing marketing agreements, taking over distributors or retail outlets, which may or may not be feasible. Very often successful international firms start by selling through agents, subsequently taking an equity position in those agents and, later still, acquiring the agency and its customer base to give the firm a strong competitive presence in the market. The United Kingdom company MediScan Ltd pursued this route in entering the Italian market. The agency route helped the company to establish a foothold in the more lucrative northern part of the country. Business there grew sufficiently and there was a possibility of expanding into southern Italy. MediScan considered selecting another agent to complement the existing agent in northern Italy. Instead it chose to establish its own sales subsidiary and recruit specialist medical sales people. This strategy corresponded with the company's stage of development. Firms sometimes also integrate forward into the market by acquiring manufacturers who would assemble or produce locally. This may be an option for MediScan at some future point.

The second way of improving marketing performance is to improve profitability, which means increasing yield, reducing costs, integrating suppliers, or focusing on key segments (Figure 20.4). Yield increases may come about through an improvement in the sales mix, e.g. promoting high-margin lines, increasing price or reducing margins in key international markets. This approach may not be possible for smaller, weaker firms in highly competitive and fragmented markets. Many firms, even smaller enterprises, would, however, have room for manoeuvre with regard to the mix of products they sell. At the other extreme the firm may decide to rationalize its product line and to rationalize segments of the market served and distribution channels. Marketing audits of successful firms often indicate that they obtain all their sales with fewer products sold to fewer customers than weaker firms. Hence, a rationalization of the number of products and customers may improve performance in some companies. Selective distribution and a clear customer focus in foreign markets may be an attractive option for some firms.

Hard and soft performance measures

A combination of four sets of measures may be used to assess international marketing performance:

- sales, profit and cash flow performance;
- market share performance;
- brand strength performance in each international market; and
- customer acquisition and retention performance in each market.

The first measure is typically based on financial reports and provides a 'hard' measure of performance. The drivers of corporate success are not, however, revealed in these hard values (Thomas, 1998). Intangible assets such as brands, market share customer franchises, sales networks, superior service capabilities, access to markets or technologies may be more important in assessing the firm's longer-term viability.

There are a number of advantages in using non-financial measures in assessing the international marketing performance of the company. Financial measures generally focus on annual or short-term performance against accounting benchmarks. They do not deal with progress against customer requirements or competitors or other non-financial objectives that may be important in achieving profitability, competitive advantage or longer-term strategic position in the market. New product or new market development or expanding organizational capabilities, for example, may be important to achieving company strategy but may change short-term financial performance.

There is often a conflict among various performance measures – good performance on one criterion may mean sacrificing performance on another. Some international marketing managers, for example, may consider that entering a particular market is a high priority because of perceived future opportunities and they may be willing to tolerate short-term losses while they learn about the new market and develop a local network of relationships (Styles, 1999, p. 28). It is necessary, therefore, to supplement accounting measures with non-financial data about strategic performance and implementation to ensure that the company communicates its objectives and provides incentives to its workers in regard to longer-term strategy.

Intangible assets such as intellectual capital or customer loyalty are neglected in traditional measures. Only hard assets receive pride of place on the balance sheet. It may be necessary to develop proxy measures to capture performance in innovation, management capability, employee relations, quality and real value as these are known to be important in determining overall company value.

Many commentators argue that non-financial performance measures can be better indicators of future financial performance. It has been shown that the performance of international companies is influenced by culture and values so it seems important to include culture, a soft measure, in measuring performance (Byrne, 2001). Even though financial performance may be the ultimate goal current financial measures may not reflect the long-term benefits of current investment in R&D, customer satisfaction and product delivery programmes.

There are difficulties in developing and applying non-financial measures. The time taken to develop and implement such measures and the costs involved may be greater than the perceived benefits and for this reason may be abandoned. Successful international firms, however, include a number of non-financial performance measures in their portfolio of performance yardsticks.

Choosing performance criteria

Success in a highly competitive world means that the company must ensure that it provides the products and services that sufficient customers want to buy. It is also important that the right quality levels are provided and that the products and services are delivered on time to where they are required. At the same time it is necessary that the company, while doing all of these things, makes a profit for its owners.

The company must, therefore, develop a set of performance criteria which allows it to measure its marketing activities and its financial position as a result of those endeavours (Katsikeas *et al.*, 2000). Profit measures, cash flow, return on investment measures are all financial criteria which show the effects of marketing activities. Financial evaluations do not identify the key success factors in the business nor do they focus on what the company is doing well or badly. Marketing performance criteria on the other hand deal with causes not effects. It is much more useful from a management point of view to discover the contribution of product innovation, customer satisfaction, product and service quality or on-time delivery in the causes of success.

There is still a strong tradition in the use of financial criteria. A fixation with financial criteria leads companies to ignore the less tangible non-financial measures but these are the real drivers of corporate success over the middle to long term. There is, however, a weakness in the non-financial performance measures. To date there has been little success in developing explicit links from marketing to financial criteria. Furthermore, companies and managers are still judged on financial criteria. Until a clear link is established it is likely that marketing criteria will continue to be treated with a degree of scepticism. This amounts to stating that when it is possible to measure what is being discussed and expressed in numbers, it may be concluded that something is then known about it. Increasingly marketing scholars have developed ways of quantifying marketing phenomena to provide a deeper knowledge of the relationships involved. Whichever set of measures is chosen it is well to recall the old adage 'you get what you measure'. In choosing performance criteria the company recognizes that the system must:

- be customer/user driven;
- support manufacturing strategy in the company;
- be capable of change;
- be simple and easy to understand;
- include financial and international marketing criteria; and
- provide positive reinforcement in the company in its international endeavours.

Benchmarking the performance

In a competitive marketing environment companies that do not evaluate their performance against the competition and pre-determined standards are likely to fail. Both these standards represent an external benchmark to evaluate performance. It is necessary to establish benchmarks so that the company can determine whether a performance gap exists. A performance analysis begins with an analysis of the current situation. A set of results-oriented performance measures are agreed by the company. A comparison is made between the actual situation and goals; the difference represents the performance gap.

As seen in the previous section competitive benchmaking information may be obtained from a variety of sources: customers, suppliers, machinery manufacturers, technical journals and the trade press. Financial benchmarks such as inventory turnover and operating profit may be found in business publications and from marketing intelligence.

Evaluating international marketing performance

Many companies acknowledge that a reliance on financial measures alone can undermine the strategies the company must pursue for long-term survival. Non-financial measures such as quality, customer satisfaction, market share, innovation, organization learning and human resources must also be considered. Nevertheless, most firms use a range of operational controls, three of which are relatively easy to measure and apply (Figure 20.5).

Sales performance analysis

Analysis of sales performance is usually performed on the basis of the relationship of the company's actual sales in a given period to planned or budgeted sales. The company first establishes an overall sales budget for a year and then divides it into components corresponding to sales territories, sales person and product group. By some criterion accepted by the company, sales quotas are established in this way and actual performance is measured against quota.

Firms also monitor foreign sales from one year to the next and use the trends to judge performance, good or poor, depending on the trend. Other firms adopt a more formal sales control approach, where sales might be measured by country or region of a foreign market, by customer and by product group. An analysis of previous sales may

Figure 20.5
Typical operational controls in international markets

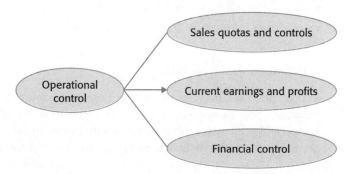

be used to establish quotas which, over time, are adjusted to accommodate changes in the market. When economic activity in a particular country is very high and developing rapidly, sales in that market are expected to grow. Similarly, a decline in the market should be reflected in a downward adjustment of the quota. The assumption behind such a sales control system is that factors causing an expansion or contraction in the market beyond the influence of the firm should not be used in evaluating sales performance. International sales growth may, therefore, overstate performance because of price escalation and market growth or it may understate performance because of experience curve effects and declining demand (Kirpalani and Balcome, 1987).

Sales-related measures may be more useful for firms in the early stage of international market development while profit-related measures may be more relevant for more experienced firms at later stages in the life cycle (Shoham, 1998). Profit measures are, however, rarely used due to measurement difficulties and the true profit position may be unknown if the firm uses any form of marginal cost pricing (Samiee and Anckar, 1998).

Current earnings and profits

The managers of marketing operations evaluated on the basis of current earnings are likely to emphasize short-run profits and neglect long-run profits. This is particularly true if managers are frequently moved from brand to brand, product to product, or market to market which would allow them to avoid the longer-term consequences of their actions. These actions could involve reducing advertising and general marketing expenditures, reducing research and development work under their control, and not spending sufficient sums on staff training and development.

Too great an emphasis on sales promotions as a short-term expedient, for example, may be symptomatic of longer-term marketing myopia. Because circumstances can be different in different markets and outside the control of management, performance measures based on sales, profits or return on investment can be misleading at best and inaccurate at worst. For this reason companies frequently compare actual results with budgeted estimates. Variances in costs and revenues can then be examined to determine whether these are affected by outside events or caused mainly by management intervention.

Financial performance criteria

For the international firm, measuring the relevant returns on foreign operations is a difficult task, since differences can arise between foreign market cash flows and cash flows back to the firm itself owing to different tax regimes and exchange controls. Furthermore, adjustment in transfer prices and credit can distort the true profitability of an investment by shifting profits and liquidity from one location to another (Shapiro, 1985). Firms use a variety of ways of measuring returns including foreign earnings, dividends, royalties and fees, interest, commissions and profits on exports.

While non-financial criteria such as market share or sales growth may be used in determining the value of a foreign market investment, many firms employ a version of

return on investment (ROI) as the means of measuring the long-run profit performance of their foreign operations. We usually associate the former approach with
Japanese firms and a dependence on ROI by US and other western firms.

Where return on investment is used, a number of comparisons are possible: comparisons with similar firms in the foreign market, with other foreign operations
controlled by the firm, with the firm's operations in the domestic market or with
targets established before entering the foreign market. A hypothetical worked example
based on ROI criteria is reported below. The appropriate measures to use in evaluating
and controlling foreign operations depend, however, on the nature of the business. For
marketing-oriented firms, market share, sales growth or the costs associated with generating a unit of sales revenue may be the most relevant measures in most circumstances.
They are especially relevant when entry to foreign markets is made by exporting.

A firm that enters foreign markets through foreign direct investment, however, may
be more concerned about unit costs of production, quality control and labour productivity and labour-related matters. Firms that enter foreign markets through the foreign
direct investment mode and equity-based strategic alliances may find return on assets
or a working capital to sales ratio most helpful.

Ultimately, all performance measures are subjective since the choice of which measure to stress in particular circumstances is a matter of judgement for the individual firm
(Shapiro, 1985, p. 231).

Having decided to expand, the company must ensure that the strategy to be followed is costed properly. It must also decide how to finance the strategy, from internal
resources or from selected external sources. Good financial management dictates that
the expansion strategy should not jeopardize the survival and growth of the company.

The costs of entering and expanding in slow-growth markets are particularly high.
Expansion for the company, even in industries which are not capital intensive,
requires large cash outlays, the postponement of income, and skilful marketing and
financial management. For success it is thus necessary to coordinate marketing strategies and financial planning. Where the company does not properly relate its marketing
strategy to its financial resources this lack of coordination can lead to the financial
collapse of the firm.

The costing and financial control of marketing strategies are difficult tasks for most
companies and can be very complicated. Marketing strategies can be difficult to quantify; they refer to the longer term and consist of numerous steps with varying impacts.
It is difficult in costing strategies to separate costs into fixed costs, variable costs, and
cash flow projections. To overcome these difficulties, successful companies attempt to
ensure that control rests with financial, marketing and general management people
since such a team effort is likely to better understand the cost implications of an international marketing strategy.

Cash flow in international markets

Most companies still use some form of profit-based measures to evaluate performance.
Other measures used in more progressive organizations are customer service, market
share and improvements in business processes. Cash flow measures are not used so
often, which reflects an emphasis on shareholder value.

The significance of cash flow to the firm in international markets, however, may be gleaned by observing the difference between profits and cash flow; profit is the difference between two sums – the price the customer pays and the total of prices the firm agrees to pay for all the inputs used in preparing the product or service for sale. Profit is the difference between agreed prices. Cash flow is the difference between money lodged in the bank and the money withdrawn from the bank. The size of the cash flow and its direction, positive or negative, depend absolutely as much upon when the money is lodged or withdrawn as upon how much is deposited or withdrawn.

It is possible to have a very profitable business but still fail owing to poor cash flow performance. The significance arises most dramatically as the firm expands into international markets. Associated with most international expansions are larger purchases of raw materials and other inputs, more sophisticated machinery, access to sources of finance, additional sales people and a concommitant delay in being paid. Attempting to grow through international market expansion has led many firms into the growth trap.

In general a faster growth in sales should produce an attractive increase in profits. There may, however, be an adverse impact on cash flow. The firm may experience impressive growth in many of its international markets with an equally impressive growth in earnings and at the same time face severe financial constraint. Cash is needed to support the business at its now larger size while awaiting payment from customers for larger sales. Consequently, during periods of rapid growth the cash flow is characteristically negative.

Timing of cash flows for international sales growth

The firm that introduces its products to a new foreign market usually finds that, initially, sales growth is slow, the firm incurs losses and cash flow is negative. While customers may be innovative there are few of them and the firm needs a lot of money to develop the market. While it is not possible to be precise about the exact nature of the relationships between sales, profits, cash flow and bank balances for all businesses, there are some general principles that apply and that can be examined (Figure 20.6).

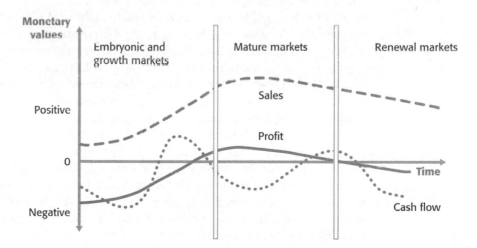

Figure 20.6
Expansion into new foreign markets – impact on key financial variables

Sales growth is generally believed to follow the traditional path of a life cycle. The life cycle of the profit–loss curve is thought to parallel the sales curve starting out as a loss and only becoming positive in the growth phase. Greatest profits are believed to occur in the mature and stable phase of market evolution.

The early losses give rise to a problem encountered by many entrepreneurial firms which expand into international markets without adequate financial resources. Early losses, or negative cash flow, may cause a significant drain on cash resources. Assuming no external financing, the cash flow position is likely to be negative for a considerable period of time, only becoming positive in the late period of the new and growing phase of the life cycle. Further expansions and the extra demands on cash, as discussed above, are likely to be reactivated, thereby pushing the cash flow curve down again. The process continues in such a cyclical fashion throughout the earlier phases of the life cycle especially, which causes great demands on the firm's cash resources. The behaviour of sales, profits, and cash flow and their interrelation is often cited in discussions of the need to have access to outside equity funds or loans and subsidies for firms attempting to internationalize. The peculiar pattern of these three key variables focuses attention on the crucial need for adequate equity in the firm contemplating an expansion in international markets. Small firms at the embryonic stage of the international life cycle often become takeover targets for larger cash-rich but less innovative firms.

Size of firm and cash flow

Managing cash flow and obtaining sufficient equity is a greater problem for smaller than for larger firms. Smaller firms need proportionally more external financing and typically have much more difficulty obtaining it. A small firm, new to exporting for example, frequently discovers that it is relatively easy to double sales in one year if what is being doubled is small. It is a much more difficult task to double sales in one year if existing sales are large. A small firm entering international markets for the first time can easily find itself in a position of doubling its sales. Consequently, smaller firms are more likely to have a continuous and urgent need for proportionally more cash to overcome negative cash flow than larger firms.

Larger firms frequently find it easier to obtain additional money under conditions of rapid growth. They usually have long-established relationships with banks and suppliers, good reputations and historical evidence of their ability to repay loans. Lenders and investors feel reasonably safe in dealing with large firms that are growing profitably. Nevertheless, large firms such as Unilever pay special attention to cash flow and ROI in their long-term marketing strategies (Exhibit 20.2).

Smaller firms, and entrepreneurial firms especially, usually find that the additional money needed is difficult to obtain. They seldom have long-established relationships; they may have little or no reputation, merely promise, and they may have only narrow evidence of their ability to manage the larger enterprise they hold as an aspiration for their firm. In such circumstances lenders and investors find it riskier to do business with smaller firms. Consequently, money that is made available to smaller firms often takes longer to procure, costs more and has conditions of control over management attached to it which may be unattractive.

Exhibit 20.2 Free cash flow and ROI at Unilever

A number of years ago, under the recently retired chief executive, Niall Fitzgerald, Unilever developed a plan that transformed the brand portfolio so that 95 per cent of revenue now comes from leading brands. The new strategy does not give hard top-line growth targets. It focuses instead on generating €30 billion in free cash flow and increasing the return on invested capital from 12.5 to at least 17 per cent by 2010. This strategy, according to Fitzgerald, 'will give the new chief executive Patrick Cescau much more flexibility as he will not have the danger of having to respond to short-term pressures'.

Source: adapted from *The Irish Times*, Friday 2 April 2004, p. 6

Strategic control in international marketing

Fundamentals of marketing control

The need to pursue marketing opportunities selectively raises the issues of finding an agreed strategic framework for marketing control. Unfortunately, there has been very little interaction of concepts and theories in marketing strategy and planning with those of finance and managerial accounting, the traditional disciplines which deal with management control. While the importance of market share objectives, market size and growth rates, and the importance of good forecasts have been recognized, procedures for marketing control have not yet been successfully related to these key factors. Though there have been very positive developments, good control systems that can be used in the implementation of marketing strategies, which include the multiple criteria discussed above, have yet to be developed. A framework for control provides a system to ensure that agreed strategies are implemented. Control and implementation are serious and complex management issues in the company.

Periodically the company decides to undertake a critical review of its overall marketing effectiveness in its various markets. Because marketing suffers from rapid obsolescence of objectives, policies, strategies and operational programmes, the company should regularly reassess its overall approach to the market. Strategic control means auditing the company's marketing activities to evaluate its marketing effectiveness. The marketing effectiveness of a company according to Kotler (2002) is reflected in the degree to which it exhibits five major attributes of a marketing orientation: customer philosophy; integrated marketing organization; adequate marketing information; strategic orientation; and operational efficiency.

Success usually means developing a marketing strategy involving a combination of initiatives by the company under each of the above headings. These initiatives may involve new or redesigned products for customers in different foreign markets, different distribution channels, expanded or improved production facilities with an emphasis on cost competitiveness, pricing with an emphasis on the ability to retaliate to influence the behaviour of competitors, and even perhaps the acquisition or establishment of associated companies in the market. All such initiatives require increased marketing expenditure.

Some of the above initiatives may be managed within the company's long-term strategy, while others would fit into annual marketing plans. Some marketing expenditures and price changes are tactical matters, the concern solely of product or brand managers or the sales force. It is the combination of these initiatives which the company uses to expand abroad which comprises the cost of the strategy.

Return on international marketing investment

Financial analysis based on return on investment is frequently used by firms to measure annual performances of foreign operations. A detailed financial analysis can decompose the elements that affect the firm's return on investment. In order to examine these issues it is necessary to recall that the formula for return on investment can be decomposed into two sub-ratios, one which measures cost control in the firm and the second which measures marketing effectiveness:

return on investment = cost control × marketing effectiveness

$$\frac{\text{net income}}{\text{total assets}} = \frac{\text{net income}}{\text{sales}} \times \frac{\text{sales}}{\text{total assets}}$$

The first ratio to the right of the equals symbol, net income divided by sales, measures cost control in the firm, i.e. the amount of gross profit the firm obtains in the market. The second ratio, sales divided by total assets, measures marketing effectiveness in the firm, i.e. the level of sales the firm obtains from the total resources at its disposal. This formula owes its origins to the DuPont Company which developed it to measure new wealth created, i.e. net income, compared with all the resources the firm could employ in the creation of that wealth, i.e. total assets.

By plotting the firm's cost-control performance against its marketing effectiveness we derive the firm's return on investment. Numerous combinations of cost-control effort and marketing effectiveness produce a given return on investment. By plotting the ratios over a number of years or country markets the firm can determine whether its emphasis on marketing effectiveness or cost control has been more fruitful. To illustrate the principles involved, the short historical performance of two hypothetical firms, ABC Technologies and XYZ Textiles, adapted from Mobley and McKeown (1987a, 1987b), is shown in Figure 20.7.

The returns on investment in Year 2 for ABC Technologies and XYZ Textiles were the same: 20 per cent. XYZ Textiles, however, achieved its 20 per cent ROI through a much more effective marketing effort; it made €3 of sales for every €1 of assets. The marketing effectiveness performance of ABC Technologies was €1 of sales for each €1 of assets but its cost-effectiveness or productive efficiency was 25 per cent compared with 5 per cent for XYZ Textiles.

Figure 20.7
Cost control and
international
marketing
effectiveness

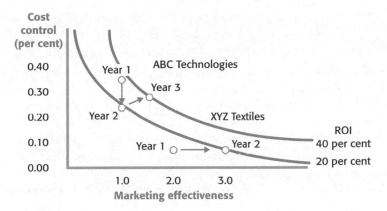

Sources: adapted from Mobley, L. and McKeown, K. (1987a) 'ROI revisited' in *Intrapreneurial Excellence*, American Management Association, pp. 1 and 4, and Mobley, L. and McKeown, K. (1987b) 'Balanced growth plans – an ROI breakthrough', in *Growth Strategies*, American Management Association, p. 3

As can be supposed, ABC Technologies, which entered a nearby foreign market for the first time during Year 1, experienced a decline in cost control between Year 1 and Year 2, while marketing effectiveness did not change to compensate for this loss. Understanding the costs of entering a new foreign market, and particularly the costs of product adaptation in high-technology firms, is a common problem. Other additional costs must also be considered, e.g. transport, selling and time costs. The result is that return on investment declined to 20 per cent. For such a business let us assume that a return of 20–25 per cent would be much too low. As a result of this analysis and a decision to seek balanced growth, ABC Technologies might decide in Year 3 to increase its return on investment to 40 per cent to satisfy profit and development requirements fully. Acknowledging this problem and the need for greater profits, ABC Technologies might, therefore, plan a balanced growth of its operations to obtain a return on investment in Year 3 of 40 per cent. As shown in Figure 20.6 it can reach its target in a balanced way by improvements on the cost side and by improved marketing effectiveness.

The foreign operation, which is evaluated on the basis of return on investment only, can, however, produce undesired results. In such an evaluative system longer-term performance may be ignored by managers. In order to boost returns essential equipment may not be replaced even when such investment is required for longer-term growth. This is so because new investments increase the asset base, the denominator in the equation above, and also because return on investment measured on a historical cost basis usually will be greater than investment measured on a replacement cost basis.

Summary

Aligning international marketing performance with planning and strategy refers to implementation and control. This means that in planning the programme the firm pays attention to difficulties that may arise subsequently in implementing plans. Successful firms institute control systems to complement and support their planning. Effective implementation of strategy in the international firm means deciding on the best short-run tactical control and long-term strategic control on the direction of the firm. In measuring international marketing performance numerous measures of efficiency can be applied: among the more common are sales quotas, asset earnings and profits, market share and market growth. One of the key variables to be managed is cash flow as the timing and sequencing of events in international markets place great pressure on cash flow; the cash flow impact is usually greater for smaller firms. Short-term financial measures such as return on investment are often used. These have the advantage that if applied over time and in different country markets the firm can monitor its performance and attribute any deviation from standard to cost or marketing factors. Most firms also apply strategic controls to their international operations; strategic control involves a much broader set of factors related to marketing, customers and competitors, and distinguishes the more successful companies from the less successful.

Questions

1. A strategic planning framework consists of a statement of the firm's vision of international markets, an evaluation of its capabilities and a set of coherent strategies. Discuss.

2. What is meant by strategy implementation for the firm in international markets? Describe the relationship between marketing strategy and its implementation. What are the key factors to be taken into account in aligning international marketing strategy with performance?

3. Outline and defend a model for evaluating performance and control in international marketing.

4. Describe the more important operational controls that can be applied in international markets.

5. Expansion into international markets should be accompanied by a financial strategy, particularly a strategy to manage cash flows. Discuss.

6. Short-term financial performance measures identify the likelihood of long-term survival in international markets. Discuss.

7. Most of the measures of strategic control are inappropriate, difficult to apply and too expensive. Some of the simpler approaches such as an ROI are acceptable. Discuss.

References

Bonoma, T. V. and Clarke, B. H. (1988) *Marketing Performance Assessment*, Boston, MA: Harvard Business School Press.

Byrne, G. J. (2001) *Culture in International Marketing*, PhD Dissertation, Department of Marketing, University College Dublin, Dublin.

Christensen, C. M. (1997) 'Making strategy: learning by doing', *Harvard Business Review*, **75** (November–December), 141–56.

Doyle, P. and Hooley, G. J. (1992) 'Strategic orientation and corporate performance', *International Journal of Research in Marketing*, **19** (1), 59–73.

Katsikeas, C. S., Leonidou, L. C. and Morgan, N. A. (2000) 'Firm level export performance assessment: review, evaluation, and development', *Journal of the Academy of Mangement Science*, **28** (4), 493–511.

Kirpalani, V. J. and Balcome, D. (1987) 'International marketing success: on conducting more relevant research' in P. J. Rosson and S. D. Reid, Eds, *Managing Export Entry and Expansion: an International Context*, New York, Praeger.

Kotler, P. (2002) *Marketing Management Analysis Planning and Control*, 11th edn, Englewood Cliffs, NJ, Prentice Hall.

Mobley, L. and McKeown, K. (1987a) 'ROI revisited' in *Intrapreneurial Excellence*, American Management Association, pp. 1 and 4.

Mobley, L. and McKeown, K. (1987b) 'Balanced growth plans – an ROI breakthrough' in *Growth Strategies*, American Management Association, p. 3.

Samiee, S. and Patrik, A. (1998) 'Currency choice in industrial pricing: a cross-national evaluation', *Journal of Marketing*, **27** (Summer), 112–27.

Shapiro, A. C. (1985) 'Evaluation and control of foreign operations' in V. H. Wortzel and L. C. Wortzel, Eds, *Strategic Management of Multinational Corporations: The Essentials*, New York, NY: Wiley, pp. 225–39.

Shoham, A. (1998) 'Export performance: a conceptualization and empirical assessment', *Journal of International Marketing*, **6** (3), 59–81.

Styles, C. (1999) 'Export performance measures in Australia and the United Kingdom', *Journal of International Marketing*, **6** (3), 12–36.

Thomas, M. J. (1998) 'Marketing performance measurement: adding value and meta value' in P. Andersson, Ed., *Proceedings*, 27th EMAC Conference, Stockholm School of Economics, 20–23 May, 355–74.

Zou, S., Taylor, C. T. and Osland, G. E. (1998) 'The EXPERF scale: a cross-national generalized export performance measure', *Journal of International Marketing*, **6** (3), 37–58.

Company index

Name index

Subject index